Whitehead and Teilhard

Whitehead and Teilhard
From Organism to Omega

Ilia Delio

and

Andrew M. Davis,

editors

ORBIS BOOKS
Maryknoll, New York 10545

Founded in 1970, Orbis Books endeavors to publish works that enlighten the mind, nourish the spirit, and challenge the conscience. The publishing arm of the Maryknoll Fathers and Brothers, Orbis seeks to explore the global dimensions of the Christian faith and mission, to invite dialogue with diverse cultures and religious traditions, and to serve the cause of reconciliation and peace. The books published reflect the views of their authors and do not represent the official position of the Maryknoll Society. To learn more about Maryknoll and Orbis Books, please visit our website at www.orbisbooks.com.

Copyright © 2024 by Ilia Delio and Andrew M. Davis

Published by Orbis Books, Box 302, Maryknoll, NY 10545-0302.

All rights reserved.

Ian G. Barbour, "Teilhard's Process Metaphysics," *The Journal of Religion* 49, no. 2 (1969), 136-59. Used with permission.

No part of this publication may be reproduced or transmitted in any form or by any means, electronic or mechanical, including photocopying, recording, or any information storage or retrieval system, without prior permission in writing from the publisher.

Queries regarding rights and permissions should be addressed to: Orbis Books, P.O. Box 302, Maryknoll, NY 10545-0302.

Manufactured in the United States of America
Manuscript editing and typesetting by Joan Weber Laflamme

Library of Congress Cataloging-in-Publication Data

Names: Delio, Ilia, editor. | Davis, Andrew M., 1987- editor.
Title: Whitehead and Teilhard : from organism to Omega / Ilia Delio, Andrew M. Davis, editors.
Description: Maryknoll, NY : Orbis Books, [2024] | Includes bibliographical references and index. | Summary: "Whitehead and Teilhard scholars imagine a philosophical and theological encounter between the two"— Provided by publisher.
Identifiers: LCCN 2024034653 (print) | LCCN 2024034654 (ebook) | ISBN 9781626986008 (trade paperback) | ISBN 9798888660553 (epub)
Subjects: LCSH: Whitehead, Alfred North, 1861-1947. | Teilhard de Chardin, Pierre.
Classification: LCC B1674.W354 W459 2024 (print) | LCC B1674.W354 (ebook) | DDC 192—dc23/eng/20240924
LC record available at https://lccn.loc.gov/2024034653
LC ebook record available at https://lccn.loc.gov/2024034654

In Memory of Joseph A. Bracken, SJ
(1930–2024)

Contents

Gratitude and Dedication   xi

Introduction: Whitehead and Teilhard
    ILIA DELIO AND ANDREW M. DAVIS   xiii

Part I
PHILOSOPHICAL
AND THEOLOGICAL CONCRESCENCE

Hold Fast the Spirit of Adventure
    Whitehead and Teilhard on God, Novelty, and the Direction
      of the Future
    DONALD WAYNE VINEY   3

Dynamic Centration
    Dipolarity in Pierre Teilhard de Chardin and
      Charles Hartshorne
    DANIEL A. DOMBROWSKI   37

Was Pierre Teilhard de Chardin a Panpsychist?
    GODEHARD BRÜNTRUP, SJ   61

Ontology of Becoming and Relative Monism
    Addressing Aporias in Whitehead and Teilhard
    PAOLO GAMBERINI   87

Our Deepest Me
    God-World Relations in Whitehead, Teilhard, and Jung
    SHERI D. KLING   101

vii

viii   Contents

Part II
SCIENTIFIC AND RELIGIOUS TRANSITION

Process Theology and the Modern World
Science, Religion, and Christology after Whitehead and Teilhard
MATTHEW DAVID SEGALL · 113

Metaphysics Beyond Earth
Whitehead, Teilhard, and the Emergence of Process Philosophical Exotheology
ANDREW M. DAVIS · 135

Wilding the Cosmos
A Decolonial and Process Approach to Space Exploration
ELAINE PADILLA · 177

Cosmic Personalization
Teilhard's Omega and the Direction of Evolution
ILIA DELIO · 211

The God of Creative Union
Renewing the Biblical Portrait of Divine Love in Teilhard and Whitehead
ROBERT NICASTRO · 245

Part III
POSSIBILITIES AND PERILS OF THE FUTURE

The Unsatisfied Theists
Pierre Teilhard de Chardin, Alfred North Whitehead, and the Future of Religion
JOHN BECKER · 265

Contents   *ix*

Cultivating Noosphere Evolution in the Spirit of Teilhard and Whitehead
STEVE MCINTOSH   279

Open Universe, Closing Window
Climate Conversation with Teilhard and Whitehead
CATHERINE KELLER   291

Teilhard, Whitehead, and the Reasons for Hope
JOHN F. HAUGHT   305

The Christic
Teilhard's Last Will and Testament
KATHLEEN DUFFY   317

Part IV
APPENDIX

Meeting with Father Teilhard de Chardin
Interview by Marcel Brion (1951)
TRANSLATED BY DONALD WAYNE VINEY   331

Teilhard's Process Metaphysics (1969)
IAN BARBOUR   347

Bibliography   373

Contributors   397

Index   403

Gratitude and Dedication

Thanks and due gratitude are owed to all who made this volume and its early prefiguring in Villanova possible. A special thanks to the staff of the Center for Christogenesis and the Center for Process Studies for their skillful organizational efforts, and to Thomas Hermans-Webster, editor and friend at Orbis Books, for his fine assistance throughout the project. This volume is dedicated to the remembrance of Joseph A. Bracken (1930–2024), who attended the original conference virtually, offered important comments and clarifications throughout, and henceforth passed away during the production of this volume. Bracken remained a model process philosopher, theologian, and friend in the tradition of Whitehead and Teilhard. His creative and rigorous engagement of science and religion throughout his career remains a testament not only to his brilliance as a scholar, but also to the potentials inherent in the process tradition of which he was a vital part. Thank you, Joe.

Introduction

Whitehead and Teilhard

Ilia Delio and Andrew M. Davis

In 1925, mathematician and philosopher Alfred North Whitehead wrote a landmark essay on religion and science in which he prophetically stated: "Religion will not regain its old power unless it can face change in the same spirit as does science. Its principles may be eternal, but the expression of those principles requires continual development."[1] Almost one hundred years later, science and religion remain culturally at odds, yielding a type of *metaphysical dysfunction* that translates into a conflicted and unhealthy planet.

The need to bring science and religion into a robust and coherent paradigm is crucial today if we are to anticipate flourishing life up ahead. Among twentieth-century thinkers Alfred North Whitehead (1861–1947) and Pierre Teilhard de Chardin (1881–1955) stand out as two bright lights of innovative ideas in this regard. Whitehead was a philosopher and Harvard University professor, while Teilhard was a trained paleontologist, a specialist of the Eocene era, who spent many years in China. Each thinker developed a system of fundamental principles that support a coherent relationship between God and world. Whitehead's mathematical and philosophical mind yielded a detailed description of dynamic systems, or what is now called process philosophy, independent of any particular culture or religion, while Teilhard's keen eye for patterns in nature led to a more explicit paradigm of Christianity and evolution.

---

[1] Alfred North Whitehead, "Religion and Science," *The Atlantic* (August 1925). In the same year this article was published as chapter 12 in Whitehead's seminal book *Science and the Modern World* (New York: The Macmillan Co., 1925).

xiii

The term *process* extends back to the age of the ancient Greek philosophers, where it was used to describe natural or biological processes like growth and aging. In the Middle Ages *process* was a term used in alchemy to refer to the procedures of turning base metals into gold or silver. The development of science in the seventeenth and eighteenth centuries resulted in more precise descriptions of sequences or processes underlying natural phenomena. Whitehead was influenced by new advances in modern science and developed a "philosophy of organism," emphasizing change over substance and permanence. Reality was envisioned as networks of interconnected and interacting processes in which interrelationships, becoming, and activity are considered essential metaphysical features of reality. Hence, the fundamental nature of reality is one of constant change and flux rather than stable substances or structures. Teilhard's ideas are consonant with those of Whitehead, but he emphasized evolution as the narrative process of reality. In his view the stuff of life is interconnected and in movement toward more complex systems of relationships, with an emerging form expressed by Christogenesis.

The rich and fecund insights of Whitehead and Teilhard are still relatively unknown in the wider world; however, the need for their ideas on the processive nature of reality is more urgent than ever, as our systems struggle to function in a rapidly changing world. The felt need for a new metaphysics to support an interconnected world, in which process thinking could support areas of ethics, politics, economics, science, and religion, led to the establishment of the Center for Process Studies in 1973 by John B. Cobb Jr. and David Ray Griffin. The center was founded to promote the study, application, and advancement of philosophical concepts, especially the work of Alfred North Whitehead. The Center for Christogenesis was founded in 2016 by Ilia Delio, who holds the Connelly Endowed Chair in Theology at Villanova University, to promote the evolutionary vision of Teilhard de Chardin.

In September 2023, The Center for Process Studies and the Center for Christogenesis collaborated with the Connelly Chair of Villanova University to host a joint conference on Whitehead and Teilhard. Fifteen scholars gathered at Villanova to present insights from Whitehead and Teilhard, to promote dialogue between these two respective areas of thought, and to engage the wider public. The contributions to this conference now appear in their revised and expanded form in the current volume. Because the book is a collection of papers that expound various ideas of Whitehead and Teilhard, we have divided it into three distinct parts: "Philosophical and Theological Concrescence," "Scientific and Religious Transition," and "Possibilities and Perils for the Future."

Philosophical and Theological Concrescence

The first five chapters situate the relationship between Whitehead's and Teilhard's thought, including the striking ways in which they not only grow together (concrescence), but also deviate from each other at different historical, philosophical, and theological depths.

In "Hold Fast the Spirit of Adventure: Whitehead and Teilhard on God, Novelty, and the Direction of the Future," Donald Wayne Viney provides a robust overview of the two thinkers. Although Teilhard referenced Whitehead at least once, neither thinker had any direct influence on the other. Nevertheless, their ideas about God, novelty, and the future reveal striking parallels and convergences. They each struggled to make sense of the dynamism of a process universe through the development of coherent frameworks from which to express their convictions of unity amid plurality, and plurality amid unity. Both argued that evolution, rather than being a purely mechanical unfolding of events, involves spontaneity, activity, and novelty that are every bit as pervasive as law, structure, and order. What is more, each of them reenvisioned the creative activity of God through a "divine lure," essential to any direction the future might take. Viney argues, however, that Whitehead and, to a lesser extent, Teilhard, left us with the unresolved problem of how novelty—arising from the creativity of creatures and with its inevitable cross-purposes and the "perishing" of the past—can be reconciled with any kind of final divine unity. This is a question particularly for Whitehead. It is here, according to Viney, that their philosophies apparently part ways. While Whitehead speaks of objective immortality in the everlasting memory of God, Teilhard speaks of a differentiating union in Omega, beyond space and time. Despite these differences, the influence of Whitehead and Teilhard continues to radiate into our own time and will continue to do so into the future.

In "Dynamic Centration: Dipolarity in Pierre Teilhard de Chardin and Charles Hartshorne," Daniel A. Dombrowski considers important similarities and differences between Teilhard and Hartshorne. In addition to Whitehead and Teilhard, Hartshorne's work remains an original expression of process philosophy and theology. In his magnum opus he indicates sympathies for Teilhard's work, particularly his positive view of religion in *xvi   Whitehead and Teilhard*

its ability to dispense with certain philosophical and theological dogmas of the Western metaphysical tradition. Among these are the primacy of being over becoming, the reduction of "freedom" in creatures to the preordained decision of divine fiat, the rejection of chance or randomness in the universe, and perhaps most important, God's unqualified immutability. Although Hartshorne's own views were not influenced by Teilhard's, Dombrowski suggests that he was encouraged by them. While Teilhard does not refer to Hartshorne's work, both men pioneered forms of process theism and, with Whitehead, are rightly seen as the most important process theists of the twentieth century. Each thinker was influenced by Henri Bergson, and according to Dombrowski, they constitute a kind of a unity-in-difference that is instructive for philosophical theists in general, and neoclassical process theists in particular. In drawing upon other important process thinkers, Dombrowski discusses Teilhard's and Hartshorne's relationship to classical theism, "creative transformation," and the impact of their views on past and present process scholarship. For Dombrowski, both men can be seen to mutually reinforce and also mutually correct each other in important ways. Among their most important affinities, Dombrowski insists, is their mutual affirmation of the Jesuit moto *ad majorem Dei gloriam* (all is for the greater glory of God). For Dombrowski, Hartshorne's "contributionism" can be seen as an attempt to intellectually defend this essential motto belonging to Teilhard's Jesuit order.

In "Was Pierre Teilhard de Chardin a Panpsychist?," Godehard Brüntrup, SJ, offers a wide-ranging discussion of panpsychism, which, although sustaining many classical antecedents, is an especially potent reaction to the Cartesian bifurcation of nature that philosophically marks the origin of modernity. From Leibniz to Whitehead to a variety of contemporary voices, panpsychism has emerged as a viable alternative to dualism and materialism in accounting for the emergence of phenomenal experience and, ultimately, conscious awareness. In addressing whether Teilhard, too, was a panpsychist, Brüntrup first attends to the modern view of nature with its legacy of dualism, including debates as to strong and weak emergence, and the nature of the physical. Countering prevalent misunderstandings of panpsychism, he then reviews several classical and contemporary arguments for panpsychism, including the genetic argument, the argument from intrinsic natures, and the historical critique of the Cartesian concept of matter. Against the backdrop of these conceptual clarifications, Brüntrup then turns to various statements of Teilhard, arguing that, when seen in the context of the classical and contemporary arguments for panpsychism, it is clear that he stands firmly in this philosophical tradition. Indeed, for Brüntrup, Teilhard, alongside Whitehead, is one of the most influential representatives of panpsychism in the twentieth century.

While Viney, Dombrowski, and Brüntrup offer different frameworks of coherence between Whitehead and Teilhard, Paolo Gamberini critically engages their philosophical theologies against the backdrop of classical metaphysics and novel panentheistic possibilities. In "Ontology of Becoming and Relative Monism: Addressing Aporias in Whitehead and Teilhard," he notes that one of the most important similarities between Whitehead and Teilhard is their understanding of God as both transcendent and immanent. Both thinkers have been interpreted as advancing panentheistic visions wherein God is viewed as the "soul" or "spirit" within which the universe is contained. God thus influences the world and is also influenced by it. Whereas Whitehead conceives God not as a static and unchanging entity, but as "creative advance into novelty," evolving with the universe, Teilhard proposes that the universe is in a perpetual state of evolution toward a point of ultimate convergence, the "Omega Point," where all creation will ultimately unify in a higher spiritual state. Both writers developed new insights on the nature of God in relation to the world. Whitehead's "process/dipolar" theism and Teilhard's "evolutionary" God each express a profoundly mutual relationship with the world. Raising some critical remarks about this relationship, Gamberini offers his own alternative panentheistic model of "relative monism." While recognizing that God's primordial nature is unconditional relativity (*relatio*), he argues that the expression of such absolute relatedness is conditional, not in Godself, but in God's relation to the world. Thus, instead of ascribing a consequent nature to God or conceiving God as the Omega Point of evolution, relative monism suggests that God is essentially creative and related to the world, albeit without being the result of becoming.

In "Our Deepest Me: God-World Relations in Whitehead, Teilhard, and Jung," Sheri D. Kling takes as her departure point St. Catherine of Genoa's mystical injunction, "My deepest me is God!" This injunction, according to Kling, finds support and rearticulation in the process-relational philosophy of Whitehead, the evolutionary theology of Teilhard, and the analytical psychology of Jung. "What would it mean if we were to really believe that we could encounter God in the very depths of our being?" Kling asks. "How would that change the way we live, and the way we look at every other thing and being in our world?" In drawing from Teilhard, Whitehead, Jung, and their influence upon a variety of thinkers, Kling discusses the nature of mysticism and matter and the problematic "monopolarity" of classical theism, which runs counter to the felt sense of divine immanence in mystical experiences. Kling demonstrates that for Whitehead, Teilhard, and Jung, God is within everything such that clean divisions between self, world, and God are far from clear and distinct. Nevertheless, God still influences the world, and the world also influences God. Indeed, for Kling, we are *enabled* to influence God and also *ennobled* in the process. In leading us from Logos, to Christ, to Self, and finally to the Christification of humanity, and the transformation of God, Kling stresses the incarnational telos of human beings in relation to God.

Scientific and Religious Transition

The next five chapters strategically draw from Whitehead's and Teilhard's thought to engage emerging topics and issues in science, religion, theology, and ethics.

In "Process Theology and the Modern World: Science, Religion, and Christology after Whitehead and Teilhard," Matthew David Segall presents a comprehensive historical and philosophical discussion of Whitehead and Teilhard as the two foremost twentieth-century contributors to process theology. In particular, he offers a Whiteheadian philosophical reflection on Teilhard's attempt at a "hyperphysics" of the human. Segall highlights Teilhard's early note in *The Human Phenomenon* that he is not attempting to do metaphysics or theology, but phenomenological science. He attempts to offer an account of the past, not in itself, but as it appears to a contemporary human observer. Like Whitehead, Segall stresses that Teilhard was in search of the cosmological conditions of human self-consciousness, a new sort of study he termed "hyperphysics." While Segall finds aspects of Teilhard's phenomenological vision of the past and mystical vision of the future deeply compelling, he argues that some aspects of his poetic synthesis of evolutionary biology and Christianity require metaphysical supplementation in light of Whitehead's cosmological scheme. When properly adjusted and mutually accommodated, however, Segall holds that a Whitehead and Teilhard–inspired synthesis of science and religion has much to offer anyone seeking a relevant and effective Christology today. By drawing out important convergences and contrasts in evolution and Christology between Whitehead and Teilhard, Segall reveals their contemporary significance to a variety of themes in current discussions of science and religion.

In "Metaphysics Beyond Earth: Whitehead, Teilhard, and the Emergence of Process Philosophical Exotheology," Andrew M. Davis argues that until recently the rapidly expanding field of exotheology, astrotheology, or cosmotheology has neglected the resources of process philosophy and theology as robust traditions affirming the mutual relevance of cosmology, theology, and metaphysics to one another. Process philosophers and theologians have not been silent on the question of other worlds and extraterrestrial life, and neither were Whitehead and Teilhard, who are widely recognized as the pillars of the modern process tradition. In an effort to further contribute to the emergence of process philosophical exotheology, Davis focuses specifically on resonant dimensions of Whitehead's and Teilhard's work, including key statements that are supportive of this endeavor. While Davis stresses that their thought provides a variety of pads from which one can launch into such a discussion, he limits the discussion to four interrelated domains: a *historical* domain concerning the advent and implications of evolutionary cosmology for theology; an *anthropological* domain targeting the shift from anthropocentrism to anthropocosmism; a *philosophical* domain clarifying contours of a living ontology for evolutionary cosmology; and a *theological* domain delineating the nature and function of God for a universe pervaded with life, mind, and value. In each of these domains Davis indicates key points of contact between Whitehead and Teilhard. Where relevant, he also draws on supplemental voices when noting the implications *beyond earth*. To conclude, Davis offers an affirmative statement of the potential of process philosophical exotheology that necessitates continual research in dialogue with the shifting landscapes of science, theology, and metaphysics.

In "Wilding the Cosmos: A Decolonial and Process Approach to Space Exploration," Elaine Padilla draws upon the process principles of Whitehead to establish an outer space ethic conducive to well-being here on earth. In doing so she addresses and offers alternatives to the spirit of colonization and conquest that continues to inform scientific uses of outer space technology. Padilla explores Whitehead's views on social progress, particularly his understanding of adventure as "the urge of the universe." She does so first as a critique of the use of force, and second as an alternative when guided by means of persuasion and love. There is a caveat for Padilla, however. Isn't Whitehead's faith in Western civilization too romantic, too modern—even Eurocentric? For this reason Padilla draws upon other indigenous voices from the darker, wilder, side of Western modernity in her analysis of adventure, especially when applied to scientific discoveries and the uses of outer-space technology. For Padilla, the divine urge of the universe, of which all

xx   *Whitehead and Teilhard*

living things partake, can also take on the form of a kind of mystical union and reverence for the wildness of earthly and cosmic life.

In "Cosmic Personalization: Teilhard's Omega and the Direction of Evolution," Ilia Delio explicates Teilhard's ideas on Omega and the noosphere in terms of complexified divinity in evolution and the emergence of a personalized holism expressed on levels of thought and action. In dialogue with different scientists, philosophers, and theologians, Delio discusses Teilhard's cosmic holism based on his affirmation of dual-aspect monism and the "whole of the whole" that is Omega. Evolution for Teilhard proceeds from matter to life to thought through the law of complexity-consciousness, which is expressed as direction in evolution. Teilhard's emphasis on matter as the place of the absolute discloses matter in its "God-bearing nature." The entanglement of God and matter is uniquely expressed in his affirmation of Christian pantheism and monism. Such a pantheism, as Delio stresses, is the basis of his personalistic universe, where true union differentiates. According to Delio, love does not absorb the other but differentiates personalities as a unitive energy. Indeed, the universe for Teilhard tends toward the "hyperpersonal," where the Christic symbolizes the collective whole in formation. It is this whole, moreover, which can be known by both science and religion in a complementary rather than contradictory manner.

In "The God of Creative Union: Renewing the Biblical Portrait of Divine Love in Teilhard and Whitehead," Robert Nicastro argues for a return to the theological primacy of love as expressed in scripture and supported by the open and relational metaphysics of Teilhard, Whitehead, and a variety of others. Contrary to popular assumptions, Nicastro insists that the biblical writers implicitly grasped that theology is the process of "faith seeking understanding." They recognized that the truth about creation is not generated simply by theological reflection alone, but also used culturally available "prescientific" knowledge to speak about God's relationship to creation in ways that were reasonable and substantive. Much like the methodology employed in the ancient world, Nicastro stresses that the principal task of contemporary theology is likewise to integrate materials from multiple disciplines into an intellectually coherent and biblically consistent system of thought. With support from multiple thinkers confirming the biblical portrait of God as open and internally receptive to the world, he argues that Teilhard and Whitehead enjoin us to embrace a new theological horizon: one that transcends inherited metaphysical categories and outgrows the dualistic split between the sacred and secular.

Possibilities and Perils of the Future

The last five chapters anticipate the future of evolution with Whitehead and Teilhard across multiple interconnected thresholds, from religion to culture, politics, ecology, and meaning in an open cosmos.

In "The Unsatisfied Theists: Pierre Teilhard de Chardin, Alfred North Whitehead, and the Future of Religion," John Becker frames his discussion by noting Teilhard's characterization of those struggling with the religious sentiment of his day not as atheists but as "unsatisfied theists." He argues that, not unlike the "nones" or the growing "spiritual but not religious" (SBNR) group today, both Teilhard and Whitehead were acutely aware of "unsatisfied theists," primarily because they were unsatisfied theists themselves. In response, both men advanced radical new visions not only of Christianity, but of religion itself. Becker stresses that Teilhard and Whitehead were also "unsatisfied scientists," who proffered an alternative to scientific materialism by incorporating other experiential dimensions. Indeed, both men were committed to a solution that was able to frame a cosmic vision. Approaches to reality must be holistic, navigating both terrains without relegating one in favor of the other. By delineating some novel trajectories for religions and their future, Becker develops Teilhard's evolutionary vision as he negotiates his scientific orientation and Catholic faith, and Whitehead's "philosophy of organism" with particular attention to the dynamism of religion. Becker insists that religiosity cannot be an exception to cosmic rules but flourishes or deteriorates under universal principles. The future of religion and its various expressions of faith is surely unknown, Becker insists, yet the visions offered by Teilhard and Whitehead offer hope.

In "Cultivating Noosphere Evolution in the Spirit of Teilhard and Whitehead," Steve McIntosh argues that the philosophies of Teilhard and Whitehead, when interpreted in generalized combination, offer a politically potent prescription for the further evolution of human culture. Analyzing the structural sequence of evolutionary emergence in the noosphere, McIntosh shows how the large-scale worldviews of modernity and postmodernity have each advanced cultural evolution in their own way. This analysis, he claims, also reveals how the tension between modernism and postmodernism expresses a dialectical relationship of thesis and antithesis. Tracing the trajectory of noosphere emergence points to the potential for a future cultural synthesis, one that transcends the worst and includes the best of these extant cultural structures. For McIntosh, this potential synthesis can be achieved by attending to Whitehead's criteria for evolutionary progress, namely, an increase in the capacity to experience intrinsic value. This synthetic move thus entails expanding the value frame of progressive postmodern culture by embracing the full diversity of valid values and viewpoints represented by the developed world's contemporary spectrum of cultural evolution. Indeed, McIntosh argues that those who understand noosphere evolution, even if partially, are called to become advocates for our culture's next evolutionary step—a transcendent and inclusive new whole through which the many can become one and increase by one.

In "Open Universe, Closing Window: Climate Conversation with Teilhard and Whitehead," Catherine Keller reflects upon the relationship between Teilhard and Whitehead against the backdrop of the current climate emergency. For Keller, it has long been too easy for Whitehead-ian theologians to minimize Teilhard's contribution to a relational theo-cosmology of becoming. Yet both have offered powerful therapy for the Western bifurcation of nature and its manifestation in the present ecological crisis. For Keller, now is the time for disciples of Teilhard and Whitehead to come together to leverage a crisis-tuned ecological Christianity in which conversation aims not at besting a competing vision but at solidarity in dif-ference. To this end Keller raises key questions for Teilhardians and White-headians to consider: What truth is there to the common presumption that the Omega Point encodes progress toward a divinely assured outcome of human history, and might therefore drain urgency from the matter of climate emergency? Can one draw promising analogies between Teilhard's Christ and Whitehead's primordial nature of God, on the one hand, and between the divine milieu and the consequent nature on the other? Does Teilhard's version of a Cosmic Christ risk a greater triumphalism than, for instance, John Cobb's Christology? How can we relate Teilhardian pantheism to Whiteheadian panentheism? Fostering unity in difference, Keller reflects upon these questions not in light of a complacent optimism but of an activating hope on a planet recently recognized to have its very tilt shifting from human water use and also having undergone the hottest week in recorded history.

In "Teilhard, Whitehead, and the Reasons for Hope," John F. Haught draws from Teilhard and Whitehead to combat the underlying nihilism of current science-inspired proclamations that both life and mind will end tragically in the evaporation of a final thought. With Teilhard and Whitehead, Haught argues that it is finally unthinkable that thought will ever finally perish since thought is a phenomenon that is inseparable from the whole cosmic story of emerging evolutionary complexity. For Haught,

Teilhard and Whitehead offer an "awaking universe" that is led forward by transcendental ideals that can never let go of our minds. Haught describes the imperishability of thought as a gift given in advance to anticipatory minds that are only now awakening to an "indestructible horizon of Rightness," or the indestructibility of being, meaning, goodness, truth, and beauty. Haught follows Whitehead in holding that it is God's will to maximize beauty, and thus to "do God's will" involves actions that beautify the world. Both Teilhard and Whitehead, he claims, inspire us in this endeavor. He insists that we are able to do God's will not only in grand ways but also in the most ordinary of ways. In doing so, we also follow the message of Pope Francis's encyclical *Laudato Si'*, which includes trusting that the meaning (and goal) of our lives is not only to contemplate beauty but to participate and continue the adventure of bringing it about.

In "'The Christic': Teilhard's Last Will and Testament," Kathleen Duffy concludes the volume by arguing that, among Teilhard's many religious essays, "The Christic" remains particularly important for two reasons. The first is that it is his last essay and thus contains his final statement of spiritual evolution and experience. The second is that he desperately wanted to write it and hoped to live long enough to do so. Having arrived in New York City in 1951 for the final phase of his many years of exile from France, he felt his life was coming to an end. Convinced of the coherence of his synthesis of science and religion, including its implications for action in the world and for the life of the church, he felt great urgency to write. In reviewing core themes of Teilhard's final essay, Duffy unfolds its dynamic and directed currents. Teilhard's awareness of the first current, which he calls cosmic emergence, traces his growing passion for Earth and was ignited during his nature walks in the countryside with his father. The second, which he calls Christic emergence, focuses on his ever-expanding love for God and arose spontaneously from the influence of his mother's deep devotion to the Sacred Heart. According to Duffy, the conjunction of the two currents evolved and transformed Teilhard's unconscious drives into deep and effective passions. By responding to their movements over a lifetime, Duffy stresses that Teilhard's cosmic sense became ever more intimate and his Christic sense ever more certain. She shows how his core doctrines of the noosphere, complexity-consciousness, Omega, Christogenesis, and others emerge in and between the two currents found in his final essay. Nevertheless, for Duffy, several serious questions remain as to how to activate and respond to the spiritual energy that floods Teilhard's universe. Despite the beauty and coherence of his Christic vision, it has yet to become widespread *xxiv   Whitehead and Teilhard*

and has not yet been able to motivate the action required to work toward union. Still, Duffy is confident that one day Teilhard's expansive vision will render the world ablaze.

Appendix: Two Documents That Add Further Context and Coherence to This Volume

The first of these two historically significant documents is Donald W. Viney's English translation of Marcel Brion's 1951 interview with Teilhard de Chardin, preceded by important historical contextualization.[2] The interview is a personal look into Teilhard's early history and emergence as a scientist, including his key ideas, which were often misrepresented in their wider cultural reception. Clarifying misunderstandings, Teilhard reiterates the core themes of his life's work, including the "unexpected possibilities held in reserve for us by the future."

The second is Ian Barbour's 1969 essay "Teilhard's Process Metaphysics," which offers a skillful and in-depth comparison of Teilhard's and Whitehead's visions of the world, God, and the future.[3] In it, Barbour draws out core themes, including reality as temporal process; the "within"; freedom and determinism; continuing creation; God and time; the problem of evil; and the future of the world. Barbour's article remains an important piece of early scholarship on the convergences and divergences of these two pioneering thinkers.

---

[2] This interview was first published in *Les Nouvelles Littéraires*, Thursday, January 11, 1951, pages 1 and 4, and has been republished in this volume with permission.

[3] Barbour's article first appeared in *The Journal of Religion* 49, no. 2 (1969): 136–59. It is republished in this volume with permission.

Part I

Philosophical and Theological Concrescence

Hold Fast the Spirit of Adventure

*Whitehead and Teilhard on God, Novelty,
and the Direction of the Future*

Donald Wayne Viney

In 1950, Teilhard encouraged his Jesuit colleague Pierre Leroy (1900–1992) with the words: "Above all, hold fast, as Whitehead says, the spirit of adventure and conquest."[1] Alfred North Whitehead (1861–1947) and Pierre Teilhard de Chardin (1881–1955) exhibited this "spirit of adventure" in diverse ways, each appropriate to his own life and his own adventurous spirit. While both men were, to greater or lesser extents, influenced by the writings of Henri Bergson (1859–1941), there is no evidence of cross-fertilization of ideas between the two. Whitehead died before Teilhard's more philosophical writings were available, and in any event he did not frequent the same scientific circles as Teilhard. As we shall see in what follows, Teilhard's metaphysical ideas predate those of Whitehead, although he apparently read or looked over Whitehead's *Science and the Modern World* and *Religion in the Making*.[2]

---

[1] "Mais, par-dessus tout, gardez, comme dit Whitehead, l'esprit d'aventure et de conquête," letter, April 19, 1950. Pierre Leroy, *Lettres Familières de Pierre Teilhard de Chardin Mon Ami Les Dernières Années 1948–1955* (Vendôme: Le Centurion, 1976), 62. Mary Lukas translates the phrase, "Hold high . . . the spirit of adventure." Pierre Leroy, *Letters from My Friend Teilhard de Chardin*, trans. by Mary Lukas (New York: Paulist Press, 1980), 52. Teilhard may have had in mind Whitehead's statement, "The death of religion comes with the repression of the high hope of adventure." Alfred North Whitehead, *Science and the Modern World* (New York: Macmillan, 1925), 276.

[2] Claude Cuénot, *Teilhard de Chardin: A Biographical Study*, trans. Vincent Colimore, ed. René Hague (Baltimore: Helicon Press, 1965), 237. Pierre Teilhard de Chardin and Lucille Swan, *The Letters of Teilhard de Chardin and Lucille Swan*, ed. Thomas M. King, SJ, and Mary Wood Gilbert (Scranton, PA: University of Scranton Press, 2001), 82.

Despite the lack of influence on each other, their ideas about God, novelty, and the direction of the future ran on parallel and sometimes convergent tracks. They struggled to make sense of the dynamisms of a universe-in-process, to find a coherent framework to speak of unity amid plurality and plurality amid unity. They argued that evolution is no mere mechanical unfolding of events. Spontaneity, activity, and novelty are as real and as all-pervasive as law, structure, and order. Moreover, each of them reconceptualized the creativity of God, considering the "divine lure" as integral to any direction the future might have. They left us, however, the unresolved conundrum of how the novelty arising from the creative activity of the creatures—which involves aims at cross-purposes and the "perishing" of the past—can be reconciled with any kind of final unity in God. Here, their philosophies apparently part ways: Whitehead to speak of immortality in the everlasting memory of God; Teilhard to speak of a differentiating union of what is uniquely personal in each of us in Omega, beyond space and time.

Adventurous Living

There was, arguably, more drama in Teilhard's life story than in Whitehead's. Even so, Whitehead's decision to accept Harvard's invitation to teach philosophy (made with his wife's approval) was intrepid. He had behind him a successful career as a mathematician and a philosopher of nature. The three-volume *Principia Mathematica* (1910–13), co-authored with his one-time student Bertrand Russell (1872–1970), is a watershed in mathematical logic. In some circles it is the main reason he is remembered. With this and other works, equally well-received, he could presumably look forward to retirement in the English countryside. Yet, the family made America their home in 1924. Whitehead immediately went to work on the articles and books that would make him as famous as a philosopher as he had been as a mathematician. In Russell's words, "In England, Whitehead was regarded only as a mathematician, and it was left to America to discover him as a philosopher."[3]

The other drama in the Whiteheads' lives, more personal than public, was the loss of their youngest son, Eric, in the First World War. His military career lasted ten months. A window to the parents' grief is in Whitehead's

---

[3] Bertrand Russell, *Portraits from Memory and Other Essays* (London: George Allen & Unwin LTD, 1956), 93.

dedication in *An Enquiry into the Principles of Natural Knowledge*: "To Eric Alfred Whitehead, Royal Flying Corps, November 27, 1898 to March 13, 1918. Killed in Action over the Forêt de Gobain giving himself that the city of his vision may not perish. The music of his life was without discord, perfect in its beauty."[4] Whitehead's other children, Jessie and North, agreed with Russell, who believed that this great loss, which affected the family and friends so deeply, had something to do with Whitehead's turn to a more accommodating attitude in his later thought to religious ideas, especially on the topics of God and immortality.[5]

Teilhard's parents certainly had their share of grief, losing five of their eleven children (two killed in the Great War) before the father's death, and a sixth before the mother's passing. In total, Teilhard outlived all but two of his siblings. These losses took place within an eventful life. From his youth as a Jesuit novice until his final days in New York City, he knew discoveries and disappointments, experienced triumphs and trials, was celebrated and silenced. He lived faithfully as a Catholic priest, but his life was never that of the cloister, or even of the settled academic. To mark some significant events: First, his participation in the digs at Piltdown in 1912 was a mixed blessing. It brought early recognition in the world of paleontology, but the happy memory was spoiled when the news broke in 1953 that Piltdown was a hoax.[6] Second, the war years were marked by terrifying scenes of slaughter at the front, yet he began composing essays in 1916 that show an indominable confidence in the future. He was a stretcher-bearer and was awarded France's top medals for bravery and valor, the Croix de Guerre and the Médaille Militaire. Third, he again achieved fame for his participation in the expedition (1929–30) that uncovered the remains of *Sinanthropus*, often called the Peking Man—actually the skull of a female, nicknamed Nelly.[7] He downplayed his role in the expedition—supervising excavations

---

[4] Alfred North Whitehead, *An Enquiry Concerning the Principles of Natural Knowledge* (New York: Dover, 1982 [1919]), iv.

[5] Victor Lowe, *Alfred North Whitehead: The Man and His Work. Vol. II: 1910–1947*, ed. J. B. Schneewind (Baltimore, MD: The Johns Hopkins University Press, 1990), 188.

[6] Stephen Jay Gould argued that Teilhard was complicit. See Stephen Jay Gould, *Hen's Teeth and Horse's Toes: Further Reflections in Natural History* (New York: W. W. Norton & Company, 1983), 201–40, chaps. 16 and 17. Since the 1990s it has been a virtual certainty that Charles Dawson was the culprit and that he acted alone. See John Evangelist Walsh, *The Science Fraud of the Century and Its Solution: Unraveling Piltdown* (New York: Random House, 1996).

[7] Pierre Teilhard de Chardin, *Le Rayonnement d'une Amitié, Correspondance avec la Famille Bégouën (1922–1955)* (Brussels: Lessius, 2011), 121.

6   Hold Fast the Spirit of Adventure

and interpreting the site—but it was yet another case of Teilhard finding himself in the middle of the major paleontological events of his time.[8]

Following the itinerary of Teilhard's travels almost makes one dizzy as, for various reasons, he zigzagged from one country to another. Early in his education as a Jesuit, he and his confrères were forced to leave France because of anticlerical politics.[9] He was first sent to the isle of Jersey, later taught elementary physics and chemistry in Cairo, and finally studied theology at Hastings. Wherever he went in these years, he used his free time to hunt for fossils. After the war he completed his doctorate in geology at the Sorbonne and taught at the Catholic Institute in Paris. Between 1923 and 1939 he made ten trips to China, stopping at various locations along the way including Africa, India, Java, and America. For the duration of the war (1939–46) he was stranded in China. His last decade was spent first in Paris (until early 1951) and finally in New York City, with several jaunts crisscrossing the Atlantic, including two trips to South Africa. Teilhard knew firsthand the evidences of early hominids, from examining (and being part of the discovery) of examples of *homo erectus* to visiting Altamira (in 1913 with Abbé Henri Breuil) and Lascaux (in 1954 with Pierre Leroy), where he saw the magnificent prehistoric cave paintings.

Much of his time in China and in America was an enforced exile by religious superiors who sought to keep him away from the intellectual life of Paris, where he had gained something of a celebrity status because of his daring ideas about the fertile relationship between the worlds of science and religion. He was continually frustrated by his religious superiors, who would not permit him to publish anything but strictly scientific works. However, his more philosophical and religious ideas found their way into both scientific circles and popular newspapers because of what he ironically referred to as his *clandestins*, ironic because they were signed and dated and known to his superiors.[10] These were copies of his works kept by his friends Simone Bégouën (1897–1960) and Jeanne Mortier (1892–1982) and duplicated on a renotype machine. Prior to 1947, when he was prohibited from further distributing them, many admirers and critics had already read them. In this way, before any of the works for which he became most famous were ever

---

[8]   Ibid., 53.

[9]   The *lois d'exception* (1901) restricted the activities of religious orders. In 1902, when the antireligious ex-seminarian Émile Combes became premier, the law was enforced and the Jesuits and other religious orders were expelled from France.

[10]   Patrice Boudignon, *Pierre Teilhard de Chardin: Sa Vie, son oeuvre, Sa Réflexion* (Paris: Éditions du Cerf, 2008), 162.

published, he was considered either a prophet or a heretic for promoting bold new ideas concerning science and faith. Teilhard willed his literary corpus to Mlle. Mortier, thereby ensuring that they were not destined for an archival cemetery; she began shepherding his works to publication immediately after his death.

Jean Piveteau (1899–1991) said that Teilhard was known during his lifetime only as a paleontologist.[11] Piveteau wished to emphasize how Teilhard's postmortem popularity tended to obscure the fact of his reputation as a well-known scientist while he was alive. While it is true that Teilhard first gained notoriety as a paleontologist, his role as a *Jesuit* paleontologist raised questions. In March 1937, Teilhard was in Philadelphia to attend a meeting with 350 other scientists at the Philadelphia Academy of Natural Sciences. On March 22, he was awarded the Mendel Medal at Villanova for recognition of his work. On the same day, the *Toronto Daily Star* reported critical remarks from a Monsignor Michael Cline. Quoting Genesis 1:27, Cline said that Teilhard's opinion was "open to challenge and denial like that of any other adventurer in the field of science." He added that God did not create man until "the house of this world was completed and furnished for his residence."[12] Teilhard was too attuned to the development of ecosystems to be swayed by such criticism. Eight years before he had written, "We have never been further than we are now from the ancient creationism that represented creatures as appearing readymade in the surroundings which received them with indifference."[13]

Five days after the *Toronto Daily Star* notice, *Newsweek* published an article about the Philadelphia science meeting, accompanied by a photograph of Teilhard, and reported journalists asking Teilhard how he reconciled his religious and scientific beliefs. He simply called it a "lack of understanding"—presumably, he was referring to the apparent conflict between science

---

[11] Nicole and Karl Schmitz-Moormann, *Pierre Teilhard de Chardin: L'Œuvre Scientifique*, 10 vols. (Olten and Freiburg im Breisgau: Walter-Verlag, 1971), xxi.

[12] "Priest Won't Agree Ape Man's Forebear: Monsignor Takes Issue with Jesuit Scholar's Opinion," *The Toronto Daily Star*, March 22, 1937.

[13] Pierre Teilhard de Chardin, *The Vision of the Past*, trans. J. M. Cohen (New York: Harper and Row, 1966), 102. On August 16, 1925, Teilhard wrote to his friend, philosopher Édouard Le Roy (1870–1954): "One cannot open a right-thinking newspaper without finding carefully reported everything that has been said or written by an incompetent person against evolutionism! Fortunately, in all the conversations I have had on this subject, even with poorly prepared people, I note, on the contrary, a real curiosity, and ultimately a real sympathy, for the accursed doctrine." Pierre Teilhard de Chardin, *Lettres à Édouard Le Roy (1921–1946): Maturation d'une Pensée* (Paris: Éditions Facultés Jesuites de Paris, 2008), 56.

8   Hold Fast the Spirit of Adventure

and religion.[14] Teilhard's notoriety was further augmented by his *clandestins,* gaining him a reputation for being a daring religious thinker. René d'Ouince (1896–1973)[15] recalls Teilhard's reception when he returned to Paris after the Second World War:

> He was received as a prophet by a crowd of those he did not even know. . . . Not simply a Parisian personality, he was a sort of movie star in the intellectual world, especially among students. Suddenly, as if by magic, his unpublished work proliferated.

A chaplain of students told d'Ouince, "If you want to pack a room full at the risk of seeing some chairs broken, just invite Jean-Paul Sartre or Father Teilhard."[16] One may grant to Piveteau that Teilhard's scientific accomplishments have too often been forgotten, but Teilhard was well enough known to nonscientists during his lifetime to merit a 1951 front-page interview in a major French literary newspaper.[17]

Near Convergent Paths

Concerning religion, Whitehead and Teilhard followed largely divergent but sometimes convergent paths. Whitehead, the youngest of four children, was raised a pious Anglican with a clergyman father. At an early age he was taught Latin and Greek. He recalled, "We read the Bible in Greek, namely, with the Septuagint for the Old Testament."[18] The best evidence concerning his religious development is that he accepted a liberal Christianity

---

[14] "Anthropology: Experts Meet but Ape-Man Link Is Still Lost," *Newsweek* (March 27, 1937), 30.

[15] From 1935 until 1973, René d'Ouince was the superior at the Jesuit house in Paris, home of the periodical *Études.* His book *Un Prophète en Procès: Teilhard de Chardin dans l'Église de son Temps* (A Prophet on Trial: Teilhard de Chardin in the Church of His Times) (Paris: Aubier-Montaigne, 1970) is one of the finest sources on Teilhard's relations with the church, written by one who was in the thick of the controversy and who was sympathetic to Teilhard's cause. For more on d'Ouince, see Gérard-Henry Baudry, *Dictionnaire des Correspondants de Teilhard de Chardin* (Lille: Chez l'Auteur, 1974), 101–3.

[16] d'Ouince, *Un Prophète en Procès,* 149.

[17] Pierre Teilhard de Chardin, "Rencontre avec le Père Teilhard de Chardin. Entretien avec Marcel Brion," *Les Nouvelles Littéraires* (Paris), January 11, 1951. See my translation in the Appendix in the current volume.

[18] Alfred North Whitehead, *Essays in Science and Philosophy* (New York: Philosophical Library, 1948), 9.

until his mid-thirties, when he sold his theological library and adopted a more agnostic, even atheistic, attitude until his mid-fifties (the time of the Great War).[19] Most of what he wrote until his move to Harvard had almost nothing to do with religion, theistic or otherwise. It was only in the works he wrote in America that he developed a non-sectarian and philosophical theism that became the inspiration for one strand of what is called process theology. Religion and God were never Whitehead's primary focus, even in his later works.[20]

As for Teilhard, he seemed never to entertain the most serious doubts about Christianity. He remained loyal to his church even as he questioned its official pronouncements and its interpretation of certain doctrines. His prewar activities (1901–12) always included interest in geology and digging for fossils. It was during his theological studies at Hastings (1908–12) that he read Bergson's *Creative Evolution* (published in 1907) and was awakened to the importance of evolution.[21] The details of Teilhard's intellectual progress on this point are murky. He *did* leave us, as it were, a transitional form in a 1911 article titled "Evolution."[22] The article outlines various ideas about evolution (also called transformism), including the evidence for them. Teilhard saw the attraction of these ideas, especially in the evidence of paleontology and in the coherence of evolutionary thinking that acknowledges the physical (not merely logical) relations among species. From the standpoint of Teilhard's mature thought, the most striking sentence is this: "[Extended] to life as a whole, transformism . . . is, and will undoubtedly always remain, a hypothesis."[23] Teilhard later adamantly opposed this idea. He said, and said often, that evolution is more than a hypothesis; it is the key to unlocking reality, a condition to which all forms of knowledge must conform.[24] Also of note is Teilhard's matter-of-fact explanation of "The

---

[19] Victor Lowe, *Alfred North Whitehead: The Man and His Work. Vol. I: 1861–1910* (Baltimore: The Johns Hopkins University Press, 1985), 136–42; Lowe, *Alfred North Whitehead: The Man and His Work. Vol. II: 1910–1947*, chap. 9.

[20] A. H. Johnson, "Whitehead as Teacher and Philosopher," *Philosophy and Phenomenological Research* 29, no. 3 (March 1969): 365.

[21] Pierre Teilhard de Chardin, *The Heart of Matter*, trans. René Hague (New York: Harcourt, Brace, Jovanovich, 1978), 25.

[22] Pierre Teilhard de Chardin, "Evolution," in Schmitz-Moormann, *Pierre Teilhard de Chardin L'Œuvres Scientifique*, 1:69–74.

[23] Ibid., 72.

[24] Pierre Teilhard de Chardin, *The Appearance of Man*, trans. J. M. Cohen (New York: Harper and Row, 1965), 211; Teilhard, *The Vision of the Past*, 87, 127, and 246; Pierre Teilhard de Chardin, *Science and Christ*, trans. René Hague (New York: Harper

10   *Hold Fast the Spirit of Adventure*

Data of Revelation" and the teachings of the church.[25] The idea of a miraculous creation of the first couple, from scratch, and of all of humanity as descended from them—the doctrine of monogenism—eventually seemed to him quite unbelievable. His response to the papal encyclical *Humani Generis* seems to leave conceptual room for a literal-minded theologian to operate, but the idea of an Adam *born adult* is, in Teilhard's words, "meaningless for modern science."[26]

During the First World War, Teilhard gravitated to his own version of process metaphysics, including revisions in the very idea of God. More and more he distanced himself from the Scholastic theology in which he had been instructed. In this way—Whitehead from the side of a suspension of faith, Teilhard from the side of passionate faith—the two scholars came to ideas about God that, if not housed in the same terminology, are most definitely in the same neighborhood of ideas.

Teilhard's metaphysical writings are chronologically prior to those of Whitehead, so I begin with them. I am using the word *metaphysics* to refer to theories about the nature of existence and its ultimate explanations. I *do not* mean to suggest that its methodology is to begin with self-evident principles and proceed deductively. Metaphysics in this sense includes the later work of Whitehead, which was an inquiry into ultimate principles that are themselves ever open to revision with the advance of knowledge and human experience. The metaphysician seeks first principles that cannot fail of exemplification. In Whitehead's words, "We can never catch the actual world taking a holiday from their sway."[27] After 1925, Teilhard was warned to confine himself to science. However, prior to that time he wrote unselfconsciously about metaphysical subjects, and he never ceased to think at that level. He struggled to name the genre of his work, calling it variously, "para- or meta-scientific" and "hyper-physics."[28] I claim that his thinking

---

and Row, 1968), 193; Pierre Teilhard de Chardin, *The Human Phenomenon*, trans. Sarah Appleton-Weber (Brighton: Sussex Academic Press, 1999), 122.

[25] Teilhard, "Evolution," 73.

[26] Pierre Teilhard de Chardin, *Christianity and Evolution*, trans. René Hague (New York: Harcourt, Brace, Jovanovich, 1971), 210.

[27] Alfred North Whitehead, *Process and Reality: An Essay in Cosmology*, corrected edition, ed. David Ray Griffin and Donald Sherburne (New York: The Free Press, 1978), 4.

[28] Teilhard, *Lettres à Édouard Le Roy*, 74; Pierre Teilhard de Chardin, *Lettres Intimes de Teilhard de Chardin à Auguste Valensin, Bruno de Solages, Henri du Lubac, André Ravier: 1919–1955*, introduction and notes by Henri de Lubac (Paris: Aubier Montaigne, 1974), 273; Teilhard, *The Human Phenomenon*, 2.

falls into the same general category as Whitehead's, so I'll not be nervous about calling it metaphysics.[29]

In his war essays Teilhard frames the idea of divine creation as "one continual gesture, drawn out over the totality of time."[30] He is not speaking merely of the way things appear to us who are caught in the temporal matrix, he is saying that God is *in fact* continually creating and thereby continually *increasing* "the absolute quantity of being existing in the universe." Thus, Teilhard can say that the pattern in which we experience the unfolding of the universe discloses "the fundamental texture of spirit."[31] In agreement with Bergson, he holds that pure nothing is a pseudo-idea.[32] In place of the traditional *creatio ex nihilo* (creation from no preexisting material), Teilhard speaks of *creative union* or *creative transformation,* which is creation by using preexistent created beings to build up completely new beings.[33] This is what Teilhard calls a *metaphysics of union.*[34]

No champion of traditional theology, especially of the Thomistic variety, could be happy about the consequences of Teilhard's mature views. First, the denial of *ex nihilo* creation entails a more Platonic account of world-making requiring a primordial "multiple" or "multitude" (Teilhard's words) that is gradually unified by God's activity. Second, the idea of "participated being" must be abandoned or at least rethought. Teilhard rejects in the strongest terms the idea that there is no more value in God-*plus*-the-creatures than there is in God existing alone. As he wrote to Mgr. Bruno de Solages (1895–1983) in 1935, "God must create in order to complete himself[35] in

---

[29] I've approached this subject from different angles in three articles. See Donald Wayne Viney, "Teilhard de Chardin and Process Philosophy Redux," *Process Studies* 35, no. 1 (Spring-Summer 2006): 15–27; "Teilhard: Le Philosophe Malgré l'Église," in *Rediscovering Teilhard's Fire,* ed. Kathleen Duffy, SSJ (Philadelphia: Saint Joseph's University Press, 2010): 76–83; and "Evolution's God: Teilhard de Chardin and the Varieties of Process Theology," *Teilhard Studies* 82 (Spring 2021): 2–4.

[30] Pierre Teilhard de Chardin, *Writings in Time of War,* trans. René Hague (New York: Harper and Row, 1968), 130.

[31] Ibid., 162–63.

[32] Ibid., 94.

[33] Ibid., 163; Teilhard, *Christianity and Evolution,* 22.

[34] Teilhard, *Christianity and Evolution,* 178 and 227; Pierre Teilhard de Chardin, *Toward the Future,* trans. René Hague (New York: Harcourt, Brace, Jovanovich, 1975), 193.

[35] Both Teilhard and Whitehead wrote in the idiom of their day, privileging male pronouns and images for God and humans quite unselfconsciously. Doubtless, had they lived long enough to consider the feminist critique of exclusive language, they would have reconsidered.

12   *Hold Fast the Spirit of Adventure*

something outside of himself."[36] Divine love *requires* relationships with the creatures and not simply a self-relation, as in the Trinity. Teilhard insists on *valorizing* the world and of acknowledging genuine creativity in the creatures. Thomistic theology says that, in the proper sense of the word, God alone creates. In contrast, Teilhard anticipates one of the central pillars of process theology: God "does not so much 'make' things as 'make them make themselves.'"[37]

At the core of Teilhard's theology is a rethinking of divine power. Thomas Aquinas paved the way for Teilhard by arguing that God cannot make logically impossible objects (for example, a circle with unequal radii), alter the past, or do something against the divine nature (for example, an evil act).[38] Teilhard extends the argument to include "physical equivalents" to the necessities of geometry and value theory: God must work within the framework of an evolutive universe that includes the creatures that make themselves. A world of such beings necessarily involves risk. Thus, Teilhard spoke of "a whole succession of inevitable risks" involved in God's creative activity.[39] This is one aspect of a Teilhardian answer to the problem of evil.

---

[36] Teilhard, *Lettres Intimes*, 302. Teilhard acknowledges to de Solages that it seems necessary, in order to save one aspect of God, to say that God need not create but, "an *absolutely free* creation seems to me altogether 'absurd' (and very difficult to harmonize with the existence and importance of the Creation-Incarnation-Redemption)" (ibid.). Henri de Lubac (1896–1991) indicates that Teilhard was never quite able to resolve the tension between these ideas (ibid., 279n72, 3). I believe the divine incarnation in the universe was uppermost in Teilhard's thinking and therefore that he gave lip service to the orthodox idea that God could choose not to create, but that he did not consider it of vital importance to Christian theology.

[37] Teilhard, *The Vision of the Past*, 25; Teilhard, *Christianity and Evolution*, 28. Before Teilhard, Jules Lequyer (or Lequier) (1814–62), who anticipated many themes of process theology, spoke of "God, who created me creator of myself." See Donald Wayne Viney, "Something Unheard Of: The Unparalleled Legacy of Jules Lequyer," *Process Studies* 51, no. 2 (Fall-Winter 2022): 143–68. In a children's book Charles Kingsley (1819–75), Darwin's friend, put these words into the mouth of Mother Carey, a personification of Nature, "Anyone can make things if they will take time and trouble enough; but it is not everyone who, like me, can make things make themselves." See Charles Kingsley, *The Water-Babies* (Stamford: Longmeadow, 1994 [1863]), 231. After Teilhard, Bergson spoke of God creating other creators, as did Hartshorne. See Henri Bergson, *The Two Sources of Morality and Religion*, trans. R. Ashley Audra and Cloudesley Brereton, with the assistance of W. Horsfall Carter (Garden City, NY: Doubleday Anchor Books, 1954 [1932]), 255; and Charles Hartshorne, *Omnipotence and Other Theological Mistakes* (Albany: State University of New York Press, 1984), 73–74.

[38] Thomas Aquinas, *On the Truth of the Catholic Faith, Summa Contra Gentiles, Book Two: Creation*, trans. James F. Anderson (Garden City, NY: Hanover House, 1956), 73–77, chap. 25.

[39] Teilhard, *Christianity and Evolution*, 31.

In addition, the element of risk implies at least a degree of openness in the future, a universe *en marche*,[40] under way, *even for God*.

With these ideas one begins to appreciate the full force of the Teilhardian vision that replaces the idea of *cosmos* (a universe made) with the idea of *cosmogenesis* (a universe in the making). For Teilhard, humans are at the apex of evolutionary development on this planet, but they (we) are still evolving. The process involves increasingly complex forms of matter associated with increasingly multiform varieties of experience. This is Teilhard's "law of complexity-consciousness" where "consciousness" (*la conscience*) stands for *every form of psychism* from the most elementary to the daylight of self-reflective awareness.[41] The very constitution of what Teilhard calls "the stuff of things" is to have both physical properties—the Without of Things (*Le Dehors des Choses*)—and qualities of experience—the Within of Things (*Le Dedans des Choses*).[42] To use the language of current philosophy, if something has the quality of a "within," there is "something that it is like" to be it, however difficult it may be for us to imagine it. For example, Charles Hartshorne (1897–2000) argued for aesthetic experience in songbirds.[43] He continually affirmed the inner life of other creatures—gorillas, honeybees, porpoises, inhabitants of other planets, and more—all the while stressing the difficulty of imagining what it is like to be them.[44] More widely known is Thomas Nagel's question, "What is it like to be a bat?"[45] Teilhard would have understood and appreciated these inquiries.

---

[40] Pierre Teilhard de Chardin, *Les Directions de L'Avenir* (Paris: Éditions du Seuil, 1973), 28.

[41] Teilhard, *The Human Phenomenon*, 25. In speaking of the most elementary forms of psychism, one is reminded of Leibniz's lowest monads existing in what he called a "stupor." Refer to his *Monadology*, #21 and #24.

[42] Sarah Appleton-Weber translates these expressions "the Inside of Things" and "the Outside of Things." I prefer Bernard Wall's "the Within of Things" and "the Without of Things." See Teilhard, *The Phenomenon of Man*, trans. Bernard Wall (New York: Harper and Row, 1959). "Inside" and "Outside" suggest too much of a spatial metaphor. The difficulty is finding language that captures Teilhard's intent and what all of us at one time or another experience. Other possibilities: *obverse* and *reverse* would indicate the two sides as distinguishable but inseparable; *public* and *private* would suggest the public observability of behavior in contrast to the privacy of one's thoughts; *experiencing* and *experienced* is also involved. Since one can experience one's own experiences as in memories of the immediate past, thereby becoming an object to oneself, the Within may well be the more inclusive category.

[43] Charles Hartshorne, *Born to Sing: An Interpretation and World Survey of Bird Song* (Bloomington: Indiana University Press, 1973).

[44] Donald Wayne Viney and George W. Shields, *The Mind of Charles Hartshorne: A Critical Examination* (Anoka, MN: Process Century Press, 2020), 95–96.

[45] Thomas Nagel, *Mortal Questions* (London and New York: Cambridge University Press, 1979), 165–80.

14   Hold Fast the Spirit of Adventure

One can endeavor to approximate the experience of other creatures imaginatively with careful attention to their environments, their habits, their interactions with others, and their physiology. However, the further down the scale of nature one moves, the more difficult the exercise becomes. For his part, Teilhard ties "the Within" to the concepts of spontaneity and freedom. He maintains that, even within so-called lifeless matter, there are tiny sparks of spontaneity that, given time, ignite into forms of life and mind. He says:

> There is no contradiction in admitting that a universe is built of "freedoms" [*libertés*] even though it outwardly appears to be mechanical—provided these "freedoms" are contained within a great enough state of division and imperfection.[46]

One advantage of Teilhard's view is that it avoids a Cartesian type of dualism of mind and matter. It also escapes the problems of what Hartshorne calls *emergent dualism,* where lifeless matter somehow evolves into matter endowed with sentience.[47] The apparently intractable problem of the emergence of mind is replaced by the more manageable problem of the emergence of different types of mentality—more manageable because it is linked with *physical* complexity in a developmental process.

Teilhard arrived at his metaphysical ideas traveling the road of evolution. Whitehead seems never to have doubted the truth of evolution. He remarks that when he was a young teenager schooled at Sherborne in Dorsetshire, it never occurred to anyone to regard the age of humankind as six thousand years. Continuity with nature, he says, was "a patent, visible fact" with "incredible quantities of fossils . . . more fossils than stones" in the surrounding area.[48] What eventually caught Whitehead's attention was the collapse of the Newtonian worldview. He was present in November 1919 at the Royal Society in London when the photographic results of measurements of the famous eclipse were announced, confirming Einstein's theory. "The whole atmosphere of tense interest was exactly that of the Greek drama: We were the chorus commenting on the decree of destiny as disclosed in the development of a supreme incident."[49]

---

[46] Teilhard, *The Human Phenomenon,* 28.

[47] Charles Hartshorne, *Creative Experiencing: A Philosophy of Freedom,* ed. Donald Wayne Viney and Jincheol O (Albany: State University of New York Press, 2011), 50.

[48] Whitehead, *Essays in Science and Philosophy,* 28.

[49] Whitehead, *Science and the Modern World,* 15.

Important as these observations were, it was not simply a question of New-tonian physics being superseded by Einsteinian physics, although this was indeed on Whitehead's mind.[50] It is, rather, a rethinking of what E. A. Burtt, in his classic study, called the metaphysical foundations of modern science.[51]

According to Whitehead, scientists and philosophers of the seventeenth and eighteenth centuries shared a view he labeled "scientific materialism," which posits a natural world of objects without sense, value, or purpose. "It just does what it does do, following a fixed routine imposed by external relations which do not spring from the nature of its being."[52] Scientific materialism involves the doctrines of "simply located" particles of inert or "vacuous" matter, devoid of any internal relations to any other part of the world. In other words, "material can be said to be *here* in space and *here* in time, or *here* in space-time, in a perfectly definite sense which does not require for its explanation any reference to other regions of space-time."[53] Whitehead called this a "fallacy" in the sense of a false conception. It is use-ful to science as an idealization or abstraction, but it is literally false. Here is an analogy: the concept of a body that is not acted upon by any external force is essential to the statement of Newton's first law of motion. It is a useful abstraction even though no such body exists or could exist.

The world of human experience, with its rich network of relationships, purposive activity, and textures of meaning, is incongruous with the world as posited by scientific materialism. To overcome this "bifurcation of na-ture" between purposeless matter and purposeful creatures, Whitehead proposed what he called throughout *Process and Reality* the "philosophy of organism."[54] According to Whitehead, the stuff of the world, *actual enti-ties* (or actual occasions), have *prehensive relations* with their surroundings, meaning they are internally related to them—they cannot be what they are apart from their environment. This is not to say that an entity is nothing more than a node where its surroundings coalesce. The word *prehension*, modeled on *apprehension*, signifies a "grasping" (as in the adjective *prehensile*) that may or may not be conscious. The actual entity is nothing beyond its activity, and this activity includes incorporating the immediate environment (composed of other actual entities) into its own being. In this way *the actual*

---

[50] Lucien Price, *Dialogues of Alfred North Whitehead*, as recorded by Lucien Price (Boston: Little, Brown and Company, 1954), 345–46.

[51] Edwin Arthur Burtt, *The Metaphysical Foundations of Modern Science* (Garden City, NY: Doubleday & Company, 1954).

[52] Whitehead, *Science and the Modern World*, 25.

[53] Ibid., 72.

[54] Cf. Whitehead, *Science and the Modern World*, 216.

entity is in the world and the world is in it. It is not a "vacuous actuality" for it is an *activity* of prehending. Whitehead used the word *feeling* as a synonym for *prehension,* thereby alerting his readers to the qualitative or affective dimensions of prehending. He characterizes the actual entity's grasping of its world as "a feeling of a complex of feelings."[55]

In two different articles, both titled "Whitehead's Revolutionary Concept of Prehension," Hartshorne argues that "prehension is one of the most original, central, lucid proposals ever offered in metaphysics."[56] According to Hartshorne, Whitehead's genius was to bring together the ideas of memory and perception as asymmetrical cause-and-effect relations[57]; memory of X or perception of X, as effects, are *necessarily* later than X as cause. Memory holds primacy since it is our clearest example of experiencing other experiences. Hartshorne asks, "What is memory if not our present experience of our own previous experiences?"[58] An entity's prehensions are a "precognitive given" in the sense that they involve influence from and incorporation of the immediate past moment in the emerging entity (the "given") *without* implying that the entity fully understands or is conscious of what has been "given" (they are precognitive). In Hartshorne's words, "To intuit or feel (a favorite word of Whitehead's here) is one thing, to think or know that and what one intuits or feels is another."[59]

The process of many elements growing into a novel actuality is called *concrescence.* In Whitehead's pithy phrase, "The many become one and are increased by one."[60] If concrescence sounds like Teilhard's metaphysics of union, it is because it is closely related to it, for concrescence, like Teilhard's creative transformation, is a *creative* process.[61] That is to say, something new enters the world that did not have any prior existence. Moreover, like

---

[55] Whitehead, *Process and Reality,* 211.

[56] Charles Hartshorne, *Creativity in American Philosophy* (Albany: State University of New York Press, 1984), 109; Charles Hartshorne, "Whitehead's Revolutionary Concept of Prehension," *International Philosophical Quarterly* 19, no. 3 (September 1979): 253–63.

[57] Alfred North Whitehead, *Adventures of Ideas* (New York: Macmillan, 1933), 305.

[58] Hartshorne, *Creativity in American Philosophy,* 106.

[59] Ibid., 105.

[60] Whitehead, *Process and Reality,* 21.

[61] In *Le Phénomène Humain,* Teilhard twice uses the word *concrescence,* although not in Whitehead's technical sense. See Pierre Teilhard de Chardin, *Le Phénomène Humain* (Paris: Éditions du Seuil, 1955), 150, 241. Bernard Wall translates the word first as *concretion* (Teilhard, *The Phenomenon of Man,* 138) and later as *concrescence* (ibid., 218). Appleton-Weber uses *concrescence* in both instances (Teilhard, *The Human Phenomenon,* 89, 152). The second instance is closest to Whitehead's meaning. Teilhard writes, "*La distribution, la succession, et la solidarité des êtres naissant de leur concrescence dans une genèse commune*" (italics in the original).

Teilhard, Whitehead explicitly contrasts his own view with one of the central ideas of classical theism, creation *ex nihilo*. According to the traditional concept, in Whitehead's telling, an "external Creator, elicit[s] this final togetherness [of the universe] out of nothing." In Whitehead's view of creativity, each event emerges from a preexisting (past) multiplicity; it is "a process issuing in novelty."[62]

Whitehead went beyond Teilhard in clarifying that concrescence must involve not only prehending other actual entities but also prehending *possibilities*.[63] In this way, there can be influence from both *what is*, and from *what could be*. This is yet another way in which actual entities are not vacuous. As with Teilhard's Within of Things, which takes many forms, one must make ample allowance for the unimaginably wide grades of the discernment of possibility, often confused and vague but occasionally clear and vivid. For example, possibilities for a dog chasing a ball are different from what they are for a human being deliberating over a difficult decision. I should add that the varieties of mentality are not necessarily discrete types. They may comprise a continuum of qualities, and therefore be infinite, as Hartshorne believed.[64]

Whitehead, like Teilhard, avoids the problem of nature as divided between mere matter-in-motion and creatures with the curious qualities of mentality. I am certain that Teilhard would also resonate to Whitehead's complaints about "misplaced concreteness," which is at the heart of the Englishman's view of philosophy as "the critic of abstractions."[65] I say this because of Teilhard's feeling for the organic developmental relations within nature and because of his distrust of the abstractions of traditional metaphysics and theology. The parallels with Teilhard begin to falter somewhat when it comes to religion. It is true that Whitehead greatly admired John Henry Newman (1801–90) and that he apparently considered the path of Catholicism. Evelyn Whitehead indicated that the doctrine of papal infallibility was a stumbling block for her husband.[66] In later life he didn't

---

[62] Whitehead, *Adventures of Ideas*, 303.

[63] Whitehead speaks of possibilities as "eternal objects" or "forms of definiteness." These forms are said to be *ingressed* (one might say instantiated) into an actual entity as it prehends them. See Whitehead, *Process and Reality*, 23. There is a considerable critical literature about the necessity of eternal objects and about their very nature. At this juncture, it is only necessary to acknowledge the importance of *discerning possibilities* as a factor in concrescence.

[64] Charles Hartshorne, *Beyond Humanism: Essays in the Philosophy of Nature* (Chicago: Willett, Clark and Company, 1937), chap. 8.

[65] Whitehead, *Science and the Modern World*, 86, 126.

[66] Victor Lowe, "A. N. W.: A Biographical Perspective," *Process Studies* 12, no. 3 (1982): 145.

18   Hold Fast the Spirit of Adventure

want to be affiliated with any church, although he said he was closest to the Unitarians.[67] The trappings and pronouncements of religion were very much a secondary concern.

Teilhard surely knew the feeling. In January 1926, he wrote to his close friend and fellow Jesuit, Auguste Valensin (1879–1953):

> In some way, *I no longer have confidence* in the outward manifestations of the Church. I believe it is by it that the divine influence will continue to reach me. But I no longer believe very much in the immediate, tangible, critical value of official decisions and directions. There are some who feel happy in the visible Church; as for me, it seems I will be happy to die to be rid of it, that is to say, to find Our Savior outside of it. I speak to you thus naively—without bitterness it seems to me—because it is true, and because I *cannot* see things otherwise.[68]

These words were penned on the heels of what has been called "the crisis of obedience." An unknown person removed from Teilhard's desk a seven-page note he had written in 1922 on the question of original sin in light of evolution.[69] The note was never intended for publication, but somehow it made its way to Rome. Wlodimir Ledóchowski (1866–1942), the Jesuit superior general, was thereby alerted to the note's possible conflict with Catholic orthodoxy. The affair came to a head in July 1925. The results were that Teilhard lost his position at the Catholic Institute in Paris and was advised to distance himself from Marcellin Boule (1861–1942) at the Museum of Natural History. On pain of official censure, he was required to sign a document agreeing to the church's position on original sin with the promise not to speak out on the subject any further. Indeed, he was not to entertain any alternative to the church's view of original sin *even hypothetically*. He was then effectively exiled to China, far from the intellectual centers of Paris.[70] While Teilhard's interchanges with Ledóchowski were

---

[67] Ibid.; and Price, *Dialogues*, 310.

[68] Teilhard, *Lettres Intimes*, 132.

[69] Teilhard, *Christianity and Evolution*, 44–55.

[70] The article by David Grumett and Paul Bentley, "Teilhard de Chardin, Original Sin, and the Six Propositions," *Zygon* 53, no. 2 (June 2018): 303–30, is essential reading. Grumett and Benley provide the content of the document that Teilhard signed. In addition, they explain Teilhard's reasons for signing it, compare his crisis of obedience to similar disciplinary measures taken by Rome against other scholars, and explain Teilhard's response to the 1950 papal encyclical *Humani Generis*. The authors make a convincing case that Teilhard's superiors could provide no conciliar justification for the proposition that he was most reluctant to accept—that "the human race takes its origin from one protopar-

gentlemanly and irenic, his correspondence with Valensin shows that he was at his most recusant when Rome was at its most intransigent.

It is misleading to call Whitehead a Christian, or at least the question requires some dialectical dancing about the meaning of Christian.[71] He took a developmental approach to religion but never assumed the trajectory to be positive. A remark in *Religion in the Making* pretty well captures his general attitude: "Religion can be, and has been, the main instrument of progress. But if we survey the whole race, we must pronounce that generally it has not been so: 'Many are called, but few are chosen.'"[72] In the case of Christianity, he speaks of "the brief Galilean vision of humility" flickering throughout the ages "uncertainly."[73] The last statement from Whitehead on religion that is extant is a talk he gave to the Augustinian Society of Cambridge, Massachusetts, on March 30, 1939. It is an occasionally searing indictment of dogmatism issuing in violent hatred. According to Whitehead, "Hatred arises when limited intelligence perceives antagonism without recognition of its own limitations."[74] The limitations include adherence to dogmatic formulae as exact expressions of truth, hubris in one's ability to discern truth, and the failure to empathize with contrary perspectives. He was particularly dissatisfied with St. Paul,[75] but more importantly with Augustine of Hippo, whom he viewed as pivotal in the church's endorsement of the persecution of heretics. Paul Kuntz remembers that some in the audience were furious: "The three Jesuit priests at my table were angry."[76] [I leave it to others to parse Whitehead's animadversions on Paul and Augustine on the question of religious intolerance. Of course, Teilhard found value in Paul's concept of the Comic Christ. What I wish to stress, however, is Whitehead's abhorrence of the traditional concept of divine power. In *Science and the Modern World*, Whitehead writes, "The presentation of God under the aspect of power awakens every modern instinct of critical reaction."[77] Later, in *Religion in the Making*, he writes:

---

ent, Adam." They conclude, "Teilhard was being required to submit to a more restrictive formula than could be justified on either historical or logical grounds" (316).

[71] See the excellent article by Paul G. Kuntz, "Can Whitehead Be Made a Christian Philosopher?" *Process Studies* 12, no. 4 (Winter 1982): 232–42.

[72] Alfred North Whitehead, *Religion in the Making*, introduction Judith A. Jones; glossary Randall E. Auxier (New York: Fordham University Press, 1996 [1926]), 37–38.

[73] Whitehead, *Process and Reality*, 342.

[74] Alfred North Whitehead, "Religious Psychology of the Western Peoples" (March 30, 1939). ADDO20 Whitehead Research Library (2019).

[75] Price, *Dialogues*, 307.

[76] Kuntz, "Can Whitehead Be Made a Christian Philosopher?" 241.

[77] Whitehead, *Science and the Modern World*, 274.

20 *Hold Fast the Spirit of Adventure*

The worship of glory arising from power is not only dangerous: it arises from a barbaric conception of God. I suppose that even the world itself could not contain the bones of those slaughtered because of men intoxicated by its attraction.[78]

No wonder that three years later, in *Process and Reality*, Whitehead refers to the idolatry of fashioning God in the image of imperial rulers.[79] Here we begin to see, once again, a convergence with Teilhard. Their respective objections to omnipotence seemed to arise from different sources—Teilhard from considerations of evolution, and Whitehead from the way it filters into society in the form of the worship of power—but their conclusions are much the same.

Whitehead constantly reworked his idea of God, most intensely between 1925 and 1929, but also up until at least 1933. The chapter titled "God" in *Science and the Modern World* was not part of the lectures (delivered in February 1925) on which the book was based. In that chapter Whitehead argues that the appearance of new actualities presupposes "an antecedent limitation among values, introducing contraries, grades, and oppositions."[80] This "principle of limitation" is God. Interestingly, Whitehead maintains that "God is not concrete, but He is the ground for concrete actuality."[81] The problem is that a *principle* limits nothing; only an *actuality* can play this role.[82] Within a year—in the lectures published as *Religion in the Making*—he referred to God as "an actual but non-temporal entity."[83] With the publication of *Process and Reality* in 1929, Whitehead speaks of God as the one non-temporal actual entity that customizes the domain of possibilities (eternal objects) for each emergent occasion.[84] The realm of all possibilities is called the Primordial Nature of God. Since the God of *Religion in the Making* and *Process and Reality* is an actual entity, it *acts and is acted upon* by the world of temporal occasions. The reception of all achieved value in the temporal world into the divine life is the Consequent Nature of God. In *Adventures of Ideas*, published in 1933, Whitehead makes explicit what is implicit at the close of *Process and Reality*. He speaks of the "everlasting

---

[78] Whitehead, *Religion in the Making*, 55.
[79] Whitehead, *Process and Reality*, 342.
[80] Whitehead, *Science and the Modern World*, 256.
[81] Ibid., 257.
[82] A. H. Johnson, "Whitehead as Teacher and Philosopher," 368.
[83] Whitehead, *Religion in the Making*, 90, 94.
[84] Whitehead, *Process and Reality*, 31, 46.

nature of God, which in a sense is non-temporal and in another [sense] temporal."[85]

Among other things, Whitehead's theism, like that of Teilhard, involves a reformed notion of divine power. God's power is twofold. In the first place, God continually acts on actual occasions not by imposing the divine will, but as "a lure for feeling," introducing possibilities for richer experiences customized for each occasion.[86] God, Whitehead says, is "the poet of the world, with tender patience leading it by his vision of truth, beauty, and goodness."[87] Process theologians often say that *God acts by persuasion rather than by coercion.* Whitehead attributes this idea to Plato's *Sophist* and *Timaeus* and calls it "one of the greatest intellectual discoveries in the history of religion."[88] To say that God does not act by "coercion" means that God does not, indeed cannot, *unilaterally* bring about the completed concrescence of any actual occasion. God provides an "initial aim" of graded possibilities around which the entity itself completes the process of its own becoming. In a metaphysical sense, it is not only God that acts persuasively and not coercively, but every actual being. The other aspect of divine power is God's openness to the creatures. Again, Whitehead writes:

> Thus, by reason of the relativity of all things, there is a reaction of the world on God. The completion of God's nature into a fulness of physical feeling is derived from the objectification of the world in God.[89]

As noted above, this is Whitehead's doctrine of the Consequent Nature of God. This passage calls to mind Teilhard's claim, mentioned previously in the letter to de Solages, that God must create something outside Godself as an act of self-completion. For both Whitehead and Teilhard, God is conceived as being in dynamic interaction with the creatures.

Both Whitehead and Teilhard recognized that the philosophical difficulties in believing in God are not simply a matter of weighing the merits of arguments for and against the existence of God. There is the prior question of definition. In *Religion in the Making* Whitehead writes: "Today there is but one religious dogma in debate: What do you mean by 'God'?"[90] In any event, there was never any question in Whitehead's mind of offering a proof

---

[85] Whitehead, *Adventures of Ideas*, 267.
[86] Whitehead, *Process and Reality*, 344.
[87] Ibid., 346.
[88] Whitehead, *Adventures of Ideas*, 213.
[89] Whitehead, *Process and Reality*, 345.
[90] Whitehead, *Religion in the Making*, 67.

22   Hold Fast the Spirit of Adventure

of God's existence. He characterizes his presentation of God as "an attempt to add another speaker to that masterpiece, Hume's *Dialogues Concerning Natural Religion*."[91] Whitehead takes God seriously *as a philosophical problem*, by adding to the dialogue—not just Hume's, but to the conversation that is Western thought—a genuinely new way of thinking about God. A question worthy of sociological study is how often people turn to disbelief because of naive, ugly, or monstrous concepts of God. In this vein Teilhard wondered whether the atheistic malaise of his time was a product of what he called *unsatisfied theism*, a failure of theology to provide a God adequate to our deepest longings.[92]

Directions of the Future

Classical theology saw the universe as a *completed product*, at least when considering things from what it took to be a God's eye view. To be sure, from our limited perspectives the future seems uncertain, but the theologians assured us that God knows in unerring detail what is to be. According to the doctrine of creation *ex nihilo*, the universe, from beginning to end, is the *effect* of divine activity as its *cause*. God's creativity, transcending the events of space and time, produces them. Room was made for creaturely secondary causes, but such was the cleverness of divine wisdom that these causes conform to God's providential plan. The rise of modern science, especially in Descartes' philosophy, introduced the metaphor of the machine for nature's processes. Later, the Deists of the eighteenth century moved God's creative act to the beginning of the universe as a quasi-temporal First Cause that

---

[91] Whitehead, *Process and Reality*, 343.

[92] Teilhard, *Activation of Energy*, 248. Charles Hartshorne often emphasized this point: "Examine unbelievers and you will often find them focusing on some more or less antiquated, discredited form of theism, not theism simply as such. Often they are rightly rebelling against some tyrant view of deity that insults or belittles human capacities and makes God far from the most lovable of conceivable beings." See Santiago Sia, ed., *Charles Hartshorne's Concept of God: Philosophical and Theological Responses* (Dordrecht: Kluwer Academic Publishers, 1990), 244. In a letter to the editor, Hartshorne writes: "So long as there are poor forms of theism, and that may be a long time, I hope there will be atheists." See Charles Hartshorne, "Tolerance Test," *Austin-American Statesman*, June 18, 1990. The occasion of his writing *Omnipotence and Other Theological Mistakes* was meeting two women who were bothered by what they saw as absurdities in the idea of God. It is true that Hartshorne wrote a lot about theistic and atheistic arguments, but reform in the concept of God was always at the center of his thinking. See Viney and Shields, *The Mind of Charles Hartshorne*, chaps. 5, 6.

set a deterministic system of cause and effect in motion. Again, the future was uncertain only from a limited perspective; if one supposed God (or LaPlace's demon) to have perfect knowledge of both the initial conditions of the universe and Newton's laws, events would unfold as omniscience had foreseen. Not being privy to such knowledge, we are obliged to act as though the future is open, making the decisions that seem to settle our fates.

Whitehead and Teilhard looked back on these ideas from a nineteenth-century perspective in which biblical chronologies were discarded or expanded and in which the time spans of prehistory seemed to lengthen by millions of years with each passing decade of new discoveries. More important still was the idea of *development* in almost every domain of inquiry. In the first edition of his book on Averroes, published in 1852, Ernest Renan (1823–92) writes:

> The characteristic feature of the nineteenth century is to . . . substitute the category of *becoming* for the category of *being*. . . . In former times everything was considered as being. . . . Now everything is considered to be in the process of being made.[93]

As Teilhard said almost a century later, "Today, positive knowledge of things is identified with study of their development."[94] Development is the idea that any particular stage of an organism, a social group, a cultural movement, presupposes previous stages that made it possible within a range of probabilities. To be sure, deterministic theories that imagined previous states as *necessitating* the stages that followed were alive in the nineteenth century; in our day they're on life support, but they remain. However, the various forms of determinism (theological or scientific) came more and more under critical scrutiny by philosophers and scientists alike—this, well before the advent of quantum physics.[95] Keenly attuned to these advances in knowledge, Whitehead and Teilhard were in the vanguard of rethinking old assumptions. The metaphysics of union and the philosophy of organism were the results.

---

[93] Ernest Renan, *Averroès et L'Averroïsme: Essai Historique*, 3rd ed., rev. and updated (Paris: Michel Lévy Frères Libraires Éditeurs, 1866), vi.

[94] Teilhard, *The Human Phenomenon*, 16.

[95] In addition to Jules Lequyer and Henri Bergson, whom I have already mentioned, one could add the names of Charles Renouvier (1815–1903), C. S. Peirce (1839–1914), William James (1842–1910), and Émile Boutroux (1845–1921). See also Ian Hacking, "Nineteenth Century Cracks in the Concept of Determinism," *Journal of the History of Ideas* 44, no. 3 (July-September 1983): 455–75.

24   Hold Fast the Spirit of Adventure

Throughout the nineteenth century the layers of the earth revealed a progression of life forms, with hominids—their fossilized bones only recently uncovered—among the last to appear, their existence spanning the tiniest fraction of the age of the planet. We have seen that Teilhard was impressed by the gradual emergence of creatures of ever more complexity and mentality. He recognized natural selection as a vital piece of the evolutionary puzzle, but he argued that it could not furnish the final explanation for the rise in complexity. If there is to be a struggle for survival in the first place, there must be "*a tenacious sense of conservation*, of survival."[96] Whitehead was aware of the related issue of how creatures of "faint survival power" came to be.[97] Like Teilhard, he was attentive to the problem of explaining the trajectory toward increasing complexification. He mused:

> Why has the trend of evolution been upwards? The fact that organic species have been produced from inorganic distributions of matter, and the fact that in the lapse of time organic species of higher and higher types have evolved are not in the least explained by any doctrine of adaptation to the environment, or of struggle.[98]

He observed that in the biosphere it is not only that populations adapt to specific environments, but that they also adapt the environment to themselves, from bird nests and beaver dams to dramatic examples of human technologies of agriculture, water management, city planning, and more. Of course, this is not news to evolutionary science. However, Whitehead—of one mind with Teilhard—thought it necessary to posit a "general counter-agency" as a kind of motive urge spread throughout the universe, too diffuse for direct observation, to explain the tendency of the elements of the universe to seek greater levels of physical complexity and psychic interiority.[99] In *The Human Phenomenon*, Teilhard's name for the counter-agency is *radial energy*.[100]

---

[96] Teilhard, *Activation of Energy*, 233–34.

[97] Alfred North Whitehead, *The Function of Reason* (Boston: Beacon Press, 1958 [1929]), 5.

[98] Ibid., 7.

[99] Ibid., 25, 27, 34, 90.

[100] Teilhard, *The Human Phenomenon*, 29. No more than Whitehead does Teilhard pretend to "provide a truly satisfactory solution" (ibid., 29) to how radial energy is related to energy as understood by thermodynamics. Suffice it to say that, contrary to some critics, he structures his speculations in ways that do not deny the fundamentals of that science. See Donald Wayne Viney, "Teilhard, Medawar, and the New Atheism," in *From*

Whitehead spoke of "the evolutionist fallacy" of supposing that fitness for survival is identical with the promotion of the art of life.[101] According to Whitehead, one must account not only for the urge to live, but also the urge to live well, and to live better.[102] These words were published in 1929 in *The Function of Reason*, Whitehead's Vanuxem Lectures at Princeton. Teilhard, in his 1950 lecture "The Zest for Living" (presented in Paris at the *Congrès Universel des Croyants*) gives a nearly exact parallel expression to these ideas when he speaks of the threefold form of psychic vitalization: "'a will to survive,' turning into a 'will to live fully,' itself taken up again in a 'will to super-live' which rises up in each one of us, unmasking its features *in the hominized state.*"[103] In evolutionary terms, what are these concepts supposed to explain?

To address this question in the case of Teilhard, it is helpful to be reminded of how his mind worked. Ursula King captures this well when she observes: "His worldview is suffused with the immensity of time and space and embedded within the great arc of evolution."[104] Of course, his primary focus was this planet, whose pre-history he knew so well. He thought on a *planetary* scale. He would have understood exactly what Marcia Bjornerud means when she says that rocks are not nouns but verbs.[105] After going from South Africa to New York via Argentina, Teilhard wrote to Leroy (November 8, 1951) of "a real shock" to see such similar geological patterns on the rims of the two southern continents. "One point for Wegener," he said, referring to Alfred Wegener's theory of continental drift, which was gaining acceptance in the 1950s. In the same letter he marveled at the thought of "the human wave" making its way from Africa, across Asia, "and down the length of the Americas—far in South America on the other side of the world!"[106] These and other observations were part and parcel of his vision of the lithosphere overlayed in the eons by a biosphere and culminating only recently in what he called the noosphere, "*the thinking envelope*

Teilhard to Omega: Co-Creating an Unfinished Universe, ed. Ilia Delio (Maryknoll, NY: Orbis Books, 2014), 134.

[101] Whitehead, *The Function of Reason*, 4.

[102] Ibid., 8.

[103] Teilhard, *Activation of Energy*, 234. I know of no evidence that Teilhard read *The Function of Reason*. This seems to be another case of Whitehead and Teilhard thinking along parallel tracks.

[104] Ursula King, "A Vision Transformed: Teilhard de Chardin's Evolutionary Awakening at Hastings," *The Heythrop Journal* 54 (2013): 596.

[105] Marcia Bjornerud, *Timefulness: How Thinking Like a Geologist Can Help Save the World* (Princeton, NJ: Princeton University Press, 2018), 8.

[106] Leroy, *Letters from My Friend Teilhard de Chardin*, 102.

26   Hold Fast the Spirit of Adventure

of the earth."[107] He was convinced that these concentric spheres showed *direction* not simply as an accident of our planet but as a result of a more general tendency at the heart of things. Herein lies the most global reason he considered radial energy as a necessary concomitant of his worldview.

There is nothing I know in Whitehead's thought that corresponds to the noosphere, but I cannot see anything in his philosophy inconsistent with it. The internet, the global network of satellite enabled communication, combined with recent advances in artificial intelligence and quantum computing, may be enough to ask in all seriousness whether we are witnessing the nascent stages of a planetary mind. On the other hand, on the whole we humans seem just as aesthetically deficient, epistemically challenged, morally undisciplined, and politically divided as we have ever been—whither beauty, truth, and goodness? Among other things, our shortsighted abuse and misuse of the environment, our failure to address the extreme concentrations of wealth in a tiny fraction of the earth's population, and our continuing fascination with pernicious forms of nationalism are among the factors that do not bode well for the long-term health of the human group. Teilhard's clarion call to put narrow identities of nation, race, and creed behind us and "to build the earth"[108] continues to compete with the noise of populous movements, race hatred, religious extremists, and the terrorist warfare of mendacious tyrants.

Having lived through two global conflicts and knowing of the horrible destructive power of nuclear weapons, Teilhard was alert to these kinds of problems. Then again, as the quotation from Ursula King suggests, Teilhard did not think in terms of years, or even centuries; he marked time using geological time scales and what is now referred to as *deep time.* As for the future, it is, as Isaiah says, and as the Christian formula has it, "world

---

[107] Teilhard first used *noosphere* in his essay "Hominization," finished in Paris and dated May 6, 1925 (Teilhard, *La Vision du Passé*, 89–90). The English translation incorrectly marks the date as May 6, 1923 (Teilhard, *The Vision of the Past*, 79), but Teilhard was in China at that time. While he was in Paris in the 1920s, Teilhard worked closely with Édouard Le Roy whose ideas often mirrored his own, and who eventually wrote about the noosphere. Teilhard's letters to Le Roy are a treasure, but they do not shed any light on the origin of the word. Teilhard also saw Vladamir Vernadsky (1863–1945) in Paris at this time, another thinker who wrote on the noosphere. See Claude Cuénot, *Pierre Teilhard de Chardin: Les Grandes Étapes de son Évolution* (Paris: Plon, 1958), 80. Teilhard remembered coining the term *noosphere,* but he added, "sait-on jamais" (one never knows). See De Lubac's note in Teilhard, *Lettres Intimes,* 151.

[108] Pierre Teilhard de Chardin, *Human Energy,* trans. J. M. Cohen (New York: Harcourt, Brace, Jovanovich, 1969), 37.

without end" (Isa 45:17), although for Teilhard it is a world of mutual construction and completion by and between God and the creatures. He was patient of this goal, pointing out that evolution directed at a definite end is not incompatible with chance as long as chance itself is directed (*hasard dirigé*), as when numerous setbacks may be suffered to achieve one's aim.[109] He traced the vector of evolutionary progress into a future to a personal center of convergence beyond space and time, which he labeled Omega or Christ-Omega.[110] Here, the metaphysics of union achieves its most eminent expression, where what is most incommunicably valuable in each of us "super-lives" in communion with God. In Teilhard's succinct formula: *True union differentiates.*[111]

Teilhard's vision is breathtaking in its scope and supremely attractive in its aim. It is worthy of a great seer, but questions remain. One may ask whether "chance" can be directed in the way Teilhard imagined. The ever-increasing multiplicity of beings in the universe with ever higher grades of freedom in the sense of enhanced abilities for choice and wider ranges of options are accompanied by greater opportunities for the flourishing of all forms of life as well as greater risks in the misuse of such liberty. Moreover, our very freedom, as a result of projects at cross purposes or simple unplanned mistakes, may result in such a degree of unpredictability as to cloud our vision of the future. As far as I know, apart from his idea of directed chance, Teilhard did not specifically address these problems. However, he did speak of the anxiety of wondering whether the future is "open or closed."[112] To illustrate, he used the analogy of trapped miners who would lose heart if there was no hope of escape—a gleam of light, a whiff of fresh air through a crevasse, the sound of rescuers. For the human group, to be "closed off" means total death, the extinction of all that we consider most worthy in ourselves. According to Teilhard, what is required to energize us is "a universe that is not only open but can also be seen to be

---

[109] Teilhard, *The Human Phenomenon*, 66.

[110] Pierre Teilhard de Chardin, *The Appearance of Man,* trans. J. M. Cohen (New York: Harper and Row, 1965), 264; and *Activation of Energy*, 146.

[111] Teilhard, "Rencontre avec le Père Teilhard de Chardin," 4. Teilhard insisted that his emphasis on "the primacy of the whole in relation to the element" is "at the antipodes either of a social totalitarianism leading to the termite mound, or of a Hindu pantheism seeking the outcome and ultimate figure of the spiritual in the direction of an identification of beings with a common background underlying the variety of events and things. Not mechanization, therefore, nor identification by fusion and loss of consciousness; but unification by laborious ultra-determination and love." Ibid.; cf. Leroy, *Letters*, 85.

[112] Teilhard, *The Appearance of Man*, 264.

centered (or, which comes to the same thing, personalizing) in the direction of the future."[113]

Teilhard is impressed by the past and what he sees as convergence toward greater complexity and consciousness, a line of development he projects into the future. It is well to recall, however, that the past is also a scene of continual extinction of species, brought on by planetary catastrophe or by competition with other forms of life. There is now talk of a new geological epoch, the anthropocene, marked by the traces of human activity, and the traces are not necessarily good. One of our least admirable qualities is the alarmingly increased rate of extinction of other species, extinctions for which *we* are responsible. Ironically, it is now clear that we may ourselves be the greatest threat to our survival. If it is true that we are creatures that *make ourselves*, it is equally true that we are capable of *unmaking ourselves*. Can our species, by virtue of qualities unique to ourselves, escape the fate of so many others? We have guaranteed that countless species will not have survived the anthropocene. But can *we* survive the anthropocene? Adopting the Teilhardian vision, or something very much like it, as a matter of faith, or of hope, cannot be unavailing. Following the line of thinking in William James's "will to believe," the trapped miners, by their very attitude and actions, can be a vital element in their own salvation.

Again, none of this is strictly inconsistent with the philosophy of organism. As far as I know, Whitehead's only speculation about the long-term future was that our universe is one in a series (or perhaps a collection) of *cosmic epochs*. If Teilhard thought in terms of *deep time*, Whitehead's mathematical mind thought in terms of what might be called *deep dimensions*.

Whitehead explains that a cosmic epoch is "that widest society of actual entities whose immediate relevance to ourselves is traceable."[114] He explains further:

> I certainly think that the universe is running down. It means that our epoch illustrates one special physical type of order. For example, this absurdly limited number of three dimensions of space is a sign that you have got something characteristic of a special order.[115]

---

[113] Teilhard, *Activation of Energy*, 174, 193.

[114] Whitehead, *Process and Reality*, 92.

[115] Whitehead, *Essays*, 90. Whitehead also expressed the idea of a universe in decay in *The Function of Reason*, 24. Here is another statement on the idea of dimensions: "The physical extensive continuum with which we are concerned in this cosmic epoch is four-dimensional. Notice that the property of being 'dimensional' is relative to a particular ovate class in the extensive continuum. There may be 'ovate' classes satisfying

If Whitehead is correct, then the order of nature that science discovers (such as physical constants, laws of attraction and repulsion, elementary particles) is not the only possible order. In metaphysics we strive to conceive the widest scope of possibilities for existence, to find what is necessary to every cosmic epoch, but we are as prone to error in this domain as in others—perhaps more so. He reminds us that geometry was once considered an affair settled in its essentials before non-Euclidian geometries demonstrated other possibilities.[116] The most general possibilities (the realm of Eternal Objects) are Whitehead's version of Plato's Forms. As Augustine had identified Plato's Forms as the *Logos* (the Mind) of God, so Whitehead locates the fund of mutually consistent possibilities for all epochs in the Primordial Nature of God.[117]

The idea of cosmic epochs pushes us to the limits of what we can conceive. It also invites us to consider our universe as one among many possible ways an epoch might unfold. Whitehead seemed resolved to adopt this super-epochal view of the universe, but this involves the concept of the birth and death of cosmic epochs, including our own. As he says, "The universe is running down."[118] What hope for escape for the trapped miners in this Whiteheadian conception? Whitehead frames the problem as a paradox:

The world is thus faced by the paradox that, at least in its higher actualities, it craves for novelty and yet is haunted by terror at the loss of the past, with its familiarities and its loved ones. It seeks escape from time in the character of "perpetually perishing."[119]

The paradox is resolved only if "novelty does not mean loss."[120] Whitehead's comments about *Process and Reality* at his seventieth-birthday celebration are revealing:

Almost all of *Process and Reality* can be read as an attempt to analyze perishing on the same level as Aristotle's analysis of becoming. The notion of the prehension of the past means that the past is an element

---

all the conditions with the exception of the 'dimensional' conditions. Also a continuum may have one number of dimensions relating to one ovate class, and another number of dimensions relating to another ovate class." See Whitehead, *Process and Reality*, 305.

[116] Whitehead, *Process and Reality*, 197.

[117] Ibid., 93.

[118] Whitehead, *Essays*, 90.

[119] Whitehead, *Process and Reality,* 340.

[120] Ibid.

which perishes and thereby remains an element in the state beyond, and thus, is objectified. That is the whole notion. If you get a general notion of what is meant by perishing, you have accomplished an apprehension of what you mean by memory and causality, what you mean when you feel that what we are is of infinite importance, because as we perish we are immortal. That is the one key thought around which the whole development of *Process and Reality* is woven.[121]

Is this one paradox explained by another: novelty does not mean loss because we die but live forevermore? Or is this the sort of fruitful oxymoron of which Whitehead was a master, and for which the teachings of the Gospels are so well known? Whitehead rejects the idea that an actual entity, by completing its concrescence, simply vanishes or becomes nothing. He continually reminds us of Plato's view in *Sophist* (240c, 257b, 258e) that nonbeing is a form of being.[122] Past actual entities exist, not only as "having been," but as factors in subsequent actual entities that prehend them, and thereby as data for others. In this way they continue to be real. Moreover, because, as we have seen, the concept of prehension is modeled on both memory and perception, it is always saturated with affectivity—prehensions are *feelings*.

Whitehead's account of how there can be truths about what has been, even when evidence from a human perspective is lost—the reality of the past—is in his doctrine of the Consequent Nature of God. In his words, "The truth itself is nothing else than how the composite natures of the organic actualities of the world obtain adequate representation in the divine nature."[123] The divine memory of the past is not simply a supercosmic stenographic record. As with all prehensions, there is the affective dimension. It is here one finds the specifically religious quality of God's Consequent Nature, or what Henry Nelson Wieman (1884–1975) called "dome and spire."[124] Whitehead says, "The world is felt in a unison of immediacy. . . . The image—and it is but an image—the image under which

---

[121] Whitehead, *Essays in Science and Philosophy*, 89.

[122] Whitehead, *Adventures of Ideas*, 285, 287, 293, 304.

[123] Whitehead, *Process and Reality*, 12.

[124] Henry Nelson Wieman and Bernard Eugene Meland, *American Philosophies of Religion* (New York: Harper & Brothers, 1936), 237–38. Wieman considered the Consequent Nature of God to be added to Whitehead's system for religious reasons. Only the Primordial Nature, he thought, could be justified philosophically. As we have seen, however, God, denuded of the Consequent Nature, is a mere principle and can neither *act* nor *be acted upon*, as is required if God is actual.

this operative growth of God's nature is best conceived, is that of a tender care that nothing be lost."[125] Whitehead's warning that the image is only an image reminds one of an oft-quoted passage in the last thing he wrote:

> This immortality of the World of Action, derived from its transformation in God's nature is beyond our imagination to conceive. The various attempts at description are often shocking and profane. What does haunt our imagination is that the immediate facts of present action pass into permanent significance for the Universe. The insistent notion of Right and Wrong, Achievement and Failure, depends upon this background. Otherwise every activity is merely a passing whiff of insignificance.[126]

If there is anything in Whitehead remotely resembling an Omega Point, this is it. Both are ideas of the universe being taken up into the reality of God. Both diverge from the classical tradition of divine simplicity by *demanding* a supreme complexity in God. As Teilhard says, the perfection of God's unification of the sum of persons born in the course of evolution is in God's complexity.[127] Finally, the completion of our lives, whether in the Consequent Nature or in Omega, as each philosopher understands these ideas, is beyond space and time, at least as far as our present experiences are concerned.

Teilhard's Omega is a divine personal center of non-divine personal centers, each of which retains what is most essential to its personality. In Omega, true union with God "differentiates," which is to say, preserves and augments, what is most precious in each person. It is much less clear whether one could say the same of Whitehead's God, even when one includes the divine Consequent Nature. I quoted above Whitehead's succinct summary of a process philosophy of nature: "The many become one and are increased by one."[128] Teilhard says something similar, but with a difference. He speaks of "the dramatic and perpetual opposition in the course of evolution between the one [*l'élément*] born of the many [*le multiple*] and the many constantly being born of the one."[129] This sounds Whiteheadian, except for the qualification in what follows. Teilhard characterizes the

---

[125] Whitehead, *Process and Reality*, 346.

[126] Whitehead, *Essays in Science and Philosophy*, 72.

[127] See Teilhard, *Human Energy*, 68.

[128] Whitehead, *Process and Reality*, 21.

[129] Teilhard, *Le Phénomène Humain*, 118; cf. Teilhard, *The Phenomenon of Man*, 111, and Teilhard, *The Human Phenomenon*, 67.

32   Hold Fast the Spirit of Adventure

rhythm of evolution between the one and the many as cruel and indifferent. Its resolution is found only in union with Omega. Teilhard writes:

> From the Spirit alone, where it reaches its *felt* paroxysm, does the antinomy become clear; and the indifference of the World for its elements transforms in immense solicitude—in the sphere of the Person.[130]

The final exemplification of "the sphere of the Person" is in Omega. Whitehead's remark on solicitude—the image of "a tender care that nothing be lost"—may perhaps show that the distance between the two thinkers, though unbridgeable, is not as great as it seems.

A number of questions remain. First, to what extent is it true in Whiteheadian terms that "nothing is lost"? One's personality as formed during a lifetime may be preserved in God's memory, but it seems that further iterations of one's personality beyond life might also be valuable. Whitehead did not foreclose on the possibility of an afterlife, but his system does not require it. Moreover, having an "afterlife" is not the same as "being immortal," which may, as Hartshorne argues, be impossible if infinite iterations of any non-divine personality is not possible.[131] The second question is whether God, conceived by Whitehead as a single everlasting actual entity, can be conceived to be a person, or even if such a God can be "felt" by us. Whitehead's own testimony, according to his student A. H. Johnson, was that he was trying to strike a balance between an overemphasis on the personhood of God in Christianity—a crude anthropomorphism—and a whittling away of the divine personality in Buddhism. He attributed personality to God but conceded that it is "a very vague concept."[132] Moreover, he said that he had not attempted to solve the problem of how an everlasting divine concrescence, which never comes to completion, can be prehended by non-divine actualities.[133] Hartshorne addressed this question by reimagining the divine actuality as a personally ordered society, a view that more clearly preserves the personhood of God but is not without its own problems, as Hartshorne himself realized.[134]

---

[130] Teilhard, *Le Phénomène Humain*, 118.

[131] Charles Hartshorne, *Wisdom as Moderation: A Philosophy of the Middle Way* (Albany: State University of New York Press, 1987), 53.

[132] Johnson, "Whitehead as Teacher and Philosopher," 366.

[133] Ibid., 373.

[134] Charles Hartshorne, *Creative Synthesis and Philosophic Method* (LaSalle, IL: Open Court, 1970), 124–25.

Whitehead could accommodate Teilhard's talk of Omega as "partially actual" and "partially transcendent," or again, as "emerged and the emergent."[135] However, by virtue of the open-ended quality of the Consequent Nature, God never reaches completion. Like the world itself, it is *ever in the making*. Whitehead's entire philosophy turns on the primacy of the aesthetic. According to Whitehead, "The teleology of the Universe is directed to the production of Beauty."[136] Aesthetic qualities, moreover, are arguably infinite in possibilities for realization. As Hartshorne argues, "Highest achievement of beauty or of value" may be no more meaningful than "highest positive integer."[137] For Whitehead, the perfect embodiment of beauty can only be in the quality of an unending process of becoming actual. To use the apt phrase of German theologian Julia Enxing, the Whiteheadian (and Hartshornean) God exhibits "perfect changes," and in this sense, perfect beauty, but not as a state of completion or as a culmination of evolution than which none greater is possible. Hartshorne provided a useful gloss on dipolar theism when he characterized God as the everlasting "self-surpassing surpasser of all."[138] Finally, the immortality Whitehead offers is more in keeping with Abraham than with Socrates, an immortality of being remembered rather than a continuation of one's personal experiences beyond the grave. In the words of a Jewish prayer: "Though all things pass, let not Your glory depart from us. Help us to become co-workers with you, and endow our fleeting days with abiding worth."[139]

---

[135] Teilhard, *Activation of Energy*, 112, 113.

[136] Whitehead, *Adventures of Ideas*, 341.

[137] Charles Hartshorne, *A Natural Theology for Our Time* (LaSalle, IL: Open Court, 1967), 19–20.

[138] Charles Hartshorne, *The Divine Relativity: A Social Conception of God* (New Haven, CT: Yale University Press, 1948), 20. *Perfect Changes* is the title that Julia Enxing chose for the book she edited with Klaus Müller, *Perfect Changes: Die Religionsphilosophie Charles Hartshornes* (Regensburg: Verlag Friedrich Pustet, 2012).

[139] Chaim Stern, ed., *Gates of Prayer: The New Union Prayerbook* (New York: Central Conference of American Rabbis, 1975), 193. As far as I know, Teilhard never addressed the strictly philosophical problem that God's Consequent Nature is supposed to solve. As noted above, the past does not simply become nothing, as if it had never been. Otherwise, we could not distinguish an imagined past from the actual past, or again, accurate or wildly inaccurate accounts of the past would be empty concepts. I am not claiming that Whitehead's theory is correct, only that the reality of the past is not something that exercised Teilhard's mind—he simply assumed its reality. If Whitehead's theory is correct, then it can be folded into Teilhard's theology. If not, Teilhard's theology is no worse off. In any event Whitehead's theory must answer a Euthyphro-style dilemma: Is the past real because God remembers it, or does God remember it because it is real? If the former, then the past is nothing more than God's memory of it, in which case there seems to be no basis for saying God's memory is accurate; if the latter, then the

Other Directions

In his twenties, Whitehead was an active member of the Cambridge Conversazione Society, also known as the Apostles. It was a select group that met to hear a paper read, to engage in open discussion, and to respond to a question concerning what had been discussed. Notes from the meetings are often cryptic and enigmatic, but Victor Lowe says of Whitehead's responses: "Throughout his Apostolic years he took a position on the side of diversity and adventure whenever the question concerned their contrast with uniformity and the *status quo*."[140] In 1886 the question posed to the group was, "Should churchmen go to Rome?" The most well-known Anglican who had gone to Rome was Newman, whom Whitehead admired. Whitehead's response to the question was this: "Yes, or in the other direction." Lowe interpreted "the other direction" to mean dropping Christian belief altogether.[141] As we have seen, Whitehead did just that, and from his mid-thirties he never again identified as Christian. But it is also true that, in his Harvard years, he developed a new philosophical theology to which some Christian theologians have resonated, and not Christians alone but some Jews and Muslims as well.[142] Whitehead found a "direction" that was not atheistic, not Catholic, not even explicitly Christian.

We know that Teilhard remained obedient to his superiors to the last. In many ways, however, he too went "in the other direction," if this means moving away from the dominant theology of the church of his time. It was precisely why he was virtually exiled from his native land, and why, despite the efforts of Kathleen Duffy and others, the *monitum* on his writings issued in 1962, reiterated in 1981, has not been lifted.[143] Fiction writer Flannery O'Connor (1925–64), a Catholic herself, read and advised others to read Teilhard. In a 1964 letter to Father J. H. McCown, she writes: "The most

---

past is independent of God's memory of it, in which case God's memory is not needed to ground its reality. For an interesting discussion of these issues, see Patrick Todd, *The Open Future: Why Future Contingents Are All False* (New York: Oxford University Press, 2021), 12–16.

[140] Lowe, "A. N. W.: A Biographical Perspective," 139.

[141] Ibid., 140.

[142] Sandra B. Lubarsky and David Ray Griffin, eds., *Jewish Theology and Process Thought* (Albany: State University of New York Press, 1996); Muhammad Iqbal, *The Reconstruction of Religious Thought in Islam* (Stanford, CA: Stanford University Press, 2012).

[143] Heidi Schlumpt, "Time to Rehabilitate Teilhard de Chardin?" *National Catholic Reporter*, January 27, 2018.

important non-fiction writer is Père Pierre Teilhard de Chardin, S.J. who died in 1955 and has so far escaped the Index although a monition has been issued on him. If they are good, they are dangerous."[144] Dangerous, yes, but also energizing.

John Haught and many others have remarked on Teilhard's influence on Vatican II, as well as the use of Teilhardian ideas in the pronouncements of recent popes.[145] As one outside the church, I can say that some version of Teilhard's ideas about evolution have never left me from when I first read and was inspired by his works as an undergraduate philosophy student in the 1970s.

Teilhard had, and still has, severe critics. Likewise, Whitehead. The prestigious philosophy journal *Mind* published scathing reviews of both *Process and Reality* and *The Phenomenon of Man*, written respectively by L. Susan Stebbing (1885–1943) and Peter Medawar (1915–87).[146] Controversial as both thinkers have been, the recent conference co-organized by the Center for Process Studies and the Center for Christogenesis, and the one like it in 2005, testify to the continuing vitality of the work of Teilhard and Whitehead.[147] In a brief 1930 review of *Process and Reality*, Wieman wrote:

> Not many people will read Whitehead's recent book in this generation; not many will read it in any generation. But its influence will radiate through concentric circles of popularization until the common

---

[144] Flannery O'Connor, *The Habit of Being: Letters of Flannery O'Connor*, ed. Sally Fitzgerald (New York: Farrar, Straus and Giroux, 1979), 570–71.

[145] John F. Haught, *The Cosmic Vision of Teilhard de Chardin* (Maryknoll, NY: Orbis Books, 2021).

[146] Stebbing maintained that "The language in which nearly the whole of the book is written is extraordinarily obscure." She found "whole sections unintelligible." See Susan L. Stebbing, "Review of Alfred North Whitehead, *Process and Reality*," *Mind* 39 (1930): 466–75. Medawar's review was published in *Mind* 70 (1961) and republished in Peter Medawar, *Pluto's Republic* (New York: Oxford University Press, 1982): 242–51. For my response to Medawar, see Viney, "Teilhard, Medawar, and the New Atheism." One of the least charitable critiques I have read maintains that the *monitum* against Teilhard's work should be lifted only for the purpose of replacing it "with a condemnation of the material heresy with which Teilhard's work is replete." See Douglas Farrow, "The Problem with Teilhard," *Nova et Vetera* [English ed.] 16, no. 2 (2018): 377–85.

[147] The Claremont School of Theology sponsored "The Shared Legacy of Teilhard and Whitehead," February 24–26, 2005. Some of the papers from that conference were published in *Process Studies* 35, no. 1 (2006). At the request of John B. Cobb, Jr., I organized a session devoted to Whitehead and Teilhard at the 6th International Whitehead Conference at Universität Salzburg, Austria, July 3–6, 2006.

man will think and work in the light of it, not knowing whence the light came. After a few decades of discussion and analysis one will be able to understand it more readily than can now be done.[148]

Wieman was probably correct about how many would read *Process and Reality*. It is not an easy book, although there are now many fine works to facilitate an understanding of it. Teilhard's *The Human Phenomenon* is almost certainly more widely read than *Process and Reality*, but, in my view, one must take account of Teilhard's unique situation of writing with one eye on what the censors would say—a barrier, he exclaimed to Valensin, like a portcullis, "Quelle herse!"[149]

What Wieman said of *Process and Reality* also applies to Teilhard's work: "Its influence will radiate through concentric circles" for years to come and many of us will work in the warmth of its light. Those lights continue to burn in this country where each man died, across the ocean from their native lands, one who moved here by choice, the other who moved because of pressure to leave his beloved Paris. Contrary to Wieman's prediction, we may continue to know whence the light came, and to reflect it for generations to come in ways that hold fast the spirit of adventure that they cherished.

---

[148] Henry Nelson Wieman, "A Philosophy of Religion: Review of *Process and Reality* by Alfred North Whitehead," *The Journal of Religion* 10, no. 1 (January 1930): 137.

[149] Teilhard, *Lettres Intimes*, 146. Teilhard's extensive correspondence is especially helpful for appreciating a less filtered version of Teilhard. For his part, with the exception of family members, Whitehead was notorious for *not* writing letters and for not answering inquiries. Bertrand Russell remarked on "one defect" of Whitehead's, "a complete inability to answer letters." See Russell, *Portraits from Memory and Other Essays*, 96. Johnson reports Whitehead as saying that he did not write letters because they "break up" his concentration. See Johnson, "Whitehead as Teacher and Philosopher," 368. Most correspondence that did exist, as well as most drafts of his writing, was destroyed by his wife after his death, according to his wishes. See Lowe, "A. N. W.: A Biographical Perspective," 137. Thanks to the Whitehead Research Project, some previously unknown works have been published, including notes from Whitehead's students. It is fair to say that we are in the early stages of reevaluating the development of Whitehead's thought based on the new material. See the especially useful account of Joseph Petek, *Unearthing the Unknown Whitehead* (Lanham, MD: Lexington Books, 2022).

Dynamic Centration

*Dipolarity in Pierre Teilhard de Chardin
and Charles Hartshorne*

Daniel A. Dombrowski

In what could be considered Charles Hartshorne's magnum opus, *Creative Synthesis and Philosophic Method,* he indicates sympathy for the work of Pierre Teilhard de Chardin.[1] The sympathy is due to Teilhard's positive view of religion, which facilitates the effort to dispense with certain dogmas of Western metaphysics. Among these are the priority of being over becoming, the reduction of "freedom" in creatures to a reiteration of what has already been decided by divine fiat, the rejection of chance or randomness in the world, and most important, the unqualified immutability of God. Although Hartshorne's own views were not really influenced by Teilhard's, it seems fair to say that he was encouraged by them. As far as I know, Teilhard does not refer to Hartshorne's work, which had been available from the 1920s (although he may have been influenced by Whitehead's work).[2] The purpose of the present article is to accentuate especially the similarities but also a few differences between these two thinkers, both of whom richly deserve to be called process theists. Indeed, they, along with Alfred North Whitehead, are arguably the most important process theists of the twentieth century. The three thinkers together (along with a few other process theists who will be mentioned, including Henri Bergson, who influenced all three) constitute something of a unity-in-difference that is very instructive for philosophical

---

[1] Charles Hartshorne, *Creative Synthesis and Philosophic Method* (LaSalle, IL: Open Court, 1970), xiv–xv.

[2] Paul Kelly, "Did Whitehead Influence Teilhard?" *Process Studies* 11, no. 2 (1981): 106–7.

38 Dynamic Centration

theists, in general. Teilhard and Hartshorne, I argue, both mutually reenforce and mutually correct each other in many ways.

We should not be surprised to hear that the French Catholic paleontologist and theologian Teilhard brings a certain sort of *excitement* to his defense of neoclassical or process theism. One example among many is his idea that baptism is important not merely because it symbolizes cleansing, but also because it symbolizes a plunge into the fire of purifying spiritual *struggle*. In this regard he is much like the process theist Nikos Kazantzakis, who also emphasized struggle.[3] But human beings are not the only ones who have to struggle. The omnipresence of God, symbolized by the Cosmic Christ in Teilhard, becomes and grows. Hence, even God (in the sense of divine actuality) is in the fray. God is co-creator of an evolutionary world, which is a different way of saying in Teilhard that creation is a process, rather than an isolated act accomplished once and for all.[4]

Joseph Donceel is astute to argue that Teilhard is to be thanked for moving away from "angelism" or a version of Platonism wherein mind or soul are metaphysically separated from matter. Rather, he thinks, Teilhard is to be seen as a dynamic hylomorphist. This designation has a family resemblance to panpsychism, which has been attributed to both Hartshorne and Teilhard. This view is connected to the thesis that creation is a process rather than a one-time event, in that with each new moment there is more to reality, both to divine reality and to nondivine reality, as material additions to the real are always animated by besouled agency of some sort.[5]

The crucial distinction here, explicit in Hartshorne but implicit in Teilhard, is between the abstract reality of God's permanent existence (*that* God exists) and the concrete actuality of God (*how* God exists from moment to moment). In Hartshorne's view, which is compatible with Teilhard's, God *always changes*. Both of these emphasized words are crucial. In fact, David Tracy thinks that this distinction between permanent divine *existence* and changing divine *actuality* is Hartshorne's greatest discovery. Hence, this Hartshornian distinction will be used as a searchlight throughout this article to illuminate certain features of

---

[3] See Daniel A. Dombrowski, *Kazantzakis and God* (Albany: State University of New York Press, 1997).

[4] Pierre Teilhard de Chardin, *Christianity and Evolution*, trans. René Hague (New York: Harcourt, Brace, and Jovanovich, 1971), 85–86; *Writings in Time of War*, trans. René Hague (New York: Harper and Row, 1968), 59.

[5] See Joseph Donceel, "Teilhard de Chardin and the Body-Soul Relation," *Thought* 40, no. 3 (1965): 371–89.

Teilhard's thought.[6] That is, the greatest contribution that Hartshorne's thought could make to Teilhard's concerns this distinction, which enables us to avoid the misguided fear, present both in Teilhard himself and in his interpreters, that there is some sort of contradiction between divine permanence and change; contradiction is avoided because these two attributes apply to different aspects of divine life.

But Teilhard can also be used to reinforce Hartshorne's thought regarding the view of God as personal, as the prime site of centration. It is crucial in Teilhard's thought that God be seen as personal, but to be absorbed into the personal life of God does not mean that one's own distinctiveness is lost. In fact, he thinks that the more we are absorbed into the personal life of God, the more we are ironically distinguished in our individuality. This is because an omniscient and omnibenevolent God would preeminently know and love us *in our idiosyncrasies*. The elements of the world become more themselves, not less, when they are organically included in the divine life. Here it is Teilhard who helps to illuminate Hartshorne's own belief in God as personal, which he distinguishes from the classical theistic God, who is a completely permanent, unmoved mover who does not change. That is, although classical theists *claim* that they believe in a personal God, it is not clear how they can do so consistently if what it means to be a person is to have a temporal order to an experiential life and to be able to "re-spond" to creaturely feelings, especially suffering feelings. Herein lies the superiority of Teilhard's and Hartshorne's neoclassical, process God to the unchanging God of classical theism. The latter cannot "re-spond" but can only "spond" from eternity in some mysterious way, in the pejorative sense of "mystery." Indeed, the impassible God of classical theism is not internally affected by creaturely suffering and hence can have only external relations to creatures, in contrast to the internal relations that characterize personal life.

I would like to make it clear that by classical theism I refer to an influential view in philosophy and theology, not to biblical theism. In fact, it is an open question as to whether classical theism or its neoclassical/process alternative does a better job of appropriating the best aspects of biblical theism, as in the concept of divine love. Classical theism has dominated the history of philosophy and theology in the Abrahamic religions, but it is not clear that it should have done so. Its monopolarity (wherein being is preferred to becoming, permanence to change, and activity to passivity) does not fit well with the concept of God as eminently loving in that God

---

[6] David Tracy, "Analogy, Metaphor, and God-Language: Charles Hartshorne," *Modern Schoolman* 62 (1985): 249–64.

40 Dynamic Centration

is alleged to love the creatures but is not at all internally affected by their suffering, whatever sort of love that might be. At the least, this sort of love is not even remotely analogous to human love, as Teilhard and Hartshorne see things.[7] The dipolarity in neoclassical or process theism includes the spirit-matter contrast, which allows a change of emphasis in the spiritual life in that the material world is given new importance, as Christopher Mooney emphasizes. On this Teilhardian/Hartshornian view, the material world is ultimately oriented toward the growth of the mental or spiritual, thus allowing the "within-ness" or "centeredness" of things to emerge and/or grow.[8]

It must be admitted that at times Teilhard wavers regarding the "new God" he discusses. He often indicates that God evolves, too, in the divine personal *inter*action with nondivine beings. However, at other times he seems to be saying that the newness in question refers to the progressive awareness of the divine life on the part of human beings. But there need not be a contradiction between these two. When Teilhard refers to "God-Above" or the transcendent God, he is referring to what Hartshorne would call the abstract essence or existence of God (the everlasting fact *that* God exists) rather than to the ever-changing actuality of God (*how* God exists), which Teilhard sometimes calls "God-the-Evolver." These designations are strongly analogous to what Whitehead means by the primordial and consequent natures of God, respectively. The persons Teilhard describes, both divine and nondivine, are clearly not the static substantial persons found in classical theism. A more accurate meaning is found when Teilhard speaks about the personal*izing* process of centration or of becoming centered.[9]

A distinctive feature of Teilhard's neoclassical or process theism that is only implicit in Hartshorne's is Teilhard's emphasis on progressive interiorization throughout evolutionary history, which is also called implosion, the opposite of explosion. This involves the process of developing an interior life or developing "centration," whereby human beings, in particular, more closely approximate a spiritual life as quotidian natural concerns are transubstantiated into love. But the spiritual life is always rooted in matter in dynamic hylomorphic (or panpsychistic) fashion. A sort of spiritual power

---

[7] See, for example, Charles Hartshorne and William L. Reese, *Philosophers Speak of God* (Chicago: University of Chicago Press, 1953), 1–25.

[8] Christopher Mooney, "Teilhard de Chardin and Christian Spirituality," in *Process Theology: Basic Writings,* ed. Ewert Cousins (New York: Newman Press, 1971), 299–320.

[9] Teilhard, *Christianity and Evolution,* 241–42; *Activation of Energy,* trans. René Hague (New York: Harcourt, Brace, and Jovanovich, 1970), 262; *Human Energy,* trans. J. M. Cohen (New York: Harcourt, Brace, and Jovanovich, 1969), 91; *Toward the Future,* trans. René Hague (New York: Harcourt, Brace, and Jovanovich, 1975), 117.

is latent in matter such that matter is the starting point of the process of spiritual ascent that has as its goal "absorption" into the dynamic life of God. "Neo-Christianity," as Teilhard uses the term, refers not so much to a new religion as to a renewed one that has fully come to terms with the reality of nature as evolutionary.[10] As Hartshorne dramatically and provocatively puts a similar point: "If theism cannot be improved upon *profoundly*, then I for one have little desire to see it survive!"[11]

Teilhard's emphasis on interiorization, implosion, and centration is obviously not meant to work against the commonplace that no person is an island. Rather, like Whitehead, he thinks that religion consists primarily in what one *does* with one's solitariness, in which he hopes to cultivate a sense of deeply social, evolutionary purpose wherein all of us together advance in wisdom, love, and justice.[12] His fear is that without a strong spiritual (centered) life one is more likely to be swept along unknowingly by the most superficial forces in society and that one would revert to the proto-interiorization found in prehuman nature. As Bergson notes, even Robinson Crusoe on his island remains in contact with other people as a result of the manufactured objects he saved from the shipwreck. Teilhard is well aware that we take our socialization with us when we retreat to an interior or centered life.[13]

Teilhard and Classical Theism

It must also be admitted that at certain times Teilhard seems to fall back into classical theistic modes of talking about the concept of God. But a charitable interpretation of his thought indicates otherwise. In at least four ways his *apparent* classical theism actually brings to light certain fascinating features of his neoclassical or process theism, which is close to Hartshorne's view.

---

[10] Pierre Teilhard de Chardin, *The Heart of Matter*, trans. René Hague (New York: Harcourt, Brace, and Jovanovich, 1978), 80, 92.

[11] Charles Hartshorne, "Ethics and the New Theology," *International Journal of Ethics* 45, no. 1 (1934): 92.

[12] See Daniel A. Dombrowski, "Religion, Solitariness, and the Bloodlands," *American Journal of Theology and Philosophy* 36 (2015): 226–39.

[13] See Alfred North Whitehead, *Religion in the Making* (New York: Fordham University Press, 1996), 16–17; Henri Bergson, *The Two Sources of Morality and Religion*, trans. R. Ashley Audra and Cloudesley Brereton (Notre Dame, IN: University of Notre Dame Press, 1977), 16.

42 Dynamic Centration

First, he speaks of an "Omega" or "Omega Point" to history, which could be interpreted to mean that the flux of history will come to an end in some sort of static divine state outside of, or beyond, time. Teilhard often gives evidence for this classical theistic interpretation. But we might be closer to Teilhard's meaning when we see him turn the word *omega* into a verb form by speaking of the process wherein something is "omegalized" or progressively transfigured by becoming more centered or more interiorized. Something similar could be said about Teilhard's use of the term *pleroma*, which refers to the natural world being brought to maturity. This might indicate a static telos to be reached at the end time, but it might also indicate (and most likely does indicate) a dynamic "pleromization" of the universe. Or again, the second coming of Christ discussed in terms of the "parousia" might refer (and most likely does refer) to human beings in any religious tradition becoming more Christlike (more interiorized, more centered) in the course of time.[14]

Henri de Lubac is helpful when he claims that in Teilhard the Pauline Cosmic Christ becomes the evolutive Christ. Whereas Paul tried to incorporate certain Stoic views into his view of God, Teilhard tries to do the same with the dynamic scientific representation of the cosmos.[15] Likewise, N. M. Wildiers[16] helps us to see that, for Teilhard, Christ is not so much a historical reminiscence, but part of the evolving and convergent cosmos. A static view of the world, by contrast, tends to conceive of Christ as an extrinsic and juridical intrusion into the world. By *Christ* Teilhard means dynamic centration or a kinetic version of the ancient Greek *logos*.

A second topic Teilhard discusses that could be interpreted as a retreat to the classical theistic concept of God concerns his use of the term *supernatural* to describe God. In the classical theistic use of this term, there is a view of the universe as two tiered, with a natural world governed by scientific laws and a supernatural world that can intervene into the natural world through miracles that violate these laws. Religious experience, on the basis of this view, involves a pole vault outside of the natural world. However, Teilhard is instructive in the way he speaks of supernaturality in terms other than those popular among classical theists. That is, he distinguishes between the supernatural and the extranatural. It is the latter term that plays into the

---

[14] Teilhard, *Activation of Energy*, 55–56, 84, 122; *Christianity and Evolution*, 177.

[15] Henri de Lubac, "The Cosmic Christ," in Cousins, *Process Theology: Basic Writings*, 257–67.

[16] N. M. Wildiers, "Cosmology and Christology," in Cousins, *Process Theology: Basic Writings*, 269–82.

hands of the classical theist. By "supernatural" Teilhard refers to something natural, but to the nth degree. The function of the supernatural is not to escape from the natural but to leaven it or to transform it. In Teilhard's view spiritual purity consists not in escaping from matter, but in entering into a deeper understanding of it. In matter is found the potential for love in the sense that matter contains within itself, at least potentially, the capacity for depth, inwardness, and care. We ourselves are examples of material beings who exhibit in rather complex ways these qualities. The supernatural is the aspect of nature in which the potential for spiritualization has already been actualized, at least to a certain extent. In this view of the concept of God, divine stability consists in the constancy of this spiritualizing process.[17]

John Haught insightfully highlights the connection between understanding what is going on in nature and right action, the latter of which includes retaining a sense of Whiteheadian adventure or Teilhardian zest for living. Unfortunately (and ironically), the idea of nature has not always been shaped by a deep sense of what is going on in the cosmos. Too often the cosmos has been depicted as either pointless or as a mere background for human action. Process thinkers, in general, have kept alive the contrasting idea that there is something afoot in the cosmos and that something momentous is at stake in the cosmos. God functions both as an inspiration to novelty and as preservative of achieved value. Supreme divine memory ensures that nothing of value is ever absolutely lost. We should therefore be impressed with the enormous *potential* in religion in that original sin and the possibility of entropic collapse are not the whole story. That which is of great consequence in the cosmos occurs too slowly, it seems, for most people to notice, as in the emergence of, and intensification of, consciousness. We ironically seem to see less when we look at the cosmos under too great a magnification. We murder to dissect, as Wordsworth and the process thinkers he influenced remind us. Teilhard is like the other great process thinkers in suggesting that much analytical thought in science and philosophy mistakes abstractions for concrete reality, thereby committing what Whitehead calls the fallacy of *misplaced* concreteness. Once again, it is ironic that science might not be sufficiently empirical if it fails to notice the presence of dramatically deeper inwardness and centeredness in nature, which Teilhard famously called the noosphere, than that which had existed previously. What is needed is a richer empiricism that notices that not only

---

[17] Teilhard, *Christianity and Evolution*, 241–42; *Hymn of the Universe*, trans. Simon Bartholomew (New York: Harper and Row, 1961), 64–65, 95; *The Divine Milieu*, trans. Bernard Wall (New York: Harper and Row, 1960), 136.

44   Dynamic Centration

consciousness, but also self-consciousness, are parts of the natural world. There is no good reason to make mental phenomena off limits to rational inquiry. When consciousness and self-consciousness are cordoned off, it becomes too easy to assume the mindlessness of nature. It is precisely in the need for a neoclassical metaphysics that Teilhard could have richly profited from a consideration of Hartshorne's thought. Matter and mind/spirit are polar tendencies within real entities in a nondualistic nature.[18]

Process theists, in general, including Hartshorne, are often quite understandably seen as theistic naturalists, on the assumption that supernaturalism refers to the classical theistic view or to supernaturalism in the pejorative sense of the term. Indeed, Hartshorne is well known for his attempt to revitalize Plato's concept of God as the World Soul who animates not this or that natural body, but who rather animates the whole natural body of the world or the cosmic body.[19] In this regard we should notice that the quintessential classical theist in the Catholic intellectual tradition, Thomas Aquinas, violates his own principle of analogy when he speaks for classical theists, in general, by describing God as a strictly supernatural being above changing nature who does not change in any way.[20] That is, Thomas's emphasis on hylomorphism in the description of natural beings should have been analogized when discussing God in terms of a divine Cosmic Hylomorph. Instead, when talking about God, he resorts to equivocity in that God is seen as completely different from natural hylomorphs. Hartshorne and Teilhard, I think, are more consistent (Thomists) in their attempt to follow through on analogical reasoning regarding the concept of God. Further, due to Hartshorne's fear of supernaturalism in the pejorative sense (which is similar to Teilhard's understandable attempt to develop a more defensible version of supernaturalism), he shies away from talk of divine miracles in the sense of a supernatural God arbitrarily intervening into, in fact, contradicting natural laws. To be precise, Hartshorne does not so much deny the existence of miracles, but rather he refuses to make them play as large a role as they play in classical theism. Classical theists *need* miracles in order to explain the relationship between the natural and the

---

[18] See John F. Haught, "What's Going On in the Universe? Teilhard de Chardin and Alfred North Whitehead," *Process Studies* 35, no. 1 (2006): 43–67; *The New Cosmic Story: Inside Our Awakening Universe* (New Haven, CT: Yale University Press, 2017).

[19] Daniel A. Dombrowski, *A Platonic Philosophy of Religion: A Process Perspective* (Albany: State University of New York Press, 2005).

[20] Thomas Aquinas, *Summa Theologiae*, Blackfriars ed. (New York: McGraw Hill, 1972), I, qq. 1–26.

supernatural; process theists do not have to resort to them to explain their version of theism.[21]

A third topic in terms of which Teilhard might be interpreted as a classical theist, but is rather very insightful in a neoclassical or a process theistic way, is his use of the concept of omnipotence to describe God or his use of the name Pantocrator to refer to God. As I understand him, however, Teilhard has in mind something somewhat different from the classical theistic concept of omnipotence, wherein God is claimed to have *all* power. Here theodicy is crucial. In the tradition of ancient Greek tragedy, Teilhard recognizes evil or suffering as natural facts. A plurality of at least partially free beings virtually ensures that frustration or perhaps even tragedy will result as freedoms clash or get in one another's way. The structure of the world as evolutionary involves uncertainty, chance, and hence risk. In this context, no being, not even a divine one, can guarantee the absence of suffering and loss without destroying altogether the free beings in question. Evil is inevitable as a secondary effect of the evolutive universe in which we live.

As Georges Crespy correctly notes, it is the "fixist" view of the world, including God, that creates the unsolvable version of the theodicy problem. Although it is a tough pill for some to swallow, one cannot eliminate the possibility of moral evil without simultaneously eliminating the possibility for moral good. Suffering and moral evil are not due to some deficiency in the divine or human creative act, but in the very structure of participative being as the power to affect others and as the power to be affected by others, in Platonic fashion.[22]

That is, completely eliminating the possibility of evil would eliminate the evolutive world itself. Evil is the expression of a plurality of nonmechanical beings and, we should note, freedom, plurality, adventure, unpredictability, and risk are, in their own ways, good things. The panoramic screen of evolutive history forces us to reconceive divine omnipotence, even if Teilhard himself continues to use this word. Perhaps he would have been better served to use Hartshornian designations such as "ideal power," "persuasive power," or "power compatible with dynamic perfection."[23] Hartshorne himself early in his career talked of divine omnipotence, but in short order he dropped this term because it did not accurately convey his concept of ideal divine power, as is evidenced in the famous (or infamous) title of one of his

---

[21] Charles Hartshorne, *Omnipotence and Other Theological Mistakes* (Albany: State University of New York Press, 1984), 119.

[22] See Plato's *Sophist* 247e.

[23] Teilhard, *The Divine Milieu*, 60; *Christianity and Evolution*, 82–85.

46   Dynamic Centration

last books: *Omnipotence and Other Theological Mistakes*. God can influence all and be influenced by all (hence the appropriateness of the designation "Pantocrator"), but this is quite different from absolutely controlling everything. If God *did* control everything, then evil would either be sent by God or at least be permitted by God, as religious skeptics have correctly urged for centuries. Classical theistic belief in divine omnipotence in the sense of God ultimately possessing *all* power creates the nastiest and insoluble version of the theodicy problem. As William Whitla notes, the divine functions in process thought as a *persuasive* (rather than *coercive*) force, which involves concepts like "concrescence" and "prehension." These have an equivalent in Teilhard in terms of "complexification" or "caritization."[24]

And fourth, Teilhard might initially seem to be something other than a neoclassical or process theist due to his frequent engagement with pantheism. The terminological issues here are complex in that he distinguishes among at least thirteen (!) meanings of the term *pantheism*, but, as I interpret his thought, his overall goal is merely to move away from the aforementioned two-tiered classical theistic view of the universe. If I am correct in this interpretation, then he might have been better served to talk about divine *world inclusiveness*, rather than about pantheism, in that pantheism (as in its Stoic or Spinozistic versions) is often assumed to be equated with both determinism and a complete lack of externality between God and the nondivine. In this regard Sion Cowell is wise to see Teilhard as a (neoclassical, process) pan*en*theist, rather than as a pantheist.

One is here reminded of Hartshorne's view throughout his scholarly career, from the 1920s until the twenty-first century, that all is *in* God (say through divine omniscience, properly understood, and through omnibenevolence), but not everything is to be *identified* with God. It should be noted that relatively early in his scholarly life Teilhard identified positively with the Platonic World Soul, which Hartshorne defended throughout his career. The World Soul is very much compatible with the panentheist position wherein the natural world is in God via divine omniscience (again, as properly understood) and divine omnibenevolence. God knows and cares for all. But the natural world is not to be identified with God, as in most versions of pantheism.[25] Further, I have noted above the importance in Teilhard

---

[24] See William Whitla, "Sin and Redemption in Whitehead and Teilhard de Chardin," *Anglican Theological Review* 47 (1965): 81–95; and John Slattery, "Pierre Teilhard de Chardin's Legacy of Eugenics and Racism Can't Be Ignored," *Religion Dispatches* (May 21, 2018).

[25] See Sion Cowell, *The Teilhard Lexicon* (Brighton: Sussex Academic Press, 2001), 141–45; and Teilhard, *Writings in Time of War*, 187.

and Hartshorne of seeing God as personal, whereas pantheism seems to be integrally connected to the view of God as nonpersonal.[26]

Among the various uses of the word *pantheism* found in Teilhard is a distinction regarding a type of pantheism in which the unity of the whole involves a fusion of the various elements found in the whole such that the distinctiveness of each element disappears. This is not the view that Teilhard (or Hartshorne) defends. Another sort of pantheism, more properly called panentheism, involves a divine whole in which the elements are not fused or annihilated but *fulfilled* by entering into a deeper and wider Center or supercenter. Here the elements are not confused but more fully differentiated because they are felt and known by an omniscient and omnibenevolent being. In this concept of God, the divine is a Center of centers. Teilhard is driven to this view by his very strong sense of the organicity of a universe that contains all of the elements in flux, a view of God that he sees as very much compatible with St. Paul's *in quo omnia constant* (in whom all things hold together—Col. 1:17). Likewise, Hartshorne is noted for frequently citing positively Paul's famous claim that we live and move and have our being in God (Acts 17:28).[27]

As before, the God-world relationship is analogous to the relationship we have with cells in our body. One of the neglected aspects of Hartshorne's philosophy is his prescient work in the 1930s in philosophy of psychology wherein, although feelings are not necessarily sensations, sensation itself is a type of feeling. In this regard David Richardson is helpful in seeing Hartshorne and Teilhard as two sides of the same coin. We feel because cells in our bodies feel or have *petite perceptions*. Sensation prehends or grasps the feelings in other individuals at a microscopic level just as analogously God feels us. There is thus a graduated intensification of interiority in nature from microscopic to mesoscopic to macroscopic (that is, cosmic) levels.[28] Jay McDaniel is like Richardson in seeing Teilhard and process thought as two sides of the same coin. Teilhard (and those he has influenced like John Haught, Thomas Berry, and Brian Swimme) focuses on what McDaniel calls "the epic of evolution tradition," which, although not the focus of most process thinkers, is nonetheless compatible with the thought of Whitehead and Hartshorne. Or again, Teilhard and those he has influenced emphasize

---

[26] See Michael Levine, *Pantheism* (New York: Routledge, 1994).

[27] Charles Hartshorne, *A Natural Theology for Our Time* (LaSalle, IL: Open Court, 1967), 9.

[28] See David Richardson, "Philosophies of Hartshorne and Chardin: Two Sides of the Same Coin?" *Southern Journal of Philosophy* 2 (1964): 107–15.

a sacramental approach to nature which, although articulated in language different from that of other process thinkers, is nonetheless compatible with process panpsychism or panexperientialism.[29]

With these clarifications in mind, we can legitimately see Teilhard as a dipolar theist who is cognizant of both activity and passivity in God (in contrast to classical theistic monopolarity, wherein God is active but not passive) as well as being and becoming in God (in contrast to classical theistic concentration on divine being and utter denial of divine becoming). God's being, on the neoclassical or process view, refers to the self-sufficiency of God's essence as the greatest conceivable and to God's necessary existence, but it does not refer to the evolutionary flux of divine actuality from moment to moment. In Teilhardian terms, there is "theogenesis."[30]

Thinking that there is a contradiction between Teilhard saying that God is a permanent being, on the one hand, and that God is forever in the process of formation, on the other, would be a mistake in that these contrasting (not contradictory) modes of discourse refer to different aspects of the divine nature. On the one hand, God is self-sufficient in existence as the being who exhibits ideal knowledge, power, and love; on the other hand, the universe contributes something that is "vitally necessary" to the divine actuality. As before, God *always* changes, whereas we change only for the finite spans of our own lifetimes. Unfortunately, Teilhard sometimes expresses guilt at defending such "contradictions," but this is perhaps because he was not sufficiently aware of Whitehead and Hartshorne, especially the latter, who could have persuaded him of the cogency of the divine existence-actuality distinction. Teilhard is correct, however, to hope for a "higher metaphysics" than the classical theistic one that persistently opts for one pole only of dipolar contrasts. In different terms, although God is self-sufficient in existence, arguing for divine "omni-sufficiency" would be a mistake. He thinks that the most authentic versions of religious tradition and experience affirm that a "bilateral and complementary" relationship exists between God and the world and that these versions are not preserved well by classical (monopolar) metaphysics. Christianity, in particular, he thinks, is given new life in the notion that a mutuality exists between the world and God that is needed in the pleromizing process.[31]

---

[29] Jay McDaniel, "Process Thought and the Epic of Evolution Tradition," *Process Studies* 35, no. 1 (2006): 68–94.

[30] Teilhard, *The Divine Milieu*, 52; *Science and Christ*, trans. René Hague (New York: Harper and Row, 1968), 174; *Christianity and Evolution*, 171; *Toward the Future*, 194.

[31] Teilhard, *The Heart of Matter*, 54; *Christianity and Evolution*, 177–79, 226–27.

Creative Transformation

As I see things, there is ample room for edifying exchange between those who are interested in Teilhard and those who are interested in Hartshorne and other process thinkers. As John Cobb details, the exchange between these two groups started in the 1960s and 1970s, then faded for a while, and was rekindled in the early 2000s. The tension between the two groups that most impresses Cobb is the fact that Teilhard sometimes gives the impression that he believes in a final supersession in the future when the material world will fade away and the mental/spiritual world will grow in complexity and value. But in many other places Teilhard seems much closer to Whitehead and Hartshorne in thinking that the mental/spiritual is firmly grounded in the physical, which is why above I talked about dynamic hylomorphism. Further, it is integral to process thought to view the future as at least partially open and not amenable to accurate prediction in the present, regardless of whether such prediction tends toward fulfillment or disaster.[32]

Cobb thinks that there is much to be learned from Teilhard regarding the idea that it is the unrealized future that is the locus for divine agency in the present. The lack of hope, for both Cobb and Teilhard, signals the destruction of zest for life in the present; hence Cobb dedicated the last third of his book *Christ in a Pluralistic Age* to Teilhard. To be specific, we should hope that the evolutionary energies that have brought life on earth to its present high level will enable us to work through present crises to a new high level. Of course, this will require creative transformation, which finds conceptual backing in all of the thinkers discussed in the present chapter, especially Teilhard and Hartshorne. Such creative transformation will no doubt require sacrifice, but not in the sense that the individual is sacrificed for the sake of the whole; in fact, the process view is that there is both preservation *and enhancement* of the individual when its contributions are made to an omniscient and omnibenevolent divine whole. Although it is true to say that we are parts of the (*totaliter*) universe, it also makes sense to say that the universe is possessed by us (*partialiter*).[33]

Despite Cobb's general agreement with Teilhard, he is correct to be a bit skittish about Teilhard's confidence that humanity is moving toward a final and positive consummation. Even though such a view has emotional appeal, it is characteristic of process thinkers (Whitehead, Hartshorne,

---

[32] See John B. Cobb, Jr., *Christ in a Pluralistic Age* (Philadelphia: Westminster Press, 1975).

[33] Ibid., 70, 179, 189, 193, 198–199, 201–2, 220, 245–46, 253–54, 257.

50   Dynamic Centration

Cobb) also to be keenly aware of the fact that life is *tragic* and there are, due to temporal asymmetry, no guarantees that all will turn out right in the end. In fact, for any being with memory life will always be tragic given the fact that there have been tragic occurrences in the past. Nonetheless, Cobb insists that human beings need a positive vision so that they can make the most of the opportunities that lie before them, given the (sometimes tragic) obstacles that are in our paths.[34]

Teilhard asserts as a fact in the phenomenology of religious experience that God is not present to us as all complete. Rather, those who experience God do so as a discovery and as part of a growing process. The dynamism of religious experience actually enhances the apophatic dimension of the concept of God, rather than detracts from it. This is because the more we think we understand divine actuality, the more we realize that something is constantly added to divine experience and as a result escapes our grasp. The "inside of things," however, enables us to enhance our understanding, such as it is. Here Teilhard attempts to mediate between polytheistic and animistic religious traditions, which deified and personified every aspect of nature, and the modernist tendency to depersonify and disenchant everything that is most admired. David Ray Griffin, for example, is a contemporary process theologian and the author of a magisterial book in which he labors along with Teilhard in the effort to "reenchant" a disenchanted and deracinated world. It is not only the great mystics who experience a Great Presence in nature, an extrahuman Energy more deeply infused into the nature of things than merely mechanical relations. Although not ubiquitous among human beings, a great number of people have experienced this Great Presence, although the labels for this presence vary greatly.[35]

Teilhard takes quite seriously the idea that something is born in the divine (actuality) when human beings love each other and that love constitutes the measure of progress in evolutionary history. God is elevated by our love, he thinks, although he does not indicate, like the process thinker Nicholas Berdyaev, whether he thinks that God is pained by our hatreds.[36]

---

[34] See John B. Cobb Jr., "Teilhard and Whitehead," *Process in Praxis* (September 1, 2021).

[35] See Teilhard, *The Divine Milieu*, 119; *The Human Phenomenon*, trans. Sarah Appleton-Weber (Brighton: Sussex Academic Press, 1999), 22, 183, 189, 209; David Ray Griffin, *Reenchantment without Supernaturalism: A Process Philosophy of Religion* (Ithaca, NY: Cornell University Press, 2001).

[36] Pierre Teilhard de Chardin, *The Future of Man*, trans. Norman Denny (New York: Harper and Row, 1964), 5–76, 79, 120; Daniel A. Dombrowski, *A History of the Concept of God: A Process Approach* (Albany: State University of New York Press, 2016), chap. 19.

Of course, God's essential nature and existence are not in need of our busy activity, but the emphasis Teilhard places on divine omnipresence (and on the related idea that God is not withdrawn from us and beyond the tangible sphere) means that such dependence is ensured regarding what Hartshorne calls divine actuality. Although we may nominally value activity over passivity, in that no self-respecting person wants to be run over, clearly our passive powers are just as crucial to a good life as the active ones. This Teilhardian and Hartshornian insight is applied in neoclassical theism in a preeminent way to the divine case. In fact, the dynamism of life equally requires both activity and passivity. Bodily life, in particular, involves passive powers to absorb food and air, but mental life also requires the absorption of information, listening to others, and so on. Teilhard resists any facile bifurcation of mind and matter if such a distinction distracts attention away from "holy matter" and the place of the material world, including our very bodies, in the spiritual life. God is revealed everywhere as the universal milieu in which the multiplicity of things in the world are indeed seen as parts of one immense world in movement that is constantly acquiring new qualities. The contrasts between activity and passivity and between mind or soul and matter involve the idea that these differing elements are in reality brought together, but not in such a manner that they are easily confused. The most important of our passive powers is the ability to receive divine influence in the midst of the material flux of events.[37]

The vibrancy of the world that is apparent in Teilhard is due to the inwardness of all things (in vastly varying degrees) in a panpsychist or panexperientialist universe. We are so accustomed to viewing things from without, a view that is understandable enough in itself, that we might fail to consider that we are not the only beings in the universe who have insides, an impulse to react to previous stimuli and to advance. Likewise, religious traditions can be viewed from without, but Teilhard has a suspicion that relying exclusively on this sort of vision leaves something significant out of the picture. To be a religious believer is to be seized by the inwardness of the religious tradition in question.

One of the features of Teilhard's thought that makes him distinctive is the way in which he weaves together the inward/outward distinction with the passivity/activity distinction. These two distinctions mutually enrich each other. The concept of God, on this interpretation, exhibits the highest expression of each of these four elements. "The basic mystical intuition

---

[37] Teilhard, *The Divine Milieu*, 15, 22, 33, 46, 67, 69–70, 73–74, 81, 91, 97, 99, 101, 103, 108, 110–11.

52   Dynamic Centration

issues in the discovery of a supra-real unity diffused throughout the immensity of the world."[38] Or again, "The world is a-building. This is the basic truth which must first be understood so thoroughly that it becomes an habitual and as it were natural springboard for our thinking. . . . A process is at work in the universe, an issue is at stake."[39] The issue at stake involves atoms as well as animals like ourselves. Evolution is holy, and not even God (especially not God!) is finished.[40]

Theodosius Dobzhansky is correct to notice that there is no straight progressive line in Teilhard in that evolution proceeds by way of active/passive "groping" (*tatonnement*), which is exhibited by beings who have both insides (*le dedans*) and outsides (*le dehors*). The price of this dipolar groping is sometimes extinction. The basic properties of all living beings—heredity and mutability—indicate that two extremes should be avoided: that we are merely lucky accidents, on the one hand, and that the appearance of human mentality was foreordained, on the other. Dobzhansky subtly mistakes things a bit when he says that in process thinkers like Hartshorne there is perfect knowledge of the past but no perfect knowledge of the future. A more accurate way to put the point would be to say that in process theism God has ideal knowledge of what has happened in the past *as well as* ideal knowledge of future possibilities or probabilities. Because, strictly speaking, there are no future actualities here to be known, it is not a mark of imperfection to fail to know the future in detail. To claim to know future determinables as already determinate is not an example of ideal knowledge, but of nescience. It is also a mistake to suggest, as Dobzhansky does, that God voluntarily limits divine omniscience and omnipotence. That is, if anything that exists has some (Platonic) power to act and to be acted upon, then no being, not even a perfect one, could have *all* power so long as there are many beings in existence. It is not the case that God falls short of perfection by not being omnipotent if the very concept of omnipotence is incoherent.[41]

Teilhard is chagrined to notice that the concept of creative transformation had no significant place in the thought of the great classical theists of the Middle Ages. Hence, this concept should be established without delay. Furthermore, the Scholastic thinkers emphasized too much the concept of

---

[38] Teilhard, *Hymn of the Universe*, 91.

[39] Ibid., 92–93.

[40] Ibid., 43, 83–84, 87, 91–93, 133; see also, Charles Hartshorne, *The Logic of Perfection* (LaSalle, IL: Open Court, 1962), chap. 7.

[41] Theodosius Dobzhansky, "Teilhard de Chardin and the Orientation of Evolution," in Cousins, *Process Theology: Basic Writings*, 229–48.

God as creator, instead of emphasizing God as the creator of free beings who in a sense make themselves. He even goes so far as to say that it is contradictory to imagine God creating an isolated being who is nonetheless a participated being who depends on others. If any being exists, then a whole interrelational world of becoming must exist. The essential relationality of things means that world-inclusiveness is part of what it would mean to be God. It is unfortunate, he thinks, that many who have been attracted to a religion of the whole have turned away from Christianity, presumably because of the Christian version of the classical theistic concept of God as supernatural, in the sense of being outside of time and immune to change as a result of natural events. By contrast, Teilhard (as well as Hartshorne) takes the Pauline view of the omnipresent, mystic body of the Cosmic Christ quite seriously. Unfortunately, classical theists did not consider the possibility that because our understanding of God obviously changes, this progressive advance might be rooted in the divine history itself.[42]

Perhaps because of the influence of Roman jurisprudence on classical theists, discourse regarding the concept of God has often resembled a legal trial between God and the creatures or among the creatures themselves when discussing God, instead of emphasizing mutuality or at least a struggle that is not internecine. At the very least we need a dynamic version of theism, whether pacific or agonistic. To put the point in spatial terms, rather than the classical theistic God as *above* us, we might be better served to think neoclassically or processually in terms of God as *ahead* of us, not as a rigid telos toward whom we must advance, but as a Whiteheadian or Hartshornian lure forward toward a better world. I think that Teilhard would agree.[43] This view is nonetheless compatible with God as omnisciently knowing all past actualities as already actualized and present realities to the extent that they are knowable. Whereas the future consists of a range of possibilities or probabilities, the present consists in the momentary process whereby future determinables are rendered determinate, the result of which is that they then become past.

The above similarities between Teilhard and Hartshorne are remarkable when the all-too-apparent differences in their disciplinary backgrounds are considered. Hartshorne was a philosopher who placed a great deal of emphasis on *a priori* rationality, including his famous rediscovery and defense

---

[42] Teilhard, *Christianity and Evolution*, 24, 28, 31–33, 59, 64, 82.

[43] Ibid., 89, 133, 212, 239.

54   Dynamic Centration

of St. Anselm's ontological argument.[44] Teilhard was not at all a philosopher but (arguably) a major figure in mystical or speculative theology. Further, although Hartshorne was raised in a Christian family and had a father who was an Anglican minister, he did not as an adult identify himself as a Christian, but rather as a philosophical (neoclassical or process) theist, in general. This is in contrast to Teilhard, who remained a devout Catholic and Jesuit priest throughout his adult life. However, the two thinkers are surprisingly alike in each having both a speculative bent, on the one hand, and expertise in empirical science, on the other. In Teilhard's case the latter was in paleontology, whereas in Hartshorne's case it was in ornithology.[45] That is, these two thinkers are alike not only in their substantive claims regarding the concept of God and the organic, evolutive character of reality, but also (surprisingly) in the rare combination of intellectual habits they brought to their different disciplinary procedures: soaring speculative flights and dense empirical observations.

As Whitehead memorably put the point regarding thinkers like Teilhard and Hartshorne: "The true method of discovery is like the flight of an aeroplane. It starts from the ground of particular observation; it makes a flight in the thin air of imaginative generalization; and it again lands for renewed observation rendered acute by rational interpretation."[46] It would be a mistake, I think, to fail to appreciate either the intellectual flights accomplished by Teilhard and Hartshorne or the safe landings found in their pragmatic success at dealing with some of the most practical issues human beings face, particularly in their ability to account consistently for the concept of divine love and how such love is compatible with there being evil in the world.

In the Postscript to *The Human Phenomenon*, Teilhard makes it clear that the universe, considered sidereally, is in the process of spatial expansion; but it is also in the process of organic involution upon itself. This is why every personal experience (whether of God or of nondivine persons) is also an experience of something else at the same time. This is what leads Bernard Lee to distinguish between the superficial presence of one person

---

[44] See Hartshorne, *The Logic of Perfection; Anselm's Discovery* (LaSalle, IL: Open Court, 1965); and Daniel A. Dombrowski, *Rethinking the Ontological Argument: A Neoclassical Theistic Response* (Cambridge: Cambridge University Press, 2006).

[45] See Charles Hartshorne, *Born to Sing: An Interpretation and World Survey of Bird Song* (Bloomington: Indiana University Press, 1973); and Daniel A. Dombrowski, *Divine Beauty: The Aesthetics of Charles Hartshorne* (Nashville, TN: Vanderbilt University Press, 2004), chap. 4.

[46] Alfred North Whitehead, *Process and Reality: An Essay in Cosmology*, corrected edition, ed. David Ray Griffin and Donald Sherburne (New York: The Free Press, 1978), 5.

in another (Whitehead's presentational immediacy) and a deeper presence (Whitehead's causal efficacy). That is, there are degrees of presence where one personal event that is *there* is transformed into a personal event *here* that takes hold in an intense manner the person (whether divine or nondivine) who is experienced. Religion dies when it no longer holds out the possibility for such adventurous prehensions.[47]

Barbour and Viney

Two more scholars should be considered whose excellent work on the connection between Teilhard and process thought (Hartshorne in particular) will help us to more fully understand the subject matter in question: Ian Barbour and Donald Viney.

Barbour isolates five ways of reading Teilhard, ignorance of which might lead us unwittingly to misinterpret him if we fail to consider or to over-emphasize one reading over another. First, it is tempting to see Teilhard primarily as an *evolutionary scientist*. In this regard Barbour is quick to point out that, although there is not much that is unscientific in Teilhard that contradicts scientific evidence, there are many statements that are nonscientific in the sense that they move beyond the self-imposed limits of what scientists would permit. Although Lamarckian ideas are mentioned in the early Teilhard, they are later rejected by him in *The Human Phenomenon*, even if he does continue to give prominence to mutations, chance, and randomness. Internal forces can influence evolution even if acquired characteristics are not inherited, as in the famous "Baldwin effect." That is, the contribution of the "within" can be defended without invoking the discredited thesis that acquired characteristics are directly inherited. The negative response to Teilhard's work on the part of some scientists is more properly about the nonscientific things that he has to say about reality, including the "within," rather than him being unscientific. This is because the thesis that the interior life of organisms contributes to evolutionary change is not to be equated with the discredited Lamarckian theory that acquired characteristics can be inherited by descendants. Teilhard himself is partly to blame here by saying that *The Human Phenomenon* should be read purely and simply as a scientific treatise.

---

[47] Bernard Lee, *The Becoming of the Church* (Mahwah, NJ: Paulist Press, 1974), 121–54, 211, 218, 227, 250.

56   Dynamic Centration

Second, Teilhard can be read as a *poet* and/or *mystic*. The magnificent sweep of his vision gives support for this sort of reading, which is better served through certain of his books, like *The Divine Milieu* or *Hymn of the Universe*. His pervasive sense of cosmic unity puts him in a tradition with St. Francis of Assisi's or Gerard Manley Hopkins's idea that the world is charged with the grandeur of God. What I am suggesting, along with Barbour, is that there is nothing wrong with seeing certain Teilhard writings as poetic or mystical, so long as one is clear about what one is doing and does not confuse what he says in these writings with other writings or with other permissible readings.[48]

Third, Teilhard can be read in the tradition of *natural theology*, where theological conclusions are drawn from evidence in the natural order, which, in Teilhard's case, involves an alleged argument from design based on a trend toward complexity, consciousness, individualization, personalization, and centration. One advantage here is that his view is compatible with the presence of much waste, chance, and failure in nature, contra the argument from design found in many classical theists, thus making it possible for a Teilhardian or a Hartshornian to avoid the Humean challenge to such arguments. In Teilhard and Hartshorne it is natural causes that produce directionality in nature, not the suspension of these causes.

Fourth, Teilhard can be read as a *Christian theologian*, who, in addition to offering a natural theology, can also offer a theology of nature, indeed, a cosmic Christology wherein "salvation" refers not to an escape from the world but to its sanctification.

And fifth, Teilhard can be read as a *process philosopher* or *metaphysician*, despite the fact that he did not have much training in philosophy beyond the Scholastic thinkers who were standard at the time. It is this reading of Teilhard with which I have been concerned in the present article, but Barbour's differentiation among the readings of Teilhard helps to put what I am doing here into context. Whereas Thomas Aquinas's basic categories were being and substance, Teilhard is like Whitehead and Hartshorne in concentrating on becoming and process (with the consequence that the dynamic aspects of the biblical God are illuminated). Thus, there is an implicit process metaphysics in Teilhard, a metaphysics that is made explicit in Whitehead and especially in Hartshorne, albeit with slightly less emphasis on cosmic unity and more on pluralism in Whitehead and Hartshorne in comparison with Teilhard. Barbour is insightful in suggesting that it is in terms of process

---

[48] Ian Barbour, "Five Ways of Reading Teilhard," *Soundings* 51, no. 2 (1968): 115–24.

philosophy that these five readings can be synthesized rather than in the terms of the other four readings. This is because a common (if implicit) process metaphysics runs through all five readings. In effect, Teilhard was much more philosophical than he was ever willing to admit.[49]

Barbour is helpful in locating why so many scholars might be skeptical of Teilhardian or Hartshornian/Whiteheadian panpsychism or dynamic hylomorphism. Although Whitehead's "subjective pole" resembles Teilhard's "within," the objects of everyday experience like stones have no subjective pole at all because they are aggregates of active singulars like atoms and molecules. These small entities *do* have subjective poles or withinness. This enables us to account for the unity of nature and the coherence of interpretive categories when trying to understand the world. It also enables us to avoid the bifurcation of nature and Cartesian dualism that bothered both Teilhard and Hartshorne/Whitehead. The apparent inertness of some stuff in nature can be explained in light of active singulars whose movements largely cancel each other out in terms of a law of large numbers, unless, of course, there is something like a central nervous system or dominant monad that can bring the sentience of the parts together in terms of a sentient whole with a greater degree of individuation and centration. As before, however, Barbour sees a bit more unity in Teilhard and a greater tendency toward pluralism in Whitehead. Hartshorne may very well occupy a moderate position in this internecine dispute in that his World Soul provides an organic unity to the cosmos more pronounced than its rough equivalent in Whitehead and perhaps less than the unity to the cosmos found in Teilhard.[50]

In addition to Barbour, another thinker who points us into the right direction in the effort to link Teilhard with process metaphysics is Donald Viney. Indeed, Viney sees Teilhard as a pioneer in process metaphysics, along with Whitehead and Hartshorne. This claim is made in full cognizance of the fact that Teilhard himself was not a philosopher, even if he was, for a while, open to the transcription of his ideas into Scholastic or Thomistic categories. (To what extent such openness was driven by a desire to placate church authority is itself an open question.) As I see things, the

---

[49] See Barbour, "Five Ways of Reading Teilhard"; and Ian Barbour, "The Significance of Teilhard," in *Changing Man: The Threat and the Promise*, ed. Kyle Haselden and Philip Hefner (Garden City, NY: Doubleday, 1968), 130–41.

[50] Ian Barbour, "Teilhard's Process Metaphysics," in Cousins, *Process Theology: Basic Writings*, 323–50. This article by Barbour is reprinted in the Appendix in the current volume.

58   Dynamic Centration

fact that Hartshorne usually called his position "neoclassical metaphysics" can help us here. To the extent that Teilhard was doing something radically "neo," he would be at odds with Scholastic categories, but to the extent that he was doing something "classical," rapprochement between substance metaphysics and process metaphysics is possible, indeed fruitful. Teilhard knew that the vector of his thinking was recognizably processual.

Viney is especially helpful in highlighting five general areas that characterize process metaphysics, all of which are very much in evidence in Teilhard's writings: First, there is a primacy of becoming over being in process thinkers generally, which is not to say that everything changes. The stable being of a thing is constituted by the series of momentary actual occasions that make it up, a view that is indebted to "saint" Bergson. Second, temporal process is asymmetrical and cumulative in that each event is an addition to the definiteness of reality. Third, existence in general has a social structure, in contrast to the Scholastic view that the blueprint for the world is eternally (and hence asocially) fixed in the mind of God. Fourth, the stuff of the universe exhibits a dipolar structure with each occasion having a physical pole and a mental/spiritual pole, to put the point in Whiteheadian terms. That is, nothing is merely physical or merely mental/spiritual. Whitehead's term for the experiential component in each actual occasion is "prehension," the closest approximation to which in Teilhard is "la conscience," as Viney helpfully notes.

And fifth, there is the process theism to which the present chapter is devoted. Here it is important to emphasize that, on a classical theistic basis, creation of the world adds more *sharers* in being, but not more being, because God is seen as the fullness of existence. Teilhard, Whitehead, and Hartshorne, however, argue that something new is added to reality at each moment, something that had never existed before, except by way of hope or anticipation or probability estimate. That is, on a classical theistic basis, a creature's possible existence and its actual existence are (mistakenly) seen as on a par. This renders any additions made to the world by creaturely creativity quite insipid.[51]

It should be noted that not even Thomas Aquinas thought that it was possible for God to do the logically impossible. Teilhard and Hartshorne add that among the logically impossible actions would be to create apart from the developmental process or to erase what has already happened in the past. We have seen that Teilhard should have avoided the word

---

[51] Donald Wayne Viney, "Teilhard and Process Philosophy Redux," *Process Studies* 35, no. 1 (2006): 12–23.

omnipotence when describing the sort of God in which he believed. Consider Viney's insightful distinction between saying that misfortune should be interpreted as good because it is God's design for an individual and God's design for an individual being the making of something good of misfortune. The former is a problematic consequence of belief in divine omnipotence. Teilhard's turn from Scholasticism was driven not only by the conviction that medieval categories were inadequate to the investigation of nature, but also by the conviction that such categories were inadequate to (or more precisely, told only half the story regarding) the concept of God. The classical theistic view of God's love as benevolent without *felt* compassion makes no sense from a process point of view.[52]

Viney admits that Teilhard is furthest from Whitehead and Hartshorne when talking about the future of evolutionary process. Although both Teilhard and Whitehead/Hartshorne were in agreement against mechanism and determinism in that rather than absolute regularity in things they saw developmental processes that introduced novel forms of matter. As Viney notes, there *is* something new under the sun; there was a time when the sun itself was new. But the contradictory of absolute regularity is not absolute irregularity; determinism and chaoticism are logical contraries rather than contradictories. To contradict absolute deterministic regularity one only needs to point to examples of partially free beings. We live in a dynamic, unfinished universe that is more than a combinatorial unfolding of what is already preordained. Because strictly speaking there are no future events (only a sketch or an outline of what might happen in the future), Whitehead and Hartshorne are a bit more reticent than Teilhard when talking about what the future will bring, although because Teilhard also subscribes to the asymmetricality of time, there is no absolute difference here.[53]

Coda

There is one final point of contact between Teilhard and Hartshorne that indicates the affinity between the two, which is deeper than either thinker would have, or perhaps could have, realized. The affinity concerns the motto of the Jesuit order to which Teilhard belonged: *ad majorem Dei gloriam* (all

---

[52] Ibid., 24–39.

[53] See Donald Wayne Viney, "Evolution's God: Teilhard de Chardin and the Varieties of Process Theology," *Teilhard Studies* 82 (Spring 2021): 1–24; and "God and the World in Teilhard," Center for Christogenesis, October 11, 2019.

60   Dynamic Centration

is for the greater glory of God). This could appropriately be seen as the motto for all Abrahamic theists (and for many other theists as well). What we should notice is that this saying *makes no sense whatsoever on the grounds of classical theism.* An unmoved mover could not in any way be affected by what we do in that this impassible being is not capable of greater glory. A strictly active being with no passive powers and only external relations to creatures would not have the passive power that is integral to love. And a purely permanent being who cannot change can neither change for the better nor for the worse, hence such a being cannot be glorified or benefited by the creatures. Of course, classical theists *say* that their God is a God of love, but they do not do a good job of showing how this could be so. Teilhard and Hartshorne knew that there is something seriously defective in the classical concept of God. Further, if the above "greater glory" refers not to God but to us, then one runs the risk of hubris or self-deification.

Hartshorne's "contributionism," in particular, is an attempt to defend intellectually the Jesuit motto that no doubt meant a great deal to Teilhard. Without God our lives are, as Whitehead put it, passing "whiffs of insignificance,"[54] given our feeble ability to remember and preserve achieved value. But in order for the value of our lives to be given lasting (even everlasting) significance by God remembering and cherishing them, we need a concept of God who is amenable to receiving our contributions by being pleased (indeed glorified) by our successes, and, it must be admitted, chagrined (indeed pained) by our failures. And these successes and failures, it should be emphasized, are temporally indexed and are hardly enacted "eternally" outside of evolutionary history.

---

[54] Alfred North Whitehead, *The Philosophy of Alfred North Whitehead*, ed. P. A. Schilpp (LaSalle, IL: Open Court, 1951), 698.

Was Pierre Teilhard de Chardin a Panpsychist?

GODEHARD BRÜNTRUP, SJ

The Cartesian Legacy

From Leibniz to Whitehead, panpsychism in modernity is a reaction to the Cartesian bifurcation of nature, which philosophically marks the origin of modernity. The beginning of modernity cannot be dated exactly, but it can be narrowed down. Newton was born in the year Galileo died (1642), exactly one hundred years after Copernicus published his *De Revolutionibus*. Descartes' *Meditations* appeared a year earlier. Perhaps the most momentous discovery of modernity was the idea of a largely empirical natural science, which set itself apart from the previously prevailing concept of Aristotelian natural science, which contained much stronger rationalistic and speculative elements. The new natural science only observes what happens. It no longer has a larger system that explains *why* everything happens the way it does. The new natural science accepts the data as *facta bruta*. It wants to organize data in a nomological context of formal relations, the fundamental laws of nature, as they are classically represented in Newtonian mechanics. Temporal dynamics can be represented by the newly discovered differential calculus, that is, the formal representation of instantaneous rates of change. Thus, it seemed a complete formal description of nature *more geometrico* had become possible. The question of the bearer of these formal relations was rejected as metaphysical. Consequently, scientists no longer wanted to, or could, say anything about the inner nature of the world, the metaphysical core that lies beyond our mathematical descriptions.

The Modern View of Nature

If natural science is understood only as the formal representation of the relations between empirical data, that is, sensory impressions, then strictly speaking a physical object is nothing more than a bundle of such sensory data or the totality of perceptions from different perspectives. Beyond that, it has no inner material or other nature. This view, which is reminiscent of Berkeley's idealism, was advocated in the twentieth century in the early days of analytic philosophy in different variants, especially in Russell's early work *Our Knowledge of the External World* (1914), but also in a different way in the phenomenalism of Carnap's *The Logical Structure of the World* (1928). However, this metaphysics of nature is by no means the one that has gained the most acceptance in modernity. The "victorious" metaphysics of nature was that of Descartes, and it is quite robustly realistic. The metaphysics of material nature that he developed conceives a set of spatially extended objects that are in relations of interaction with one another. The material world is characterized exclusively by the modes of extension: form, size, movement in space. These attributes of a spatial substance, the *res extensa*, were not external to it, but determine its very essence. For Descartes, the distinction between substance and attribute is not a real distinction, but rather a purely conceptual distinction in the mind. The basis of the scientific representation of nature is therefore the analytic geometry founded by Descartes, which allows problems of classical geometry to be solved independent of observation using the methods of linear algebra. The formal description of planetary orbits only became possible on this basis. In addition, linear algebra later made it possible to transcend completely the realm of the intuitive—for example in the theory of n-dimensional vector spaces. Then came mathematical analysis developed by Leibniz and Newton, which made it possible to calculate functions of real numbers, their continuity, integration, and differentiability. Physics conceived in this way became the fundamental discipline in the study of nature. This concept was significantly expanded, but not fundamentally changed, by Minkowski's four-dimensional space-time formalism and the resulting general theory of relativity with its inclusion of a constitutive time dimension. This brings us to the present day. Despite this imposing structure, the mind found no place in this picture of nature. The independent existence of mind is either denied (reductive or eliminative physicalism) or is juxtaposed to the material world—as *res cogitans* or as the subject of (post-)Kantian philosophy—in an unmediated way. Thus, even today, this legacy of dualism is alive and well, even if it is often not visible at first glance. This was the situation Teilhard de Chardin encountered as the predominant intellectual milieu in his time. In his *The Heart of Matter* he describes how he gradually overcame this Modern mindset:

> Until that time my education and my religion had always led me obediently to accept—without much reflection, it is true—a fundamental heterogeneity between Matter and Spirit, between Body and Soul, between Unconscious and Conscious. These were to me two "substances" that differed in nature, two "species" of Being that were, in some incomprehensible way, associated in the living Compound; and it was important, I was told, to maintain at all costs that the first of those two (my divine Matter!) was no more than the humble servant of the second, if not, indeed, its enemy. Thus the second of the two (Spirit) was by that very fact henceforth reduced for me to being no more than a Shadow. In principle, it is true, I was compelled to venerate this shadow but, emotionally and intellectually speaking, I did not in fact have any live interest in it. You can well imagine, accordingly, how strong was my inner feeling of release and expansion when I took my first still hesitant steps into an "evolutive" Universe, and saw that the dualism in which I had hitherto been enclosed was disappearing like the mist before the rising sun. Matter and Spirit: these were no longer two things, but two states or two aspects of one and the same cosmic Stuff.[1]

What he describes in this passage is exactly the intuition that motivated the reemergence and renaissance of panpsychism in the twentieth century. It is not simply a Kantian turn to the subject because the subject no longer stands opposite the material world; rather, the material world is conceived as a world of subjects. The mind is not a counterpart to the material world, but an essential part of it. This "move" is intended to enable a "post-modern" philosophy, which overcomes the dualism to whose legacy materialism, dualism, and even Kantian idealism are still committed. Whitehead spoke of a "reformed subjectivist principle" that was to overcome modernity without falling back into a purely objective metaphysics of a pre-modern pattern. Pierre Teilhard de Chardin is an ally of Whitehead's in overcoming the bifurcation of nature. Their views are astoundingly similar.

---

[1] Pierre Teilhard de Chardin, *The Heart of Matter*, trans. René Hague (New York: Harcourt, 1980), 26.

The Legacy of Dualism

The arguments for dualism developed in the Cartesian tradition have the following basic structure:

1. There is an insurmountable epistemic gap between the mental facts of conscious experience and the purely physical facts.
2. If there is an insurmountable epistemic gap between mental and physical facts, then there is also an ontological gap between the two realms.
3. So monistic physicalism is wrong.

Even today, arguments critical of materialism often have precisely this structure. A much discussed one is that of the *ex hypothesi* perfect neuroscientist named "Mary," who knows all the facts about color perception in the brain. However, Mary has never seen a color herself. Let's assume she has worn glasses with small integrated black and white monitors all her life. Can Mary now deduce from this complete knowledge of the physical principles of color perception what it feels like to see the color blue, for example? Our intuition is that knowledge of what a perception of blue feels like cannot be derived from knowledge of the neurophysiology of color perception. Mary must have experienced a color perception to know these facts of phenomenal color experience. So, there is an epistemic gap between facts of conscious experience and purely physical facts. If one concludes from this epistemic asymmetry that the physical facts are different from the mental facts, then one has argued against physicalism in the style of the Cartesian tradition. If we call the time at which Mary first has a color perception "t" then we can reconstruct the argument as follows:

1. Mary knows all the physical facts about color perception before t.
2. Mary learns something at t.
3. Mary acquires propositional knowledge at t.
4. Mary learns a new fact at t.
5. There are facts about color perception that are not physical facts about color perception.
6. If physicalism is true, then there are no nonphysical facts about color perception.
7. Thus, physicalism is wrong.

This argument is open to attack in several places, especially the thesis that Mary really learns new facts. However, the finer points of the argument are not the issue at this point.[2] The thesis of interest here is that the physical realm can be completely described without recourse to phenomenal consciousness, that is, that the brain can be completely described as a physical entity without ever coming to speak of phenomenal experience. The Cartesian tradition has drawn far-reaching ontological consequences from this. The fundamental thesis of both dualism and physicalism is that the physical substances of which the more complex physical bodies are composed do not contain phenomenal experience.[3] The physical is, by its fundamental nature, non-phenomenal. This physical-contains-nothing-phenomenal-thesis can be stated thus: "Physical matter is something that by its fundamental nature is entirely without phenomenal experience." The basic material from which our world is composed is purely physical and not mental. This raises the question of how a being with conscious experience can be assembled from these completely experience-free building blocks. In principle, there are four possible answers to this question:

1. Strictly speaking, there is no phenomenal experience, no conscious experience. There is only complexly arranged non-phenomenal matter.
2. Phenomenal experience exists independently of the basic physical building blocks and does not emerge from them.
3. Phenomenal experience emerges suddenly and radically from a completely non-phenomenal basis.
4. There is phenomenal experience even in the basic building blocks. Consciousness is part of the physical world from the beginning.

Panpsychism chooses the fourth strategy. Teilhard de Chardin, I argue, also endorses the fourth strategy, not the third one, as one might think. The third strategy, the emergence of consciousness from an entirely non-mental realm, will be discussed here, but only in as much as necessary to demarcate it clearly from panpsychism. There is no systematic reason to discuss the first two strategies here. These are reductive or eliminative physicalism on the one hand and dualism on the other. Teilhard de Chardin clearly opposed both.

---

[2] Peter Ludlow, Yujin Nagasawa, and Daniel Stoljar, *There's Something about Mary: Essays on Phenomenal Consciousness and Frank Jackson's Knowledge Argument* (Boston: MIT Press, 2004).

[3] Galen Strawson, *Consciousness and Its Place in Nature: Does Physicalism Entail Panpsychism?* (Exeter, UK: Imprint Academic, 2006).

Emergence

At first glance the emergence thesis is a very attractive one. Aren't there a multitude of emergent levels in nature? Living organisms are systems that maintain a complex functional order by absorbing energy from the environment. The laws that govern the development of living things cannot be directly traced back to the fundamental laws of physics. Here, we must certainly speak of something novel, an emergent level, albeit in a weak sense. Emergence is weak here because we can, without major conceptual problems, assume that a perfect knowledge of the physical structures of living beings implies knowledge of their biological properties such as metabolism and procreation. *Weak* emergence is to be distinguished from *strong* emergence. Weakly emergent novel properties are necessitated by the base level with strong modal force (across all possible worlds). Even God could not create a physical duplicate of a living being that lacks the properties of living beings. Weak emergence thus presupposes a strong concept of reduction, which can be described as micro-reduction. Reducibility in this sense is only given if the properties to be reduced can be derived from the knowledge of the components on the reduction level alone. It should therefore be possible to understand (deduce) fully that the emergent properties necessarily arise from the basic properties of the system's components alone. From an ideal epistemic point of view, the base level is therefore "researchable" (scrutable) in terms of the conditions within it that necessitate the emergence of novel properties at a higher (weakly emergent) level. The connection between the two levels is therefore a conceptual one; the conditional connection is so strong that it could be inferred independently of additional experience (*a priori*) in the case of ideal knowledge. In this *weak* sense, many macroscopic objects of everyday life are emergent.

Weak emergence also allows for genuine novelty. The impression of novelty is created by the dissimilarity of the emergent properties to the basal properties. Weakly emergent system properties are not among the basal properties of the building blocks of the universe. They appear for the first time at a certain level of complexity in the development of the universe. There are usually no clear demarcation lines as to when exactly an emergent property first appears, but rather a continuous transition. The impression of novelty only arises when the intermediate stages that are similar to each other are neglected and two systems that are further apart in their complexity are considered. The similarity relation is not transitive. If A is similar to B, and B is similar to C, then A does not necessarily have to be similar to

C. So even if all intermediate stages in the stage structure of the world are similar to their neighbors, distant stages can be very dissimilar. If you combine hydrogen and oxygen to form H2O, and do this in sufficient quantities, you will eventually obtain a liquid and thus the emergent system-property "liquid" will arise. There is no precise answer to how many elementary particles are needed to create a liquid. The transition is blurred. However, the liquid stuff is emergent in a weak sense. The individual hydrogen and oxygen particles are not liquid. They are too small to have such macro properties. For scientists, however, the emergence of these properties is not mysterious. Water is liquid because the attraction of positive and negative charges of the water molecules creates hydrogen bonds, which restrict the mobility of the molecules; they clump together a little, so to speak.

The higher-level system property "is alive" is, of course, not as easy to attribute as "is liquid," as we use "life" to describe a whole bundle of very complex processes such as metabolism, reproduction, and self-sustaining repair of damage. However, all these processes are nothing more than complex functional patterns in physical processes, which can in principle be broken down into their small chemical and ultimately physical building blocks. Here too, the transition between nonliving and living systems cannot be clearly defined (viruses). The impression of a radical break only arises if one compares very complex living systems with inorganic systems. However, the impression often arises that life is emergent in a strong sense. This is probably due to the fact that criteria such as reaction to stimuli are assumed to be typical criteria of life and are associated with the fact that the living being senses or experiences something. However, the phenomenal content of sensing or experiencing is precisely the problem at issue here. If we introduce experience into the picture, weak emergence collapses. How could the complex configuration of non-experiencing parts ever necessitate the emergence of experience?

According to the Cartesian bifurcation, phenomenal experience could emerge from mindless matter only in a process of a very strong emergence; mindless matter alone cannot necessitate the emergence of the mind. The relevant emergence laws cannot be deduced from the knowledge of the basic level alone. This type of emergence is quite different from that of "liquid" or even "alive." Weak emergence means that the combination of many small functional structures results in a larger pattern, which then has functional properties that its substructures did not have. It is only a matter of an increase in functional complexity within a homogeneous ontological framework. Weak emergence is therefore the appearance of new properties

68   Was Pierre Teilhard de Chardin a Panpsychist?

that are dissimilar to those of the basic level in many respects. However, this dissimilarity is only relative, since weak emergence is still within the framework of a category of attributes, for example, that of functional structures in space. One could therefore also speak of *intra-attribute emergence* instead of weak emergence.

However, the qualitative content of a sensation cannot be characterized purely functionally by relations of physical entities in space.[4] Phenomenal experiences do not fit into the ontological framework of purely functionally determined physical entities. An emergence in which entities of a completely new metaphysical category suddenly appear is not comprehensible. Even a being with ideal cognitive abilities could not derive these surprising leaps into a completely other metaphysical realm. They must be accepted as *facta bruta*. One can then also speak of *inter-attribute emergence*, in which properties that belong to a completely different attribute class suddenly appear. If, for example, functionally undefinable phenomenal qualities of the mental emerge from a purely functional-spatial physical level, then two completely different attributes are placed in a brute relationship of emergence. The intellectual strain that such a concept of emergence entails can be illustrated with another example. Let us assume that, in addition to concrete entities in space and time, there are also abstract entities, like numbers, which do not exist in space and time. A radical "Pythagorean" emergence thesis would be that our world fundamentally consists of abstract mathematical entities. According to this theory, if these abstract entities are arranged in a complex way, then suddenly concrete spatio-temporal entities emerge from the abstract realm. However, the transition from an abstract to a concrete entity is not intelligible. Analogously, the transition from entities that, by their fundamental nature, are entirely without phenomenal experience, to entities endowed with phenomenal experience, is equally unintelligible. The following dilemma arises: either emergence is conceived weakly and mentality is simply a higher-level physical property like "liquid"; or the concept of emergence is so strong that anything can emerge from anything. The dependence between the base level and the emergent properties then becomes unintelligible.

In a somewhat more technical vocabulary, this relationship can also be explained using the concept of supervenience. Weakly emergent properties are in a strong sense supervenient with respect to their basic properties.

---

[4] See Godehard Brüntrup, "Zur Kritik des Funktionalismus," in *Ist der Geist berechenbar? Philosophische Reflexionen*, ed. Wolfgang Köhler and Hans-Dieter Mutschler (Hrsg.) (Darmstadt: Wissenschaftliche Buchgesellschaft, 2003).

There is no possible world that is an isomorphic one-to-one image of our physical world, but in which water-stuff is not liquid. The physical level forces the weak emergence of the supervenient levels (chemical, biological) with necessity. Therefore, this type of emergence of higher-level properties is not in itself mysterious, even if in complex cases it may not be known to us in detail. In the case of conscious experience, however, there is an "upward opacity" so that one, in principle, is unable to grasp how the purely physical level, void of any phenomenal experience, could force the occurrence of higher-level emergent experiential properties.

There is no *a priori* connection between the physical and phenomenal levels if the physical level is characterized purely functionally. This insight is shared even by most physicalists today. For conscious experience to occur, additional facts are needed to explain supervenience of the mental on the physical. These additional facts, which go beyond the physical facts, could allow for an emergentist version of dualism. Special psycho-physical emergence laws govern the existence of minds. Physicalism is defeated. How can physicalists account for the mind without resorting to such an emergent dualism? David Chalmers has argued that they can meet this challenge by extending his concept of the physical so that it already contains the additional facts that enable conscious experience to occur. This is a form of panpsychism, which he labeled Russellian monism. It is worth taking a slightly closer look at Chalmers's argument to determine the exact logical place for this argumentative move.[5]

Two Concepts of the Physical

Recall that the basic premise is that the fundamental physical facts do not contain facts of phenomenal experience (that is, experience does not occur in the world of physics). Chalmers's basic idea is that a world is conceivable (possible) in which all the fundamental physical facts of our world are copied one to one, but in which there is no phenomenal experience.

---

[5] David Chalmers, *The Conscious Mind: In Search of a Fundamental Theory* (Oxford: Oxford University Press, 1996). See also Strawson, *Consciousness and Its Place in Nature*; Daniel Stoljar, *Ignorance and Imagination: The Epistemic Origin of the Problem of Consciousness* (Oxford: Oxford University Press, 2006); Gregg Rosenberg, *A Place for Consciousness: Probing the Deep Structure of the Natural World* (Oxford: Oxford University Press, 2004); David Ray Griffin, *Unsnarling the World-Knot: Consciousness, Freedom, and the Mind-Body Problem* (Berkeley: University of California Press, 1998); and Michael Lockwood, *Mind, Brain, and the Quantum: The Compound 'I'* (Oxford: Balckwell, 1989).

70   Was Pierre Teilhard de Chardin a Panpsychist?

He calls this the world of "metaphysical zombies." This somewhat striking name comes from the fact that in this world, of course, all strongly supervenient facts of chemistry, biology, and so on would also arise in perfect copy to our world. This means that we ourselves would also appear in this world, but without conscious experience; we would be a kind of living dead, metaphysical "zombies."

In its simplest form, the argument looks like this:

> Let us define P as the logical conjunction of all physical facts (or simply: the set of all physical facts) and let us take Q to be any fact of qualitative, phenomenal experience (or simply: a fact of phenomenal experience).
> 1. It is conceivable that <P and not Q>.
> 2. If it is conceivable that <P and not Q>, then it is metaphysically possible that <P and not Q>.
> 3. If it is metaphysically possible that <P and not Q>, then physicalism is false.[6]

However, the representative of scientific essentialism will not agree with this. The sciences discover the essence of things and therefore metaphysically exclude certain logically conceivable possibilities (in Chalmers's classification: type-B materialism). According to the type-B materialist, the mistake lies in the fact that we work with primary intensions (level of sense) in the case of epistemic possibilities and with secondary intensions (level of reference) in the case of metaphysical possibilities. In the first case we regard a world as actual; in the second case we regard a world counterfactually. If we consider Putnam's twin earth, where XYZ is in the lakes and rivers, as actual, then "water is not H2O" is a true proposition there, if by water we mean "the stuff that is in the rivers and lakes, drinkable, transparent, and so on." This is an epistemic possibility. If we consider the meaning of water to be fixed by our actual world (rigid designator) and then counterfactually consider the twin earth with XYZ in the rivers and lakes, then the sentence "water is not H2O" is false. In this case, "water is H2O" expresses a necessary truth (in Kripke's sense), that is also true in twin-earth. Let us call possibility in connection with primary intensions "1–possibility" and possibility in connection with secondary intensions "2–possibility."

---

[6] David Chalmers, "Consciousness and Its Place in Nature," in *Philosophy of Mind: Classical and Contemporary Readings*, ed. David Chalmers (New York: Oxford University Press, 2002), 247–72.

Now Chalmers can state his argument more precisely:
1. <P and not Q> is conceivable.
2. If <P and not Q> is conceivable, then <P and not Q> is 1–possible.
3. If <P and not Q> is 1–possible, then <P and not Q> is 2–possible.
4. If <P and not Q> is 2–possible, then materialism is false.
5. Materialism is false.

For (3) to be true, it is assumed that both P and Q have primary intensions and secondary intensions that coincide. In the case of Q, that is, qualia such as pain, this is unproblematic. Something that feels like pain is pain. In the case of P, however, the situation is more complicated. Physical entities are defined by their functional role. One could say that the primary intension of "mass" picks out whatever plays the mass role in a given world. The secondary intension of "mass," on the other hand, is tied to the filler of the mass role in our world in such a way that in a world where something else occupies that role, that filler is not mass. Against this background, premise (3) can be rejected. In this case there would be worlds indistinguishable from ours in their physical functional structure, but in which something else would be the intrinsic bearer of these functional roles. What could that be? What can be the intrinsic bearer of all functional roles? The only entirely intrinsic properties we know are the properties of phenomenal experience. In our world the phenomenal mind is intrinsic, that is, not definable relationally. The view that the intrinsic nature of matter, the ultimate carrier of the functional roles, has a phenomenal, i.e. mental, character is that of panpsychism. Thus, we now have an argument for panpsychism:

Chalmers's argument for panpsychism has the following structure:
1. <P and not Q> is conceivable.
2. If <P and not Q> is conceivable, then <P and not Q> is 1–possible.
3. If <P and not Q> is 1–possible, then <P and not Q> is 2–possible or panpsychism is true.
4. If <P and not Q> is 2–possible, then materialism is false.
5. Materialism is false or panpsychism is true.

So, if one wants to avoid the refutation of materialism as a consequence of the argument, then the assumption of panpsychism provides a loophole. However, this then means that the language of physics in our world refers to something (secondary intension) whose essence it does not fully grasp. The

72 Was Pierre Teilhard de Chardin a Panpsychist?

nature of the physical is not fully revealed by the terminology of physics. The description in the functional language of physics leaves out one crucial aspect of physical reality, and it is precisely this aspect that is the ontological basis of all phenomenal facts. We must therefore introduce two concepts of the physical: first, a concept of the physical as conceived by physics, and then another concept of the physical that goes beyond what the language of physics can directly grasp. This "meta-physical" concept of the physical has (proto-)mental properties built-in.[7] Galen Strawson accordingly distinguishes "realistic physicalism," which describes the whole nature of the physical, from a mere "physicSalism" which is merely the perspective of physics as empirical science (the emphasized letter S is the s in the English word *physics*). According to Strawson, a realistic physicalism must accept and integrate the undoubted fact of the existence of phenomenal experience. Since inter-attribute emergence is incomprehensible, and a reductive explanation of phenomenal experience in purely functional terms is not possible, the only way out for a realistic physicalism is to regard phenomenal experience as a fundamental aspect of the physical itself.[8]

One could argue that neutral monism is another alternative. The core thesis is that mental and physical properties emerge from a unified origin that is neither mental nor physical. Influential variants of neutral monism were advocated by Ernst Mach and Bertrand Russell.[9] However, if this underlying, neutral level does not contain any proto-mental properties, the familiar problem arises again. How can a mental entity emerge from something that has nothing in common with the realm of the mental? So, if neutral monism admits proto-mental properties on a neutral basis, then it is only an interesting variant of the broadly panpsychist position.

A Misunderstanding of Panpsychism

The spontaneous reaction to theories of this kind is incredulous amazement, because they contain the thesis that the fundamental entities that make up

---

[7] See Daniel Stoljar, "Two Conceptions of the Physical," in *Philosophical and Phenomenological Research* 62, no. 2 (2001): 253–81.

[8] Strawson, *Consciousness and Its Place in Nature*; Thomas Nagel, *Mortal Questions* (Cambridge: Cambridge University Press, 2006), chap. 13.

[9] Ernst Mach, *Die Analyse der Empfindungen und das Verhältnis des Physischen zum Psychischen* (Darmstadt: Wissenschaftliche Buchgesellschaft, 1991); Bertrand Russell, *The Analysis of Matter* (London: Routledge, 1992).

the universe have mental properties. However, the idea that electrons, for example, have sensations like tiny persons is obviously absurd. However, panpsychism is an important position in the history of philosophy; just think of names such as Spinoza or Leibniz. Panpsychist approaches have been advocated by influential philosophers from the pre-Socratics to the present day.[10] The danger of anthropomorphism was clearly seen by most proponents of panpsychism. Thus, a clear distinction is often made between conscious experiences in the full sense and their primitive predecessors. Leibniz distinguished perception from fully conscious apperception, Whitehead introduced the term *prehension* to describe non-sensory perceptions that lie far below the threshold of conscious attention. For Whitehead, the mental properties of simple actual entities were above all creativity, spontaneity, and a certain informational receptivity toward the environment. He regarded this receptivity as a kind of "feeling" that is dissimilar to our conscious feeling. Other contemporary panpsychists also attribute the ability of representation to very simple entities. One example of this is physicist David Bohm.[11] The problem here, however, is that in analogy to the human experience of waking consciousness and dreamless sleep, we regard consciousness as either fully given or entirely nonexistent. This basic intuition can be abandoned, however, as it is itself an anthropomorphism. We humans cannot imagine consciousness in other species such as bats or worms, nor can we imagine which sensations are still somehow perceived in our body below the level of complex waking consciousness.

The logical structure of all these arguments is based on the non-transitivity of the similarity relation. Let us assume a stratification of reality. Between the lowest level of elementary particles and levels of highest complexity, such as a human being, there are many intermediate levels. In terms of their mental properties, each level is similar to its neighbors. However, since similarity is not transitive, it is possible that distant levels are no longer similar in terms of their mental properties. Not only can the complexity of the mental properties decrease radically, but also the intensity and temporal frequency. Therefore, panpsychism does not imply the absurd thesis that the

---

[10] See David S. Clarke, *Panpsychism: Past and Recent Selected Readings* (Albany: State University of New York Press, 2004); David Skrbina, *Panpsychism in the West* (London: MIT Press, 2005); and *Mind That Abides: Panpsychism in the New Millennium* (Amsterdam: John Benjamins, 2009).

[11] David Bohm and B. J. Hiley, *The Undivided Universe: An Ontological Interpretation of Quantum Mechanics* (London: Routledge, 1993).

mental properties of the lowest layers of complexity, that is, the elementary particles, must be conceived according to the model of human subjectivity.[12]

After having located the origin of the renaissance of panpsychism in the contemporary philosophy of mind, we wish to look briefly at two historically influential arguments for panpsychism. The genetic argument and the argument from intrinsic natures. Both will be useful in then answering more fully whether Teilhard de Chardin was a panpsychist.

The Genetic Argument for Panpsychism

The genetic argument is based on the intuition *ex nihilo nihil fit*—nothing can come from nothing, or more specifically, nothing can give which it does not possess. In his essay "Panpsychism," Thomas Nagel argued that the emergence of mental properties of higher organisms should be explainable from the properties of their smallest components. However, these sought-after properties could not be of a physical nature, as one would then not understand how the mental can arise.[13] In the background of the genetic argument is a train of thought that has also been called the absence-of-analysis argument. It states that the emergence of phenomenal experience from a world in which there are no proto-forms of experience remains completely incomprehensible. Gregg Rosenberg, who developed a detailed panexperientialist theory, has presented this argument in a rather intuitive form.[14] It is based on the idea of cellular automata: A cellular automaton consists of points or "cells" in an abstract space that have certain properties. Roughly speaking, you can imagine a chessboard pattern. Each square on the chessboard is a cell. The decisive factor is that the cellular automaton develops step by step over time. The properties change according to certain rules. Let us introduce two primitive properties as an example: Each cell can be either "off" or "on." We also assume three rules:

1. If exactly two neighbors of a cell are "on," it retains its "on" or "off" property unchanged in the next step.
2. If exactly three neighbors of a cell are "on," then the cell itself is "on" in the next step.
3. In all other cases, the cell is "off" in the next step.

---

[12] Godehard Brüntrup, "Is Psycho-physical Emergentism Committed to Dualism? The Causal Efficacy of Emergent Mental Properties," *Erkenntnis* 48, nos. 2/3 (1998): 133–51.

[13] Nagel, "Panpsychism," in *Mortal Questions*, 187–89.

[14] Rosenberg, *A Place for Consciousness*, 13–76.

Now imagine a huge chessboard with such cells. Such a world consists of a large number of elementary particles and laws that determine the interaction of the elementary particles. "On" and "off" are the basic properties of this world, the three rules are its fundamental laws of nature. It is immediately apparent that the cellular automaton is a simple model of a physical theory. In contemporary physics we have more than one type of fundamental elementary particle (bosons and fermions), and these have more than two properties (spin, charge, mass, and so forth). But the basic structure is still very similar to the simpler case. In principle, it should therefore be possible to implement a very complicated cellular automaton on a computer, which in its complexity comes quite close to our physical world.

It has already been proven that even relatively simple cellular automata can produce an enormous variety of complex patterns. In cellular automata, patterns emerge relatively quickly that extend over several cells and show a tendency toward non-trivial self-replication. Research has shown that even the well-known self-replicative patterns of DNA can be simulated in this way. This is why these cellular automata are also called *life worlds*. To explain the emergence of these complex patterns in our cellular automata, we do not need to extend its basic ontology. All higher-level properties are nothing other than complex patterns that can be completely derived from the rule-governed interaction of the elementary parts. The argument against physicalism that thus arises is an argument that points to a lack of analysis, a lack of intelligibility of the emergence of consciousness. It has the following structure:

1. The facts of the cellular automaton contain no facts about phenomenal consciousness, neither *a priori* nor *a posteriori*.
2. If the facts of the cellular automaton do not contain facts about phenomenal consciousness, then purely physical facts do not contain facts about phenomenal consciousness either.
3. So purely physical facts do not contain facts about phenomenal consciousness.

The argument can also be developed differently:

1. The fundamental properties of the cellular automaton are defined solely by their dynamic relations.
2. Facts of phenomenal consciousness are intrinsically qualitative facts that are not determined purely by their dynamic relations.
3. Facts about dynamic relations do not contain (neither *a priori* nor *a posteriori*) intrinsic qualitative facts.

4. So, the facts about phenomenal consciousness are not contained in the facts of the cellular automaton.

This argument gets by without speculation about metaphysically possible worlds and is therefore in some respects preferable to Chalmers's argument (zombies). It formulates the central intuition that purely functionally defined entities have no compelling conceptual connection with the emergence of a qualitatively determined perspective of experience. The same formal structure could also relate to other or even no qualitative phenomenal contents at all. Let us briefly reconsider our example with the properties "on" and "off." How are they defined? Only by the fact that they are different and that they develop in time according to the three rules. This is a purely structural-functional view of reality that has no place for qualitative experience. This is exactly how physics works. But aren't there purely intrinsic properties in physics? Mass might be a candidate. But having mass is the property that something has when it takes on a certain functional role, which is determined by the relation of force and acceleration: $m=F/a$. What about rest mass? It is a consequence of general relativity that only an isolated system has a coordinate-independent mass. Since a non-isolated system continuously exchanges energy-momentum with its environment, the mass at a certain point in time should also depend on the observer's determinations of simultaneity, that is, be relatively determined. In quantum mechanics, mass is ultimately explained by the Higgs mechanism. Thus, if you only dig deep enough, you will eventually arrive at purely functional determinations.

If one accepts this absence-of-analysis argument, then the force of the genetic argument is obvious. Let us assume that the physical world is free of any proto-forms of qualitative experience at its lower levels. If we further assume that evolution proceeds in comprehensible small steps, that is, does not make any incomprehensible leaps, it then follows from the absence-of-analysis argument that the genesis of consciousness remains inexplicable. The relevant way out here is precisely to assume proto-forms of experience on all levels of the physical world. This was Chalmers's way out. William James expressed this idea classically: If evolution is to proceed smoothly, then consciousness must have been present in some form at the very origin of things.[15]

---

[15] William James, *The Principles of Psychology*, Vol. I. (New York: Dover, 1950), 149.

The Argument from Intrinsic Natures for Panpsychism

The other argument is that from intrinsic natures. An intuitive way to present it is the problem of circular interdependence of purely formal systems.[16] Let us consider a purely formal structure like a chess game. It consists of circularly interdependent types: pawns, knights, kings, and so on. Each type is precisely defined by the moves it is allowed to make in the game as a whole. Without the context of the game, none of these types could exist. But the reverse is also true: without these individual types, the game as a whole could not exist. We have a circular structure here. Each part of the game presupposes the whole game; the whole game presupposes each part. This circularity is harmless because every concrete implementation of the game of chess is based on external properties that introduce the game piece by piece. For example, we have different, distinguishable physical objects that stand for the individual types. We have a chessboard that occupies a certain position in space relative to the players. If the game of chess takes place on a computer, then there are certain physical states within the computer that, extrinsic to the logical structure, give the game a foothold and position in reality. The existence of the chess game is dependent on these external properties and relations.

The formal structure needs a support that is external to the categorical nature of the formal structure. In every level of scientific theories one finds such closed systems of circularly interdependent conceptualization. The reason why this is harmless is that for every functional conceptualization of a scientific theory there is an external level that anchors the formal description in reality. Normally this is done by going one level deeper, for example, from the computer program to the hardware, from the biological level to the level of molecular biochemistry. The same phenomenon of circular definitions can be found in physics, since here, as already shown, the entities are also defined by their functional role. A physical entity, say an electron, is defined by the causal role it plays in the whole of physical reality, and the whole of physical reality is defined by individual types of physical entities that occur in it.

But which level is extrinsic to physics, so that physics could be realized or grounded by it? What sustains the contrasts and relations of physics?

---

[16] See Rosenberg, *A Place for Consciousness*, chap. 12; John Haugeland, "Pattern and Being," in *Dennett and His Critics*, ed. Bo Dahlbom (Oxford: Oxford University Press, 1993), 53–69; Wilfried Sellars, "Some Reflections on Language Games," in *Science, Perception, and Reality* (New York: Humanities Press, 1963), 323ff.

78   Was Pierre Teilhard de Chardin a Panpsychist?

If all physically described entities are defined interdependently via their causal roles, then the question arises as to what properties the *bearer* of these causal roles should have. What grounds physics? Every functionalist level of description requires a level of realization or instantiation. If the physical level is the ultimate, fundamental level, then there are no carriers for it. One might claim that there are always finer and more basic physical levels, and that one never thus comes to an end. However, Planck's quantum of action seems to set a clearly defined limit to the division of physical reality into ever smaller building blocks.

One possible way out would be to look for carriers that are external to any functionally characterized physical system and that by their nature are not functional but absolutely intrinsic. The only candidate for such an ultimate carrier of the physical with which we are familiar are the properties of phenomenal experience. This is an idea that Sir Arthur Eddington already formulated as follows: "Physics is the realization of structural forms, not the realization of content. An unknown content runs through the entire physical world, which is undoubtedly the basis of our consciousness."[17] We will see that Teilhard de Chardin had a similar intuition. Bertrand Russell had also pointed out that physics grasps but the formal, mathematically representable structures of reality, while everything we know about the intrinsic properties of reality is derived from mental experience.[18] The argument from intrinsic natures for panpsychism thus states that there is no purely relational reality, and that the best candidates for the intrinsic properties we are looking for are (proto-)mental properties.

The Historical Critique of the Cartesian Concept of Matter

What are the intrinsic properties of the entities of our actual world, and to what extent do the intrinsic properties in turn determine the external, relational properties? Leibniz's metaphysics advances the thesis that all external properties must be grounded in intrinsic properties. The best candidates of intrinsic properties that can guarantee this are those that enable a mental representation of the external world. Leibniz thus arrives

---

[17] Arthur Eddington, *Space, Time, and Gravitation* (Cambridge: Cambridge University Press, 1920), 200; see Alfred North Whitehead, *Adventures of Ideas* (New York: The Free Press, 1967), 132.

[18] Russell, *The Analysis of Matter*, 270, 402; see also Timothy Sprigge, *A Vindication of Absolute Idealism* (London: Routledge, 1983).

at a panpsychism in which each monad is a "living mirror" that mentally represents the universe from its perspective. This is a thought that Teilhard explicitly relates to. The crucial point is that the mechanistic concept of causal influence was replaced by that of mutual information. The whole of spatial reality was constructed by the fact that each monad had a point of perspective from which it represented reality. Space is therefore not a given container but is constituted as an experienced and represented space. The monads do not simply passively reflect a space, but it is their activity that constitutes the spatial relations.

This idea can also be developed independently of Leibniz's monadology. The criticism of the Cartesian concept of *res extensa* expressed by many authors had very similar basic intuitions to those found in Leibniz. The mental is seen as that which grounds all physical relations. The following analysis of abstraction will try to make this point: An abstract structure in itself is not metaphysically fundamental, but it is rather derived from concrete individual things. In this sense, an abstract structure is "incomplete." A concrete entity with a geometric shape, say a cube, has a certain edge length, is made of a certain material, and so forth. The abstract cube, on the other hand, only has the negative property of not having a specific edge length and not being made of a specific material. One of the main temptations of scientific thinking is to take the abstract structures that can be mathematically determined for reality itself. This mistake is what Whitehead characterized as the "fallacy of misplaced concreteness" and concluded that one of the main tasks of philosophy was precisely to criticize one-sided abstractions. The modern, Cartesian image of matter is precisely such an abstraction. For Descartes, a material substance consists only of modes of extension (form, size, movement in space). The fact that this image of the material world is an abstraction can be illustrated by a thought-experiment.[19] Unger claims that two completely different worlds, if considered purely as abstract modes of extension, are indistinguishable: The first world, the *particle* world, is one in which elementary particles move through empty space according to the physical laws of that world. The second world, the *plenum* world, is one in which tiny empty spaces instead of particles move through a filled space according to the same physical laws. In their formal characteristics, the two worlds are indistinguishable. If the particles have no intrinsic nature they remain, to use another of Whitehead's expressions, "empty entities." *Empty* here means that they are underdetermined. The formal structure needs some

---

[19] Peter Unger, *All the Power in the World* (Oxford: Oxford University Press, 2006), 33.

concrete realization to become real. Our concrete world is therefore more than just a structured arrangement of modes of extension.

This criticism of the Cartesian view of matter was well known in Modern philosophy, perhaps more so than today.[20] In the fourth part of David Hume's *A Treatise of Human Nature*, there is a section entitled "On Modern Philosophy." This cabinet piece of skeptical argumentation is a reckoning with the Cartesian concept of matter. Hume argues here that if we subtract all experiential properties such as sound, color, taste, and smell (the so-called secondary properties) from the mind-independent external world, the entire external world becomes completely unintelligible. If we subtract the experiential qualities (sensible qualities) from the mind-independent external world, then, according to Hume, nothing remains to which one can attribute a concrete mind-independent existence. Hume goes on to show that the central intuition of materiality, namely solidity and impenetrability, cannot be explicated without the assumption of qualitatively intrinsic properties. This idea was taken up by the contemporary panpsychist Freya Mathews.[21]

Leibniz had also criticized the untenability of the Cartesian concept of matter. Extension can be determined purely relationally, but what then is the nature of the relata? According to Leibniz, pure extension cannot be understood in itself. Extension is not a primitive concept, but one that can be further analyzed. It can be analyzed in plurality, continuity, and coexistence of parts at a point in time.[22] Pure extension is nothing but a repetition of what is spread out. But this is not enough to explain the nature of the substance that is extended and repeated. Its concept is prior to that of its repetitive expansion.[23] Extension is a relative concept that cannot be explicated on its own, but only in relation to that which is or will be extended: "Extensionem non esse absolutum, quoddam praedicatum, sed relativum ad id quod extenditur sive diffunditur."[24]

The early Kant also criticized the modern concept of matter for being purely relational and not knowing any intrinsic natures. It remains un-

---

[20] Robert Adams, "Idealism Vindicated," in *Persons: Human and Divine*, ed. Peter van Inwagen and Dean Zimmerman (Oxford: Oxford University Press, 2007), 35–54.

[21] Freya Mathews, *For The Love of Matter: A Contemporary Panpsychism* (Albany: State University of New York Press, 2001), 30ff.

[22] Gottfried Wilhelm Leibniz, *Die philosophischen Schriften von Gottfried Wilhelm Leibniz*, hg. von Carl Immanuel Gerhardt, 7 Bde., Berlin 1875–1890 (Hildesheim: Olms, 1978), 169–70.

[23] Ibid., 467.

[24] Ibid., 394.

clear what the substances are that stand in these relations.[25] In his critical philosophy Kant argues that a purely relational concept of matter as an impenetrable extension is not intelligible in a classical metaphysical understanding.[26] Kant writes:

> We are acquainted with substance in space only through forces which are active in this and that space, either bringing other objects to it (attraction), or preventing them penetrating into it (repulsion and impenetrability). We are not acquainted with any other properties constituting the concept of the substance which appears in space and which we call matter. As object of pure understanding, on the other hand, every substance must have inner determinations and powers which pertain to its inner reality. But what inner accidents can I entertain in thought, save only those which my inner sense presents to me? They must be something which is either itself a thinking or analogous to thinking.[27]

Kant thus argues here, quite similarly to Russell, that although the intrinsic nature of the physical external world is unknown to us, we can assume with good reason that the inner nature of things can be thought analogous to the mental (to "thinking"), which we know from our own experience. It seems that even Kant saw that the only way out of the modern predicament was panpsychism. Now, endowed with these conceptual clarifications, we can finally turn to Teilhard de Chardin again.

Pierre Teilhard de Chardin as Panpsychist

The question we wanted to ask was whether Teilhard de Chardin took a similar position. Is he a "Russellian monist" in Chalmers's sense of the term? Is he arguing along the lines of Leibniz and Whitehead that the modern concept of matter is "vacuous"? Does he even take the position that the mental is the intrinsic nature of the physical? The autobiographical quotation from *The Heart of Matter* mentioned above suggests that he does. He

---

[25] Immanuel Kant, *Metaphysicae cum geometria iunctae usus in philosophia naturali, cuius specimen I. continet monadologiam physicam* (Academy edition, 1756), 480.

[26] Immanuel Kant, *Critique of Pure Reason*, trans. Norman Kemp Smith (New York: St. Martin's Press, 1965), B 340.

[27] Ibid., B 321–22.

wants to overcome dualism by relocating the mental *into the heart of matter*. Teilhard de Chardin considers dualism and the modern bifurcation of mind and matter as disastrous:

> In the first place, under the cosmos-system, a fatal dualism was inevitably introduced into the structure of the universe. On one side lay spirit, and on the other matter: and between the two there was nothing but the affirmation of some unexplained and inexplicable coupling together—in other words there was ultimately no more than a verbal inter-dependence, which too often was akin to a subjection of one to the other.[28]

He sees the overcoming of dualism and materialism as a "third way" (*via tertia*), a bipolarism of matter and spirit, in which the extremes are intimately connected with each other:

> Ever since man, in becoming man, started on his quest for unity, he has constantly oscillated, in his visions, in his ascesis, or in his dreams, between a cult of the spirit which made him jettison matter and a cult of matter which made him deny spirit: omegalization allows us to pass between this Scylla and Charybdis of rarefaction or the quagmire. Detachment now comes not through a severance but through a traversing and a sublimation; and spiritualization not by negation of the multiple or an escape from it, but by emergence. This is the via tertia that opens up before us as soon as spirit is no longer the opposite extreme but the higher pole of matter in course of super-centration. It is not a cautious and neutral middle course, but the bold, higher road, in which the values and properties of the two other roads are combined and correct one another.[29]

While matter enables functional and causal connections, it is not the basis of the mental. On the contrary: the mental as the intrinsic nature of the material grounds the existence of matter:

> Strictly speaking, if matter is defined as "something with no vestige of consciousness or spontaneity," it does not exist. Even in pre-living

---

[28] Teilhard de Chardin, *Activation of Energy*, trans. René Hague (San Diego/New York: Harcourt, 1971), 258.

[29] Ibid., 53.

particles, we saw, we must conceive some sort of curvature which prefigures and initiates the appearance of a freedom and a "within."[30]

For me, matter was the matrix of consciousness and all around us matter, born of consciousness, was constantly advancing towards some ultra-human.[31]

Matter does not ground itself. Consciousness is the "stuff" that permeates the entire physical world. This is the very thought that was developed by physicist and panpsychist Sir Arthur Eddington in his *Space, Time, and Gravitation* (1920) as seen above.

"Consciousness" (that is to say the tension of union and desire) has in my eyes become the "fundamental element/ the very stuff of the real, the veritable 'ether'; . . . All present-day physics of matter is merely the study of a wave motion."[32]

But this is not meant to be an affirmation of radical idealism. The material is spiritualized, but not eliminated or downgraded to a mere phenomenon:

Matter, it is true, is not the formal instrument of the union and interplay of the monads; but it is matter that gives the things of this world their radical capacity of entering into higher or lower syntheses, under one and the same Spirit. The essence (the formal effect) of materiality would appear to be to make beings capable of unification.[33]

The material aspect of reality enables connection and relatedness through time:

In each one of us, through matter, the whole history of the world is in part reflected.[34]

---

[30] Ibid., 122.

[31] Teilhard, *The Heart of Matter*, 45.

[32] Teilhard de Chardin, *Letters to Léontine Zanta*, trans. Bernard Wall (New York: Harper & Row, 1969), 87.

[33] Teilhard de Chardin, *Writings in the Time of War*, trans. René Hague (New York: Harper & Row, 1968), 267.

[34] Teilhard de Chardin, *The Divine Milieu*, trans. Bernard Wall (New York: Harper & Row, 1965), 59.

84   Was Pierre Teilhard de Chardin a Panpsychist?

This close connection between matter and spirit is intended to radically overcome the bifurcation of matter and spirit.

> There is neither spirit nor matter in the world; the "stuff of the universe" is spirit-matter.[35]

Teilhard de Chardin introduces panpsychism by philosophical arguments that cannot be tested by direct empirical evidence because the mentality at the lowest level is too "small."

> But—interiority, the rudiment of consciousness, exists everywhere; it is only that if the particle is extremely simple, the consciousness is so small that we cannot perceive it.[36]

He chooses a model of panpsychism that is close to Russell's in his *The Analysis of Matter* (1927). The mental is the inside of the granular physical.

> Since the stuff of the universe has an internal face at one point in itself, its structure is necessarily bifacial; that is, in every region of time and space, as well, for example, as being granular, co-extensive with its outside, everything has an inside.[37]

Teilhard de Chardin thus sees himself in agreement with the latest developments in philosophy and physics, which regard the mind as the "essence" of matter. Here he could be referring to Russell, Whitehead, Bergson, and Eddington.

> Conforming to recent views which point towards the idea of a spiritual essence of matter.[38]

A reference to Leibniz's *Monadology* is also clearly recognizable. The monads each represent the whole universe in their own individual way.

---

[35] Teilhard de Chardin, *Human Energy*, trans. J. M. Cohen (San Diego/New York: Harcourt, 1971), 57–58.

[36] Teilhard, *Activation of Energy*, 156.

[37] Teilhard de Chardin, *The Human Phenomenon*, trans. Sarah Appleton-Weber (Brighton: Sussex Academic Press, 1999), 24.

[38] Teilhard, *Human Energy*, 130.

At every degree of size and complexity, the cosmic corpuscles or grains are not only, as physics recognizes, centers of universal dynamic radiation but, somewhat like human beings, they possess and represent . . . a small "inside" (however diffuse or fragmentary it may be . . .) in which is reflected, in more or less rudimentary form, a particular representation of the world: psychic centers in relation to their own selves and, at the same time, infinitesimal psychic centers of the universe.[39]

But it is not the static view of Leibniz, primarily, but rather the dynamic view of Whitehead where the monads are internally linked by internal relations and dynamically determine each other.

The phenomenon of man forces us to see the universe as made up of psychic nuclei, each one of which acts as a partial centre in relation to the world and is therefore potentially co-extensive with the universe: to take this view is obviously to go back to Leibniz's monads. While, however, in the static universe of monadology, the cosmic particles "have neither doors nor windows," from the evolutionary standpoint adopted by centrology, they are seen to be in threefold solidarity one with another, within the centrogenesis in which they are born.[40]

But how can the relationship between matter and spirit be thought of more precisely? Teilhard de Chardin defines the relationship as follows:

Every individual cosmic particle can be represented symbolically in our experience as an ellipse constructed around two foci of unequal and variable intensity—one, F1, of material arrangement, the other, F2, of psychism; F2 (consciousness) appearing and increasing initially as a function of F1 (complexity) but soon revealing a persistent tendency to react constructively on F1, in order to super-complexify it and become increasingly individualized itself.[41]

Even more specifically, Teilhard de Chardin developed a model of two cosmic *energies*, one psychic and the other physical. Together they determine the nature of the cosmos.

---

[39] Teilhard, *Activation of Energy*, 101.

[40] Ibid., 104.

[41] Teilhard de Chardin, *Toward the Future*, trans. René Hague (San Diego/New York: Harcourt, 1975), 183–84.

Briefly, the "trick" consists of distinguishing two sorts of energy: the one primary (psychic or radial energy) escaping from entropy; the other secondary (physical or tangential energy) obedient to the laws of thermodynamics—the two energies not being directly transformable into each other but mutually interdependent on each other in function and evolution (the radial increasing with the arrangement of the tangential and the tangential only becoming arranged when activated by the radial).[42]

This spiritualization of matter is intended to lead to a new philosophy of life and even to a new cosmically based ethics. Panpsychism become a first philosophy on which an entire edifice can be built.

The idea, developed above, of a spiritualizing moleculization of matter, does more than throw light on the stuff of the universe, in its internal structure. The same shaft of light correspondingly brings out, in their main lines, a whole new philosophy of life, a whole new ethical system, and a whole new mysticism.[43]

The quotations given here show that Teilhard is firmly situated in the tradition of panpsychism. There are close links to Leibniz, Bergson, Russell, and in particular, Whitehead. Unlike Whitehead, however, he does not develop a systematic philosophical cosmology comparable to *Process and Reality*. His thoughts are often aphoristic and, more often than not, work with metaphors rather than with clearly defined terms. In addition, his philosophical thoughts are often embedded in theological speculation. However, if seen in the context of the classical and contemporary arguments for panpsychism presented earlier, it becomes clear that he is standing in this philosophical tradition. There can be no doubt that Teilhard de Chardin was one of the most influential representatives of panpsychism in the twentieth century.

---

[42] Teilhard de Chardin, *The Appearance of Man*, trans. J. M. Cohen (New York: Harper & Row, 1965), 265n1.

[43] Teilhard, *Activation of Energy*, 49.

Ontology of Becoming and Relative Monism

Addressing Aporias in Whitehead and Teilhard

Paolo Gamberini

Alfred North Whitehead and Pierre Teilhard de Chardin were two of the most influential thinkers of the twentieth century, and their ideas continue to shape contemporary philosophy and theology. Both were interested in reconciling the findings of modern science with traditional religious beliefs, and they both developed new understandings of the nature of God.

One of the most significant similarities between Whitehead and Teilhard is their understanding of God as both transcendent and immanent. Both thinkers have been seen as compatible with panentheism, where God is viewed as the soul or the spirit within which the universe is contained, continuously influencing and being influenced by it.

Whitehead's process theology aligns with this notion as he conceives of God as a "creative advance into novelty" that evolves alongside the universe, rather than as a static and unchanging entity.[1]

Pierre Teilhard de Chardin proposed that the universe is in a state of evolution toward a point of ultimate convergence, which he referred to as the Omega Point. At this Omega Point, all creation would unify in a higher spiritual state.

As contained "in God," the world not only derives its existence from God but also returns to God, while preserving the characteristics of

---

[1] Alfred North Whitehead, *Process and Reality: An Essay in Cosmology*, corrected edition, ed. David Ray Griffin and Donald Sherburne (New York: The Free Press, 1978), 28.

88 Ontology of Becoming and Relative Monism

being a creature. Accordingly, the relations between God and world are (in some sense) bilateral.[2]

But what does this "in some sense" mean for panentheists and how do Whitehead and Teilhard articulate the mutuality implied in the concept of God?

Whitehead and Teilhard: Between Panentheism and Monism

Whitehead and Teilhard avoid ascribing to God an external relationship to the world, and consequently, both reject Aquinas's classical theory of the *relatio non ex aequo* in dealing with God's relation to the world. Both Whitehead and Teilhard uphold a concept of God that is dipolar and grounded on the idea that the relationship between God and the world should be internal to God's being and at the same time mutual (*ex aequo*).

According to Whitehead, God is present within every moment of experience, actively influencing and guiding the ongoing processes of the universe. Whitehead affirms that God and world coexist and codetermine one another:

> The transcendence of God is not peculiar to him. Every actual entity, in virtue of its novelty transcended its universe, God included.[3]

Whitehead's process-relational panexperientialism, however, does not identify God with the universe. There is an aspect of God's nature that remains transcendent, thus providing the ultimate ground for its being. This fundamental force that underlies all of reality is "creativity." While being the ground of all beings, Whitehead avoids identifying "God" with "creativity." God is only the non-temporal instance of such force and God's actuality is significantly and continuously shaped and limited by what creatures decide to be.[4]

---

[2] Niels Henrik Gregersen, "Three Varieties of Panentheism," in *In Whom We Live and Move and Have Our Being: Panentheistic Reflections on God's Presence in a Scientific World*, ed. Philip Clayton and Arthur Peacocke (Cambridge: Eerdmans Publishing, 2004), 22.

[3] Whitehead, *Process and Reality*, 94.

[4] "[God] does not create the world, he saves it; or, more accurately, he is the poet of the world, with tender patience leading it by his vision of truth, beauty, and goodness." Ibid., 346.

Whitehead favors a view of God as a persuasive, relational force that invites and empowers creatures to participate in the ongoing processes of the universe. "In this sense, God is the great companion—the fellow-sufferer who understands."[5] Whitehead's theology favors a sort of monistic understanding of reality in which the ultimate reality, "creativity," is differentiated as God and the world.

Teilhard's panentheistic view of God shares with Whitehead the idea that God has two aspects: one is transcendent and self-subsisting (the trinitarian God), and the other is immanent.[6] Teilhard states that the Omega Point "must be independent of the collapse of the powers with which evolution is woven." God is not only *the term* of the series, but "is also outside the series."[7] "I see in the World a mysterious product of completion and fulfilment for the Absolute Being himself."[8] The Omega Point, the point of convergence of all that is, presupposes

> behind it, and deeper than it, a transcendent—a divine—nucleus. . . . [It is] necessarily an auto-center. . . . In virtue of this center of himself he subsists in himself, independently of time and space.[9]

Although God is self-sufficient, there is something in the world that *affects* God.[10] That means that God is in some sense changed by the world and the

---

[5] Ibid., 351. Whitehead clearly states: "It is as true to say that God is one and the World many, as that the World is one and God many. It is as true to say that, in comparison with the World, God is actual eminently, as that, in comparison with God, the World is actual eminently. It is as true to say that the World is immanent in God, as that God is immanent in the World. It is as true to say that God transcends the World, as that the World transcends God. It is as true to say that God creates the World, as that the World creates God." Ibid., 348.

[6] Teilhard's view of God is similar to the *Anima mundi*, the Soul of the World or the Spirit. See Ewert Cousins, "Teilhard and the Theology of the Spirit," *CrossCurrents* 19 (1969): 159–77. As a soul permeates the body, so is Christ permeating the world, although transcending the world, as the soul the body.

[7] Pierre Teilhard de Chardin, *The Human Phenomenon*, trans. Sarah Appleton-Weber (Portland, OR: Sussex Academic Press, 1999), 192–93.

[8] Pierre Teilhard de Chardin, *The Heart of Matter*, trans. René Hague (New York: Harcourt Brace Jovanovich, 1979), 54.

[9] Pierre Teilhard de Chardin, *Activation of Energy*, trans. René Hague (New York: Harcourt Brace Jovanovich, 1970), 145–46.

[10] "All around us, and within our own selves, God is in process of 'changing,' as a result of the coincidence of his magnetic power and our own Thought." Teilhard, *The Heart of Matter*, 53.

90   *Ontology of Becoming and Relative Monism*

universe adds something to God. "The universe contributes something that is vitally necessary to [God]."[11] The relationship between the transcendent and the immanent aspect of God is mutual.[12]

Although Teilhard de Chardin is not typically associated with monism, his understanding of God as having two aspects can be considered inclined toward monism. "An exact conjunction is produced between the old God of the Above and the God of the Ahead."[13] There is just "one process"—identified as God's evolution—in which the Omega Point is the unifying force that draws all created finite beings toward itself and bringing all the disparate elements of creation into "one" single, integrated whole. According to Rahner's expression, God is the Absolute future,[14] the God of Evolution.[15]

What distinguishes Teilhard's monism is the idea of *differentiation* in this creative unifying process. God pushes the Universe to differentiate and evolve with greater complexity so that finite beings find their fulfillment without being dissolved into a single, undifferentiated whole. The unifying process of interconnectedness integrates all aspects of creation into "one," without reality losing its multiplicity.

> The more together, they become the other, the more they become "themselves," in that mysterious Center of our centers I have just called "Omega."[16]

---

[11] Pierre Teilhard de Chardin, *Christianity and Evolution* (New York: Harcourt Brace Jovanovich, 1971), 177.

[12] "God acts in the present not by overwhelming and dissolving the world, but by 'going before' it as an endless source of opportunities for its becoming more." John Haught, *The Cosmic Vision of Teilhard de Chardin* (Maryknoll, NY: Orbis Books, 2021), 19–20. According to Haught, we need to distinguish a *metaphysics of the future*—as Teilhard represents—from a *metaphysics of the past* (envisioned by science) and a *metaphysics of the eternal present* (as classical metaphysics has proposed). The last two metaphysics consist in a "deterministic" worldview of reality. Science reduces everything to the atomistic components and classical metaphysics reduces everything to the omniscient and omnipotent God who controls everything and exercises divine power over creation. The beginning and the End are not identified in God as the Alpha and Omega. God is more Omega than Alpha. There is a disproportion between the two in favor of the Omega Point. Ibid., 39–44.

[13] Teilhard, *The Heart of Matter*, 99.

[14] Karl Rahner, "Marxist Utopia and the Christian Future of Man," in *Theological Investigations*, vol. 6, trans. Karl and Boniface Kruger (Baltimore: Helicon, 1969), 62–63.

[15] Teilhard, *Christianity and Evolution*, 239–40.

[16] Teilhard, *The Human Phenomenon*, 191.

The Divine Milieu enables creatures "*to be united* (that is to become the other) *while remaining oneself*."[17] God's evolution shuns both absorption and dispersion.[18]

The universe is not simply a collection of separate entities, but rather one single process of development and growth that is characterized by a constant increase in complexity and consciousness that finally converge and find unity in the pleroma. There is consummation in the Cosmic Christ but not dissolution in the Omega Point.[19]

> The substantial *one* and the created *many* fuse without confusion in a *whole* which, without adding anything essential to God, will nevertheless be a sort of triumph and generalization of being.[20]

What Teilhard states ("without adding anything essential to God") apparently contradicts what he often says regarding the *mutual dependence* and *completion* of God and the world.[21]

> [God] in some way "transforms himself" as he incorporates us. . . . God is in process of "changing," as a result of the coincidence of his magnetic power and our own Thought.[22]

God is "partially immersing himself in things, by making himself an 'element.'"[23] While being self-subsistent, God immerses Godself in creation, so that he may embody creation within Godself.[24] God and the world will be constituted into an organic complex pleroma, called a "pantheism of differentiation."[25]

As it was for Whitehead, creativity plays an essential role in Teilhard's evolutionary vision of reality. Creativity is the process by which the universe

---

[17] Pierre Teilhard de Chardin, *The Divine Milieu: An Essay on the Interior Life* (New York: Harper and Row, 1960), 116.

[18] The universe does not converge toward a great Whole "in which individuals were supposed to become lost like a drop of water, dissolved like a grain of salt, in the sea." Teilhard, *The Human Phenomenon*, 186. The more each being becomes itself and more distinct from the others, the closer it comes to them in Omega.

[19] Pierre Teilhard de Chardin, *Toward the Future*, trans. René Hague (New York: Harcourt Brace Jovanovich, 1973), 209–11.

[20] Teilhard, *The Divine Milieu*, 122.

[21] Teilhard *The Heart of Matter*, 54.

[22] Ibid., 53.

[23] Teilhard, *The Human Phenomenon*, 211.

[24] Teilhard, *Toward the Future*, 196.

[25] Ibid., 201.

constantly generates new forms of complexity and diversity, the driving force behind all of reality. For Teilhard, as it is for Whitehead, creativity is the substance in which the whole reality consists, and it is realized through the mutual relationship of God and the world, "so that [God] may be attained by us and himself attain us (that is to say, receiving from the World, in relation to us, a sort of *esse tangibile*)."[26]

Relative Monism

As I have previously highlighted, Whitehead and Teilhard distance themselves from the idea of the Unmoved Mover of classical theism. To accomplish that, Whitehead introduces the distinction between the *primordial* and the *consequent* natures of God, the immutable aspect of the essence of God, and its mutability. The same happens in Teilhard's distinction between God and the Omega Point. God is influenced by creatures. At the same time, Teilhard avoids both collapsing God's transcendence and ultimacy into the mutuality and reciprocity between God and the world. The Omega Point is the term of the series and at the same time it is also "outside" the series.[27]

How to reconcile these two aspects?[28] If *God becomes God* through the effects that the world has on Godself, how can it be still asserted that the action of creatures on God is made possible by God himself. Does God undergo a move from potentiality to actuality by relating the divine self to creatures? If these two aspects or modes of the Godhead, *being* and *immutability* (x) on one side, and *becoming* and *mutability* (y) on the other

---

[26] Teilhard, *The Heart of Matter*, 200–201.

[27] Teilhard, *The Human Phenomenon*, 193.

[28] As the process theologian Joseph Bracken says: "The becoming of God is understood as a continuous evolution of the three persons in knowledge and love, which means that each of them is in a condition of continual 'growth.'" Joseph A. Bracken, *Christianity and Process Thought: Spirituality for a Changing World* (New Brunswick: Templeton Press, 2006), 20. God is not yet God or *fully* God, and thus Exodus 3:14 is interpreted: *God is he who will be.* Such an understanding of God's being is usually balanced by another statement which affirms that God does not need his creatures to become himself, but calls them into existence freely, simply out of love. Interaction with creatures does not totally actualize God's being and act. God is not only the one who *will be* but also the one who *is* and who *was.* Bracken expresses these two opposite theses in this way: "God, to be clear, never began to exist at a certain point, like the present finite occasions. But God, too, exists only by virtue of creativity, just as God radically conditions the way creativity operates in the world." Joseph A. Bracken, *The Divine Matrix: Creativity as Link between East and West* (Eugene, OR: Wipf & Stock, 2006), 54–55.

side, refer to the same reality (Godself), how to avoid the emergence of a contradiction?

A possible way out is to posit immutability (x) and mutability (y) *not* "absolutely" but "relationally": x=x+y. As Karl Rahner formulates: "God can become something. He who is not subject to change in himself can himself be subject to change in something else."[29] "Although he is immutable in and of himself, he himself can become something in another."[30]

There are two ways in which "mutability" can be ascribed to God's immutability. First, by regaining the original meaning of Aristotle's *energeia*, which means "activity," we find no *static* understanding of being, but rather eternal movement: "*ousia* is nothing but *energeia*: the divine has activity as its essential nature, and therefore what it is—its essential being—is the very principle of being itself."[31] By saying that God's being is not static, we are not necessitated to introduce potentiality into God's being. *Dynamis* indicates a "capacity" and "power" and not a "potentiality" in God. This is what Nicholas of Cusa calls "possest," the actual existence of possibility, to be able to be itself.[32] *Dynamis* is not *kinesis*, "motion" or "change" (from one state to another). By defining God as *dynamis*, we simply ascribe to Godself an ongoing self-transcendence, an *ekstasis* of love, constantly communicating Godself to beings.

The second way in which "mutability" can be ascribed to God's immutability is by acknowledging that the "otherness" ascribed to creation has no standalone existence, and it is totally and radically identified with its *relatedness*-to-God. As Thomas Aquinas puts it: "Creation in the creature is only a certain relation to the Creator as to the principle of its being." Creation in its passive meaning does not belong to the category of "change" or "movement" but of "relation."[33] By saying that in God the relation to the creature is not a

---

[29] Karl Rahner, *Foundations of Christian Faith* (New York: Crossroad, 1987), 220.

[30] Ibid., 221.

[31] Aryeh Kosman, *The Activity of Being: An Essay on Aristotle's Ontology* (Cambridge, MA: Harvard University Press, 2013), 85.

[32] *Posse* means "potentiality" and *est* "actuality." By *possest* Nicholas of Cusa means realized "possibility" and "power" of being. Both "potentiality" and "power" are included in the notion of "possest." For an analysis of the notion of *posse* in Cusa's works, see Jasper Hopkins, "Cusanus und die sieben Paradoxa von posse," in *Nikolaus von Kues: De venatione sapientiae*, MFCG 32 (Treves: Paulinus, 2010), 67–82. Peter J. Casarella inquires in his study on the concept of *possest* Cusa's relation to Aristotelian and Thomistic notions of actuality and possibility. See Peter J. Casarella, "Nicholas of Cusa and the Power of the Possible," *American Catholic Philosophical Quarterly* 64 (1990): 7–34.

[33] Thomas Aquinas, *Summa theologiae*, I, q. 45, art. 2, *ad secundum*. "Creation signified actively means the divine action, which is God's essence, with a relation to the creature. In God relation to creatures is not a real relation, but of reason; whereas the relation of the creature to God is a real relation." Ibid., I, q. 45, art. 3, *ad primum*.

94   *Ontology of Becoming and Relative Monism*

real relation does not mean that God is not connected to the world.[34] God's relation to creatures can be "real" and "actual" as long as creation does not add anything to God's being.[35] If creation does not add anything to God, that means that God is not other than creation, as Nicholas of Cusa says: "As the Not-Other, God is one and not one with everything else."[36] That means the relationship between God and the world is asymmetrical.

Both Whitehead and Teilhard rightly saw that relation to "createdness" internally—and not simply externally *or* accidentally—qualifies God's being, but both lacked in articulating how God's and creatures' being *are* and at the same time *are not* identical at all. God's *infinite* being encompasses the *finite* being of createdness, but not vice versa. For this reason, from the standpoint of the finite (*sub specie creaturae*) God is "other" than creatures, but from the standpoint of the infinite (*sub specie dei*) God is "not-other" than creatures.[37]

I will refer to Bernard of Clairvaux, Nicholas of Cusa, and Rahner in order to articulate what in Whitehead and Teilhard still remains aporetic. In his *De consideratione libri quinque* Bernard of Clairvaux says that "God is the Being of Himself and of everything" (*Deus suum ipsius est et omnium esse*). "Suum" qualifies both the Being of God (*ipsius*) and of all (*omnium*).[38] Created being does not belong to itself (*ab alio*) as God's being does (*a se*).[39] Created being has no standalone existence, but the being attributed to God

---

[34] "The core criticism is that classical theism, in making God supernaturally immutably perfect and impassible, has made him static, inert and totally unrelated to the world and man." T. G. Weinandy, *Does God Change? The Word's Becoming in the Incarnation* (Still River, MA: St. Bede Publications, 1985), 128.

[35] Ibid, 95. "[While] God in his ontological nature cannot be 'really related' to the world because such a relation would affect his immutable nature, he can intentionally be actually and personally related through knowledge and love. Clarke, Hill, Wright, et al, maintain that one can in a true sense call this kind of relation 'real' since it is one that actually is part of reality. They also hold that God's personal knowledge and love of the world and man can in a sense change with the advance of history and man's personal response to him, but this change in no way affects his perfect ontological being in himself. While some modifications may be necessary, these articles have the merit of being scholarly attempts that elucidate God's personal relationship to man from within the classical Christian tradition." Ibid., 95n110.

[36] Clyde Lee Miller, "God as *li Non-Aliud*: Nicholas of Cusa's Unique Designation for God," *Journal of Medieval Religious Cultures* 41 (2015): 38.

[37] "And this divine infinity means that God is not other than creatures." Ibid.

[38] Bernard of Clairvaux, *De consideratione libri quinque ad Eugenium* III, liber V, caput 6, § 13, quoted by A Monk of the West, *Christianity and the Doctrine of Non-Dualism* (Hillsdale, NY: Sophia Perennis, 2004), 13.

[39] "Being properly pertains to God, *suum ipsius, et omium esse*: it does not belong to me to be who I am; he who I am is not I; I am not what I am." (A Monk of the West, *Christianity and the Doctrine of Non-Dualism*, 16).

and to creatures is the same and not other than God's being, although in two different modes: infinite and finite.[40] For this reason, Nicholas of Cusa speaks of createdness (finite) as a created god (*deus creatus*), a finite infinity. "For the Infinite Form is received only finitely, so that every created thing is, as it were, a finite infinity or a created god."[41]

We cannot "separate" the created being (y) from the Godhead. "Createdness" can be *indirectly* attributed to "uncreatedness," without merging God (x) and creation (y) as in pantheism (x=y) or uncritically assuming the *communicatio idiomatum* of traditional Christology.

We may refer here to what Rahner says about the core truth of the incarnation of the Logos:

> The God who is not subject to change in himself can change in something else, can become man. We may not regard this process by which one changes in something else as a contradiction to God's immutability, nor allow this changing in something else to be reduced to asserting a change of something else. Here ontology has to be adapted

---

[40] According to Nicholas of Cusa "The divine Not-Other is not other than that created thing, and in that sense God is 'the same' as it." Miller, "God as *li Non-Aliud*," 31. We may compare the relation between God and creatures to possible combinations of number 10, such as: 8+2; 15–5; 2x5; 10–2; 9+1; and so forth. If 8+2 is equal to 10, we do not say that only 8+2 is 10. If 10 were to see itself, by seeing itself it would see all the numbers and their possible combinations of 10. Number 10 is the complication of combinations, Nicholas of Cusa would say. As 10 is not something in "2x5" but everything (*totum*), so God is not "other" or "something" in *this* single creature but everything (*totum*), "not-other" than it. "If you consider [God] as He is in things, you consider things to be something in which He is. And in this regard, you err. . . . For it is not the case that the being of a thing is another thing, as a different thing is [another thing]; rather, its being is derivative being. If you consider a thing as it is in God, it is God and Oneness." Nicholas of Cusa, *On Learned Ignorance: A Translation and an Appraisal of De Docta Ignorantia* (Minneapolis: The Arthur J. Banning Press, 1981), 67. God is *totum* in every single creature (single operation), but it would be false to say that God is *totaliter* in *this* or *that* single creature, as if there were an *absolute* identity between God and creation. God encloses every single being and each being is permeated by God, but *this* or *that* being does not comprehend God's being. God transcends not only all *creaturely* distinctions (*this* or *that*) but also what makes the distinction between God and createdness. "God and the world are not two things to be added together. Neither are they two things that are 'really' one thing. . . . Nicholas of Cusa, whose characterization of God as *non aliud*—'not another thing'—in relation to the world expresses the heart of this point. . . . This *non aliud* principle, or what I have called—in what I know is a rather awkward phrase—'non-dual non-identity,' is at the heart of the relation between the infinite and the finite." Rowan Williams, *Christ the Heart of Creation* (London: Bloomsbury Continuum, 2018), XIV.

[41] Cusa, *On Learned Ignorance*, 64.

96 *Ontology of Becoming and Relative Monism*

to the message of faith and not be schoolmaster to this message. If the mystery of the Incarnation is transposed into the dimension of the finite alone, the mystery in the strictest sense would really be eliminated.[42]

In terms of Rahner's theology, we speak of formal causality between God and createdness. Since God is the absolute reality, God is not only *the giver* of being, according to the efficient causality, but *the gift* itself. In efficient causality the effect is always different from the cause; in formal causality the cause is an essential element of the effect.

God in his absolute being is related to the created existent in the mode of formal causality, that is, that he does not originally cause and produce something different from himself in the creature, but rather that he communicates his own divine reality and makes it a constitutive element in the fulfillment of the creature.[43]

Such fundamental element in createdness is nothing but God's being—as Bernard of Clairvaux and Nicholas of Cusa state—in finite form. Speaking of "the Divine in Evolution," Teilhard de Chardin refers to the "formal causality" in order to address the evolutive understanding of the relationship between creation *in progress* and the God (we may say "the Future") toward whom the cosmos is aiming.

God is not conceivable (either structurally or dynamically) except in so far as he coincides with (as a sort of "formal" cause), but without being lost in, the center of convergence of cosmogenesis.[44]

The "Noumenal" (*Divinitas*) and "Phenomenal" (*Deus*) Aspects of God

In the formulation of what I call relative monism, I recognize Whitehead's insight in distinguishing two aspects of God's nature: *primordial* and *consequent*. God's divinity (*divinitas*) is formally distinct from the other aspect of God, the *creator* (*deus*), which represents instead God as conditioned or influenced by the world. Whitehead identifies this aspect as the *consequent*

---

[42] Rahner, *Foundations of Christian Faith*, 221.

[43] Ibid.

[44] Teilhard, *Christianity and Evolution*, 239.

nature of God and Teilhard as the Omega Point (Christ), whereas divine creativity (*divinitas*) is the *un*conditional and *un*caused aspect of Godself, or what Nicholas of Cusa identifies with God's "non-otherness" and Tillich with "*the* unconditional," to be distinguished from God (*deus*).[45] "The *creator* God" (*deus*) and the world (*creatio*) *de*fine and determine each other "within" the immanent and mutual relativity (MR), but this MR is made possible by the absolute relativity (AR) of the unconditional divinity. Divine creativity is the nature of absolute relativity, out of which emerge both *the* God who creates the world (AR —> MR) and the world that is created. "The" God *creator* (*deus*) represents that aspect of God which Whitehead identifies as the *consequent* nature of God and Teilhard as the Omega point. God and Omega Point are in mutual relationship with the world, and both are *affected* and *increased* by the contribution and interplay with creation. Creatures do add something to God (Whitehead) and to Omega Point (Teilhard). As between the whole and its parts there is a biunivocal relationship and dependence from each other, so there is the same mutual relationship between God and the world.

> The model of relational holism based on implicate order and divine entanglement means that God affects the world and world affects God. God can change and grow. . . . God and world are a complementary pair and, together, they form a unified whole.[46]

But *the* God (*deus*) or Omega Point that can be said to be entangled and "not-yet" fulfilled is *not* the divine creativity (*divinitas*), out of which both God *the* creator and *world* emerge. The *determinate* and *concrete* totality in which God and creation are *mutually* related is *not* to be identified with the *in*determinate, *absolute*, *un*related relatedness of the Godhead (*divinitas*). These two aspects, (x) and (x+y), are *formally* distinct, but *are* (=) the same reality (x=x+y).[47]

---

[45] "Where is the unconditional to be found? Tillich's answer is that *God* is unconditional, which is how God is God, but the unconditional itself cannot be identified with or restricted to God. Why not? Because the unconditional is always and everywhere and cannot be shut up inside a word or a being, not even a Supreme one." John D. Caputo, *What to Believe? Twelve Brief Lessons in Radical Theology* (New York: Columbia University Press, 2023), 19.

[46] Ilia Delio, *The Not-Yet God: Carl Jung, Teilhard de Chardin, and the Relational Whole* (Maryknoll, NY: Orbis Books, 2023), 83.

[47] "'Creativity' simply designates the activity of creating, or the power to create—to bring something new into being. It does this, moreover—and this is a very important point—without in any way implying that creating requires or presupposes a creator, a

98   *Ontology of Becoming and Relative Monism*

The ultimate and "noumenal" substance of reality is *infinite relativity*, whose "nature" (*divinitas*) is *creativity*, whereas God—the *creator*—represents the totality of reality as "phenomenal" and "determinate."[48] "Creativity" represents the "*in*determinate" aspect of God's nature, its "*un*relatedness" or "asymmetry." This transcendental aspect is the ineffable or "noumenal" side of God. As the two sides of the moon—visible and invisible—are not separated but are the *same* moon, so these two aspects—noumenal and phenomenal, transcendent and immanent—are the same Godhead.[49]

Nicholas's insight into the Mystery of God as "not-other"[50] may guide us also in discerning what Teilhard grasps of God's Oneness. According to Teilhard, God is like a brazier of fire, but such fire does not destroy the

---

being who does the creating: creativity, the bringing into being of something novel, may be going on in this or that situation or context; whether there is some specifiable cause of this or not is a separate question." Gordon D. Kaufman, "Confucian and Christian Conceptions of Creativity: A Christian View of Creativity: Creativity as God," *Dao* 6 (2007): 106.

[48] The totality of determinate beings has two aspects. The first aspect (*phenomenal*) is to be identified with the totality in mutual relationship with its determinations, and therefore is itself determinate. This *phenomenal* dimension of totality is traditionally called *summum ens*, the ground of all beings, the creator God (*deus*). The *noumenal* aspect of the totality is what defines the determinates without by these being defined, the *back*ground or the depth of all beings, the infinite, the *divinitas*. The finite does not "add" something to the infinite, being the infinite "*in*determinate," although the infinite is not "other" or "separated" from the totality of determinations. If this were the case, the infinite would be something "other" than the finite, therefore an "other" (Being) not among but beyond (*supra*) the *other* finite beings. The indeterminate aspect of totality, instead, is not "other" than the finite beings. The infinite cannot be identified with and by any of its determinations. Between the indeterminate aspect of the totality (Godhead) and its determinate aspect (God *and* the world) there is a *relative* identity (x=x+y).

[49] The distinction between "indeterminate" and "determinate" totality is analogous to the distinction between "creativity" and "creator," "Godhead" (*divinitas*) and "God" (*deus*). In Sermon 56 (*Nolite timere eos qui corpus occidunt*), Meister Eckhart thus describes this distinction between *Godhead* and *God*. "God and Godhead are as different as heaven and earth. I say further: the inner and the outer man are as different as heaven and earth. But God is loftier by many thousands of miles. God becomes and unbecomes. . . . God becomes when all creatures say 'God'—then God comes to be." Bernard McGinn, *The Complete Mystical Works of Meister Eckhart* (New York: Crossroad, 2007), 293–94. In Sermon 60, the trinitarian distinctions in God are derived from such simple ground, the silent desert of the Godhead in which there is no distinction of Father, Son, or Holy Spirit. Ibid., 311.

[50] "The place wherein Thou art found unveiled is girt round with the coincidence of contradictories, and this is the wall of Paradise wherein Thou dost abide. The door whereof is guarded by the most proud spirit of Reason, and, unless he be vanquished, the way in will not lie open. Thus 'tis beyond the coincidence of contradictories that Thou mayest be seen, and nowhere this side thereof." Nicholas of Cusa, *The Vision of God* (New York: Frederick Ungar, 1978), 44.

many in an amalgam, thus making them an indistinct "One."[51] Instead of merging beings in an undifferentiated whole, the movement towards personification and unification—as Teilhard says—grows in no competitive way with the differentiations of the many.[52] By such noncompetitive understanding of the relationship between the one and the many, God and the world, *created* being does not compete with *God's* being, since creation is nothing but God's being. Nothing exists "outside" God's creative essence. Created beings subsist in God's being and "all that exists in God, is God" (*quidquid est in Deo Deus est*).[53]

Alfred North Whitehead and Pierre Teilhard de Chardin developed a new understanding of the nature of God in relation to the world. Whitehead's "process/dipolar" and Teilhard's "evolutionary" concept of God envision God in a mutual relationship with the world. Their mutual understanding of the panentheistic relationship between God and the world generates aporias about the nature of God that can be overcome by critically retrieving the classical understanding of the *creatio ex nihilo*. The panentheistic model

---

[51] "When we try to understand and express in physical terms the way in which the mystical body (the pleroma) is held together, there is, of course, one extreme we must avoid if we are not to 'founder in our faith.' We should not do what could be read into the language censured in some mystics (Eckhart, for example) and try to make of the consummated Christ a being so unique that his subsistence, his person, his 'I', takes the place of the subsistence, the personality, of all the elements incorporated in his mystical body. This concept of a hypostatic union extended to the whole universe (which, incidentally, is simply Spinoza's pantheism) is not in itself either contradictory or absurd; but it conflicts with the whole Christian view of individual freedom and personal salvation." Teilhard, *Christianity and Evolution*, 69.

[52] "It is therefore an error to look for the prolongation of our being and of the noosphere in the direction of the impersonal. The future of the universe can only be hyperpersonal—in the Omega Point." Teilhard, *The Human Phenomenon*, 184–85.

[53] Aquinas, *Summa theologiae*, I, q. 27, art. 3, *ad secundum*. Thomas Aquinas argues that we may approach the understanding of createdness *in* God's essence from two different perspectives (*Quaestiones disputatae "De Potentia,"* q. 13, art. 16, arg. 24, English translation by Richard J. Regan): "We should say that one says in two ways that a creature is in God. One says it in one way as in the cause governing and preserving the existing of a creature to say that the creature is from God. For we understand that a creature is preserved in existing only insofar as it already has existence in its own nature, as the existing of a creature is distinguished from God. And so a creature being in God in this way is not the creative essence. One says in a second way that a creature is in God as in the power of its active cause or in the one who knows it, and so the creature in God is the very divine essence, as Jn 1:13 says: 'What was made was life in him.' And although a creature being in God in this way is the divine essence, there are many creatures, not only one, in the essence in this way since God's essence is the sufficient means to know different creatures and sufficient power to produce them." Thomas Aquinas, *The Power of God* (Oxford: Oxford University Press, 2012), 88–89.

of relative monism, while recognizing the *unconditional* relativity (*relatio*) of creativity, does not ascribe to God a consequent nature or conceive God as the byproduct of evolution, but suggests that the Godhead is essentially creative and, therefore, related to the world.

Our Deepest Me

God–World Relations in Whitehead, Teilhard, and Jung

SHERI D. KLING

It is said that St. Catherine of Genoa ran through the streets shouting the Italian equivalent of "My deepest me is God!" In Ursula King's book of selected writings of Pierre Teilhard de Chardin, she shares a very similar statement from his work *Writings in Time of War*: "The deeper I descend into myself, the more I find God at the heart of my being; the more I multiply the links that attach me to things, the more closely does he hold me." Teilhard then connects this interior presence to the second person of the Trinity as a God who "pursues" through humanity an incarnational "task."[1]

What would it mean if we were really to believe that we could encounter God in the very depths of our being? How would that change the way we live, and the way we look at every other thing and being in our world? In this chapter I draw from Teilhard, Alfred North Whitehead, and Carl Jung to show that not only is our "deepest me" God, but that divine Seed is the living Source that fuels the task of our own creative transformation and through us the transformation of God.

Mystics, Matter, and Monopolarity

King describes Teilhard as "a great contemporary Christian mystic in the best tradition of Christian mysticism, but also a mystic in search of a new

---

[1] Ursula King, comp. and intro., *Pierre Teilhard de Chardin: Writings*, Modern Spiritual Masters Series (Maryknoll, NY: Orbis Books, 1999), 50–51.

mystical way, a new spirituality open to the rhythm of the contemporary world and its ongoing development."[2] Like many medieval women mystics and Persian poets, Teilhard writes in passionate and ecstatic tones to describe God, often using metaphors of fire or blazing light to express what he intuited and experienced.

He describes his spiritual awakening as a process through which "the world gradually caught fire for me, burst into flames . . . until it formed a great luminous mass, lit from within. . . . I began to feel myself drawn by matter—or, more correctly, by something which 'shone' at the heart of matter."[3] While much of the Christian mystical tradition has denigrated the body (along with women and matter in general) and sought instead the transcendence of earthly embodied life to the life of the spirit, Teilhard saw the holiness at the heart of every thing. He wrote that "underneath matter's veil of restless movement and multiplicity" was revealed a "glorious unity."[4]

In his book *Process Mysticism* philosopher Daniel A. Dombrowski seeks to rescue mysticism from the "dangerous world-denying tendency that is fueled by both ascetical and apophatic negativities"[5] and argues that classical theism is inadequate to the reality of religious experience. In his critique of classical theism's concept of God, Dombrowski draws attention to *monopolarity* as particularly problematic. If God monopolizes only one side of any dipolarity where the other is deemed to be inferior, then a "perfect" God who does not change or passively receive cannot be in real relationship with the world and its creatures. Such monopolarity denies God the "excellences" of the opposite pole that are not accepted as divine within classical theism.[6]

My purpose in this chapter is not to expand upon Dombrowski's critique of classical theism regarding mystical experience. Instead, I want to send tap roots into the aquifers of philosophy, theology, and psychology to access living water from such thinkers as Whitehead, Teilhard, and Jung, who do provide us adequate frameworks for understanding how we might encounter God at our depths. With them, we might quench our thirst with truths like that of Teilhard, who says that "purity does not lie in separation from, but in a deeper penetration into the universe."[7]

---

[2] Ibid., 20.

[3] Ibid., 30–33.

[4] Ibid., 43.

[5] Daniel A. Dombrowski, *Process Mysticism* (Albany: State University of New York Press, 2023), 7.

[6] Ibid., 12–13.

[7] King, *Teilhard*, 42.

God within Every Thing

When we look deeply into the cosmos through Whiteheadian eyes, we find that God can be found at the initiation of every new moment of experience. In a world where new subjectivities arise from the objective past, it is God's initial aim at satisfaction that kick starts every event into existence. As Bernard Lee writes, "He adds Himself to the actual ground from which every creative act takes its rise. The world lives by the incarnation of God in itself."[8] The immanent subjective aliveness of divinity is the necessary active presence of God's vision for the becoming of each moment. Once that moment actualizes its own subjective aim, it perishes and becomes the objective past from which the next moment arises. But it also is taken up and everlastingly held in God's tender embrace and memory. Nothing we do is ever lost. Whitehead's dipolar God relationally presences God's self as conceptual vision and subjectivity on a moment-to-moment basis, and then receives the world's "fullness of physical feeling" through its objectification within God.[9] This is the world's offering of enjoyment to God's divine life. For Whitehead, God and the world are mutually immanent.[10]

In process theology, experience begins at the intersection of the future of God and the past of the world. In Jung's psychology, the human psyche is formed through the meeting of the subjective self and the objective psyche. In both, the individual confronts and is changed by a larger, transpersonal, and objective Reality. The ego—or the conscious aspect of the psyche—is the seat of the *subjective* self, but it is the archetypal Self or the God-image within that which is the "seat of *objective* identity" and the "inner empirical deity."[11] Not substantial, the Self is dynamic, processive, and lures the individual toward wholeness through the integration of shadow material and the union of opposites.

Edward Edinger describes this Self as the "central generative point" where "transpersonal energies flow into personal life."[12] Also rejecting monopolarity, Jung suggests we can "imagine him as an eternally flowing

---

[8] Bernard J. Lee, *The Becoming of the Church: A Process Theology of the Structures of Christian Experience* (New York: Paulist Press, 1974), 96.

[9] Alfred North Whitehead, *Process and Reality: An Essay in Cosmology*, corrected edition, ed. David Ray Griffin and Donald Sherburne (New York: The Free Press, 1979), 345.

[10] Ibid., 348.

[11] Edward F. Edinger, *Ego and Archetype: Individuation and the Religious Function of the Psyche* (Boston: Shambhala, 1992), 3.

[12] Ibid., 4.

104   Our Deepest Me

current of vital energy that endlessly changes shape just as easily as we can imagine him as an eternally unmoved, unchangeable essence."[13] While each moment meets God at the beginnings of its experience, we might say that the human psyche meets God at the depths of experience. Because such encounters do not come from a source that is "intrusive" or "foreign to life," writes John P. Dourley, both Jung and Paul Tillich saw such religious experience as healing rather than as splitting.[14]

Teilhard saw God as "the most intimate presence" incarnated within a world that is illuminated by the "great fire of the spirit"; in this world, all things carry "the rudiments of immanence, a spark of the spirit."[15] God is found in our innermost depths for Teilhard *because* Christ assumed real flesh. Therefore, matter has a *"cosmic role as the basis, lower in order but primordial and essential, of union."*[16] He writes:

> God reveals himself everywhere, beneath our groping efforts, as a *universal milieu*, only because he is the ultimate point upon which all realities converge. . . . It follows that all created things, every one of them, cannot be looked at, in their nature and actions, without the same reality being found in their innermost being—like sunlight in the fragments of a broken mirror—one beneath its multiplicity, unattainable beneath its proximity, and spiritual beneath its materiality.[17]

None of these thinkers were dualists. They did not denigrate or isolate the body; rather, they saw it as intimately interconnected with the entire world. For Whitehead, "our bodies lie in the field of nature."[18] In *Adventures of Ideas*, he writes:

> We cannot determine with what molecules the brain begins and the rest of the body ends. Further, we cannot tell with what molecules the body ends and the external world begins. The truth is that the brain

---

[13] C. G. Jung, *Psychology and Religion: West and East*, trans. R.F.C. Hull, corrected, vol. 11, *The Collected Works of C. G. Jung*, Bollingen Series (New York: Pantheon Books, 1963), 361.

[14] John P. Dourley, *The Psyche As Sacrament: A Comparative Study of C. G. Jung and Paul Tillich* (Toronto: Inner City Books, 1981), 9.

[15] King, *Teilhard*, 23, 31, 57.

[16] Ibid., 52.

[17] Ibid., 72.

[18] Alfred North Whitehead, *Modes of Thought* (New York: The Free Press, 1968), 114.

is continuous with the body, and the body is continuous with the rest of the natural world.[19]

Jung says something very similar in his autobiography, *Memories, Dreams, Reflections*:

> At times I feel as if I am spread out over the landscape and inside things, and am myself living in every tree, in the splashing of the waves, in the clouds and the animals that come and go, in the procession of the seasons. There is nothing . . . with which I am not linked.[20]

For Jung, the body is inherently interwoven with a psyche that is made of "living processes"; the individual human psyche is a series of images held together by the cohesive force of the ego.[21] At the same time, it is the archetype of the Self—the God-image within—that serves as the unifying point for body, soul, mind, and spirit, forming an "integrated whole."[22] Therefore, when we plunge into our depths, we are diving down deep into our bodies, and even into the world itself.

In a very resonant way Teilhard writes: "My own body is not these cells or those cells that *belong exclusively* to me: it is *what*, in these cells *and* in the rest of the world, feels my influence and reacts against me. *My* matter is not a *part* of the universe that I possess *totalier*, it is the *totality* of the Universe possessed by me *partialiter*."[23] In fact, it is through this Universe, through nature, that Teilhard believed he was "immersed in God,"[24] and diving into nature was taking a "baptismal plunge."[25]

Early on, Teilhard fell in love with both God and matter. He saw God as a "presence" that was not "abstract" but that was, he recounts, a "deep-running, ontological, total current which embraced the whole universe in

---

[19] Alfred North Whitehead, *Adventures of Ideas* (New York: The Free Press, 1933), 225.

[20] C. G. Jung, *Memories, Dreams, Reflections*, trans. Clara Winston and Richard Winston (New York: Pantheon Books, 1963), 225.

[21] Jung, *Psychology and Religion*, 11:8:323.

[22] Robin Robertson, *Jungian Archetypes: Jung, Gödel, and the History of Archetypes*, rev. ed. (New York: iUniverse, 2009), 209.

[23] Pierre Teilhard de Chardin, *Science and Christ* (New York: Harper & Row, 1965), quoted in John B. Cobb, Jr., and David Ray Griffin, *Process Theology* (Louisville, KY: Westminster John Knox Press, 1976), 115.

[24] King, *Teilhard*, 49.

[25] Ibid., 157.

106   *Our Deepest Me*

which I moved."[26] God takes shape within things,[27] and is "in union with matter."[28] According to King, Teilhard saw spirit and matter not as two different things, but as "two states or two aspects of one and the same cosmic stuff."[29] Yet he stressed "the primacy of spirit, or, which comes to the same thing, the primacy of the future."[30]

Logos, Self, and Christification

Whitehead, Teilhard, and Jung are all considered developmental thinkers, and teleology plays a key role in their writings. While Whitehead's future is open, with only *possibilities* for each moment envisioned by God, Teilhard describes an ultimate Omega Point where evolution is headed. In this purposive movement toward the future, what role for humanity is enabled—and *ennobled*—by the God within our very depths? To answer this question, I lead us from Logos, to Christ, to Self, and finally to the Christification of humanity and the transformation of God.

Earlier, I described God's presence within each moment of experience as the initial aim. This aim comes from what Whitehead describes as the Primordial Nature of God, and John Cobb and David Ray Griffin link the Primordial Nature to the Logos.[31] They also argue that "the *incarnate* Logos is Christ. In this broadest sense, Christ is present in all things." Though the presence of Christ is less apparent in inanimate objects that merely repeat their pasts, "Christ is present to a greater or lesser extent as the creature decides for or against the Logos."[32] According to Lewis Ford, if we believe in classical theism's omnipotent God, we might ask why God chose Israel or why Jesus; yet, a process explanation might suggest that God calls every person, but we each can choose how to respond and to what degree. Our own positive response to God's initial aim "enables God to intensify that call and to develop it further. . . . In Jesus' life we see fulfilled God's aim as reaching beyond his own life into the lives of all of us."[33]

---

[26] Ibid., 39.

[27] Ibid., 44.

[28] Ibid., 61.

[29] Ibid., 40.

[30] Ibid., 41.

[31] Cobb and Griffin, *Process Theology*, 98.

[32] Ibid., 98–99.

[33] Lewis S. Ford, "The Power of God and the Christ," in *Religious Experience and Process Theology*, ed. Bernard Cargas and Harry J. Lee (New York: Paulist Press, 1976), 85–86.

According to King, Teilhard was inspired by Bergson's *Creative Evolution* to see the universe as an "immense stream of evolutionary creation where every reality is animated by a 'christic element.'"[34] While Cobb and Griffin link Christ to the initial aim as the creative love of God,[35] Teilhard similarly paints his "universal Christ" as "the organic, dynamic, deeply personal and fiery center of love in the universe, the point of convergence for all things and people."[36] His Christ-Omega is a "furnace of fire, energy, life, and light" that is also present within all being, gives all being its ontological value, and is the center of all physical and spiritual growth.[37] For Teilhard, this pervading presence is the "incarnate Word" or Logos.[38] Jesus was born from the physical world of matter because the Christ or Logos had *already incarnated* within creation from the very beginning. Teilhard writes:

> The first act of the incarnation, the first appearance of the cross, is marked by the plunging of the divine unity into the ultimate depths of the multiple. Nothing can enter into the universe that does not emerge from it. Nothing can be absorbed into things except through the road of matter. . . . The redeemer could penetrate the stuff of the cosmos, could pour himself into the life-blood of the universe, only by first dissolving himself in matter, later to be reborn from it.[39]

This active presence of the Christ within all matter initiates, like the yeast within the loaf, each thing's physical and spiritual maturation, a process that Teilhard terms "Christification." Christification is "a fire with the power to penetrate all things—and which was now gradually spreading unchecked."[40]

There are hints of Christification within Jungian thought. According to Morton Kelsey, Jung believed that the purposive development seen in human life "is likely to be close to the inner meaning of the universe."[41] Mirroring Teilhard, analyst June Singer describes the persuasive energy of individuation as feeling "as if one were being drawn toward a center

---

[34] King, *Teilhard*, 14.

[35] Cobb and Griffin, *Process Theology*, 100.

[36] King, *Teilhard*, 83.

[37] Ibid., 83–89.

[38] Ibid., 96.

[39] Ibid., 98.

[40] Ibid., 102.

[41] Morton T. Kelsey, *Encounter with God: A Theology of Christian Experience* (New York: Paulist Press, 1988), 106.

of great luminosity . . . a source of light and energy that has no limits."[42]
This center, for Jung, is the archetypal Self, the "visible form" or image that
symbolizes—and *participates in*—that which is "ineffable" and ultimately
inaccessible to consciousness.[43] I have suggested elsewhere that the archetypal Self may be the historic route of our initial aims.[44] Jung understood the
Self to be a "psychological God-image," and although he did not typically
speak of a God beyond the psyche, he felt strongly that there must be an
"original behind our images" of God.[45] When we look at the Christ-event
psychologically, Christ "represents a totality . . . which corresponds to the
total personality that transcends consciousness."[46] This *imago* in the human
psyche is linked to the historical Christ because Jung believed he *exemplified* the archetypal Self.[47]

In a 1957 letter to Rev. David Cox, Jung explains why this archetypal totality is linked to Jesus. "If this collective archetype had not been associated
with Jesus he would have remained a nameless Zaddick [Jewish spiritual
leader]. . . . It is not the Jewish rabbi and reformer Jesus, but the archetypal
Christ who touches upon the archetype of the Redeemer in everyone and
carries conviction."[48] But Jung purposefully uses the term *Self*; he writes:
"Because I am talking to Hindus as well as Christians, and I do not want
to divide but to unite. . . . There is no reason whatsoever why you should
or should not call the beyond-Self Christ or Buddha or Perusha or Tao or
Khidir or Tifereth. All these terms are recognizable formulations of what
I call the 'Self.'"[49]

Jung describes the psyche as compensatory, where the collective unconscious presents the conscious ego with symbolic material mediated by the
archetypal Self. This Self draws each of us toward wholeness through the
compassionate integration of our naturally opposing energies of conscious
and unconscious elements. When brought to consciousness, this material
can then be integrated into the personality, thereby developing a whole and

---

[42] June K. Singer, *Boundaries of the Soul: The Practice of Jung's Psychology*, rev. ed. (New York: Anchor Books, 1994), 209–10.

[43] Jung, *Psychology and Religion*, 11:360.

[44] Sheri D. Kling, *A Process Spirituality: Christian and Transreligious Resources for Transformation* (Lanham, MD: Lexington Books, 2020), 191–203.

[45] Jung, *Psychology and Religion*, 11:360.

[46] C. G. Jung, *Aion: Researches into the Phenomenology of the Self*, vol. 9, pt. 2, *The Collected Works of C. G. Jung*, Bollingen Series (New York: Pantheon Books, 1959), 37.

[47] Ibid.

[48] Jerry R. Wright, "Dreams and the Archetypal Christ," Natural Spirituality Regional Gathering, Toccoa, Georgia, February 12, 2011.

[49] Ibid.

Sheri D. Kling   109

unique individual that is capable of real relationship. Cobb and Griffin seem to point to something similar when they describe "creative transformation" as a movement toward "original styles of life and social organizations" and connect that to the "peculiarly effective presence of Christ."[50]

In an essay entitled "Jung and Christology," G. Clarke Chapman connects Jung's thinking to Joachim of Flora, who saw the cosmos progressing from the ages of the Father and Son to an age of the Spirit with an anticipated heaven on earth. This kind of cosmic trinitarianism "charts the process of human maturation—for both the individual psyche and for the race as a whole."[51] For Jung, Christ plays a pivotal role in the evolution of the collective unconscious by throwing us into a "new phase." Echoing Teilhard, Jung believed that Christ's incarnation was an ongoing process that required "continuation and completion" *through* humanity. As Chapman indicates:

> [Jung] saw God's sonship not as immutable, but eschatological—a continuing process of actualization. . . . [Jesus] would stand forth as the fully Human One, suffering and mortal, but proleptically the human self embodied, who called forth a completed selfhood in the rest of us. His divine/human oneness is a mystery already given, yet it also awaits completion through the Christification of the whole human family.[52]

When we are willing to withdraw our projections from the external figure of Jesus and internalize what the Christ means within each of us—echoing the process idea of creative transformation—then, writes Chapman, we mark "the transformation of God as well as humanity."[53] This idea of divine transformation is strongly present in process thought. Cobb and Griffin describe Christ as creative transformation and the initiator of novelty, with novelty playing a key role in the enjoyment of God. Ford describes a God that welcomes surprises, because "then there is a challenge, something to which he can respond, something he can interact with." It is this sense of adventure that brings with it an element of novelty, and this, then, becomes an offering that the world can provide to God. "Whitehead's argument,"

---

[50] Cobb and Griffin, *Process Theology*, 101.

[51] G. Clarke Chapman, "Jung and Christology," *Journal of Psychology and Theology* 25, no. 4 (December 1, 1997): 419.

[52] Ibid., 422, 425.

[53] Ibid., 421–22.

110   Our Deepest Me

writes Ford, "is that the world and God are each the instruments of novelty for the other."[54]

Ford describes this cooperative and mutually transformative relationship as a "fellowship with God and Christ" that we are invited to enter in order to "heal our brokenness and isolation." Furthermore, it is "fulfilled in the emergence of the body of Christ," which Ford understands as "a new product in the evolutionary development of the world which is also God's creative advance."[55] Chapman, too, recognizes a resonance between the telos for humanity described in Jungian psychology, Teilhardian theology, and process thought: "Like Teilhard de Chardin and process theology, [Jung] envisioned a cosmic evolutionary momentum, a panentheism that invites our cooperation with the divine. With the survival of the planet hanging in the balance, readers are exhorted to join the grand Christification of humanity."[56]

Again, we need not understand this as Christian exclusivism. If this presence of God as initial aim, Logos, or Christ within our "deepest me" is a universal *image Dei*, and if that image is the immanent and transcendent Self that mediates our creative transformation through individuation and the actualization of novelty, and if that novelty transforms both the world and God, then this is a universal and transreligious phenomenon. It is, as Norman Pittenger writes, what "God is always and everywhere up to, what God is always and everywhere doing, and what God is always and everywhere seeking to achieve in the world—with which God is unfailingly related and with which God is in a relationship of mutual influence."[57] This is both life-giving and ennobling news for humanity. It means that not only is our "deepest me" God, drawn through luminous love toward an even greater union with God, but also that the value we actualize in this world is of supreme importance to God and actually intensifies God's experience and enjoyment as well as our own. This is the incarnational task for which we have been born.

---

[54] Ford, "The Power of God and the Christ," 81.

[55] Ibid., 91.

[56] Chapman, "Jung and Christology," 421–22.

[57] W. Norman Pittenger, *The Lure of Divine Love: Human Experience and Christian Faith in a Process Perspective* (New York: Pilgrim Press, 1979), 65.

Part II

Scientific and Religious Transition

Process Theology and the Modern World

Science, Religion, and Christology after Whitehead and Teilhard

Matthew David Segall

After almost two centuries of passionate struggle, neither science nor faith has managed to diminish the other; quite the contrary, it becomes clear that they cannot develop normally without each other, for the simple reason that they are both animated by the same life.
—Pierre Teilhard de Chardin, *The Human Phenomenon*

Philosophy frees itself from the taint of ineffectiveness by its close relations with religion and with science, natural and sociological. It attains its chief importance by fusing the two, namely, religion and science, into one rational scheme of thought.
—Alfred North Whitehead, *Process and Reality*

Pierre Teilhard de Chardin and Alfred North Whitehead are perhaps the two foremost twentieth-century contributors to evolutionary cosmology and process theology. Whitehead's theological ideas developed as a consequence of his work in mathematical logic, physics, philosophy of science, and cosmology, without concern for the offense they might cause to any religious orthodoxies. Still, his creative conception of the God-World relation has been heartily taken up and developed by many American Protestant theologians, and increasingly by thinkers inspired by other faiths. Teilhard, on the other hand, was a paleontologist and Jesuit priest whose evolutionary

113

114   *Process Theology and the Modern World*

revision of the dogma of original sin brought him censure from the Catholic Church. Not unlike the Sun-centric Giordano Bruno had enjoined Catholic Scholastics to look again at the motions of the heavens, the Omega-centric Teilhard called his fellow priests to turn their Christology away from a truncated vision of the past toward an evolutionary convergence in the future. Lucky for Teilhard, the Inquisition had by then retired its tradition of burning heretics at the stake. Regardless, his heart was already engulfed in the inferno of evolution.

Teilhard composed his masterwork, *The Human Phenomenon*, while in China between 1938 and 1940, just as the Second World War was beginning to rage in Europe. He was no stranger to the horrors of war, having served as a stretcher-bearer in the French army during the Great War. His experience fighting for survival and tending to wounded comrades on the front lines of over eighty battles did not deflate but buoyed his faith in the future. In July 1918, he prayed:

> Was there ever, my God, a humanity more like, in the shedding of its blood, to a sacrificed victim—more ready, in its ferment, to receive creative transformation—more rich, in what it unleashes, in energy that can be sanctified—more close, in its agony, to the supreme communion?[1]

Earlier in the war he had had a mystical encounter with a painted face of Christ whose outlines dissolved to encompass the whole world. Teilhard could not say whether the divine face expressed "indescribable agony or a superabundance of triumphant joy," but he reports seeing the expression once more "in the glance of a dying soldier."[2]

Two decades later, as younger men again slaughtered one another on the battlefield, Teilhard was engaged in an inner battle of the spirit to share his vision of evolution and what it portends for humanity. Just as Germany was invading France in 1939, Teilhard wrote to friends of his efforts "as his part in the combat—war being sublimated into a work to form new eyes, to enable the world to see and to become more."[3] He insists in an author's

---

[1] Pierre Teilhard de Chardin, *Writings in Time of War* (New York: Harper and Row, 1968), 223.

[2] Pierre Teilhard de Chardin, *Hymn of the Universe* (New York: Harper and Row, 1969), 41.

[3] Pierre Teilhard de Chardin, *The Human Phenomenon* (Portland, OR: Sussex Academic Press, 2003), xxiv.

note added in 1947 and in his prologue to *The Human Phenomenon* that the book is not an attempt to do metaphysics or theology but phenomenological science. He attempts to offer an account of the past, not in itself, but as it appears to a contemporary human observer, "so that the world may be true for us at this moment."[4] Like Whitehead—who sought "evidence for that conception of the universe which is the justification for the ideals characterizing the civilized phases of human society"[5]—Teilhard was in search of the cosmological conditions of human self-consciousness, a new sort of study he christened "hyperphysics."[6] It may be that part of Teilhard's insistence that his treatise be interpreted strictly as a work of natural science was a plea to his Jesuit censors. He is careful to note on page one that "beyond this first scientific reflection, essential and ample room remains for the more advanced reflection of the philosopher and the theologian."[7] Regardless, the Society of Jesus ultimately refused to allow him to publish the book because of its unmistakable theological content.[8]

This chapter offers a Whiteheadian philosophical reflection on Teilhard's attempt at a hyperphysics of the human. While I find aspects of Teilhard's phenomenological vision of the past and mystical vision of the future deeply compelling, I argue that some aspects of his poetic synthesis of evolutionary biology and Christianity require metaphysical supplementation in light of Whitehead's cosmological scheme. But properly adjusted and mutually accommodated, I believe a Whitehead and Teilhard inspired synthesis of science and religion has much to offer anyone seeking a relevant and effective Christology for our perilous times.

Convergence

Anyone whose faith is wed to dogmatic tradition will inevitably resist novelties in speculative theology. A recent critic of Teilhard's attempt to evolutionize Christianity, Catholic philosopher and mathematician Wolfgang Smith, has argued that Teilhard's scientific claims are as fictional as his theological innovations are heretical.[9] On Smith's reading, evolutionary

---

[4] Ibid., 6.
[5] Whitehead, *Modes of Thought* (New York: The Free Press, 1938), 105.
[6] Teilhard, *The Human Phenomenon*, 2.
[7] Ibid., 1.
[8] Ibid., xxii.
[9] Wolfgang Smith, *Theistic Evolution: The Teilhardian Heresy* (Brooklyn, NY: Angelico Press, 2012).

116   Process Theology and the Modern World

theory (which he very narrowly identifies with neo-Darwinism) has been refuted by intelligent design, and nothing can or need be added to St. Augustine's doctrine of original sin or Thomas Aquinas's teachings on the relationship between reason and revelation.

While the church fathers remain worthy of careful study, intelligent-design theorists have simply lost the plot, providing a great example of how not to mix scientific theory and theology. It is apparent that human consciousness, and with it our knowledge of the universe, has continued to evolve over the millennia. It is also important to remember that St. Thomas himself was initially a controversial figure. His efforts to integrate newly translated Aristotelean texts on natural science with Catholic doctrine met resistance from many church leaders of the time, who sought to censure him. Indeed, Thomas Berry once remarked that the magnitude of the alterations proposed to Christian self-understanding by Teilhard rival those introduced by St. Thomas.[10] In the anthropocene, the Earth itself has been transformed entirely by the application of our science and technology. In such a situation Christians cannot but find themselves in need of a "refashioned Christology . . . to solve the apparent conflict that henceforth exists between the traditional God of revelation and the 'new' God of evolution."[11]

As for the general theory of evolution (which preceded and continues to be refined after Darwin) and Teilhard's poetic phenomenological approach to science, Smith's and others' criticisms can be at least qualified, if not refuted, particularly if we allow Whitehead to come to Teilhard's philosophical aid. The difficulty with Teilhard's claim to have produced a scientific treatise was summed up sixty years ago by the paleontologist George Simpson in his mostly sympathetic review of *The Human Phenomenon*: "Imprecision or contradiction in definition is one of the constant problems in the study of the Teilhard canon."[12] Whitehead is recorded by his Harvard students as having made similar remarks about Henri Bergson, a shared influence on both Teilhard and himself. Whitehead takes Bergson's side in the latter's famous dispute with Einstein about the difference between duration and clock-time, but complains that Bergson "phrases it so that you never can be quite sure what he means." And yet, he continues, "Bergson has a merit

---

[10] Thomas Berry, "Teilhard de Chardin in the Age of Ecology," interview by Jane Blewett, YouTube, 4:00–4:20. See also Thomas Berry, "Teilhard in the Ecological Age," in *Teilhard in the 21st Century: The Emerging Spirit of Earth*, ed. Arthur Fabel and Donald St. John (Maryknoll, NY: Orbis Books, 2003), 60.

[11] Pierre Teilhard de Chardin, *Christianity and Evolution* (New York: Houghton Mifflin Harcourt, 2002), 212.

[12] George Gaylord Simpson, *Scientific American* 202, no. 4 (April 1960): 204.

greater than clearness," namely, "philosophical originality—putting things [in a way] which he feels and sees; whether he can make them clear or not."[13] A similar case can be made for the value of Teilhard's vision, but can his theory of the Omega Point really be considered scientific?

Though Teilhard calls his attempt to "make others see" a purely scientific project, his phenomenology nonetheless reaches beyond mere appearances to the within of things. By attempting to place human consciousness "wholly and completely in the context of appearances,"[14] Teilhard is turning the mirror upon the act of knowing itself. In this way he hopes to "break through and go beyond appearances"[15] to the very source of our seeing.

As Thomas King writes:

In placing man [in the framework of phenomenon and appearance] Teilhard does not mean the flat veneer of colors that strike the retinas. Rather he wants to show the meaning that haloes man when he is placed in the context of a vast cosmic movement.[16]

Teilhard sees more than the bare sensory impressions of David Hume. His vision of the cosmos is one where every body (whether atomic, molecular, cellular, plant or animal) has an "internal propensity to unite."[17] The meaning of our perceptions is in the movement of matter itself, as "the subject is unquestionably no longer the human monad, but the world."[18] Instead of cutting the mind off from reality, Teilhard nearly identifies mind and nature by showing that one can come to know the world only "by being co-extensive with it," or by "becoming to some degree one body with it."[19] Our minds partake in the things themselves, and the things in us. Our bodies are not limiting containers, isolating us from the universe: "Every cosmic particle, be it the smallest electron, is strictly co-extensive with the totality of space and time."[20] Bodies are rather living expressions of our interiority,

---

[13] Paul Bogaard and Jason Bell, eds., *The Harvard Lectures of Alfred North Whitehead, 1924–1925: Philosophical Presuppositions of Science* (Edinburgh: Edinburgh University Press, 2017), 299.

[14] Teilhard, *The Human Phenomenon*, 3.

[15] Pierre Teilhard de Chardin, *Letters from a Traveler* (New York: Harper, 1962), 70.

[16] Thomas King, *Teilhard's Mysticism of Knowing* (Fayetteville, NC: Seabury Press, 1981), 46.

[17] Teilhard, *The Human Phenomenon*, 188.

[18] Pierre Teilhard de Chardin, *Toward the Future* (New York: Harcourt, 1975), 50.

[19] Teilhard, *Christianity and Evolution*, 61, 100.

[20] Teilhard, *Toward the Future*, 169n4.

118   *Process Theology and the Modern World*

as Teilhard puts it elsewhere,[21] converging almost verbatim on Whitehead's view that "the human body is that region of the world which is the primary field of human expression."[22] The convergence with Whitehead goes further:

> The living organ of experience is the living body as a whole. . . . The plausible interpretation of such experience is that it is one of the natural activities involved in the functioning of such a high-grade organism. The actualities of nature must be so interpreted as to be explanatory of this fact. . . . We cannot tell with what molecules the body ends and the external world begins. The truth is that the . . . body is continuous with the rest of the natural world. Human experience is an act of self-origination including the whole of nature, limited to the perspective of a focal region.[23]

Though Teilhard goes to great lengths to assure the reader of *The Human Phenomenon* that the theory he lays out therein is not a work of metaphysics, a case can be made that Teilhard is turning the positivist approach to science inside out. Instead of bare and meaningless sensory impressions (patches of color, measurable angles, and so on) being the only and the most primitive form of experience from which all our knowledge is derived, he recognizes within the human being a "cosmic sense" or feeling of deep connection between what is interior and personal, and what is exterior and supposedly impersonal. The human being is "the universe . . . become conscious of itself."[24] As Whitehead would refer to it, Teilhard is describing a kind of "non-sensuous perception"[25] of the whole history of the universe coiling itself up within him. This is not a "solitary introspection, where beings are only seen as closed in on themselves in their 'immanent' operations."[26] Rather, every granule is constituted "by that which is commonly called the 'beyond it' rather than by its center."[27] In other words, the immanence of the feeling of the within is part of a perpetual movement, or transience, that takes the granule in question beyond itself "to become part of a growing

---

[21] Teilhard, *Toward the Future*, 169n4.

[22] Whitehead, *Modes of Thought*, 22.

[23] Alfred North Whitehead, *Adventures of Ideas* (New York: The Free Press, 1933), 225.

[24] Pierre Teilhard de Chardin, *Human Energy* (New York: Harcourt, 1969), 102.

[25] Whitehead, *Adventures of Ideas*, 180.

[26] Teilhard, *The Human Phenomenon*, 22.

[27] Pierre Teilhard de Chardin, *Let Me Explain* (New York: Harper and Row, 1972), 185.

common movement of life."[28] Teilhard is correcting a "fallacy of misplaced concreteness" (as Whitehead calls it) in the thinking of modern philosophers from Descartes and Hume to Kant. Instead of seeing the world only as it appears through the highly conceptualized, abstraction-prone mind of the philosopher, he returns "to the deepest recesses of the blackness within"[29] and discovers there that "it is through [the] most incommunicably personal in us that we make contact with the universal."[30]

It will already be clear to students of Whitehead's theory of prehensive unification and account of the object-subject-superject vector of experience[31] that his categoreal scheme can bring much conceptual clarity and coherence to Teilhard's mystical insights. As Whitehead summarizes his view, it amounts to an inversion of modern philosophy as typified by Kant's transcendental idealism: "For Kant, the world emerges from the subject; for the philosophy of organism, the subject emerges from the world—a 'superject' rather than a 'subject.'"[32] Whitehead also articulates a novel theory of perception inclusive of the causal efficacy of our visceral feelings, a source of contact with cosmic energies and memories of deep time that has long been neglected by philosophers.[33]

Contrast

Teilhard the priest and paleontologist gave us a new gospel of evolution and an inspiring vision of the human future. Whitehead the mathematical physicist and philosopher, equally aware of humanity's newly discovered cosmogenetic context, provided no less in the way of vision. But his cosmology is tempered by a radically empirical speculative method and an elaborate and revisable categoreal scheme. He offers not an eschatological destination but a way of making sense of natural science, art, spirituality, and the rest of human experience in a divinely inhabited world-in-process. Though this section emphasizes a contrast in their perspectives, this should be taken in Whitehead's sense of contrast as a way beyond contradiction to prehensive unification, seeking some intensification of our own vision as a consequence

---

[28] King, *Teilhard's Mysticism of Knowing*, 26.

[29] Ibid., 92.

[30] Teilhard, *Christianity and Evolution*, 97–98.

[31] Alfred North Whitehead, *Process and Reality: An Essay in Cosmology* (New York: The Free Press, 1929), 29, 45–47.

[32] Ibid., 88.

[33] Ibid., 120–21.

120 Process Theology and the Modern World

of attempting to think with a priest-scientist and a mathematician-philosopher about the complex unity of anthropocosmogenesis.

Even if we define natural science in the expanded, unbifurcated, organic sense that Whitehead does—as the study of relational patterns evident in the nexus of entities disclosed to sense perception including the colors of dawn and the harmonies of birdsong as much as the masses of atoms and wavelengths of light—Teilhard's study of the human phenomenon oversteps a strictly scientific purview. He laments that for convenience's sake the science of his day

> has provisionally taken the stance of ignoring the question of how to link the two energies of body and soul together in a coherent way. But caught here as we are, for better or worse, in the logic of a system where the inside of things has just as much or even more value as their outside, the difficulty confronts us. It is impossible to avoid the encounter: we must move ahead.[34]

Whitehead was also eventually compelled to move ahead from his early philosophy of science into a speculative cosmology integrating human consciousness and nature as studied scientifically within a broader organic metaphysics. But he did so while maintaining the special function of the natural sciences as a study of those aspects of experience that remain at least hypothetically "closed to mind."[35] Despite affirming that "nature can be thought of as a closed system whose mutual relations do not require the expression of the fact that they are thought about,"[36] Whitehead explicitly denies that his philosophy of science commits him to any metaphysical division of mind from nature. He also affirms that there are other ways that minds relate to themselves and to nature that do not involve sense perception directly or indirectly. Finally, his definition of natural science as "excluding any reference to moral or aesthetic values"[37] is not at all a denial of the importance of Goodness and Beauty in any final accounting of reality, or of the devotion to Truth motivating all scientific inquiry. It is just that he would consider such an accounting a matter to be taken up in philosophical cosmology and theology, rather than by a special scientific investigation:

---

[34] Teilhard, *The Human Phenomenon*, 29.
[35] Alfred North Whitehead, *The Concept of Nature* (Cambridge, UK: Cambridge University Press, 1920), 4.
[36] Whitehead, *The Concept of Nature*, 3.
[37] Ibid., 5.

The values of nature are perhaps the key to the metaphysical synthesis of existence. But such a synthesis is exactly what I am not attempting [in this treatise on the concept of nature]. I am concerned exclusively with the generalisations of widest scope which can be effected respecting that which is known to us as the direct deliverance of sense-awareness.[38]

That said, Teilhard's phenomenological method can be fruitfully compared to the participatory scientific method practiced by Goethe, speculatively elaborated in the *Naturphilosophie* of Schelling and later clarified and expanded by Rudolf Steiner[39] (who edited Goethe's scientific papers). Whitehead's philosophy of organism is also resonant with Goethean science and *Naturphilosophie*, but still he cautions against claiming scientific knowledge beyond what we are aware of in sense perception. This is a check on the metaphysical overreach of any scientific materialism claiming science could even in principle explain consciousness, but also on any absolute idealism claiming a mental explanation of nature. Qualitative science is possible under Whitehead's definition, but as Goethe also cautioned, whether doing qualitative or quantitative science we must pay due attention to the subtle interplay between observation and speculation, lest our "imagination . . . [sweep us] away on its wings before [we know our] feet have left the ground."[40]

Does Teilhard really *see* the psychic curvature of the universe with his eyes? Or is he *seeing into* the deeper tissues of imaginal experience weaving us back, body and soul, to the birthplace of the All? To say Teilhard is doing speculative cosmology and mystical theology is not to diminish the importance of his achievement in the slightest, but it does allow us to maintain the practice of scientific hypothesis formation and experimentation as a distinct enterprise. Goethe could observe the life cycle of plants and the daily rhythm of the sun, allowing him to describe empirically the dynamic polarities evident in the metamorphosis of leaf and light. Teilhard cannot step out of cosmic history to see the terminus of the curve he traces from its dispersion in matter through the socialization of life into the personal unity

---

[38] Whitehead, *The Concept of Nature*, 5.

[39] See, for example, Rudolf Steiner, *The Philosophy of Freedom* (East Sussex, UK: Steiner Press, 2011). See also Rudolf Steiner, *Nature's Open Secret: Introduction to Goethe's Scientific Writings* (Great Barrington, MA: Anthroposophic Press, 2000).

[40] Johann Wolfgang von Goethe, *Scientific Studies*, ed. and trans. Douglas Miller (New York: Suhrkamp, 1988), 14.

122   *Process Theology and the Modern World*

kindling in his heart-mind. While intensely suggestive and alluring to our powers of feeling and willing, especially when connected to the revelation at the core of his Christian faith, Teilhard's leap to Omega seems, to my thinking at least, unjustified. Further, his certainty on this point undoubtedly contributed to blinding him to the ecological destructiveness of industrial technologies and the ethical horrors of eugenics.[41] Whitehead's more cautious definition of scientific knowledge does not diminish the import of religious vision but allows for a more differentiated philosophical integration of science and religion. As he puts it in *Process and Reality*:

> Religion is centered upon the harmony of rational thought with the sensitive reaction to the percepta from which experience originates. Science is concerned with the harmony of rational thought with the percepta themselves.[42]

Stripped of its scientific claims and religious apologetics and read instead as speculative cosmology, Teilhard's approach shares much with Whitehead's. Like Whitehead, Teilhard is searching for generic characteristics that apply to atomic elements and living cells as much as to human consciousness.[43] He seeks "to discover the universal underlying the exceptional."[44] Teilhard affirms that "all energy is essentially psychic."[45] Also, like Whitehead, he recognizes two poles or faces of cosmic process, what he calls tangential and radial forms of energy. Akin to Whitehead's physical pole, tangential energy refers to the exchange of mechanical forces; akin to Whitehead's mental pole, radial energy centers itself around the lure of the future.[46] While Whitehead grants there is reason to suspect that nature "contains within itself a tendency to be in tune,"[47] and while he recognizes a gradual movement in the evolution of the universe and in the history of civilization

---

[41] For an ecological critique of Teilhard, see Thomas Berry, "Teilhard in the Ecological Age," in Fabel and St. John, *Teilhard in the 21st Century*, 57–73. On the issue of eugenics, Teilhard's numerous comments can only read as shocking to contemporary eyes. And yet, for a species aware of and possessing the technology to transform itself, the question is less about whether eugenics itself is a good or evil idea, but about how to *evolve on purpose* while avoiding the evils of racism and classism.

[42] Whitehead, *Process and Reality*, 16.

[43] Teilhard, *The Human Phenomenon*, 13.

[44] Ibid., 24.

[45] Ibid., 30.

[46] Teilhard, *The Human Phenomenon*, 30.

[47] Whitehead, *Adventures of Ideas*, 251.

from brute force to persuasive love as the primary mode of relationship,[48] his vision lacks any hint of the necessity with which Teilhard seems to affirm the Omega Point. Where Teilhard prophesizes "a definite limit and term to the elementary value and to the sum total of radial energies,"[49] Whitehead remains skeptical of any final state of order "beyond which there can be no progress.... This belief in a final order, popular in religious and philosophic thought, seems to be due to the prevalent fallacy that all types of seriality necessarily involve terminal instances."[50]

Excursus on Evolution

Bracketing the idea of evolution's end in a Christogenetic curve of curves, Whitehead and Teilhard share a sense of the time-developmental genesis of the Earth and broader cosmos as essential to scientific understanding. Evolution must be integrated not just in biology but "as the guiding methodology of all branches of science," according to Whitehead.[51] For Teilhard, evolution becomes "a general condition to which all theories, all hypotheses, all systems must henceforth bow and satisfy if they are to be thinkable and true."[52] But neither was particularly attached to Darwin's theory of natural selection as the prime explanation of evolutionary process. Whitehead does not at all doubt the general Darwinian observation that a struggle for existence means the fittest eliminate the less fit.[53] But as he points out, this obvious fact offers no explanation for how more complex organisms, comparatively deficient in survival power, could ever have evolved.[54] Both Teilhard and Whitehead detect an upward trend in evolution, a great "counter-agency"[55] to the entropic dispersion of preliving matter that is driving the living world into greater complexity and deeper consciousness. The universe not only falls but through its radial centers

---

[48] Ibid., 69ff. See also Andrew M. Davis, ed., *From Force to Persuasion: Process-Relational Perspectives on Power and the God of Love* (Eugene, OR: Cascade, 2024).

[49] Teilhard, *The Human Phenomenon*, 32.

[50] Whitehead, *Process and Reality*, 111.

[51] Alfred North Whitehead, *Science and the Modern World* (New York: The Free Press, 1925), 101.

[52] Teilhard, *The Human Phenomenon*, 152.

[53] Alfred North Whitehead, *The Function of Reason* (Boston: Beacon Press, 1958), 2.

[54] Ibid., 3, 7.

[55] Ibid., 25.

124   Process Theology and the Modern World

climbs toward the materially improbable, as though evincing an "inverse form of gravitation."[56]

While it was still possible for Daniel Dennett to argue in the mid-1990s that "evolution is a mindless, purposeless, algorithmic process," making Teilhard's orthogenetic vision a "loser" among scientific hypotheses,[57] the state of the life sciences several decades later looks quite different. Dennett's neo-Darwinian horse, while leading the paradigmatic pack for much of the latter half of the twentieth century, has since lost its stride. Genetic reductionism failed to deliver on its promise to explain life. Weismann's trump card against Lamarckian ideas—that the barrier between somatic and germ cells prevents any possibility of inheritance of acquired characteristics—has been severely qualified if not nearly demolished by more recent research in niche construction, epigenetics, lateral gene transfer, and developmental biology.[58] Rather than viewing evolution as driven by genetic algorithms, contemporary biology is coming to terms with the fact that genes are tools used by living cells, which like all organisms are not passive victims of fixed environmental conditions but agents participating in their own evolution.[59]

While Whitehead and Teilhard agree that the emergence of cellular life constitutes something of a "psychic mutation"[60] bursting through to a new phase of evolution, wherein reactions are no longer determined by the past but are "adapted to the capture of intensity" and "the clutch at vivid immediacy,"[61] they refrain from drawing any sharp boundaries between the living and nonliving worlds. Both see the germ of consciousness already implanted in the most primordial energetic rhythms, such that "the root principles of life are, in some lowly form, exemplified in all types of physical existence."[62] Life thus constitutes a massive acceleration, but not the origin,

---

[56] Teilhard, *Toward the Future*, 187.

[57] Daniel Dennett, *Darwin's Dangerous Idea* (New York: Simon and Schuster, 1995), 320.

[58] Neuhof Moran, Michael Levin, and Oded Rechavi, "Vertically- and Horizontally-Transmitted Memories—The Dading Boundaries between Regeneration and Inheritance in Planaria," *Biology Open* 5, no. 9 (2016): 1177–88.

[59] Michael Levin, "Darwin's Agential Materials: Evolutionary Implications of Multiscale Competency in Developmental Biology," *Cellular and Molecular Life Sciences* 80 (2023): 142. See also Michael Levin, "The Computational Boundary of a 'Self': Developmental Bioelectricity Drives Multicellularity and Scale-Free Cognition," *Frontiers in Psychology* 10 (2019): 2688. See also Alfonso Martinez Arias, "Cells, Not DNA, Are the Master Architects of Life," *Noema* (May 30, 2023).

[60] Teilhard, *The Human Phenomenon*, 50.

[61] Whitehead, *Process and Reality*, 105.

[62] Whitehead, *The Function of Reason*, 21.

of the cosmic urge toward complexification of expression and intensification of experience. Teilhard acknowledges that life "can advance only by endlessly feeling its way,"[63] pointing to chirality (that is, the contingent asymmetry of certain biomolecules shared by all living cells) and the fanning out of divergent branches of terrestrial biogenesis as examples of how "life exhausts only a part of what might have been."[64] But his sense of the role played by possibility in evolutionary trajectories only goes so far. Where Whitehead affirms open-ended creative advance with only a "particular providence for particular occasions,"[65] Teilhard detects a "single rising tide beneath the rhythm of the ages"[66] directing all life and mind on Earth toward a universal providential destination.

Although Darwin is usually credited with having discovered the theory of evolution, he rarely if ever used the word. In fact, "evolution" never appears in *The Origin of Species* (until the sixth edition) or in *The Descent of Man*. Evolution, from the Latin *evolvere*, means the *un-*rolling of the *in-*rolled, the *de-*velopment of the *en-*veloped. Until at least the mid-nineteenth century, evolution was usually discussed by naturalists only in reference to what is today called ontogenesis, or the development of an individual from a preformed seed or egg. The main problem was how to account for the development of individual living beings without violating the theological truth that God's act of creation took place only once. This early doctrine of evolution held that every developing organism was merely the "unrolling of something already given."[67] The notion that species themselves changed in any way over time was not considered.

The theory of evolution familiar to most twenty-first-century students of biology, while being prefigured in the speculative writing of Descartes,[68]

---

[63] Teilhard, *Toward the Future*, 171.

[64] Teilhard, *The Human Phenomenon*, 55.

[65] Whitehead, *Process and Reality*, 351.

[66] Teilhard, *The Human Phenomenon*, 59.

[67] Etienne Gilson, *From Aristotle to Darwin and Back Again: A Journey in Final Causality, Species, and Evolution*, trans. John Lyon (Notre Dame, IN: University of Notre Dame Press, 1984), 50. Gilson's historical study of the place of teleology in biology is instructive despite his disdain for Teilhard's revision to the Catholic doctrine of original sin, dismissing it as "theology-fiction." See Gilson's *Les Tribulations de Sophie* (Paris: J. Vrin, 1967), 97.

[68] Descartes writes: "We come to know much better the nature of Adam and that of the trees of Paradise if we have examined how children are formed bit by bit in the wombs of their mothers and how plants spring from their seeds, than if we only considered what they were when God created them . . . we might be able to see clearly that the stars and the earth and at length the entire visible world could have been produced, as it were, from several seeds . . . if we describe it only as it is rather than as we believe

126   *Process Theology and the Modern World*

Comte de Buffon,[69] and Kant,[70] did not gain widespread acceptance until Lamarck, Alfred Russel Wallace,[71] and Darwin gave it a more secure theoretical and empirical basis. Better termed *transformism,* the general theory "affirms that animal or vegetable species have changed in the course of time, no matter how these changes are explained."[72] Only the proposed mechanism underlying this change separates Darwin and Lamarck, who are otherwise in complete agreement against creationism.

Lamarck developed his theory in a time when scientists were not concerned that presenting their work in a philosophical manner would in any way discredit them in the eyes of their audience.[73] Darwin, by contrast, avoided the expansive reasoning characterizing such works and instead focused only on what could be derived from assembling masses of particular facts. Nonetheless, Lamarck must be credited with having first made the idea of transformism plausible.

In his main work, *Zoological Philosophy*, Lamarck writes:

> Since all living bodies are productions of nature, she must herself have organized the simplest of such bodies, endowed them directly with life, and with the faculties peculiar to living bodies. [And] by means of these direct generations formed at the beginning both of the animal and vegetable scales, nature has ultimately conferred existence on all other living bodies in turn.[74]

---

that it was created." *Principles of Philosophy* (part III, ch. I, 45–46), quoted in Gilson, *From Aristotle to Darwin and Back Again*, 40.

[69] Comte de Buffon discusses the implications of admitting that species are related to each other within larger families: "All animals have issued from only one single animal which, over the course of time, has produced, through perfecting itself and through degeneration, all other races of animals." *Natural History of Animals*, quoted in Gilson, *From Aristotle to Darwin and Back Again*, 48.

[70] Kant writes: "Perhaps a succession of millions of years and centuries is to flow by before the sphere of developed nature in which we find ourselves grows to the perfection now inherent in it." *Universal Natural History and Theory of Heaven* (Arlington, VA: Richer Resources Publications, 2008), 107.

[71] Unlike Darwin, with whom he co-discovered natural selection, Wallace came to understand the reality of evolution as evidence of cosmic purpose. See *The World of Life: A Manifestation of Creative Power, Directive Mind and Ultimate Purpose* (London: Chapman and Hall, 1914).

[72] Gilson, *From Aristotle to Darwin and Back Again*, 41.

[73] Ibid., 42.

[74] J. B. Lamarck *Zoological Philosophy*, trans. Hugh Elliot (New York: Bill Huth Publishing, 2006), x.

Lamarck recognized that species are not fixed essences but changing forms. He attempted to explain the reason for the changes in terms of a variation in the surrounding environment. Here, he and Darwin are in agreement. However, Lamarck, according to Gilson, "does not mean that the environment acts directly on the organism, but that it forces the organism to modify itself in order to adapt to the new surroundings."[75]

Darwin's theory of natural selection, in contrast, appeals only to a pre-given environment to explain the changes seen in organisms. The only quality Darwin saw as intrinsic to organisms themselves was the desire to survive and reproduce in ruthless competition with others. Lamarck thought an organism adapted either by making "new parts . . . by the efforts of its interior feeling," or by making "more frequent use of some of its parts which previously it used less, thus greatly [developing] and [enlarging] them."[76] Darwin's theory of natural selection, in contrast, offers little if any evolutionary autonomy to organisms (the little they do have would come via sexual selection). Under the theory of natural selection a change in the form of a species was the result of a series of random genetic variations selected for by the harsh realities of a given environment.

Lamarck's attempt to explain evolution by way of acquired characteristics, which are learned within the single lifetime of an individual due to its needs and desires and then passed on to offspring, is still a teleological view of the living world. It is similar to Aristotle's understanding of organisms, which "working from within by their substantial form, progressively shape their matter according to the type of perfected being which they tend to become."[77] Dispensing with the idea of each species having been created ready-made by a transcendent God, Lamarck instead "has caused the finality of God's thought to descend into the interior of nature."[78]

We see here an affinity in the thought of Lamarck, Teilhard, and Whitehead, as each sees evolution as an inwardly creative process motivated by a drive toward perfection. Darwin's theory of natural selection left no room for directionality or for an efficacious and affective *within* helping guide the development of the *without*. Further, in Whitehead's view, the emphasis on competition in the Darwinian doctrine has found unsavory social application:

---

[75] Gilson, *From Aristotle to Darwin and Back Again*, 44.
[76] Lamarck, *Zoological Philosophy*, 235.
[77] Gilson, *From Aristotle to Darwin and Back Again*, 46–47.
[78] Ibid., 48–49.

The contrast between the dominant theories of Lamarck and Darwin made all the difference. Instead of dwelling on the brotherhood of man, we are now directed to procure the extermination of the unfit.[79]

That said, the mechanism of natural selection that Darwin discovered was in no way denied by Teilhard or Whitehead. The issue is rather straightforward: while few mechanists admit purpose in nature, there are just as few finalists who would deny the many natural functions of organisms displaying a mechanical aspect.[80] But what "would the mechanical energies themselves be without some *within* to feed them?"[81] Teilhard and Whitehead are at a loss to understand how the trajectory of evolution, whether cosmic or biological, could advance without accepting some kind of fundamental impetus driving it forward from within. But again, Teilhard does not deny Darwin's mechanisms; he merely finds that they alone are incapable of explaining the plain facts. Teilhard insists that

> life proceeds not only by strokes of luck, but strokes of luck that are recognized and grasped, that is, psychically selected. . . . Understood correctly, Neo-Lamarckian "antichance" is not merely the negation, but on the contrary, the utilization of Darwinian chance. There is a function of complementarity between the two factors—a "symbiosis," one might say.[82]

Christogenesis

In addition to the integration of chance and decision, Whitehead affirms with Teilhard that "a satisfactory cosmology must explain the interweaving of efficient and final causality."[83] But to my mind, Whitehead strikes a better balance between the contingency and necessity of future progress. In Whitehead's scheme, telos is unmistakably evident in the decisions of individual occasions of experience and in the enduring biological organisms they compose. In the larger arc of cosmic and Earth evolution, he notes an overall aim at intensified Beauty, but insists upon its epochal variation (that

---

[79] Whitehead, *Adventures of Ideas*, 36.
[80] Gilson, *From Aristotle to Darwin and Back Again*, 105.
[81] Teilhard, *The Human Phenomenon*, 97.
[82] Ibid.
[83] Whitehead, *The Function of Reason*, 28.

is, the aim at Beauty is realized in various ways with various types of order severally dominant in different cosmic epochs).[84] Rather than imprisoning creatures in the curvature of Omega, Whitehead recognizes "a factor of anarchy" in their self-creative decisions.[85] Here his Jamesian inheritance of pluralistic realism shows itself, as Whitehead resists both idealist and evolutionary Absolutes in favor of a radically empirical acknowledgment that, in James's words, we live in a "strung-along unfinished world in time."[86]

Still, for James, as for Whitehead, once life has hominized and become self-conscious, the question of what human beings decide to do with their earthly freedom becomes acute. "When we come to mankind, nature seems to have burst through another of its boundaries."[87] In another sense, according to James, "philosophies are intimate parts of the universe, [expressing] something of its own thought of itself. . . . Our philosophies swell the current of being, add their character to it."[88] In the human, reflective thought breaks through the surface of biological instinct, generating Teilhard's new noospheric layer of the Earth.[89] And so, Teilhard's faith in the Christogenesis of humanity may be understood if not as a hyperphysical inevitability then at least as a meta-moral possibility, if only we may learn to love one another as members of one complex body. His vision is an invitation to participate in a "common faith in a future of the earth."[90]

> For that man [who recognizes Christogenesis as the end of anthropogenesis], everything, in every element and event of the universe, is bathed in light and warmth, everything becomes animate and a fit object for love and worship.[91]

Teilhard's call for the renewal of Christian faith involves a threefold transformation of its main dogmas. He insists that we come to relate to the divine as (1) vast and mysterious as the Cosmos; (2) immediate and all-embracing as Life; and (3) linked to our human efforts on the Earth.[92]

---

[84] Whitehead, *Adventures of Ideas*, 201, 265.

[85] Whitehead, *The Function of Reason*, 33.

[86] William James, *A Pluralistic Universe* (New York: Longmans, Green, and Co., 1909), 128.

[87] Whitehead, *Modes of Thought*, 26.

[88] James, *A Pluralistic Universe*, 317.

[89] Teilhard, *Toward the Future*, 173.

[90] Ibid., 203.

[91] Ibid., 204.

[92] Teilhard, *The Heart of Matter*, 212.

130 Process Theology and the Modern World

The first requirement is a result of Teilhard's own experience as a scientist learning about the immensity and complexity of the universe. As his knowledge of nature increased, his former faith began to seem childish. This tension between scientific facts and religious revelation allowed him, throughout his life, to share in the anxieties felt by so many nonbelievers. But like many Christian natural philosophers before him, he was able to find a way to bring together the Bible and the Book of Nature. For Teilhard, there is "a secret message explanatory of the whole of Creation . . . allowing us to feel God in everything we do and in everything that is done to us": the cosmos is Christ incarnate.[93] It is this secret that, when revealed within one's heart (for it cannot be outwardly seen), demonstrates the conjunction of both humanity's heavenly and earthly attractions. The vast universe, inclusive of the mass of humanity, becomes the mysterious body of God.

The second requirement stems from Teilhard's plea for priests to engage more fully with the world rather than remaining merely "the people who bury you."[94] He finds it imperative that believers must not only study within religion in order to defend it, but must apply their passionate religiosity to other fields, especially to science, where the disheartening metaphysical assumptions of materialism are so often the default dogma. The natural world, studied religiously as Christ incarnate, becomes another source of divine revelation. As Owen Barfield remarks in a similar spirit, "There will be a revival of Christianity when it becomes impossible to write a popular manual of science without referring to the incarnation of the Word."[95]

To meet the second requirement, Teilhard also calls for a renewed appreciation of the power of love, from which duty-based moral theory has tended to recoil. There is no more powerful force than love in the lives of human beings, and a religion that does not embrace its transformative potential has no future.

The third requirement is related to the second but is aimed specifically at the potential otherworldly tendencies of Christianity, concerned more with the salvation of separate souls than with the collective evolution of the Earth. Earthly life cannot be understood as a mere passage to the next

---

[93] Ibid., 216.

[94] Ibid., 217.

[95] Owen Barfield, *Saving the Appearances: A Study in Idolatry* (Middletown, CT: Wesleyan University Press, 1988), 164. The trick, of course, is not to succumb to the creationist temptation to imagine God as an external engineer who designed nature from beyond nature. God creates by living and dying with the evolving creatures of the world.

world. There is nothing more important in Christianity than the incarnation: the entrance of the divine fully into this world. It expresses God's willingness to suffer and die for the redemption of every creature and for creation as a whole.

In order to feel at home on Earth, and to take responsibility for its flourishing, it is also important to remember that what is below is like what is above, that eternity participates in time, and that matter is spirit *in nuce*. Humanity, barely conscious of its own role in the matter, finds itself in the midst of one of Earth's major evolutionary transitions, a decisive moment whose window is closing. If we find a way to have faith in the future, we may feel that the presence of Omega is already with us, luring us onward despite the apparent improbability of success.

According to N. M. Wildiers, the central concern of Teilhard's Christology is the problem of secularization.[96] Religion has not been able to keep pace with the psychosocial transformations precipitated by modern science and technology. Whitehead also noted the urgency of the philosophical task of secularizing the concept of God's functions in the world.[97] Nearly a century later, tired debates between religion and science continue to rage, signaling the difficulty of the task. To the extent that human beings need meaning as much as food to live, the task is now something of an emergency. Modern people generally lack an intellectually convincing and ethically motivating vision of our purpose on this planet. Consumer capitalism is happy to fill the void. If only it could. The point is not to pretend to offer some deductive solution to the world in the vein of Spinoza or Hegel, but "a cluster of axial lines of progression," as Teilhard put it.[98]

One of the most striking convergences in Teilhard's and Whitehead's work concerns their shared intuitions about how theology must shift from imagining God as an impassive substance to God as a relational process. In Teilhard's terms, he seeks to replace the traditional Scholastic "metaphysics of being" with a "metaphysics of union" or "unification."[99] He grants at least the initial pole of God a self-subsistent unity, which he describes as haloed by a necessary circumference of multiplicity or "creatable nil," which "by passive potentiality of arrangement" or unification provides "a possibility of being, a prayer for being: a prayer . . . which it is just as though God

---

[96] Teilhard, *Christianity and Evolution*, 9.

[97] Whitehead, *Process and Reality*, 207.

[98] Teilhard, *Toward the Future*, 164.

[99] Ibid., 193.

132   *Process Theology and the Modern World*

had been unable to resist."[100] Teilhard could here be said to have rendered into poetry Whitehead's metaphysical account of God's primordial envisagement of eternal objects, "abstracted from his commerce" with the world but "yearning after concrete fact."[101] Teilhard goes on to describe the requirements of divine creation or actualization of passive possibilities in terms that again correspond remarkably well with Whitehead's notion of God's consequent nature: "In order to create . . . God has inevitably to immerse himself in the multiple, so that he may incorporate it in himself. . . . No creation without incarnational immersion."[102] For Teilhard, as for Whitehead, God does not create by fiat, but by "magnetic influence."[103] God's initial aim at unification reverberates within each unit, "in unison of becoming with every other creative act,"[104] luring each creature toward what would be most beautiful for it by reflecting its greatest potential back to it. Both account for evil in the same way, by admitting that God is not all-powerful in the sense of forcefully contending tit-for-tat in the disputes of finite creatures. How a creature decides to respond to the divine lure is out of God's hands, though whatever happens, God will love what can be loved in it, dismissing the rest into triviality.[105]

Despite these resonances, Whitehead's account of a dipolar divinity offers no hint of the providential climax evident in all Teilhard's writing on the subject of Omega. Unlike the primordial nature, which despite knowing all possibilities has as yet no one else to know with, Whitehead describes the consequent nature as a growing consciousness and "fellow-sufferer."[106] Making one last effort at convergence between these two leading lights of process thought in the last century, might we then say that the intensity of God's consciousness and power of love depends in some measure upon our human willingness to participate in personalizing all our earthly relations? Can we coevolve on purpose while steering clear of the evils of eugenics?[107] Doing so will require an as yet unachieved coordination among each of our highest ideals: the Goodness of religion, the Beauty of art, the Justice of politics, and the Truth of science. "The essential criterion of truth," according to Teilhard, "is its power of developing indefinitely," not only without

---

[100] Teilhard, *Toward the Future*, 194–95.
[101] Whitehead, *Process and Reality*, 33–34.
[102] Teilhard, *Toward the Future*, 196, 198.
[103] Ibid., 197.
[104] Whitehead, *Process and Reality*, 345.
[105] Ibid., 346.
[106] Ibid., 390.
[107] Teilhard, *The Human Phenomenon*, 202.

contradiction but such that all its partial statements form an ever more complementary whole.[108] In Whitehead's terms,

> truth itself is nothing else than how the composite natures of the organic actualities of the world obtain adequate representation in the divine nature . . . which evolves in its relationship to the evolving world without derogation to the eternal completion of its primordial conceptual nature. . . . There can be no determinate truth, correlating impartially the partial experiences of many actual entities, apart from one actual entity to which it can be referred.[109]

God (whether perceived as real or conceived as ideal) thus plays a crucial role in human evolution, not as sole Creator out of nothing of an entirely capricious creation, but as common Mediator and creative goad within a multifarious world-in-process. In Teilhard's and Whitehead's heart-minds, God becomes the shared referent of all finite truth-claims, infinite in the capacity to instigate novelty and to swell with love in an integral embrace of the good that emerges. They offer not only a theological intervention upon outworn dogmas stunting human growth, but their work is also a theological invitation to a scientifically informed and mystically inspired "love of evolution."[110]

---

[108] Teilhard, *Toward the Future*, 165.
[109] Whitehead, *Process and Reality*, 12–13.
[110] Teilhard, *Toward the Future*, 205, 202.

Metaphysics Beyond Earth

Whitehead, Teilhard, and the Emergence of Process Philosophical Exotheology

ANDREW M. DAVIS

The history of philosophical and theological reflection concerning other worlds and extraterrestrial life stretches from antiquity and continues today in dynamic forms.[1] As revealed most recently by the new James Webb Space Telescope, modern cosmology has not ceased to haunt our imaginations with the infinite scales of the cosmos and our merely finite position within them. Current theological discourse employs various designations—whether exotheology, astrotheology, or cosmotheology—extending from equally various philosophical frameworks, as scholars continue to debate the nature of life and mind, its potential pervasiveness in the universe, and the impact of discovery on philosophical and theological worldviews.[2]

---

[1] See, for example, Steven J. Dick, *Life on Other Worlds: The 20th-Century Extraterrestrial Life Debate* (Cambridge: Cambridge University Press, 1998) and *Plurality of Worlds: The Extraterrestrial Life Debate from Democritus to Kant* (Cambridge: Cambridge University Press, 1982). Next to Dick, see Michael J. Crowe, *The Extraterrestrial Debate: Antiquity to 1915* (Notre Dame, IN: University of Notre Dame Press, 2008) and *The Extraterrestrial Life Debate, 1750–1900: The Idea of a Plurality of Worlds from Kant to Lowell* (Mineola, NY: Dover Publications, 1999). For a more recent contribution to the discussion, see Pierre Connes and James Lequeux, *History of the Plurality of Worlds: The Myths of Extraterrestrials Through the Ages* (Cham, Switzerland: Springer, 2020).

[2] Recent contributions include Richard Playford, Stephen Bullivant, and Janet Siefert, *God and Astrobiology* (Cambridge: Cambridge University Press, 2024); Andrew Davison, *Astrobiology and Christian Doctrine: Exploring the Implications of Life in the Universe* (Cambridge: Cambridge University Press, 2023); Paul Thigpen, *Extraterrestrial Intelligence and the Catholic Faith: Are We Alone in the Universe with God and the Angels?* (Gastonia: Tan Books, 2022); Olli-Pekka Vainio, *Cosmology in Theological Perspective:*

136   *Metaphysics Beyond Earth*

Until recently, this rapidly expanding field has neglected the resources of process philosophy and theology as robust traditions affirming the mutual relevance of cosmology and theology to each other.[3] This affirmation is not insignificant. As Lewis S. Ford argued in the first sustained article on extraterrestrial life from a process perspective (1968), theology and cosmology *must* be relevant to each other *if* any exotheology or astrotheology is possible at all.[4] Moreover, Whitehead reminds us that neither theology nor cosmology can proceed without *metaphysics*: "You cannot shelter theology from science, or science from theology, nor can you shelter either of them

---

Understanding Our Place in the Universe (Grand Rapids, MI: Baker Academic, 2018); Jonathan M. S. Pearce and Aaron Adair, *Aliens and Religion: Where Two Worlds Collide: Assessing the Impact of Discovering Extraterrestrial Life on Religion and Theology* (Onus Books, 2023); Joel Parkyn, *Exotheology: Theological Explorations of Intelligent Extraterrestrial Life* (Eugene, OR: Pickwick, 2021); Adam Pryor, *Living with Tiny Aliens: The Image of God for the Anthropocene* (New York: Fordham University, 2020); Ted Peters et al., *Astrotheology: Science and Theology Meet Extraterrestrial Life* (Eugene, OR: Cascade, 2018); Derek Malone-France, "Hell Is Other Planets: Extraterrestrial Life in the Western Theological Imagination," in *Social and Conceptual Issues in Astrobiology*, ed. Kelly C. Smith and Carlos Mariscal, 21–53 (Oxford: Oxford University Press, 2020); David A. Weintraub, *Religions and Extraterrestrial Life: How Will We Deal with It?* (Cham, Switzerland: Springer, 2014). Constance Bertka, *Exploring the Origin, Extent, and Future of Life: Philosophical, Ethical, and Theological Perspectives* (Cambridge: Cambridge University Press, 2009); Thomas F. O'Meara, *Vast Universe: Extraterrestrials and Christian Revelation* (Collegeville, MN: Liturgical Press, 2012); David Wilkinson, *Science, Religion, and the Search for Extraterrestrial Intelligence* (Oxford: Oxford University Press, 2013); Guy Consolmagno and Paul Mueller, *Would You Baptize an Extraterrestrial?: . . . and Other Questions from the Astronomers' In-box at the Vatican Observatory* (New York: Image, 2018).

[3] For the first full-scale explorations of the topic from various perspectives internal to process philosophy and theology, refer to Andrew M. Davis, *Metaphysics of Exo-Life: Toward a Constructive Whiteheadian Cosmotheology* (Grasmere: SacraSage, 2023); and Andrew M. Davis and Roland Faber, *Astrophilosophy, Exotheology, and Cosmic Religion: Extraterrestrial Life in a Process Universe* (Lanham, MD: Lexington, 2024).

[4] Consider Ford's comments: "Unless I can make some kind of cosmological statements about God's relationship to the world, to space and time, to physical processes, can I say anything at all about how God might be related to such beings?" Contrary to the subjective confines of Rudolf Bultmann's existential theology, the issue of extraterrestrial life "entails cosmological assertions bearing on our scientific understanding of the universe. For we must show the possibility of God's involvement in the emergence of other forms of intelligent life before any claim can be entertained concerning their existential standing before God, and this task invites dialogue with scientific accounts of evolutionary processes." Lewis S. Ford, "Theological Reflections on Extraterrestrial Life," in Davis, *Metaphysics of Exo-Life*, 156, 159.

from metaphysics, or metaphysics from either of them. There is no shortcut to truth."[5] Cosmology, theology, and metaphysics *inform each other*.

The neglect of process philosophy and theology is further compounded by the many unacknowledged statements process philosophers and theologians have historically made on the topic of other worlds and extraterrestrial life.[6] These statements, however, also extend from Alfred North Whitehead (1861–1947) and Pierre Teilhard de Chardin (1881–1955), who are widely recognized as the founding pillars of the modern process tradition. Since its inception, therefore, it can be said that process theology has been an *implicit* form of exotheology. As John B. Cobb Jr. and David Ray Griffin wrote in 1976, "Process theology intends to think through the meaning for our existence and actions of the space-time scales that scientific cosmology suggests."[7] Wedded inexorably to these modern space-time scales is the natural question as to whether life and mind is a rare phenomenon on our planet alone, or utterly pervasive as an inherent part of the cosmos. Indeed, John F. Haught recognized in 2001 that process theology in the tradition of Whitehead and Teilhard is already "inherently open to being developed into a 'theology after contact.'" This is due, Haught notes, not only to its embrace of a universe "still in the process of being created," but also to its teleological conception of this process in terms of aesthetic purposes.[8]

Thus, in an effort to further contribute to the emergence of process philosophical exotheology, this chapter focuses specifically on resonant dimensions of Whitehead's and Teilhard's work, including key statements that are supportive of this new endeavor. While their thought provides a variety of pads from which to launch such a discussion, I seek to limit us to four interrelated domains: (1) a *historical* domain concerning the advent and implications of evolutionary cosmology for theology; (2) an *anthropological* domain targeting the shift from anthropocentrism to anthropocosmism;

---

[5] Alfred North Whitehead, *Religion in the Making* (Cambridge: Cambridge University Press, 1926), 67.

[6] For a historical review of these statements, see Davis, *Metaphysics of Exo-Life*, app. A.

[7] John B. Cobb, Jr., and David Ray Griffin, *Process Theology: An Introductory Exposition* (Louisville, KY: Westminster Press, 1976), 146.

[8] See John F. Haught, "Theology after Contact: Religion and Extraterrestrial Intelligent Life," *Annals of the New York Academy of Sciences* 950 (2001): 306–7. These themes of cosmic becoming and aesthetic teleology are central to recent proposals in Davis and Faber, *Astrophilosphy, Exotheology, and Cosmic Religion*.

138   Metaphysics Beyond Earth

(3) a *philosophical* domain clarifying contours of a living ontology for evolutionary cosmology; and (4) a *theological* domain delineating the nature and function of God for a universe pervading with life, mind, and value. In each of these domains I aim to focus on key points of contact between Whitehead and Teilhard. Where relevant, I also draw on supplemental voices when noting the implications *beyond earth*. To conclude, I offer an affirmative statement of the potential of process philosophical exotheology that necessitates continual research in dialogue with the shifting landscapes of science, theology, and metaphysics alike.

Historical: Cosmology and Theology in Transition

I begin by setting the historical backdrop that mutually informs Whitehead's and Teilhard's cosmological attention. It is clear that both men developed their work in light of the revolutionary advent of evolutionary cosmology that profoundly challenged formerly static conceptions of the universe and longstanding scientific and theological convictions. Whitehead, for example, captures this changing cosmological tide, saying "On a grand scale, our cosmology discloses a process of overpowering change, from nebulae to stars, from stars to planets, from inorganic matter to life, from life to reason and moral responsibility." These evolutionary disclosures, moreover, have forever changed our approach to existence: "We can no longer conceive of existence under the metaphor of a permanent depth of ocean with its surface faintly troubled by transient waves. There is an urge in things which carries the world far beyond its ancient conditions."[9] Similarly, Teilhard is adamant that we "must of necessity proceed from the fundamental change of view which since the sixteenth century has been steadily exploding and rendering fluid what had seemed to be the ultimate stability—our concept of the world itself. To our clearer vision the universe is no longer an Order but a Process. The cosmos has become a Cosmogenesis."[10] Indeed, both men write in light of this profound transition and demonstrate ample awareness of this new cosmological consciousness.

Whitehead points to the "countless star-systems" of our universe, each with a detailed history that is far beyond our own. With respect to our own planetary history, he insists that "historical knowledge tells us of ages

---

[9] Alfred North Whitehead, *Science and Philosophy* (Paterson: Littlefield, Adams & Co., 1964), 211.

[10] Pierre Teilhard de Chardin, *The Future of Man* (New York: Doubleday, 2004), 261.

in the past when, so far as we can see, no living being existed on earth."[11] Remarkably, life itself did emerge through biological evolution on our small planet, but biological evolution was antedated by billions of years of cosmological evolution that formed our planet and those of the wider solar system. Being attuned to recent cosmological discoveries, Whitehead was aware of "new planets." "The story is typical of the previous discovery of Neptune," he states, "and of many discoveries of the faint members of double stars."[12] Ours is hardly the only planet orbiting a star in this immense universe. Fully acknowledging the reality of our cosmological de-centering, Whitehead insists: "The human race consists of a small group of animals which for a small time has barely differentiated itself from the mass of animal life on a small planet circling round a small sun. . . . The universe is vast."[13]

Whitehead does, of course, recognize our unique differentiation from animals with respect to science and philosophy (and theology). "Among living things on this planet, so far as direct evidence reaches, Science and Philosophy belong to men alone," he states.[14] Yet even here, these disciplines are set against the vast multiplicities of a cosmos in becoming. Whitehead, in fact, fully acknowledges that philosophy and theology ignore our modern cosmological standing to their own peril and irrelevance. The Copernican principle of mediocrity is a fact, and we have only begun to engage these de-centerings in our philosophical and theological disciplines:

> Any system of thought based on this earth of [ours] . . . is extremely limited in its conceptions—either theology or philosophy—and most of them have been. We know now that our earth is an insignificant planet swinging round a second-rate sun in no very important part of the universe. The response to that knowledge of first-rate people talking together . . . should be immeasurably larger than it is.[15]

Whitehead here points to the need of philosophers and theologians to incorporate fully the fact of our cosmological de-centering, and thus, the

---

[11] Alfred North Whitehead, *Science and the Modern World* (New York: The Free Press, 1967), 91.

[12] Alfred North Whitehead, *Adventures of Ideas* (New York: The Free Press, 1967), 126. Whitehead references a recent discovery made at the Lowell Observatory in Arizona.

[13] Whitehead, *Science and Philosophy*, 129.

[14] Whitehead, *Adventures of Ideas*, 140.

[15] As recorded by Lucien Price, *Dialogues of Alfred North Whitehead* (Jaffrey: David R. Godine, 2001), 237.

140   *Metaphysics Beyond Earth*

terrestrial contingency of our religious and theological convictions. Although he does not overtly encourage (or scorn) theology with respect to the topic of other inhabited worlds (as Teilhard does below), he nevertheless does show concern for the "tale of the Christian religion" and its further evolution through incorporation of the new revelations of cosmology. It is in this context that he offers his own suggestions as to how Protestant theology should continue to develop. "Protestant theology should develop as its foundation an interpretation of the Universe which grasps its unity amid *its many diversities* [emphasis added]," he states. "The interpretation to be achieved is a reconciliation of seeming incompatibilities."[16] Note that included in these "many diversities" is the possibility of a *diversity of life* in the universe. Given what has happened on our planet, Whitehead's wonder naturally extends *beyond it*:

> Who would have ever dreamed . . . when this earth was a mere molten mass, of any such forms of life as have appeared? The method of nature seems to be by the production of novelty—some totally unexpected turn of origination. By and by the earth cooled, and the seas appeared; eons later, plant life and animals. . . . And finally, man . . . after perhaps a million years. And who that watches the heavens can doubt that forms of life just as amazing exist on other planets? The nebulae, too, have their life cycles; come into being, are obliterated, and pass into some other form.[17]

Whitehead knows well that religious and theological acceptance of these cosmological conditions did not always come easy, nor was the current scientific paradigm necessarily open to the many speculative possibilities rising from them. For example, he references the reigning pope who "had forbidden the expression of Copernican opinions" and instead made use of the "entirely irrefutable argument" from divine omnipotence in navigating the geocentric-heliocentric controversy: "God being omnipotent, it was as easy for him to send the sun and the planets around the earth as to send the earth and the planets round the sun."[18] He notes that the church also expressed hostility to Galileo because of "the ravages made by the telescope on the sacred heavens." "It must be remembered that the heaven, which

---

[16] Whitehead, *Adventures of Ideas*, 170, 172.

[17] As recorded by Price, *Dialogues of Alfred North Whitehead*, 193–94. Whithead's timescale here requires adjustment, however.

[18] Whitehead, *Science and Philosophy*, 239.

Christ had taught is within us, was by the popular sentiment of medieval times placed above us," he states. "Accordingly, when the telescope revealed the moon and other planets reduced to the measure of earth, and the sun with evanescent spots, the shock to sentiment was profound."[19]

Whitehead thus speaks of a certain "disruption of Western Christianity" with the rise of the "new cosmology" as typified by figures like Copernicus and Versalius. "It was an age of ferment," he states, "Nothing was settled, though much was opened—new worlds and new ideas."[20] In addition to Galileo's persecution, Whitehead points to Giordano Bruno as "the martyr" of speculative imagination. "The cause for which he suffered was not that of science," Whitehead stresses, "but that of free imaginative speculation." As is well known, Bruno's imaginative rebellion included a rejection of the geocentric universe and an affirmation of an infinite universe with infinite populated worlds. According to Whitehead, "His death in the year 1600 ushered in the first century of modern science in the strict sense of the term. In his execution there was an unconscious symbolism: for the subsequent tone of scientific thought has contained distrust of his type to general speculativeness."[21]

More so than Whitehead, Teilhard gives consistent attention to new cosmological discoveries concerning the developments of planets, stars, and other astral magnitudes of space-time. What is more, he repeatedly acknowledges the existential toll these discoveries have placed upon us both psychologically and religiously. Historically, he notes early indications that an immovable geocentric cosmos was giving way to *cosmogenesis*. "We are astonished, or simply smile, at the anxiety the Church experienced when she first came up against Galileo's system," he states. "In fact, the theologians of the time were quite correct in their *presentiment*," the "collapse of geocentrism" signaled that the "evolutionist point of view" was emerging.[22] In this early stage of Galileo, "it may have seemed that the stars alone were affected. But soon the Darwinian stage showed that the cosmic process extends from sidereal space to life on earth; with the inevitable result that, in the present phase, Man finds himself overtaken and borne on the whirlwind which his own science has discovered and, as it were, unloosed."[23]

---

[19] Ibid., 240–41.

[20] Whitehead, *Science and the Modern World*, 1.

[21] Ibid.

[22] Pierre Teilhard de Chardin, *Christianity and Evolution* (Orlando: Harvest/Harcourt, 2002), 37n1, 36.

[23] Teilhard, *The Future of Man*, 261.

142   *Metaphysics Beyond Earth*

Teilhard describes the toll of this cosmological whirlwind in terms of "the inner terrors of metamorphosis" and a "malady of multitude and immensity," the very rule of which is a "feeling of futility" in the universe.[24] Consider his extended judgments, which evoke precisely these *feelings*:

> No doubt you have gazed up at the sky on a fine winter's night and, like innumerable human beings before you, had an impression of a serene and tranquil firmament twinkling with a profusion of small, friendly lights, all apparently at the same distance from yourself. But telescopic and spectroscopic observation, and increasingly exact calculations, are transforming this comfortable spectacle into a vision that is very much more unsettling, one which in all probability will profoundly affect our moral outlook and religious beliefs when it has passed from the minds of a few initiates into the mass-consciousness of Mankind as a whole: immensities of distance and size, huge extremes of temperature, torrents of energy. . . . But the shock is even greater when we learn that these myriads of suns scattered in the void are no more than the grains forming a supergrain of infinitely greater magnitude, and that this in its turn is no more than one unit amid a myriad of similar units! Imagination is confounded. . . . Yet this is what we learn, beyond any possibility of doubt, from the Milky Way and other galaxies.[25]

> The enormity of space is the most tangible and thus the most frightening aspect. Which of us has ever in this life really had the courage to look squarely at and try to 'live' a universe formed of galaxies whose distance apart runs into hundreds of thousands of light years? Which of us, having tried, has not emerged from the ordeal shaken in one or other of his beliefs? And who, even when trying to shut his eyes as best he can to what the astronomers implacably put before us, has not had a confused sensation of a gigantic shadow passing over the serenity of his joy?[26]

This "gigantic shadow" of which Teilhard speaks is directly related to the sense of being, as Whitehead expressed above, an "insignificant planet

---

[24] Pierre Teilhard de Chardin, *The Phenomenon of Man* (London: Harper & Row, 1959), 226–28.

[25] Teilhard, *The Future of Man*, 92–94.

[26] Teilhard, *The Phenomenon of Man* (London: Harper & Row, 1959), 227.

swinging round a second-rate sun in no very important part of the universe." In other words, this *shadow* is our incontrovertible *cosmological de-centering*. "Today we know, with absolute physical certainty, that the stellar universe is not centered on the earth," Teilhard insists, "and that terrestrial life is not centered on mankind."[27] Like Whitehead, Teilhard's wonder stretches from life on our planet to life *beyond it:*.

> Thousands of centuries before a thinking being appeared on our earth, life swarmed on it, with its instincts and its passions, its sufferings and its deaths. And it is almost impossible to conceive that, among the millions of the Milky Ways which whirl in space, there is not one which has known, or is going to know, conscious life.[28]

Of this, Teilhard is quite adamant, calling the man who believes himself to be alone, or in a "special position" in the universe, a *cosmological solipsist*. This man "reminds us of the philosopher who claims to reduce the whole of the real to his own consciousness, so exclusively as to deny true existence to other men.[29] Put differently, when we consider "what we now know about the number of 'worlds' and their internal evolution," Teilhard states, "the idea of a *single* hominized *planet* in the universe has already become in fact (without our generally realizing it) almost as *inconceivable* as that of a man who appeared with no genetic relationship to the rest of the earth's animal population."[30] What is more, in ways that far surpass Whitehead (no doubt because he was a priest), Teilhard raises pertinent questions about the implications for terrestrial theology:

> Confronted with this fantastic multiplicity of astral centres of "immortal life," how is theology going to react, if it is to satisfy the anxious expectations and hopes of all who wish to continue to worship God "in spirit and in truth"? It obviously cannot go on much longer offering as the only *dogmatically certain* thesis one (that of the uniqueness in the universe of terrestrial mankind) which our experience rejects as *improbable*.[31]

---

[27] Teilhard, *Christianity and Evolution*, 38.
[28] Ibid., 38.
[29] Ibid., 43.
[30] Ibid., 231.
[31] Ibid., 232.

144 *Metaphysics Beyond Earth*

Although Teilhard cautions us to not treat "the plurality of extra-terrestrial mankinds" as a certainty, he is nevertheless adamant that "there is no question . . . of having to *begin work on a theology for these unknown worlds*" [emphasis added]. "We must at least . . . endeavour to make our classical theology open to (I was on the point of saying 'blossom into') the possibility (a positive possibility) of their existence and their presence," he states.[32] This is a remarkable claim, for it is Teilhard's early call for the development of "exotheology" as a deliberate vocation of the church. Only now is this call being heard by mainstream theological ears.[33] In Teilhard's time, however, it was falling on deaf ears and blind eyes. With fury, he stresses that "the theologians" were content to "shut their eyes" to the revelations of astronomy. In a letter to his friend Pierre Leroy, he employs a volcanic metaphor when stressing the failure of theology to face up to the fact that the universe erupts with other inhabited worlds:

> How, I repeat, is it that they [the theologians of the church] cannot see that under these conditions, the "plurality of inhabited worlds" has once and for all ceased to be an imagination . . . , and that from now on it is a "greater probability" which the Christian Weltanschauung must satisfy. (All this without rushing to the unthinkable escape hatches of galaxies which are not affected by original sin (!!), or a terrestrial redemption affecting all the galaxies!!!) On this point, as on many others . . . the theologians are serenely sitting on the top of a volcano or over an abyss which they do not see, because they refuse to admit that two and two make four (even in the favorable cases where they are capable of counting up to two, . . .).—I'm completely done with the theologians![34]

Similarly, in a letter to Bruno de Solages, Teilhard insists that

---

[32] Ibid., 234.

[33] Refer to Peters, *Astrotheology*; Parkyn, *Exotheology*; Davison, *Astrobiology and Christian Doctrine*; and Thigpen, *Extraterrestrial Intelligence and the Catholic Faith* as recent contributions.

[34] Letter from Teilhard to Pierre Leroy, May 31, 1953, in Pierre Leroy, *Letters from My Friend Teilhard de Chardin*, trans. Mary Lukas (Mahwah, NJ: Paulist Press, 1976), 171–72. I thank Don Viney for bringing this quotation to my attention. Through personal correspondence, Viney further notes: "I looked at the French and Teilhard's statement about being completely done with the theologians could be translated with stronger language."

the probability of the existence of [other] Noospheres has become such that any religion that excludes (or even does not positively admit) the structural eventuality of a plurality of thinking centers will no longer account for the dimensions of the World that we know. This is why I insist that we must have, sooner or later, a new Nicaea defining the cosmic face of the Incarnation.

Underlying these provocative, yet pioneering, statements is also Teilhard's strong critique of the Aristotelian foundations of Scholastic theological conviction. "But *the* present Aristotelian theology (theology of Cosmos, and not of Cosmogenesis) has certainly become too narrow, asphyxiating," Teilhard states.[35] As seen above, he seeks not just becoming, but *genesis*, not merely a cosmos, but *cosmogenesis* where real evolutionary novelty takes place. The advent of cosmogenesis requires a transition from terrestrial theology to *exotheology*.

Given Teilhard's statements, it is clear that he was concerned for particular Christian doctrines in light of other inhabited worlds.[36] While Whitehead shows no comparable concern in this regard, it is worth noting that subsequent process theologians, including Norman Pittenger (1905–1997) and Lewis Ford (1933–2018), who were the earliest commentators on extraterrestrial life from a process perspective, draw on both Whitehead and Teilhard in expressing the cosmic shapes that Christian doctrine might take given varieties of extraterrestrial life in the universe.[37] For our purposes it is interesting to note that Ford, although clearly drawing on Whitehead's metaphysics in his trailblazing article, never actually names him; he does, however, mention Teilhard in the context of his speculations regarding a possible "convergence of world-civilizations."[38] Indeed, we will find Teilhard suggesting precisely this possibility below.

This first historical domain offers an important contextualization for this discussion. Both Whitehead and Teilhard show keen attention to the transit and transitions of cosmology and theology, both historically and up

---

[35] From Pierre Teilhard de Chardin, *Lettres intimes de Teilhard de Chardin à Auguste Valensin, Bruno de Solages, Henri de Lubac, André Ravier 1919–1955* (Paris: Aubier Montaigne, 1974), 459–60. Thanks again to Don Viney for referring me to this letter, the translation of which is his own.

[36] See, for example, several chapters in Teilhard, *Christianity and Evolution*.

[37] For a review of these statements, see Davis, *Metaphysics of Exo-Life*, apps. A and B. See also *Astrophilosophy, Exotheology, and Cosmic Religion*, introduction and epilogue.

[38] See Ford, "Theological Explorations of Extraterrestrial Life," 176.

146   Metaphysics Beyond Earth

to their current time. These transitions continue into our own time with still-newer revelations coming from the James Webb Space Telescope, revelations that are again "ravaging" what we know (or thought we knew) about the universe.[39] As in Whitehead's and Teilhard's time, these transitions require us to soberly confront the full implications of our cosmological de-centering for our terrestrial worldviews. Still, it is important to see that neither Whithead nor Teilhard understood our cosmological de-centering to be the *whole* story concerning our place in the universe. For both men, it is only *part* of the story—and not the most significant part. Moving to our second domain, we will see that the reason for this is their commitment to "see" human existence and experience as itself revelatory of the deepest principles of nature.

Anthropological:
From Anthropocentrism to Anthropocosmism

Both Whitehead and Teilhard share strong critiques of the tendency among scientists and philosophers to "abstract" or "bifurcate" human beings from our rightful standing *in and as nature*. That we are an *expression* and not a deviation from what the universe is ultimately up to is at the heart of their speculative cosmological efforts. Put differently, that humanity is an *exemplification* rather than an exception to everything that is going on in the universe constitutes the essential methodological starting point for both men. Indeed, while our cosmological de-centering is a fact, our *metaphysical re-centering* is required if we are to pierce the deepest nature and character of things, whether terrestrial, extraterrestrial, or divine. Such a conviction, however, does not naively repeat anthropocentric or anthropomorphic suppositions; rather, it is based in their shared conviction that human beings

---

[39] See, for example, Ben Turner, "James Webb Telescope Spots Thousands of Milky Way Lookalikes That 'Shouldn't Exist' Swarming across the Early Universe," *LiveScience* (2023); Keith Cooper, "8 Ways the James Webb Space Telescope Is Already Revolutionizing Astronomy," Space.com (2022); Adam Mann, "The James Webb Space Telescope Prompts a Rethink of How Galaxies Form," *PNAS* 120, no. 32 (2023). Among these ravages are even suggestions that the Big Bang did not happen or is an inadequate understanding of cosmic origins. See, for example, Segall's short blog, "Are There Alternatives to the Big Bang?" *Footnotes2Plato* (2022), which includes a recent video presentation by plasma physicist Timothy E. Eastman titled, "Big Bang? Multiple Universes? How Do Scientists Know?" at the Cobb Institute. See also, Paul M. Stutter, "As Creation Stories Go, the Big Bang Is a Good One," *Nautilus* (2022); and Michael J. Disney, "Modern Cosmology: Science or Folktale," *American Scientist* 95, no. 6 (2007).

are *anthropocosmic* and thus revelatory of the deeper rhymes and rhythms of evolutionary ontology, both on this planet, and also *beyond it*.

In justifying the naming of his magnum opus *The Phenomenon of Man*, Teilhard clarifies that its first purpose is to "assert that man, in nature, is a genuine fact falling (at least partially) within the scope of the requirements and methods of science." Its second purpose is "to make plain that of all the facts offered to our knowledge, none is more extraordinary or more illuminating." He stresses that "my only aim, and my only vantage-ground in these pages, is to try to see; that is to say, to try to develop a *homogeneous* and *coherent* perspective of our general extended experience of man. A *whole* which unfolds."[40] Although he stresses that is he not offering a "metaphysical system," he nevertheless expresses the *re-inclusion* of human existence and experience in ways that take on a profoundly metaphysical character, and one that shows strong resonances with that of Whitehead.[41] "The pre-eminent significance of man in nature, and the organic nature of mankind; these are two assumptions that one may start by trying to reject, but without accepting them, I do not see how it is possible to give a full and coherent account of the phenomena of man," Teilhard states.[42] Truly, for Teilhard, the human being *in* nature is far more significant than has been recognized. He makes this point poignantly in his concluding comments to his Foreword to *The Phenomenon of Man*:

> When studied narrowly in himself by anthropologists or jurists, man is a tiny, even a shrinking, creature. His overpronounced individuality conceals from our eyes the whole to which he belongs; as we look at him our minds incline to break nature up into pieces and to forget both its deep inter-relations and its measureless horizons: we incline to all that is bad in anthropocentrism. And it is this that still leads scientists to refuse to consider man as an object of scientific scrutiny except through his body.
>
> The time has come to realise that an interpretation of the universe . . . remains unsatisfying unless it covers the interior as well as the exterior of things; mind as well as matter. The true physics is that

---

[40] Teilhard, *The Phenomenon of Man*, 34–35.

[41] For a classic comparison of key dimensions of Whitehead and Teilhard's metaphysics, see Ian Barbour, "Teilhard's Process Metaphysics," *The Journal of Religion* 49, no. 2 (1969): 136–59. Republished in the Appendix in the current volume.

[42] Teilhard, *The Phenomenon of Man*, 30.

148 Metaphysics Beyond Earth

which will, one day, achieve the inclusion of man in his wholeness in a coherent picture of the world.

I hope I shall persuade the reader that such an attempt is possible, and that the preservations of courage and the joy of action in those of us who wish, and know how, to plumb the depths of things, depend upon it.

In fact, I doubt whether there is a more decisive moment for a thinking being than when the scales fall from his eyes and he discovered that he is not an isolated unit lost in the cosmic solitudes, and realizes that a universal will to live converges and is hominised in him.

In such a vision man is seen not as a static center of the world—as he for long believed himself to be—but as the axis and leading shoot of evolution, which is something much finer.[43]

Despite the reality of our cosmological periphery, for Teilhard, human existence and experience are, nevertheless, the "key to the universe." "Man is not the centre of the universe as once we thought in our simplicity, but something much more wonderful. . . . Man alone constitutes the last-born, the freshest, the most complicated, the most subtle of all the successive layers of life."[44] Put differently, he insists that mankind "represents, individually and socially, the most synthesized state under which the stuff of the universe is available to us," and correlatively, "he is at present the most mobile point of the stuff in the course of transformation."[45] Summarizing his anthropocosmism, Teilhard insists that "the *human monad*, is, like every monad, *essentially cosmic*."[46]

Similar to Teilhard, we find Whitehead actively countering scientific abstractions through a re-centering of human experience as the very focal point of metaphysics and cosmology. Using the language of "speculative philosophy," he defines metaphysics as "the endeavor to frame a coherent, logical, necessary system of general ideas in terms of which every element of our experience can be interpreted."[47] Alternatively, metaphysics, he states, "endeavors to express the most general concepts adequate for the all-inclusive universe," with the "primary metaphysical data" being the

---

[43] Ibid., 35–36.

[44] Ibid., 31, 224.

[45] Ibid., 281–82.

[46] Pierre Teilhard de Chardin, "Cosmic Life," *The Library of Consciousness* (1916).

[47] Note here that Whitehead does use the language of "system," whereas Teilhard above appears to shy away from such an attempt.

world of which we are "immediately conscious."[48] Where human life and experience is a *fully natural* expression of the cosmos, Whitehead rightly notes the oddity of unilateral or lopsided readings of the human relation to nature. Consider his emphasis on the need to *reverse* this when considering factors essential to the emergence of life in the universe:

> Mankind has gradually developed from the lowliest forms of life, and must therefore be explained in terms applicable to all such forms. But why construe the later forms by analogy to the earlier forms[?] Why not reverse the process? It would seem more sensible, more truly empirical, to allow each living species to make its own contribution to the demonstration of factors inherent in living things.[49]

For Whitehead, this anthropic cosmological reversal should be applied not simply to attempts to understand the various forms of life that have evolved on this planet, but also to the wider stretches of the cosmos that necessarily condition these forms. Note again his concern for a *converse* approach to nature through human bodily life:

> It is the accepted doctrine in physical science that a living body is to be interpreted according to other sections of the physical universe. This is a sound axiom; but it is double-edged. For it carries with it the converse deduction that other sections of the universe are to be interpreted in accordance with what we know of the human body.[50]

This claim is profound in its implications: human experience is relevant to (and revelatory of) the wider stretches of the cosmos—its billions of planets, its pulsating star systems, and its (likely) many evolved forms of life. In an imaginative statement, Whitehead ponders the remote ages of a lively universe anticipating the birth of life:

> Our historical knowledge tells us of ages in the past when, so far as we can see, no living being existed on earth. Again it also tells us of countless star-systems, whose detailed history remains beyond our ken. Consider even the moon and the earth. What is going on

---

[48] Alfred North Whitehead, *Process and Reality: An Essay in Cosmology,* corrected edition, ed. David Ray Griffin and Donald Sherburne (New York: The Free Press, 1978), 3; Whitehead, *Religion in the Making,* 72-73.

[49] Alfred North Whitehead, *The Function of Reason* (Princeton, NJ: Princeton University Press, 1929), 11.

[50] Whitehead, *Process and Reality,* 119.

150   *Metaphysics Beyond Earth*

within the interior of the earth, and on the far side of the moon! Our perceptions lead us to think that something is happening in the stars, something happening within the earth, and something happening on the far side the moon. Also they tell us that in remote ages there were things happening.[51]

For Whitehead, human experience is *internally connected* to what is happening in countless star systems, or in the interior of the earth, or on the far side of the moon. This is what *metaphysically follows* from the claim that human beings are a fully natural expression of the universe. Indeed, Whitehead would put it in an even stronger fashion, saying: "Any doctrine which refuses to place human experience outside nature, must find in descriptions of human experience factors which also enter into the descriptions of less specialized natural occurrences. If there be no such factors, then the doctrine of human experience as a fact within nature is mere bluff."[52] Since human experience as a fact in nature is far from "bluff," Whitehead insists that "the human body provides our closest experience of the interplay of actualities in nature." He thus concludes that we must "finally construe the world in terms of the type of activities disclosed in our intimate experience."[53] The *activities* disclosed in our experience are connected to what is *happening* in the stars.

As with Teilhard, this is not just romantic sentiment (though romance certainly belongs to the universe). While Whitehead has at times been charged with *anthropomorphizing* the cosmos, this is a mistake. As should be clear from his foregoing statements, he is not *naively* conceiving the cosmos in terms of human form or characteristics. On the contrary, human beings are necessarily expressive of the deeper contours of cosmic evolution. Neither is this conviction blindly anthropocentric; rather, it is *anthropocosmic* in its refusal to bifurcate human beings from their inherent cosmological context. Despite our cosmological de-centering, Whitehead too recognizes that to begin to approach human existence and experience as a part of, and not apart from, this universe is to marvel at the fact that "in being ourselves we are more than ourselves." With Teilhard, Whitehead also affirms a *finer* side to human life as *belonging* to this universe because our "experience, dim and fragmentary as it is yet sounds the utmost depths of reality."[54] What

---

[51] Whitehead, *Science and the Modern World*, 89–90.
[52] Whitehead, *Adventures of Ideas*, 184–85.
[53] Alfred North Whitehead, *Modes of Thought* (New York: The Free Press, 1968), 115.
[54] Whitehead, *Science and the Modern World*, 18.

then, for Whitehead, are these "utmost depths of reality" like? How, for Teilhard, should we characterize the nature and character of the "stuff of the universe"? We move now from the anthropocosmic to the ontological.

Philosophical:
Living Ontology for Evolutionary Cosmology

The fact that we are part and parcel of nature is not insignificant for Whitehead and Teilhard, for it gives us an essential place to start when attempting to discern what the ontological constituents of nature are like. In this regard, each employs a method that I term *retrospective induction*, that is, the imaginative endeavor of *descending downward* from our experience through levels of reality to see (in at least part) what they too must be like at the most fundamental level. For both men, this method is based in the conviction that there is *metaphysical uniformity* or continuity across nature that is always and everywhere presupposed across cosmic evolution. In Teilhard, this is a method of "backward extrapolation" or what he describes as a movement "refracted rearwards along the course of evolution."[55] As shown above, Whitehead too seeks a "reverse" or "converse" approach to nature which, as we will see, also follows this retrospective method. A certain ontological conviction persists for both men. Teilhard captures it vividly: "*In the world, nothing could ever burst forth as final across different thresholds successively traversed by evolution (however critical they be) which has not already existed in an obscure and primordial way.*"[56]

It is important to stress at this point that Whitehead's and Teilhard's deeply organic visions were not *just* a result of strategic philosophizing downward from human experience. Both also sought to stay close to the empirical data of the natural sciences (Teilhard literally digging in the dirt!) and what this data was ultimately suggesting. Both men rejected mechanistic materialism as a *dead ontology* that is unable to account for the rise of life, mind, and value in the evolutionary process. They both saw that the sciences were beginning to reveal the world to be a layered multiplicity of organisms *within* organisms across vast and various scales of evolutionary emergence and complexity throughout nature. A new organic universe was emerging,

---

[55] Teilhard, *The Phenomenon of Man*, 16, 60. We will see further below that "backward extrapolation" is Julian Huxley's designation of Teilhard's method.

[56] Ibid., 71.

152   *Metaphysics Beyond Earth*

the nature of which Teilhard describes as "both organic and atomic."[57] "This world of 'organic compounds' is ours," he states. "We live among them and are made of them."[58] For Whitehead too, "The field is now open for the introduction of some new doctrine of organism."[59] Akin to Teilhard, he insists that his "philosophy of organism" is an "atomic theory of actuality."[60] The contributions of Whitehead and Teilhard are both unique and compelling. Deep into their metaphysical soil we find a *living ontology* where life, mind, and value are never wholly absent from nature. Such a conviction, moreover, is not insignificant when considering the aims of evolution, and indeed, the achievements of these aims *beyond earth.*

Life

Whitehead and Teilhard *breathe life* back into ontology. It is significant that they both reject clear divides between living and nonliving entities, with Whitehead stressing that there is "no absolute gap between 'living' and 'nonliving'" organic systems, and Teilhard admitting that at atomic depths "all differences seem to become tenuous" so that "we can no more fix an absolute zero in time (as was once supposed) for the advent of life."[61] For both men, it can be said that prior to the emergence of what we recognize as highly evolved "living" organisms, there are still-more-fundamental organisms that exhibit active evolution, dynamic response, and purposive internal relations to their environment. While experience appears to demonstrate that organisms may be living or nonliving, *nonliving* does not mean *dead.* Teilhard writes:

> For a long time we have known how impossible it is to draw a clear line between animal and plant on the unicellular level. Nor can we draw one . . . between "living" protoplasm and "dead" proteins on the level of the very big molecular accumulations. We still use the word "dead" for these latter unclassified substances, but have we not already come to the conclusion that they would be incomprehensible

---

[57] Pierre Teilhard de Chardin, "The Position of Man in Nature and the Significance of Human Socialization," *The Library of Consciousness* (1947).

[58] Teilhard, *Phenomenon of Man*, 70.

[59] Whitehead, *Science and the Modern World*, 36.

[60] Whitehead, *Process and Reality*, 27.

[61] Ibid., 102; Teilhard, *The Phenomenon of Man*, 77.

if they did not possess already, deep down in themselves, some sort of rudimentary [life]?[62]

Non-life, or what Teilhard calls "pre-life," can be said to be the *limit case* of life, but it may be quite wrong to insist it is *lifeless*. "In a coherent perspective of the world," he states, "life inevitably assumes a 'pre-life' for as far back before it as the eye can see," and is thus present in an elementary form at the lowest level of nature.[63] Speaking within the context of Whiteheadian ontology, Lewis Ford described life as a *degree concept,* saying, "The decisive difference between living and [nonliving] matter . . . is the difference between novel and habitual response. This may well be a matter of degree, such that what we designate as living may simply be those instances where novelty dominates over habit."[64] Here Ford echoes Whitehead's own intuition that "an organism [can be considered] 'alive' when in some measure its reactions are inexplicable by any tradition of pure physical inheritance."[65] This novel reactionary ability, however, so highly expressed in human life and freedom, is *never wholly absent* even at the far-side of his primitive ontology. As Whitehead stresses, "The root principles of life are, in some lowly form, exemplified in all types of physical existence."[66] Teilhard, too, sees the movement from pre-life to life as one of degree and complexification: The "Universe from top to bottom" is "a single, immense coiling movement successively generating nuclei, atoms, molecules, cells and metazoa—the special properties of Life being due solely to the extreme (virtually *infinite*) degree of complexity attained at its level."[67]

Thus, for both Whitehead and Teilhard, the atomic constituents of nature are more accurately described as *alive,* not dead. The fundamental organisms of Whitehead's ontology are conceived as *living events* whose status as "living" is grounded in the temporal dynamics of their individual and collective becoming, response, and relationality to their universal environment.[68] As a hallmark of process metaphysics, becoming is more fundamental than being, and it is these spatio-temporal events—what Whitehead terms "actual occasions" or "actual entities"—that are the

---

[62] Teilhard, *The Phenomenon of Man,* 77.
[63] Ibid., 57.
[64] Ford, "Theological Explorations of Extraterrestrial Life," 166.
[65] Whitehead, *Process and Reality,* 104.
[66] Whitehead, *The Function of Reason,* 21.
[67] Teilhard, "The Position of Man in Nature."
[68] See Whitehead, *Modes of Thought,* 150–52.

living ontological base of his evolutionary cosmology. Indeed, it is not false to say that these events are *coming alive* in each and every moment for Whitehead.

In holding to "a world that is *being born* instead of a world that *is*," Teilhard in no way reserves these statements only to higher achievements of evolution; rather, they must retrospectively apply to the very depths of ontology.[69] *Cosmogenesis* in this way presupposes a deeper *ontogenesis* such that the universe is *always giving birth*. He offers a similar vision to Whitehead where "duration permeates the essence of every being" so that "every particle of reality, instead of constituting an approximate point in itself, extends from the previous fragment to the next in an invisible thread running back to infinity." That Teilhard conceives this process as *living* is supported by his conviction that "life is not an epi-phenomenon in the material universe, but the central phenomenon of evolution."[70] As he stresses, "life as a universal function of the cosmos" is one of the original thematic points of *The Phenomenon of Man*.[71]

For both Whitehead and Teilhard, therefore, a *living processual ontology* forms the antecedent condition that renders cogent the evolution of all higher life achieved throughout cosmogenesis. For both men, moreover, this is not insignificant when considering what evolution is ultimately about. We might put it this way: Where *life* in a primitive processual form belongs inexorably to the universe as such, *there is no meaning to evolution beyond the higher achievement, complexification, and intensification of life*. This has been demonstrated on our planet, and it will necessarily occur on other planets where conditions are ripe. While Teilhard insists that "we have no idea either of the chemistry or the morphology peculiar to the various extra-terrestrial forms of life," he nevertheless speculates as to the prevalence of hominized "extra-terrestrial 'mankinds'" saying, "At an average of (at least) one human race per galaxy, that makes a total of millions of human races dotted all over the heavens."[72] Whitehead too holds that "the forms of life which might be lived on other stars millions of light-years away and millions hence could be infinite and admit every possibility that the imagination could conceive."[73]

---

[69] Teilhard, *The Future of Man*, 80.
[70] Teilhard, "The Position of Man in Nature."
[71] Teilhard, *The Phenomenon of Man*, 303.
[72] Teilhard, *Christianity and Evolution*, 232.
[73] As recorded by Price, *Dialogues of Alfred North Whitehead*, 280.

Mind

In addition to breathing life back into ontology, Whitehead and Teilhard also *infuse mind* back into ontology. For both men, the "livingness" of the processual constituents of reality is not only linked to their durational nature—the fact that they are becoming (or *being born*)—but also to the fact that their becoming *is* the becoming of atomic *mentality*. Both hold to a form of panpsychism or panexperientialism that renders logically cogent the evolution of mind throughout nature, not least in human beings. Note how Julian Huxley speaks to Teilhard's panpsychism in terms of his retrospective induction from human experience:

> Comparative study makes it clear that higher animals have minds of a sort, and evolutionary fact and logic demand that mind should have evolved gradually as well as bodies and that accordingly mind-like . . . properties must be present throughout the universe. Thus, in any case, we must infer the presence of potential mind in all material systems, by backward extrapolation from the human phase to the biological, and from the biological to the inorganic.[74]

Just as "pre-life" for Teilhard is not *lifeless*, the "potential mind" of which Huxley speaks is not *mindless*. "We are logically forced to assume the existence in rudimentary form (in a microscopic, i.e. an infinitely diffuse, state) of some sort of psyche in every corpuscle," Teilhard insists, "even in those (the mega-molecules and below) whose complexity is of such a low or modest order as to render it (the psyche) imperceptible."[75] Whitehead also counters scientific abstractions of mind from nature through retrospective logic from human experience. As with Teilhard, the result is the extension of "mental operations" throughout nature:

> Scientific reasoning is completely dominated by the presupposition that mental functionings are not properly part of nature. Accordingly it disregards all those mental antecedents which mankind habitually presuppose as effective in guiding cosmological functioning . . . this sharp division between mentality and nature has no ground in our fundamental observation. We find ourselves living within nature. . . .

---

[74] Huxley, "Introduction," in Teilhard, *The Phenomenon of Man*, 16.
[75] Teilhard, *The Phenomenon of Man*, 301–2.

156   *Metaphysics Beyond Earth*

> I conclude that we should conceive mental operations as among the
> factors which make up the constitution of nature.[76]

While Teilhard will often use the language of *consciousness* for the domain
of psyche at very low levels of reality, he clarifies that this term "is taken in
its widest sense to indicate *every kind of psychism* [emphasis added], from
the most rudimentary forms of interior perception imaginable to the human
phenomenon of reflective thought."[77] In making this important distinction
Teilhard guards himself against common critiques of panpsychists who are
charged with incredulously extending consciousness to all things. Using the
notion of "experience" rather than "consciousness," Whitehead is perhaps
better positioned to avoid this challenge, for, as he insists, "consciousness
presupposes experience and not experience consciousness."[78] Thus, *experience*
goes all the way down in nature, but consciousness does *not*. For both men,
consciousness is a late emergent phase in the evolution of very complex
"living" organisms involving incredibly layered synchronizations of psychic
energy that finally bloom into what Teilhard above calls "reflective thought"
and Whitehead simply the "function of knowing."[79] The evolutionary late-
ness of consciousness notwithstanding, in the primitive form of psychical
activity, the place of mind in nature remains *irreducible* for both men.

What is ontologically entailed in the extension of mind throughout
nature? To speak of mentality in all things is also to assume an *organic
interiority* and not just exteriority as conceived in mechanistic-materialistic
conceptions of the universe. Where there is interiority, there is also room
for *freedom and creativity* in nature. For Whitehead, each event is "dipolar,"
having both a "physical pole" that inherits via efficient causation from the
objectified past world, and a "mental pole" that agentially "decides" via final
causation among unsettled possibilities for its own becoming. For him, the
physical and the mental *belong together* in the "concrescence" (growing together) of each occasion of experience. Teilhard also insists that co-extensive
with the *without* of nature is also a *within* and that nature shows "*a double
aspect to its structure*" where exteriority *and* interiority ascend the evolutionary scale together.[80] Against materialist and idealists alike he affirms with
Whitehead a *dual aspect monism* where mind and matter are "the two aspects

---

[76]   Whitehead, *Modes of Thought*, 156.
[77]   Teilhard, *The Phenomenon of Man*, 57n1.
[78]   Whitehead, *Process and Reality*, 53.
[79]   Whitehead, *Science and the Modern World*, 144, 151.
[80]   Teilhard, *The Phenomenon of Man*, 56.

or connected parts of one and the same phenomenon."[81] He speaks not simply of an external "tangential energy" that achieves a certain conformal or determinative consistency in the physical universe, but also an interior "radial" or "psychic" energy that draws each durational occurrence forward into possibly, complexity, and further mental centricity.[82]

It is clear that both men are concerned to reconcile dualistic bifurcations between the mental and the physical, the interior and the exterior, the determined and the free in the universe. Indeed, Whitehead holds that "however far the sphere of efficient causation be pushed in the determination of components of [an event's] concrescence—its data, its emotions, its appreciations, its purposes, its phases of subjective aim—beyond the determination of these components there always remains the final reaction of the self-creative unity of the universe."[83] This statement might be seen as his own elaboration of Teilhard's base conviction that the universe shows itself to be "determinate *without*, and 'free' *within*," even at the lowest level of ontology.[84]

Both life *and* mind therefore are tangled concomitants in Whitehead's and Teilhard's ontology. As the primordiality of "life" alters our entire vision of the nature of evolution, so too does an affirmation of panexperientialism: *there is no meaning to evolution beyond the higher achievement, complexification, and intensification of mental experience and, thus, the higher achievement of novelty and freedom throughout the universe.* As with life, relocating mind in ontology has much bearing on whether mind is to be found *beyond* earth. As Charles Hartshorne recognized, a panpsychist or panexperientialist view "implies the eternal existence of finite minds of some kind in the universe," adding that one of the many ways this might be verified is "by the discovery of other inhabited planets."[85] Alongside life, if mind too is a corresponding ontological primitive, then a vast and bewildering spectrum of life, mind, intelligence, and sentience necessarily pervades the universe. Consider the further reaches of Whitehead's cosmological wonder:

I see no reason to suppose that the air about us and the heavenly spaces over us may not be peopled by intelligences, or entities, or

---

[81] Ibid., 61.

[82] Ibid., 64–65.

[83] Whitehead, *Process and Reality*, 47.

[84] Teilhard, *The Phenomenon of Man*, 57, 149.

[85] Charles Hartshorne, *Beyond Humanism: Essays in the Philosophy of Nature* (Eugene, OR: Pickwick, 2017), 256.

158   Metaphysics Beyond Earth

forms of life, as unintelligible to us as we are to the insects. In the scale of size, the difference between the insects and us is nothing to that between us and the heavenly bodies; and—who knows?—perhaps the nebulae are sentient entities and what we can see of them are their bodies. That is not more inconceivable than that there may be insects who have acute minds, though . . . their outlook would be narrower than ours.[86]

Whitehead here situates human existence and experience along a spectrum of life and mind in the universe. This vast spectrum runs from the heavenly magnitudes above us, to the insects below us, and to the air that we breathe. "We are part of an infinite series," he states, "and since the series is infinite, we had better take account of that fact, and admit into our thinking these infinite possibilities."[87]

We find Teilhard entertaining these possibilities still further. Because cosmogenesis presupposes a deeper ontogenesis which *is* noogenesis, he holds that the likelihood of a "cloud of thinking stars" is *practically certain.*[88] In fact, Teilhard giddily speculates as to our ability to detect extraterrestrial noospheres:

The most unexpected is perhaps what we should most expect. Under the increasing tension of the mind on the surface of the globe, we may begin by asking seriously whether life will not perhaps one day succeed in ingeniously forcing the bars of its early prison, either by finding the means to invade other inhabited planets or (a still more giddy perspective) by getting into psychical touch with other focal points of consciousness across the abyss of space. The meeting and mutual fecundation of two noospheres is a supposition which may seem at first sight crazy, but which after all is merely extending to psychical phenomena a scope no-one would think of denying to material phenomena. Consciousness would thus finally construct itself by a synthesis of planetary units. Why not, in a universe whose astral unit is the galaxy?[89]

---

[86] As recorded by Price, *Dialogues of Alfred North Whitehead*, 233–34.
[87] Ibid., 234.
[88] Teilhard, *Christianity and Evolution*, 231.
[89] Teilhard, *The Phenomenon of Man*, 286.

Here we may have found the likely inspiration that led Lewis Ford to imagine a kind of Teilhardian "convergence of world-civilizations" in the cosmos.[90] Despite the heights of his imaginative wonder, however, Teilhard soberly descends and admits that terrestrial and spatial bottlenecks forever bar such possibilities. In so doing, he can be seen to offer one of the principal responses to the "Fermi Paradox" as to why we have not yet encountered extraterrestrial life and intelligence if indeed it pervades the universe.[91]

> The human organism is so extraordinarily complicated and sensitive, and so closely adapted to terrestrial conditions, that it is difficult to see how man could acclimatise himself to another planet, even if he were capable of navigating through interplanetary space. The sidereal durations are so immense that it is difficult to see how in two different regions of the heavens, two thought systems could co-exist and coincide at comparable stages of their development. For these two reasons among others I adopt the supposition that our noosphere is destined to close in upon itself in isolation, and that it is in a psychical rather than a spatial direction that it will find an outlet, without need to leave or overflow earth.[92]

It remains an open question whether Whitehead and Teilhard would have encouraged the efforts of SETI (Search for Extraterrestrial Intelligence) and METI (Messaging Extraterrestrial Intelligence) in our time.[93] As John Haught rightly states, Teilhard's "bold thoughts could be stretched to an age of SETI." If he were alive today, Haught thinks, Teilhard would likely pay "closer attention" to these pioneering agendas of cosmic communication.[94] The same could be said of Whitehead. Whether or not contact can ever be made with intelligent extraterrestrial civilizations, however, Whitehead's

---

[90] Ford, "Theological Explorations of Extraterrestrial Life," 176.

[91] For different entry points into the paradox, see Milan M. Cirkovic, *The Great Silence: Science and Philosophy of Fermi's Paradox* (Oxford: Oxford University Press, 2018); and Duncan H. Forgan, *Solving Fermi's Paradox* (Cambridge: Cambridge University Press, 2019).

[92] Teilhard, *The Phenomenon of Man*, 287.

[93] For various perspectives on these efforts, refer to H. Paul Schuch, ed., *Searching for Extraterrestrial Intelligence: SETI Past, Present, and Future* (Chichester: Springer/Praxis, 2011).

[94] John F. Haught, *The Cosmic Vision of Teilhard de Chardin* (Maryknoll, NY: Orbis Books, 2021), 7.

160   *Metaphysics Beyond Earth*

and Teilhard's ontologies of life and mind make it *"practically certain"* that they are in fact *there.*[95]

Value

In addition to breathing life and infusing mind back into ontology, Whitehead and Teilhard also *reawaken value* in ontology. For both men, the very concepts of life and experience are vacuous without the concept of *value* and *value attainment.* Thus, evolution is characterized not only by the rise of life and experience, but also by the concomitant rise of value. Rejecting clearly the modern divide between fact and value, Whitehead is adamant that "we shall never elaborate an explanatory metaphysics unless we abolish this notion of valueless, vacuous existence."[96] He instead praises the poetic response offered by nature poets like Wordsworth, Shelley, and Coleridge to "lifeless" nature as portrayed by scientific materialism. Notice again how Whitehead moves retrospectively from human value-experience to value-experience as pervasive throughout the events of nature:

> Remembering the poetic rendering of our concrete experience, we see at once that the element of value, of being valuable, of having value, of being an end in itself, of being something which is for its own sake, must not be omitted in any account of an event as the most concrete actual something. "Value" is the word I use for the intrinsic reality of an event. Value is an element which permeates through and through the poetic view of nature.[97]

As the most fundamental sparks of life and experience, actual occasions are not valueless for Whitehead, but valuable *in and for themselves.* They are permeated with *intrinsic value* in their very reality of becoming. The world bears witness to "the becomingness of real values," Whitehead states, and "existence, in its own nature, is the upholding of value-intensity."[98] The rise of the world process is a *value process* presupposing real *standards of value* and also *possibilities of achievable value* that are resident in the nature of things. Just as life and experience go all the way down in nature, therefore, so also does *value.* Thus, Whitehead's philosophy should not only be deemed

---

[95] Teilhard, *Christianity and Evolution*, 231.

[96] Whitehead, *The Function of Reason*, 24.

[97] Whitehead, *Science and the Modern World*, 93.

[98] Alfred North Whitehead, "First lecture," *Whitehead Research Library* (1924), 19; *Modes of Thought*, 111.

panexperientialism, but also what Victor Lowe calls "pan-valuism."[99] As Nathaiel Barrett has recently argued, Whitehead's panexperientialism is also a "pan-axiological view of nature."[100]

Indeed, Whitehead conceives the very becoming into being (concrescence) of every occasion as a *living valuational process* where possibilities of value are experientially felt (prehended), actualized, and then transferred on to the birth of subsequent occasions. Far from maintaining the modern divorce of fact from value, Whitehead actively mends it: "Everything has some value for itself, for others, and for the whole. This characterizes the meaning of actuality."[101] The rise of the evolutionary process shows definitively that value is inherent in the *making of fact*, and fact is the *attainment of value*. The upward trend of evolution has clearly nurtured an *increase in the ability of life and mind to experience intrinsic worth*.

Although Teilhard does not stress the ontological mending of fact and value in the same way as Whitehead, he certainly does see value as necessarily attendant in the rise of complexity and consciousness in the evolutionary process. "The most categorical and the dearest to us is certainly that of the *infinite value of the universe and its inexhaustible store of richness*" [emphasis added], he states.[102] This "inexhaustible store of richness" might be likened to the bottomless depths of possibility and value that are made manifest or actual throughout cosmic evolution. He thus encourages our appreciation of (and trust in) "the value of sacred evolution as an instrument of beatification, and the eternal hope it contains."[103] Evolution is a sacred process *because* of the value of its achievements in complex life and mind, and it has realized a trajectory of value-realization that is evident in ourselves and *trustworthy* as it carries us into the "unexpected possibilities held in reserve for us by the future."[104]

As a *process of beatification*, evolution has engendered the realization and appreciation of values inherent in the nature of things. Considered retrospectively, Teilhard speaks of "the degree of consciousness attained by living creatures" as a "parameter to estimate the direction and speed of

---

[99] Victor Lowe, *Alfred North Whitehead: The Man and His Work. Vol. I: 1910–1947*, ed. J. Schneewind (Baltimore: Johns Hopkins University Press, 1990), 168, 270.

[100] Nathaniel F. Barrett, *Enjoyment as Enriched Experience: A Theory of Affect and Its Relation to Consciousness* (Cham, Switzerland: Palgrave, 2023), 345.

[101] Whitehead, *Modes of Thought*, 111.

[102] Teilhard, "Cosmic Life."

[103] Ibid.

[104] "Meeting with Father Teilhard de Chardin," interview by Marcel Brion, trans. Donald Wayne Viney, in *Les Nouvelles Littéraires* (January 11, 1951), 1, 4. Republished in the Appendix in the current volume.

162 *Metaphysics Beyond Earth*

Evolution" as oriented toward "absolute values."[105] It is a "qualitative value which expresses itself—like all biological progress—by the appearance of a specifically new state of consciousness," he states.[106] Moreover, it is the connection between consciousness, complexity, and "absolute values" that should govern our assessment of what is occurring in the ascendent rise of evolution:

> Thus the rising scale conforms both to the ascending movement towards higher consciousness and to the unfolding of evolutionary time. Does not this suggest that, by using the degree of complexity as a guide, we may advance very much more surely than by following any other lead as we seek to penetrate to the truth of the world and to assess, in terms of absolute values, the relative importance, the place, of all things?[107]

Teilhard's emphasis here on the "relative importance" of all things is a nice connecting point to Whitehead, for whom "importance" and "matter of fact" ultimately require each other, and find complicated expression in the evolution of moral consciousness and action.[108] Indeed, for both Whitehead and Teilhard, the inherent value of nature supports the *genuine evolution* of morality in human and—by extension—extraterrestrial experience.

Whitehead holds that aesthetic value is the deepest form of value applicable to the universe. It is in this context that he affirms that "the moral order is merely certain aspects of the aesthetic order" realized in human life.[109] Just as consciousness *crowns* experience at high evolutionary levels, so too does morality *crown* aesthetics. As Whitehead states, "There is that other form of beauty, which is rightness of conduct," that has arisen in the course of civilizational evolution. Moral progress has been a reality involving the "growth, slow and wavering, of respect for the preciousness of human life." Whitehead deems this "the humanitarian spirit" that has gradually emerged in "the slow sunrise of a thousand years."[110]

Whitehead, however, also reveals himself to be a strong critic of the static codification of morality in an evolutionary universe. "The purest conservative

---

[105] Teilhard, "The Significance of Man in Nature."
[106] Teilhard, *The Phenomenon of Man*, 295.
[107] Teilhard, *The Future of Man*, 101.
[108] Whitehead, *Modes of Thought*, 4.
[109] Whitehead, *Religion in the Making*, 91.
[110] Whitehead, *Adventures of Ideas*, 148, 83.

is fighting against the essence of the universe,"[111] he states, and moral codes are case in point.

> Moral codes have suffered from the exaggerated claims made for them. The dogmatic fallacy has here done its worst. Each such code has been put out by a God on a mountain top, or by a Saint in a cave, or by a divine Despot on a throne, or, at the lowest, by ancestors with a wisdom beyond later question. In any case, each code is incapable of improvement; and unfortunately in details they fail to agree with each other or with our existing moral intuitions. . . . The details of these codes are relative to the social circumstances of the immediate environment—life at a certain date on "the fertile fridge" of the Arabian desert, life on the lower slopes of the Himalayan Mountains, life on the plains of China, or on the plains of India, life on the delta of some great river.[112]

It is significant for our purposes that Whitehead's comments also extend *beyond earth* to life on other planets and in other star systems.

> Each society has its own type of perfection, and puts up with certain blots, at that stage inevitable. Thus the notion that there are certain regulative notions, sufficiently precise to prescribe details of conduct, for all reasonable beings on Earth, in every planet, and in every star-system, is at once to be put aside. That is the notion of the one type of perfection at which the Universe aims. All realization of the Good is finite, and necessarily excludes certain other types.
>
> But what these codes do witness to, and what their interpretation by seers of various races throughout history does witness to, is the aim at a social perfection. Such a realized fact is conceived as an abiding perfection in the nature of things, a treasure for all ages. It is not a romance of thought, it is a fact of Nature.[113]

The rise of the "humanitarian spirit" is a fact of cosmic evolution, and while we should resist any simple mapping of "our morality" onto possible extraterrestrial moralities, Whitehead does indicate that other planets might awaken to the contextual call of the Good, or to the aim at particular social

---

[111] Ibid., 274.
[112] Ibid., 290.
[113] Ibid., 291.

164   Metaphysics Beyond Earth

perfection, or indeed, to any of the wider aesthetic and rational values that belong to the fabric of reality. In this regard Whitehead may very well agree with David Ray Griffin:

> On other planets with the conditions for life to emerge and to evolve for many billions of years, we should expect there to be some with creatures that, no matter how different in physical constitution and appearance, would share some of our capacities, such as those for mathematics, music and morality, or, more generally, truth, beauty and goodness.[114]

Like Whitehead, Teilhard also holds that moral intuition dawns with the advent of higher consciousness in the evolutionary process. This consciousness has involved "a progressive realization of the universality of the things surrounding each of us." "The proof that the growing coextension of our soul and the world, through consciousness of our relationship with all things, is not simply a matter of logic or idealization," he states, "but is part of an organic process . . . —the proof is that it expresses itself in a *specific evolution of the moral value of our actions*."[115] In contrast to morality in static cosmologies, Teilhard notes the basis of obligation and duty in a processual cosmos:

> So long as our conceptions of the universe remained static the basis of duty remained extremely obscure. To account for this mysterious [moral] law which weighs fundamentally on our liberty, men had recourse to all sorts of explanations, from that of an explicit command issued from outside to that of an irrational but categorical instinct. In [an] evolutionary scheme of the universe, such as we have here accepted, the answer is quite simple. For the human unit the initial basis of obligation is the fact of being born and developing *as a function of a cosmic stream*. We must act, and in a certain way, because our individual destinies are dependent on a universal destiny. Duty, in its origins, is nothing but the reflection of the universe in the atom.[116]

Both duty and destiny are aligned for Teilhard, but they are also deeply obscure both individually and collectively. "Individual moral perfection is still to be measured by steadfastness in pursuance of the known good (and

---

[114] David Ray Griffin, *Panentheism and Scientific Naturalism: Rethinking Evil, Morality, Religious Experience, Religious Pluralism, and the Academic Study of Religion* (Claremont: Process Century Press, 2014), 88.

[115] Teilhard, *The Future of Man*, 8.

[116] Quoted in Haught, *The Cosmic Vision of Teilhard*, 56.

therefore relative)," he states.[117] Although he readily admits that there is nothing simple or clear about collective morality in an evolutionary context, his conviction that life *does* have a moral objective and summit in the universe remains strong:

> In its present state Morality offers a painful spectacle of confusion. Apart from a few elementary laws of individual justice, empirically established and blindly followed, who can say what is good and evil? Can we even maintain that Good and Evil exist while the evolutionary course on which we are embarked has no clear direction? Is striving really a better thing than enjoyment, disinterest better than self-interest, kindness better than compulsion? Lacking a lookout point in the Universe, the most sharply opposed doctrines on these vital matters can be plausibly defended. Meanwhile human energy, being without orientation, is lamentably dissipated on earth. . . . But is it not in itself a consolation and a strength to know that Life has an objective; and that the objective is a summit; and that this summit, toward which all our striving must be directed, can only be attained by our drawing together, all of us, more and more closely and in every sense—individually, socially, nationally, racially?[118]

While Teilhard's comments here are restricted to life *on earth*, it stands to reason that there may be stellar civilizations whose moral advance and cohesion are far more advanced than our own. Neither Whitehead's nor Teilhard's anthropocosmism assumes that *human* life, mind, and value are the pinnacle of evolution beyond which there can be no beings *more* alive, *more* intelligent, or *more* axiologically sensitive and/or expressive. This would merely repeat a form of cosmological solipsism they both seek to avoid. Human life, experience, and value remain an essential retrospective *clue* as to the nature and character of evolution, but we need not (and likely are not) its highest exemplification. This notwithstanding, the addition of value to their ontologies of life and experience sheds still further light on the nature of cosmic evolution. Just as there is no meaning to evolution beyond the higher achievement of life and mind, there is equally *no meaning to evolution beyond the higher achievement of value.*

It is worth stressing here that regardless of whether we can ever know if intelligent extraterrestrials share our own terrestrial morality or aesthetics,

---

[117] Teilhard, *The Future of Man*, 8.
[118] Ibid., 83.

166 Metaphysics Beyond Earth

the reawakening of intrinsic value in nature, as differently expressed in both Whitehead and Teilhard, provides a fruitful metaphysical context from which to develop a wider "extraterrestrial ethic" in an age of space exploration. Neither Whitehead nor Teilhard developed a systematic ethics; however, as a sizable literature continues to develop under various headings—whether astroethics, cosmocentric ethics, or astropolicy—it is clear that they have much to offer this discussion.[119] The potential of Whitehead's aesthetic (kalogenic) ontology in particular has recently been sounded by Brian Henning and, before him, Frederick Ferré in this regard.[120] "As some humans consider 'colonizing' other planets, mining asteroids, and possibly interacting with extraterrestrial life, it is urgent that we develop an adequate extraterrestrial ethic," Henning states. "We need to move beyond geocentric ethics, toward a cosmocentric ethics, and Whitehead's organicist environmental metaphysics is an ideal basis for doing just that. . . . We take our ethics—and our metaphysics—with us as we move into and beyond our solar system."[121] Indeed, Henning's is an important call for the development of *metaphysics beyond earth* when confronting all manner of ethical issues raised by our still-nascent space age.

Theological:
God as Beginning and End, Alpha and Omega

Having now passed through the shared historical, anthropological, and philosophical domains of Whitehead's and Teilhard's work with respect to other worlds and extraterrestrial life, the time has come to consider what they

---

[119] Refer, for example, to James S. J. Schwartz and Tony Milligan, eds., *The Ethics of Space Exploration* (Cham, Switzerland: Springer, 2016); Steven J. Dick, *Astrobiology, Discovery, and Societal Impact* (Cambridge: Cambridge University Press, 2020), chaps. 8–9; Smith and Mariscal, *Social and Conceptual Issues in Astrobiology,* parts IV and V; Peters, *Astrotheology,* part 5; Octavio A. Chon Torres et al., *Astrobiology: Science, Ethics and Public Policy* (Beverly, MA: Scrivener, 2021); and Mark Lupisella, *Cosmological Theories of Value: Science, Philosophy, and Meaning in Cosmic Evolution* (Cham, Switzerland: Springer, 2020).

[120] See Brian G. Henning, *Value, Beauty, and Nature: The Philosophy of Organism and the Metaphysical Foundations of Environmental Ethics* (Albany: State University of New York Press, 2023); and Frederick Ferré's superb trilogy: *Being and Value: Toward a Constructive Postmodern Metaphysics* (Albany: State University of New York Press, 1996); *Knowing and Value: Toward a Constructive Postmodern Epistemology* (Albany: State University of New York Press, 1998); and *Living and Value: Toward a Constructive Postmodern Ethics* (Albany: State University of New York Press, 2001).

[121] Henning, *Value, Beauty, and Nature,* 209–10.

each offer *theologically*. As with the preceding domains, we find deep resonances between them. Both men affirm a dynamic and participatory view of God that seeks to *complement* rather than contradict an evolutionary cosmos and what it achieves on all levels. In doing so, they share strong criticisms of static and non-relational metaphysical categories that essentially make God and the world the antithesis of each other. For both men, a becoming universe requires that God's relation to cosmic evolution be conceived as *organic and interior* such that God and world are *united* to each other rather than opposed. They both affirm that God only creates through evolution and point to the need to adjust classical divine attributes to be consistent with the fact of evil as an inherent shadow side of the evolutionary process. What is more, they both affirm forms of divine dipolarity where God is both the *unchanging ground of possibility and value* presupposed by cosmic evolution (primordial nature/Alpha) and its *changing fulfillment and transformation* (consequent nature/Omega). Ultimately, both also affirm that it is truer to say there is *someone*, and not merely something, in evolution, and that divine love necessary seeks plurality, plenitude, and pleroma throughout the cosmos. These theological innovations not only complement the previous historical, anthropological, and philosophical domains, but also provide the final divine justification for a universe abounding in extraterrestrial life.

At the heart of Whitehead's and Teilhard's philosophical theologies is a robust critique of classical metaphysical notions that render the existence of the world, and God's relationship to it, wholly disjointed. These notions come principally from Aristotle and Aquinas and are ensouled within what Teilhard calls a "metaphysics of Being/Esse." "Ever since Aristotle there has been almost continual attempts to construct 'models' of God on the lines of an outside Prime Mover, acting *a retro* [from the past]," Teilhard states.[122] Note his criticism: "In the metaphysics of *Esse*, pure act, once posited monopolizes all that is absolute and necessary in being; and, no matter what one does, *nothing* can justify the existence of participated being."[123] He elaborates:

> It is sound Scholastic philosophy, as everyone knows, that being, in the form of *Ens a se* [Being in itself], is posited exhaustively and repletively, and instantaneously, at the ontological origin of all things. Following this in a second phase, all the rest (i.e., "the world") appears in turn only as an entirely gratuitous supplement or addition: the guests at the divine banquet.

---

[122] Teilhard, *Christianity and Evolution*, 240.
[123] Ibid., 178.

168   *Metaphysics Beyond Earth*

Strictly deduced from a metaphysics of potency and act, this thesis of creation's gratuitousness was acceptable in the Thomistic framework of a static universe.[124]

As seen in the first historical domain, our conception of the universe has changed from a static cosmos to an unfolding cosmogenesis and, for Teilhard, a concomitant change is required of our understanding of God. "Since the emergence in our consciousness of the 'sense of evolution' it has become impossible to conceive . . . anything but an organic Prime-Mover God, *ab ante* [from the future]," Teilhard insists.[125] "Supposing . . . we replace a metaphysics of *Esse* by a metaphysics of *Unire* [Union]?" he asks. From this perspective, "the created [world] which is 'useless,' superfluous, on the plane of being, becomes essential on the plane of union."[126] Teilhard thus seeks the *union* of God and the world in an evolutionary cosmos.

We find remarkably similar sentiments coming from Whitehead in his criticism of the development of the classical doctrine of God:

The notion of God as the "unmoved mover" is derived from Aristotle. . . . The notion of God as "eminently real" is a favourite doctrine of Christian theology. The combination of the two into a doctrine of the aboriginal, eminently real, transcendent creator, at whose fiat the world came into being, and whose imposed will it obeys, is the fallacy which has infused tragedy into the [history] of Christianity.[127]

Note Whitehead's comparable characterization of this God, which makes what Teilhard above called "participated being" wholly "useless":

[God] became the one absolute, omnipotent, omniscient source of all being, for his own existence requiring no relations to anything beyond himself. He was internally complete. . . . God was eminently real, and the World was derivatively real. God was necessary to the World, but the World was not necessary to God. There was a gulf between them.[128]

For Whitehead, this "gulf" between God and the world is ultimately a result of faulty metaphysics that assume God to be the "great exception" to

---

[124] Ibid., 224–25.
[125] Ibid., 240.
[126] Ibid., 178.
[127] Whitehead, *Process and Reality*, 342.
[128] Whitehead, *Adventures of Ideas*, 169.

the evolutionary nature of the world. Like Teilhard, he appeals to the need for God and the world to be *unified*: "What metaphysics requires . . . is a solution which exhibits the World as requiring its union with God, and God as requiring his union with the World."[129] Whitehead, too, therefore, affirms a metaphysics of *Unire* between God and the world.

One of the necessary consequences of upholding a metaphysics of union in an evolutionary cosmos is a thoroughly reframed understanding of divine power and creation. Teilhard draws out the implications in ways that further wed God and the world together and also have important consequences for the whence and why of evil:

> The organic vastness of the universe obliges us to rethink the notion of divine *omni-sufficiency*. . . . From the same angle . . . we have to make a further readjustment in our thought as it affects the idea of *omnipotence*. In the earlier conception, God could create, (1) instantaneously, (2) isolated beings, (3) as often as he pleased. We are now beginning to see that creation can have only one object: *a universe*; that (observed *ab intra* [from within]) creation can be effected only by an *evolutive process*. . . . The recognition that "God cannot create except evolutively" provides a radical solution for our reason to the problem of evil (which is a direct "effect" of evolution).[130]

For Teilhard, the possibility of evil is necessarily linked to the fact that God only creates through co-creative evolution where the world too has real agency, freedom, and creativity that cannot be revoked through divine omnipotence. *Risk* is inherent in evolution. Classical theology faces pressing questions: Why a creation at all if God is ultimately self-sufficient? Why an evolutionary process requiring "pain and labour" if God could have created instantaneously "isolated beings" ex nihilo?[131] One might just as well argue that God *did* do so on *only one isolated planet*. In this way a kind of cosmological solipsism could be justified via divine omnipotence in a static and non-relational cosmos. As Teilhard emphasizes, however, this is hardly *our* universe. By rethinking omnipotence, affirming that creation is only through evolution, and expanding "creation" to mean the *all-inclusive universe itself*, Teilhard bars these retrograde conclusions and affirms the union of God and *the Universe* with the vast extraterrestrial plentitude it contains.

---

[129] Ibid., 168.
[130] Teilhard, *Christianity and Evolution*, 178–79.
[131] Ibid., 225.

170 Metaphysics Beyond Earth

Whitehead again shows a remarkable similarity to Teilhard on these points. He further emphasizes the incoherence of traditional affirmations of omniscience and omnipotence in light of evil and imperfection, and the collaborative nature of the God-world relationship toward the achievement of risky, but worthwhile, ends:

> It was a mistake . . . to conceive of God as creating the world from the outside, at one go. An all-foreseeing Creator, who could have made the world as we find it. . . . Foreseeing everything and yet putting into it all sorts of imperfections. . . . There is a general tendency in the universe to produce worth-while things, and moments come when we can work with it and it can work through us. But that tendency in the universe to produce worth-while things is by no means omnipotent. Other forces work against it. God is in the world, or nowhere, creating continually in us and around us. This creative principle is everywhere, in animate and so-called inanimate matter, in the ether, water, earth, human hearts. . . . This creation is a continuing process.[132]

As process theologians have emphasized, God knows all that can be known of past and present actuality, but what is *not yet actual* God only knows in the mode of open and undetermined possibly. Moreover, as evidentially befits a slow evolutionary process, divine power is *always persuasive* and never coercive in nature. This insight dates back to Plato and constitutes what Whitehead insists is "one of the greatest intellectual discoveries in the history of religion."[133] Indeed, it would seem that the inconceivable *patience* of evolution offers empirical support for Plato's ancient discovery.[134] While Whithead above only mentions "earth," it is clear that, like Teilhard, his notion of "creation" is not restricted to our planet alone but is utterly cosmic in scope. "Our concept of this world has enlarged to that of the universe," he states. "I have envisioned . . . a God of the universe."[135] As noted above, for Whitehead, this is a universe that harbors forms of life on other stars, the possibilities of which are infinite and beyond imagination.[136]

---

[132] As recorded by Price, *Dialogues of Alfred North Whitehead*, 370.

[133] Whitehead, *Adventures of Ideas*, 166.

[134] See, for example, various expressions and applications of persuasive divine power in Andrew M. Davis, ed., *From Force to Persuasion: Process-Relational Perspectives on Power and the God of Love* (Eugene, OR: Cascade, 2024).

[135] As recorded by Price, *Dialogues of Alfred North Whitehead*, 218.

[136] Ibid., 280.

As a further result of their commitment to God's *union* with the universe, Whitehead and Teilhard also reject classical affirmations of divine simplicity and impassibility. This is seen in their mutual affirmations of divine "dipolarity," wherein real distinctions of both nature and function are affirmed within God and in God's relationship to the world. While this appears much more explicit in Whitehead, it can also be discerned in Teilhard. Still, for both men, God remains fundamentally unified.

For Teilhard, there are "dual-aspects" not simply to his universe, but also to his God. On the one hand, he insists that "there is a pole [to the universe] which is supreme in attraction and consistence . . . we have called Omega."[137] Omega in and of itself is God as "entirely self-sufficient"; yet Teilhard also maintains that "the universe *contributes something that is vitally necessary to him*."[138] "[God] in some way 'transforms himself' as he incorporates us," Teilhard states. "God is in process of 'changing,' as a result of the coincidence of his magnetic power and our own Thought."[139] Although transcendent and complete, evolution is also pictured as being summed up in God and as *adding* to God's life through *actualized value* that is forever preserved. Haught comments on Teilhard's dipolar vision in this regard:

> There has to be *an eternal ground of all the possibilities* [emphasis added] that become actualized in the course of the unfolding of the world, whether as life, consciousness or spirit. The ultimate source of these possibilities can be nothing less than . . . God. Second, cosmic process and human action can have deep significance only if there exists a transcendent principle that is *preservative* of all events that make up cosmic process.[140]

Teilhard's God is at once the *evaluative storehouse of possibility* and the *appreciative preservation of actuality*, the beginning and end, of all that is accomplished in evolution. This dipolar affirmation can further be read into Teilhard's expression of theogenisis as having two phases. In the first phase "God posits himself" as "frontal being reflecting itself, self-sufficient, upon itself." As Haught expressed above, this can be likened to God as grounding and entertaining the infinite wealth of possibly and value the divine nature

---

[137] Teilhard, *The Phenomenon of Man*, 291.

[138] Teilhard, *Christianity and Evolution*, 177.

[139] Pierre Teilhard de Chardin, *The Heart of Matter* (New York: Harcourt Brace Jovanovich, 1979), 53.

[140] Haught, *The Cosmic Vision of Teilhard de Chardin*, 57.

172   *Metaphysics Beyond Earth*

sustains. In the second phase God "envelopes himself in participated being, by evolutive unification of pure multiple . . . born."[141] God then enters into the world process as partaker and participant.

While these two phases of theogenesis reflect God as Alpha and Omega, it is important to stress that Teilhard does not picture God as *first* Alpha, *then* Omega in some chronological sense. Rather, God is Alpha and Omega, both *now* and *then*. While Omega has often been presented as primarily a future promise in Teilhard's universe, it is clear that Omega is also *ever-present* through its immanent attraction of the evolutionary process forward. As Teilhard insists, Omega is *"already in existence* and operative" with an existence that should "be manifest to us here and now through some traces . . . by partially immersing himself in things, by becoming 'element,' and then, from this point of vantage in the heart of matter assuming . . . leadership of what we now call evolution."[142] For Teilhard, however, this is *true leadership* that also implicates and affects the divine Leader.

The two phases of theogeneiss also undergird the *transcendent union* and *immanent differentiation* that Teilhard finds amenable to an authentic *pantheistic* affirmation. He distinguishes two kinds of pantheism. In the first kind, "the unity of the whole is born from fusion of the elements—as the former appears, so that latter disappear." In the second, "the elements *are fulfilled* by entering a deeper center which . . . supercenters them into itself." He continues: "In virtue of the principle . . . that union does not confuse the terms it unites, but differentiates them, the second form of pantheism is the only one which is intellectually justifiable and mystically satisfying."[143] Teilhard similarly defends "an absolutely legitimate form of pantheism" over and against traditional religious anxiety:

> To put an end once and for all to all the fears of "pantheism," constantly raised by certain upholders of traditional spirituality as regards evolution, how can we fail to see that, in the case of a *converging universe* such as I have delineated, far from being born from the fusion and confusion of the elemental centres it assembles, the universal centre of unification (precisely to fulfil its motive, collective and stabilising function) must be conceived as pre-existing and transcendent. A very real "pantheism" if you like (in the etymological meaning of the word) but an absolutely legitimate pantheism—for if, in the last

---

[141] Teilhard, *Christianity and Evolution*, 178n4.
[142] Teilhard, *The Phenomenon of Man*, 291, 294.
[143] Teilhard, *Christianity and Evolution*, 136–37.

resort, the reflective centres of the world are effectively "one with God," this state is obtained not by identification (God becoming all) but by the differentiating and communicating action [of God] (God all *in everyone*).[144]

Teilhard's complications of "pantheism" here have led some (but not all) interpreters to instead speak of "panentheism" as a more adequate rendering of his position, where both union and differentiation are preserved in the God-world relationship.[145]

Whereas Teilhard's statements of dipolarity are more subdued and implicit, Whitehead is open and explicit in his affirmations. Holding to the union of God and the world, he famously insists that "God is not to be treated as an exception to all metaphysical principles, invoked to save their collapse. He is their chief exemplification."[146] Among the many implications of this conviction is that God too is to be conceived as "dipolar" in both nature and function: "Analogously to the [mental and physical] poles of every occasion," Whitehead states, "the nature of God is dipolar."[147] Viewed from the divine mental pole—what Whitehead calls the "primordial nature"—God is the "unlimited conceptual realization of the absolute wealth of potentiality." Here, Whitehead envisions God as the *transcendent ground of all possibility*. Akin to Teilhard's transcendent pole of the universe, which is "supreme in attraction," Whitehead's primordial nature is "the lure for feeling, the eternal urge of desire" that inaugurates every event in the world process with a vision of possibility (an "initial aim") relevant to its own becoming. Viewed from the physical pole—what Whitehead calls the "consequent nature"—God is "consequent upon the creative advance of the world" so that there is "a reaction of the world on God." Although God's primordial nature is "unchanged by reason of its final completeness," God's consequent nature "evolves in its relationships to the evolving world."[148] For Whitehead too, therefore, God is "the beginning and the end" in that God *gives possibility and purpose* via

---

[144] Teilhard, *The Phenomenon of Man*, 309–10.

[145] For two relevant discussions, see John Cooper, *Panentheism: The Other God of the Philosophers* (Grand Rapids, MI: Baker Academic, 2013), chap. 6; and Daniel A. Dombrowski, *A History of the Concept of God: A Process Approach* (Albany: State University of New York Press, 2016), chap. 22.

[146] Whitehead, *Process and Reality*, 343.

[147] Ibid., 345.

[148] Ibid., 343, 12.

174   Metaphysics Beyond Earth

the primordial nature and *receives actuality and value* via the consequent nature.[149] Ian Barbour notes the similarities with Teilhard in this way:

> Whitehead's idea of God's "primordial nature," like Teilhard's Alpha, refers to God's eternal purposes for the world; the "consequent nature" like Teilhard's Omega, includes the world's contribution to God. For Teilhard, however, Omega is primarily in the future, though it exerts an attraction on the present. For Whitehead, the two aspects represent two contributing roles of God which are abstractions from his unity.[150]

The interplay of the primordial and consequent natures makes for a "notion of God" that Whitehead describes as "immanent in the actual world, but transcending any finite cosmic epoch—a being at once actual, eternal, immanent, and transcendent."[151] While Whitehead acknowledges "an air of paradox, or of pantheism," it is also clear that he seeks to avoid extremes associated with the "monotheistic doctrine of God, as essentially transcendent and only accidentally immanent," on the one hand, and "the pantheistic doctrine of God, as essentially immanent and in no way transcendent," on the other.[152] Akin to Teilhard, this has led many interpreters (but not all) to also label his position panentheism as the wavering balance between these extremes.[153]

Before concluding this discussion, it is worth emphasizing that for both Whitehead and Teilhard, "God" is not simply an impersonal "principle" at work in the evolutionary process. Teilhard speaks firmly, saying, "Either the whole construction of the world presented here is vain ideology or, somewhere around us, in one form or another, some excess of personal, extrahuman energy should be perceptible to us if we look carefully, and should

---

[149] Ibid., 343.

[150] Barbour, "Teilhard's Process Metaphysics," 343.

[151] Whitehead, *Process and Reality,* 93.

[152] Whitehead, *Adventures of Ideas,* 236, 121.

[153] See, for example, Charles Hartshorne and William L. Reese, eds., *Philosophers Speak of God* (Amherst: Humanity Books, 2000); and Griffin, *Panentheism and Scientific Naturalism.* For a summary of alternative views, see Andrew M. Davis, *Mind, Value, and Cosmos: On the Relational Nature of Ultimacy* (Lanham, MD: Lexington, 2020), chap. 10. For an in-depth study of both Whitehead and Teilhard via differing panentheistic conceptualities, see Valerian Mendonca, "Panentheistic Interconnectedness: On the Revival of Metaphysics in A. N. Whitehead and P. Teilhard de Chardin," PhD diss., Katholieke Universiteit Leuven, 2019.

reveal to us the great Prescence."[154] Put differently, for Teilhard, there is a "palpable influence on our world of *an other*"—a "supreme Someone" who affects, and is affected by, evolution.[155] Still, this *Someone* is not obvious; we must look *carefully*.

The language of "someone" and the resulting implications of "person-hood" in God are less explicit in Whitehead, yet he does speak in ways that gesture in this direction, albeit tentatively. In describing "the intuition of immediate occasions as failing or succeeding in reference to the ideal relevant to them," so that "there is a rightness attained or missed," he insists that "this is a revelation of character, apprehended as we apprehend the characters of our friends. But in this case it is an apprehension of character permanently inherent in the nature of things."[156] Whitehead underscores the fact that "character" belongs not to an impersonal something, but to a *some-one* (a friend). Analogously, the "permanent character" of which he speaks might be fittingly related to Teilhard's "supreme Someone." He is quick to note, however, that we have "no direct intuition of such an ultimate personal substratum to the world." Rather, this belief is based upon an inference that, as most Christian theologians have insisted (whether rightly or wrongly), is "sufficiently obvious" based upon "individual personal experience."[157]

Finally, both men recognized that when operating from within the context of *someone*, guidance and love become interpretive notions that are less available in the context of *something*. Thus, where Teilhard speaks of "God as providence, directing the universe with loving, watchful care," Whitehead speaks of "the love of God for the world . . . [as] the particular providence for particular occasions." God is not only likened to a "friend" for Whitehead, but to "the great companion—the fellow sufferer who understands."[158] For both men, a process metaphysics of *Unire* underscores love as an utmost value. "As one might expect in a universe built on the plane of union and by the forces of union," Teilhard states, "love . . . is undoubtedly the single higher form toward which . . . all other sorts of spiritual energy converge" in evolution.[159] This final insistence on divine love, I submit, is essential for Whitehead's and Teilhard's process philosophical exotheologies. As the theological tradition has long held, it belongs to the

---

[154] Teilhard, *The Phenomenon of Man*, 292.

[155] Ibid., 290, 298.

[156] Whitehead, *Religion in the Making*, 50.

[157] Ibid., 51–52.

[158] Teilhard, *The Phenomenon of Man*, 293; Whitehead, *Process and Reality*, 351.

[159] Teilhard, *Christianity and Evolution*, 186.

176   *Metaphysics Beyond Earth*

nature of love to *necessarily overflow*, to *give of itself* on behalf of the existence and multiplication of others. For both men, immanent to the obvious drive for plurality, plenitude, and pleroma in our universe is an admittedly less obvious, yet universally present, *Someone*, who "slowly and in quietness operate[s] by love."[160]

Conclusion

This discussion has aimed to contribute further to the emergence of process philosophical exotheology by highlighting resonant historical, anthropological, philosophical, and theological domains in the work of its two foundational figures. While the importance of Whitehead's and Teilhard's contributions remain underappreciated in current discussions of extraterrestrial life, this is also changing. Teilhard offered an early call: "There is no question . . . of having to begin work on a theology for these unknown worlds."[161] This work has started and needs to continue. Whether characterized as astrotheology, cosmotheology, or exotheology, the field is now ripe for the contributions of present and future process philosophers and theologians. As the James Webb Space Telescope permits us to "see" ever deeper into the vastness of space, it serves us to always remember the shifting interrelations between science and theology and the ways in which they mutually inform each other. Let us also not forget the necessity of metaphysics as a complement to both. "There is no shortcut to truth,"[162] Whitehead reminds us, neither on this planet, nor on those *beyond* it.

---

[160] Whitehead, *Process and Reality*, 343.
[161] Teilhard, *Christianity and Evolution*, 234.
[162] Whitehead, *Religion in the Making*, 67.

Wilding the Cosmos

A Decolonial and Process Approach to Space Exploration

Elaine Padilla

No more than a year ago, I had the pleasure of moving near the edge of the Claremont Hills Wilderness Park at the base of the San Gabriel Mountains and the Angeles National Forest. Being that it is just a few steps from home, I hike it regularly. As I start my ascent, the sounds of the town are slowly drowned by the silence that inhabits the wilderness. The sonorous chirps of birds make possible the letting go of the linguistic formulas and proper grammar of my own thoughts. A rhymeless rhyme also conjures the smells of sage mixed with the morning dew that saturates the air, while not too distantly homes, cars, roads, electric poles and cables, reception towers and the like, take on a diminutive form. The domesticated becomes a wild refuge.

My dog, Magnus, usually accompanies me and often beckons me to sit, to wait, to be still, and to enjoy all that the moment is gifting us by being the first to lie down. So, I choose to lie down on the ground facing upward right next to him. My legs bend as I seek to touch the ground with my feet. Then the sky above opens before us. I feel we are being inhabited by a vital space, a living space that is wildly free, autonomous, even as we dwell in this highly urban surround. I ask: What meaning can be found in a universe that collapses into the nooks and crannies of this highly urbanized and compacted sprawl of the metro area of Los Angeles? Here the earthen cosmos and intimate instances shrink into one millisecond, a moment in space. The wilderness becomes cosmic as much as the cosmos becomes wild.

I close my eyes and imagine the concrescence of myriad entities acquiring the metaphysical character of unity—*one actual entity*—as perhaps

178 *Wilding the Cosmos*

Alfred North Whitehead also once did. I imagine him closing his eyes in wonderment of this complex entity, then seeking a consciousness of becoming integral to each concrescence from then onward. Perhaps, similarly, an untamed wilderness and cosmos inhabited him so that he too could become untamed, so that his imagination could run wild. Yes, I imagine that Whitehead experienced such a mystical union with the *all in all*. As he possibly did, in this enveloping, concrescent unity, I become aware of the potentially new being embraced by all things past and of being persuaded by a divine, erotic impulse that urges me to experience life with zest! To employ Whitehead's terminology, the "production of novel togetherness"[1] occurs because of "the divine element in the world, by which the *barren inefficient disjunction* [emphasis added] of abstract potentialities obtains primordially the efficient conjunction of ideal realization."[2] I am humbled by the thought of abstract potentialities symbolized in the wildly barren desert at the edge of my neighborhood being infused by myriads of galaxies and acquiring meaning as the universe becomes a "solidarity of many actualities"[3] in the integrative event of Magnus and me. This cosmic yonder being surprisingly embedded in the now of the present urbanized zone and proximate wilderness invites me to wonder.

I am provoked to wonderment before such sublime phenomena but also feel compelled to inquire how such complex unity could become an alternative path to the pervasive use of force globally. Particularly, for me, by considering liberational and decolonial thinking to be inquiring companions to process philosophy, I *wonder* how a unified way of existence has led to what Mariana Ortega describes as *ontological expansiveness* or the expansion of Being permitted for the privileged few and restricted for the colonized others.[4] This would be the expansiveness of Europeans employed against peoples whose ways of being human have been cast to what Walter Mignolo has called "the darker side of western modernity," meaning where coloniality has established the one, global power of modernity with the use of blunt force since the fifteenth century.[5] Now that outer space has become the next

---

[1] Alfred North Whitehead, *Process and Reality: An Essay in Cosmology*, corrected edition, ed. David Ray Griffin and Donald W. Sherburne (New York: The Free Press, 1978), 21.

[2] Ibid., 40.

[3] Ibid.

[4] See Mariana Ortega, *In-Between: Latina Feminist Phenomenology, Multiplicity, and the Self* (Albany: State University of New York Press, 2016).

[5] Walter D. Mignolo, *The Darker Side of Western Modernity: Global Futures, Decolonial Options* (Durham, NC: Duke University Press, 2011), 3.

frontier of conquest and colonization, one needs to grapple further with the implications of such use of force for the purposes of space supremacy by our own nation.

In drawing upon process principles to establish an outer-space ethic conducive to well-being here on earth, this chapter addresses and offers alternatives to the spirit of conquest that continues to inform scientific uses of outer-space technology. To these ends the chapter explores Whitehead's views on social progress, particularly his understanding of adventure as "the urge of the universe."[6] I do so first as a critique of the use of force, and second, as an alternative when guided by means of persuasion and love. There is a caveat, however. Isn't Whitehead's faith in Western civilization too romantic, too modern—even Eurocentric? For this reason, other voices from the darker, wilder, side of Western modernity will also inform my analysis of adventure, especially when applied to scientific discoveries and the uses of outer-space technology. The urge of the universe, of which all living things partake, can also take on the form of mystical union and reverence for earthly and cosmic life.

The *Res Extensa* of the Non-*Humanitas*

But science, as equipped by Descartes, gave intellectual status to a point of view which has had very mixed effects upon the moral suppositions of modern communities. Its good effects rose from its efficiency as a method for scientific researchers within those limited regions which were then best suited for exploration. *The result was a general clearing of the European mind away from the stains left upon it by the hysteria of remote barbaric ages* [emphasis added]. This was all to the good, and was most completely exemplified in the eighteenth century.[7]

Whitehead, in his critique of the influence that philosophy exerted upon modern science, rightly faults the scientific method developed during the seventeenth century. This century was a transitional period, as the early modern method began with the fifteenth century (as a response to Scholasticism) and matured in the eighteenth century, with dire results visible in

---

[6] Alfred North Whitehead, *Adventures of Ideas* (New York: The Free Press, 1967), 295.

[7] Alfred North Whitehead, *Science and the Modern World* (New York: The Free Press, 1925), 195.

180   Wilding the Cosmos

the nineteenth and subsequent centuries. Modern science was reanimating Greek civilizational "principles of aesthetics and reason" to which Whitehead attributes, among others, "racial inheritances, dividing the living and the dead."[8] Here lies a critical point in Whitehead's critique, even when not explicitly challenging the geopolitical ailments of the start of the modern period. As I will demonstrate below, these ailments also remain at play in the development of outer-space technology. Racial configurations that inform the split between things living and things dead have set the tone for the scientific knowledge and use of technology and have become the apex of a civilization driven by domination.

In reference to the extract above, who are the remote and barbaric beings from whose culture and knowledge the European mind sought to purify itself? Certainly, there was some barbarism in the Middle Ages, the clearing of which led to growth in human consciousness of itself, as with the development of human rights initiated during the early modern period, like the Valladolid Debate between Bartolomé de Las Casas and Juan Ginés de Sepúlveda (1550). But how has the Cartesian ego, which arose from the colonial underbelly of the sixteenth century, informed definitions of barbarism and savagery based on the encounter with the *wild-other* in need of civility via domestication, and how did these attitudes influence scientific methods that emphasized the human spirit of *exploration*?

At this juncture one needs to place Whitehead's challenge to modern science at the start of the modern period—as Europe was conquering the Americas, Africa, and Asia—in order to specifically address matters of coloniality. For Mignolo, modernity has maintained an aura of supremacy over barbarism by establishing and maintaining the fallacy of a *modern civilized/colonial savage* divide.[9] This divide occludes modernity's dependence on the totalitarian systems of colonization for its successes in technological advancement, an exaltation of the modern mind still figuratively washing its hands from the system of coloniality that it established. Furthermore, the concept of racial configurations developed in antiquity, and instrumental in the Middle Ages (for example, Aristotelian racism adopted by Scholasticism), paved the way for colonization and made possible the development of scientific methods based on *insiders* versus *outsiders* and the face of *otherness* developed through both conquest and slavery.

---

[8] Ibid., 140.

[9] See, for example, Mignolo's introduction in *Local Histories/Global Designs: Coloniality, Subaltern Knowledges, and Border Thinking* (Princeton, NJ: Princeton University Press, 2000).

Native American Jamake Highwater, quoting from Whitehead, points to how "the major advances of civilization are processes that all but wreck the societies in which they occur."[10] One reason that Highwater gives for this wreckage is the singular way the term *civilization* has been defined over against the technology, history, religious beliefs, and leisure activities of Indigenous peoples. Racially, the Indigenous were described as primitive, savage, ape-like, and cavernous. He avers: "The more lowly in comparison to the white male who places himself at the crown of creation," the more Indigenous peoples and their lands were fit for the "aggressiveness of the West."[11] The European claim to an indisputable right to superiority "no matter the loss in customs, property, rights, and survival of others"[12] set the basis for the racialization of science. European-sameness imposed views on progress that reiterated "the idea that only one cultural path leads out of the ancestral cave, and therefore all peoples must progress through the same evolutionary stages in a prescribed succession of steps if they are to attain what the West calls maturity and high civilization."[13]

To clarify, Whitehead overtly indicts the *subjectivism* characteristic of the individualization of religious experience in his analysis of modern science (for example, by faith alone) and not colonialism and much less the racialization of Indigenous peoples. Accordingly, for Whitehead, the start of the Reformation translated into egotism bolstered by an intellectualized gnosis that was applied to science and that ascribed supremacy to, I would say, a European kind of rationality to the detriment and exclusion of other forms of rationality, now racialized as inferior (European rationality/non-European irrationality). René Descartes (1596–1650) is a key figure to whom Whitehead rightly attributes this turning point. One fallacy that summarizes Whitehead's critique is the *simple location* of matter and mind as "independently existing substances" in time and space, which undergirds the modern view of a "materialistic, mechanistic nature, surveyed by cogitating minds."[14] Cartesian thinking led to two evils: "one, the ignoration of the true relation of each organism to its environment; and the other, the habit of ignoring the intrinsic worth of the environment which must be allowed its weight in any consideration of final ends."[15]

---

[10] Jamake Highwater, *The Primal Mind* (New York: Harper & Row, 1944), 36.
[11] Ibid., 23.
[12] Ibid., 38.
[13] Ibid., 23.
[14] Whitehead, *Science and the Modern World*, 145.
[15] Ibid., 196.

182 *Wilding the Cosmos*

With Descartes, therefore, modern science, which was already influenced by the belief in the progress of a *racialized* civilization, severed the ties of the universe from its complex systems of relations and turned it into a *totality* generated by the soul. This, to me, ultimately grants an ontological expansion of the European *Humanitas* from one edge of the Atlantic to another, and toward the skies. Accordingly, the Cartesian virtue of self-consciousness or consciousness "of its own existence as a unit entity,"[16] which Whitehead impugns (albeit too romantically), is also a privilege that has been exclusively applied to the *mind* of highly developed nations, a Supreme sense of Being over the rest of the nations that must now be dependent on their scientific methods and technological advancements.

In support of this claim, one needs to dig deeper into Whitehead's argument on the purification or clearing of the European mind, for it can extend to the domestication of spaces, as when wild spaces are cleared of disordered elements presumed to be clogging the advance of civilization. Another aspect that Whitehead addresses and that can be fruitful in challenging the above Cartesian view is *force* in the implementation of order, wherein civilization or domesticity is attained via *domination*. Specifically, according to Whitehead, "war, slavery, and governmental compulsion exemplify the reign of force."[17] Indeed, such civilizations have relied on "the sway of conquerors over conquered populations, and upon the rule of individual masters over slaves," a dominance that also extends to men ruling over women.[18]

On these two specific critiques—the Cartesian split and the concept of civilization by force—Whitehead's views of modern science and politics also acquire a liberational tone. When extending Whitehead's critique to what occurred in the Americas, it can be argued that European gnosis became equivalent to the supreme mind that could survey the lands and tabulate its species, while the barbaric or savage acquired the natural and mechanistic or utility qualities. Enrique Dussel, primarily targeting the Cartesian axiom of *cogito, ergo sum* in terms of the effects of coloniality in Latin America, addresses the matter of bodies inhabiting the outer geographical edges of modernity whose experiences of dispossession came by means of the violence that began in 1492. Domestication rendered them non-*Humanitas* as the whole earth was becoming a Cartesian *res extensa*, or an extension of

---

[16] Ibid., 141.
[17] Whitehead, *Adventures of Ideas*, 83.
[18] Ibid.

Europe's "I discover" and "I conquer" that denies the conquered their own exteriority (visibility).[19]

As a liberation philosopher, Dussel also departs from Whitehead, for whom "commerce is the great example of intercourse in the way of persuasion." For Dussel, with modernity also came the worship of the Christian God of capital that emerged not only from the Catholic Inquisition, but also from the Protestant ethic. In a more precise manner than Whitehead, Dussel draws attention to how mechanization became synonymous with the bodies of the non-*Humanitas*, since they were deemed more fit for labor than for rational thinking. Stripped from their gods and their sacredness, the Indigenous in Latin America, and later the Africans and American Indians, were no longer "*someone* distinct" but rather a being for plunder. The God of "I conquer," as Dussel states, also establishes a kind of *mimetic desire* that prompts society to hoard without limits and to impose money as a universal medium of value.[20] In the Americas, the value of flesh was weighed according to the balances of this system, corrupting every area of society.

Concerning natural environments, during colonial times the Americas (and Africa) were viewed as dark forests where savages and wild beasts could hide. There, civilized men would need to avert many dangers and the temptation to succumb to savagery, even when conquest was the true aim. Mark Woods in his book *Rethinking Wilderness* concludes that mastery over nature "became worldwide as European nations began their colonization of much of the world, beginning in the fifteenth century, and this 'completes the intellectual divorce of humankind from nature.'"[21] This would also be a Lockean ideal, declaring all "wilderness," especially that of the New World, as a gift from God meant for labor and privatization.[22]

Once conquered, the wild, new world could be paradoxically romanticized, perceived as a paradise, a Garden of Eden, and, as with some apocalyptic views in vogue at the time, a suitable land upon which to build the kingdom of God through its domestication.[23] The Europeans sought

---

[19] Enrique Dussel, *Beyond Philosophy: Ethics, History, Marxism, and Liberation Theology* (Lanham, MD: Rowan and Littlefield Publishers, 2003), 221.

[20] Ibid.

[21] Mark Woods, *Rethinking Wilderness* (Peterborough, Ontario, Canada: Broadview Press, 2017), 25.

[22] See, for example, John Locke's views on private property in his *Second Treatise of Civil Government* (1960), chapter 16.

[23] See *Apocalyptic Spirituality: Treatises and Letters of Lactantius, Adso of Montier-En-Der, Joachim of Fiore, the Spiritual Franciscans, Savonarola*, trans. and intro. Bernard McGinn, pref. Marjorie Reeves (New York: Paulist Press, 1979), esp. 97–148.

184   Wilding the Cosmos

to create societies that would mimic European civility. They were driven by an imaginary of economic gain through conquest of the wild. With the exponential increase of urbanization and decrease in the wilderness, Americans began to set up fences to preserve it and protected it from their own human harm.[24] For instance, in the United States, thinkers like Ralph Waldo Emerson, Henry David Thoreau, and John Muir, to name only a few, advocated for its preservation and pointed to the aesthetic, religious, and spiritual values inherent in wilderness.

But, with the US Wilderness Act in 1964, the term *wild* also became difficult to define. Parks and monuments gave options of reaching remote and untouched areas—an experience of the wild—from a hotel window.[25] Certainly, not all environmentalists have agreed on this concept of preservation, with some arguing that "wilderness preservation fails to preserve wilderness," and can be elitist, androcentric, ethnocentric, Eurocentric, and racist.[26] Indeed, the National Parks System was established as Indigenous peoples were displaced, relocated, dispossessed, and killed, and as the newly "unoccupied" lands were appropriated by the federal government.

Ironically, as tribal groups were being removed from their lands so that the wilderness could be protected from being *untrammeled*, the romanticism of the nineteenth century for wild spaces also led to what Highwater describes as "an upsurge in the study of primal cultures":

> The ignoble *savage* became noble—primal peoples were now depicted as living in perfect relationship with nature without strife or greed because they were deemed naturally good and unspoiled by the ravages of civilization. . . . [They] were thus balanced between two impossible images: innocence or evil, loftiness or lowness, perfection or imperfection. Nowhere in the precepts of the eighteenth-century religious rationalism or the nineteenth-century romanticism was there room for them to be simply human.[27]

Another irony is that economy, as Joseph R. Desjardins warily indicates, has also played a major role in the management of the wilderness through

---

[24] Mark Woods, "Wilderness," in *A Companion to Environmental Philosophy*, ed. Dale Jamieson (Malden: Blackwell Publishing, 2001), 352.

[25] Woods, *Rethinking Wilderness*, 26.

[26] Ibid., 11.

[27] Highwater, *The Primal Mind*, 27.

decisions made in Congress. Many of these decisions have hindered "long-range, rational, and efficient policy" due to the wants of diverse and opposing interest groups that Congress felt responsible for satisfying.[28] For example, for over one hundred years, and by the mid-1980s, the main mission of the US Forest Service has been "to furnish a continuous supply of timber," even as the Multiple-Use Sustained Yield Act (1960) requires that the forests be managed for recreational purposes and for the protection of waterways, fish, and wildlife.[29] The need for timber significantly increased with World War II because of the high demand for housing that privately owned timberlands could not provide. Also, the dependence on the sale of timber for the management of these resources put the national forests at risk of being under the control of those who "are willing to pay the most" for what the forests produce.[30] Several ways that it supplies this timber is through "fire suppression, research, and other custodial duties."[31] There are also forms of access like roads that make possible outdoor recreation and the sale of timber but that adversely affect the protection of wildlife and other natural resources.

How, then, to thwart the dominant aspects of civilization (many of which have become tools of racialization) from expanding to the next stages in scientific development of technology for the exploration of outer space when every area of society is so pervasively under the spell of *force*? One needs to explore the reasons for Whitehead's warning against cultivating a spirit of adventure that is heartlessly guided by domination, and yet add another against an advance in civilization that creates and is indifferent to inequality. Technology has vastly outpaced social progress. Domesticity remains an expression of a legal system ruled by elites who are blinded and indifferent to the ever-widening gaps that it creates on the path to "progress" and "development." Wealthy nations and individuals, driven by the same systems of coloniality, continue to keep some groups of the human collective impoverished and malnourished and deprive thousands of species of healthy and thriving ecosystems.

Ivan Vlasic provides the example of the widening trend of the "'capability gap' between a few technologically and economically advanced countries and

---

[28] Joseph R. Desjardins, *Environmental Ethics: An Introduction to Environmental Philosophy* (Boston: Wadsworth Cengage Learning, 2006), 53.

[29] Ibid., 50.

[30] Ibid., 54.

[31] Ibid., 50.

186   Wilding the Cosmos

the rest of the family of nations."[32] Much of the international "cooperation" (for example, agreements and initiatives) on outer space favors highly developed nations like the United States, which conspicuously holds most of the membership, and dominates the initiatives brought before specialized agencies of the United Nations. Furthermore, such "cooperation" often aims at transforming much less technologically developed nations into consumers. Bilateral agreements forged under the guise of being mutually benefiting commonly prevent disadvantaged nations from their autochthonous utilization of natural and human resources such as local knowhow and scientists who are well equipped to manage and protect the local resources.

Limitations to developing sustainable and equitable approaches to outer-space law are also due to the exorbitant allocation of resources on "the conquest of this new frontier"[33] at the expense of developing programs that alleviate inequality locally, nationally, and globally. As Vlasic states, "The political, economic, and psychological cost of the arms race makes it almost difficult to initiate any major joint program of space utilization which would benefit the needy peoples of the world."[34] For instance, the allocation of the resources of military technology in highly developed countries (for example, the focus on security) detracts from targeting far-reaching needs for food and healthy environments. Other issues that are also ignored when considering the "humane aspirations of the world community" are racial and gender inequalities compounded by the destruction of natural habitats needed for world flourishing.[35]

Is the dark cosmos the next wild expanse awaiting domestication through domination? Is the clearing of an alien wildness with a materialistic philosophy that establishes the limits of discourse concerning the dwelling of all beings, including exoplanetary beings, another casting of outer space to the *res extensa*? Outer space would then remain ruled by the rubrics of coloniality that sharply split *Humanitas* from non-*Humanitas*. Taming space or harnessing cosmic elements in ways similar to how wild or savage territories of Indigenous and Afro peoples were conquered here on earth condemns future chances for developing structures of cooperation by means of persuasion to the perils of annihilation.

---

[32] Ivan Vlasic, "The Relevance of International Law to Emerging Trends in the Law of Outer Space," in *The Future of the International Legal Order*, vol. 2: *Wealth and Resources*, ed. Richard A. Falk and Cyril E. Black (Princeton, NJ: Princeton University Press, 1970), 319.

[33] Ibid., 266.

[34] Ibid., 292.

[35] Ibid., 293.

Elaine Padilla   187

Outer Space:
The Last Frontier?

Today, the Cartesian axiom *cogito, ergo sum* has morphed into ego-politics with the idea of the technological revolution here on earth extended to the skies, a technology that, as Mignolo critiques, is not at the service of humanity but is putting humanity at its service.[36] The focus has been on the *homo faber* as the one who *fabricates* outer space by domestication through technological thinking that mirrors the one systemic power on earth. Global political agendas continue to fail to recognize the value of autonomy and flourishing of other life forms. The progressive transformation of outer space, for example, into the human image has been one major outcome of scientific advancements on technology that, while exemplary of human curiosity and creativity, have become mirrors for human admiration of itself. Thus, human sights need to steer toward vulnerable life forms other than human, and sympathetically become conscious of the "numerous trajectories of [nature's] entities and their relationships with one another" that are evident in the environments that humans inhabit and beyond.[37]

To Infinity and Beyond!

A trope emblematic of the spirit of conquest in the American imaginary is the cowboy, and the popular film that depicts its evolution into a rocket man is *Toy Story* (five versions 1995–2026), albeit, as a benign hero who saves humanity from annihilation. As the narrative progresses, the wound between being earthbound and heavenward is progressively healed, yet in such a manner that redemption is achieved by transcending earth-boundaries. The audience is presented with two tropes—the cowboy Woody and the rocket man Buzz Lightyear. At first, Woody and Buzz envision space antithetically. Woody, the cowboy (with all the cowboy gear except a gun), leads the toy-community and tends to daily matters of recreation and play, and even concerns himself with the welfare of the members of the toy-community. But Buzz is aimed heavenward. With his battery-powered wings and sonar sounding arm-weapon, he can fly "to infinity and beyond!" as he pulverizes any enemy that gets on his path.

---

[36] Mignolo, *Darker Side of Western Modernity*, 15.
[37] Keekok Lee, *The Natural and the Artefactual: The Implications of Deep Science and Deep Technology for Environmental Philosophy* (Oxford, MA: Lexington Books, 1999), 203.

188   *Wilding the Cosmos*

The tension between the past and the future of the toys' identities also makes possible an evolution in the consciousness of the child named Andy even beyond the film series that evolves into *Lightyear* (2022). Play goes back and forth, from a hand-held and manually wound cowboy that keeps peace in the land and sets order upon disorder, to a toy that elevates the child's imagination to the stars and planets above, eventually facing enemies solely in outer space. In addition, the film exposes the child to the challenges of technology such as constructing an identity produced *en masse* as well as the classic philosophical debate between transcendence and economy, and between chaos and order.

More poignantly, even as an imaginary play, *Toy Story* depicts two aspects in the human thirst for expanding new horizons: the conquest of the southwestern frontiers at the hands of the American cowboy, followed by the unquenching desire for the American domination of outer space represented in Buzz. In particular, Buzz symbolizes the human desire to imaginatively fly above the constraints of gravitation and freely traverse outer space with the mission to protect human life from extinction.

Subsequently, the drive for supremacy is shrouded by the myth that humanity will be saved through a cowboy-like technology. Believers in this messianic technology have argued that the challenges of today, such as pollution, scarcity of natural resources and food, and wealth inequality, can be overcome by building space colonies, as with Gerard O'Neil.[38] At the same time humanity is being prepared to face hostile life forms in outer space for which military might will be essential. So, a future redemption from any enemy forces would paradoxically be the result of purely benign actors, hence the belief in a human will that ultimately bridles its own technological prowess.

While not discussing the *Toy Story* series of films and *Lightyear*, Lee Worth Bailey traces the evolution of the "space cowboy" who as an archetypical hero surpasses the plain "rancher herding cattle" and the mythic nineteenth-century, gun-shooting cowboy in North American culture.[39] The Western cowboy led the pioneers to possess and domesticate the farthest and wildest frontiers. The use of gun powder as a mass-produced technology became symbolic of the "conquest of natives and of vast land" as well

---

[38] See Lee Worth Bailey, *The Enchantments of Technology* (Urbana: University of Illinois Press, 2010), 139–40; see also Gerard O'Neil, *The High Frontier: Human Colonies in Space* (New York: Morrow, 1977).

[39] Ibid., 122.

as of "crude phallic power over the more subtle but beautiful forces of the feminine and native Mother Earth."[40]

Certainly, the space cowboy also flies on the winged mythos of prior conquerors of the wild. The daring and bold voyage across oceans and seas initiated by Christopher Columbus at the turn of the fifteenth century, while some philosophers have described it as a meaningful expression of human adventure (including Whitehead), has made it possible for space cowboys to not only cross endless frontiers in the Americas, but also transgress many earthly limits. Elevation now allows for reaching for the infinite. As if "mounting on angel's wings," the conquest over earth's gravitation "offers vastly expanded spectacles of reality—seemingly ultimate reality—in outer space."[41] Quite the search for other paradisiacal forms of life that ironically remain under *the threat of falling*!

Furthermore, outer-space technology continues to be developed for the sake of military supremacy. For example, the dream of flying, from the start, has been overshadowed by a technology that aims at the domination of air space. Soon after Wilbur Wright demonstrated flying over an hour in France in 1908 and Orville Wright flew in Washington DC that same year, warplanes began to be mass produced (1909). About two decades later, after the invention of planes by the Wright brothers, and after Charles Lindbergh was the first to fly solo across the Atlantic (1927), bomber planes were flying across vast distances, as with the Boeing B-17 designed in the 1930s, one of the most used aircrafts in World War II.

Today, *the threat of falling* is illusorily averted by the weaponization of outer space. It is no secret that in the United States billions of dollars are invested yearly in national missile defense systems for the control of the dark, wild universe. The next Manifest Destiny is winning major conflicts soon carried in outer space, as Senator Bob Smith of New Hampshire (2001–2003) once declared, right as the United States was facing high alerts in security threats due to 9/11 and contemplating war against Iraq.[42] On February 2020, in his State of the Union Address, former president Donald J. Trump similarly stated: "Now we must embrace the next frontier, America's Manifest Destiny in the stars."[43] A picture-perfect example

---

[40] Ibid.

[41] Ibid., 124.

[42] See SpaceRef Editor, "Comments on Senate Floor regarding Space by Sen. Bob Smith," *SpaceRef* (November 20, 2002).

[43] See "Remarks by President Trump in State of the Union Address" (February 4, 2020).

190   *Wilding the Cosmos*

of this is Amazon founder Jeff Bezos, who wore the aviation glasses and cowboy hat of Amelia Hart for the news conference on the launching of his privately funded space vessel.[44]

Domesticating the Wild

Together with the impulse of conquest, one needs to acknowledge the human impulse of dwelling via domestication. Humans build structures, such as houses and roads, and develop systems and networks, some of which aim at cultivating good living. A large portion of technology has been essential in promoting this aim by preventing natural degradation, protecting species, improving environmental conditions, creating alternatives to human over-dependence on fossil fuels, and the like. In aiming at good living, humans have also sought to stretch their boundaries on earth and reach far-flung distances in outer space through their scientific discoveries.

This impulse toward flourishing derives from an innate urge that is characteristic of all living beings. Whitehead attributes this urge to a *feeling* of *transcendence* essential for adventure that stirs civilizations toward progress. Adventure particularly derives from an innate urge for zest in life bequeathed by the divine Eros of the Universe that thrives through modes of peace or harmony of diverse elements, becoming one actual entity that also surpasses all entities in what Whitehead calls the "Unity of Adventure."[45] The Eros of the Universe thus urges each living being toward "the realization of an ideal perfection" upon having prehended or received "all possibilities," yet as each entity belongs to a specific social milieu. Thus, an *ideal end* is meant as an expression of beauty that is not for the benefit of one entity alone, or as an event abstracted from this adventurous unity.[46]

In other words, to be alive is to dwell adventurously by inviting and welcoming novelty in outworn structures and systems! "Life refuses to be embalmed alive!"[47] Thus, domestication (*domus*), if viewed as the "original sin" that has separated us from a paradisiacal world of nature and the cosmos, is not only erroneous, as David Macauley argues,[48] but also impractical,

---

[44] See Noa Bronstein, "Jeff Bezos' Cowboy Hat Photo Links Him to a Lineage of Images Depicting a Desire to Colonize and Claim," *Toronto Star*, special issue, February 21, 2020.

[45] Whitehead, *Adventures of Ideas*, 295.

[46] Ibid.

[47] Whitehead, *Process and Reality*, 339.

[48] David Macauley, "Be-wildering Order: On Finding a Home for Domestication and the Domesticated Other," in *The Ecological Community: Environmental Challenges*

because humans have always built—and will continue to build—dwellings that guarantee their survival and also enable them to engage their natural environments and cosmic spaces with a deep sense of curiosity, awe, and novelty.

Certainly, there have been enough examples of robust understandings of the *oikos* that have maintained a healthy boundary between the domestic and the wild to demonstrate the potential of cultivating alternative meanings of human dwelling. During biblical times attitudes toward the wild varied from secluded spaces where jackals and evil reigned, to spaces of solitude where selected holy men, like Moses and Jesus, would strip themselves of vainglory and encounter the divine. This view has remained in place throughout the history of Christianity. As with the monastics, those who have befriended the wild have also endured many trials in purifying their souls from the impulse toward egotism, greed, and aggrandizement. Today, environmental ethicists like Larry Rasmussen have emphasized the practice of *enkrateia* or reduction of consumption by cultivating simplicity, as taught by St. Francis of Assisi in the thirteenth century.[49]

Today, also, outer-space technology is being developed for humanitarian and beneficial purposes. Vlasic provides the examples of artificial satellites used for "weather forecasting and cloud survey, for global transmission of voices and data, for transcontinental television broadcasting, for mapping and navigation, and for scientific investigation of the earth environment and of the solar system."[50] Some of these artificial satellite capabilities can be put into greater service of humanity. Vlasic also hopes for future programs targeting the alleviation of natural shortages through education, sustainable forms of agriculture and engineering, sanitation and medicine in less-developed countries, detection of environmental changes and insect invasions, soil conservation and crop-acreage-control programs, and detection of catastrophic weather patterns, among others. He incisively states the following about outer-space exploration: "There are few enterprises that could do more for the cause of international understanding and for peace in outer space than having scientists from different countries work together in the greatest adventure undertaken by man."[51]

---

for Philosophy, Politics, and Morality, ed. Roger S. Gottlieb (New York: Routledge, 1997), 106.

[49] Larry Rasmussen, "Drilling in the Cathedral," *Dialog: A Journal of Theology* 42, no. 3 (August 2003): 202–25.

[50] Vlasic, "The Relevance of International Law," 320.

[51] Ibid., 323.

192 Wilding the Cosmos

Still, there are no guarantees that human adventures always produce harmonious and beautiful outcomes. Often domestication of the environment, even if being a natural impetus for dwelling adventurously, lacks any reference to the very *oikos* (*oikumene*) that grounds it. Definitions of wildly inhabited spaces, for example, derive from egocentric tendencies that perceive unknown worlds as lacking control, hence their need for domestication, which requires the human *will* to create an orderliness suitable for meeting human necessities without grasping and honoring the complexity of interconnections comprised in the universe to which these wild spaces belong.

Commonly, this sense of order does not consider the uncommon ways in which *oikos* is defined by Indigenous or native peoples. One example is how the social progress toward home ownership is a foreign concept for many of them. The Maori believe that one belongs to the land, hence land cannot be acquired, sold, bought, or traded.[52] The term *belong* refers to being bound to the land by birth. The bond between person and land produces an allegiance, an attachment, a dependence that connotes intimacy, mutuality, and an identity that is inherently tied to the land of birth. In particular, American Indians "don't actually own their land; the federal government does," as Jonna Higgins-Freese and Jeff Tomhave argue.[53] Highwater has also challenged the use of the term *wilderness* as an opposite to dwelling, as though it were something other than "the natural state of the world."[54] Wilderness connotes that nature needs taming and harnessing, as when requiring cleanliness. Soiling oneself or being dirty in the English language renders nature obscene, hence the forceful way the wild is manicured or cast out so that humans can be kept safe from it.

Additionally, domestication is commonly reduced to the crude impulse for gratification in bottomless desire. Highwater laments the loss of "moving toward an eternal pole" as a guiding principle essential to understanding nature and the cosmos, as well as the peoples who view both as sacred.[55] Subsequently, *control*, in the sense of what Macauley calls "weeding out the wild"[56] within and beyond human spaces, weeds out the good and the sacred of domestic life and adversely affects all flourishing.

---

[52] Laurie Anne Whitt, et al., "Indigenous Perspectives," in Jamieson, *A Companion to Environmental Philosophy*, 5.

[53] Joanna Higgins-Freese and Jeff Tomhave, "Race, Sacrifice, and Native Lands," in *This Sacred Earth: Religion, Culture, and Environment*, 2nd ed., ed. Roger S. Gottlieb (New York: Routledge, 2004), 719.

[54] Highwater, *The Primal Mind*, 5.

[55] Ibid., 41.

[56] Macauley, "Be-wildering Order," 107.

Concerning the loss of sacredness of exoplanetary life, one example is the future of terraformation on other planets such as Mars—even if attaining these goals are *light-years* in the future. The inhospitable environment of Mars, Keekok Lee avers, must be "terraformed to render it fit for human colonization."[57] This effort toward Martian terraformation he describes as "the process of consciously and deliberately transforming a planet which does not possess the conditions—chemical, physical, geological—necessary for life to become one which can support not only plant but also animal, including, human life. In other words, to create a biosphere where none exists, turns Mars into an earth-like planet."[58]

Lee ponders the ethics of terraforming Mars. For anything emerging in it would be viewed as abiotic, meaning purely technological, useful insofar as it would make possible human life. Its forms of existence would be completely under human manipulation and control which would beg the question of the need for any present and future decisions based on values or morality. Unlike our planetary environment, Mars' biosphere and settings, if technology allows it, would not attain value in-itself and for-itself; hence, it could potentially become a colony, in other words, a territory solely dedicated to multiple forms of *slavery*.

Furthermore, the colonial views of the wild as savagery (for example, terrorism) continue to shape the systematic construction of a facade of sameness, a manicured society in which technology has become increasingly a totalitarian or dictatorial arm of domestication—the utmost expression of ego-politics. The domestication of the next frontier—outer-space colonization—is a result of international decisions being made here on earth that are mostly focused on national *security* issues that outer space appears to guarantee. A totalitarian system fortified with military dominance seems essential to the scientific development of technology, for it claims to advocate for human well-being while seamlessly occluding its instrumentation in guarding national interests. Thus, a human adventurous spirit reaching for the stars has been equated with "the quest for military supremacy" supplementing surveillance and wars.[59] Rather than opening humans to infinite

---

[57] Keekok Lee, "Colonization," in Jamieson, *A Companion to Environmental Philosophy*, 494.

[58] Ibid.

[59] Vlasic, "The Relevance of International Law," 281. One example is the "use of military personnel for nonmilitary missions," which allows for a variety of military uses of outer space that do not require compliance with international laws set by the UN General Assembly (277). Another example is the International Satellite Consortium

194   Wilding the Cosmos

possibilities, the messianic heroism of technology walls domestic life from the wild elements now represented by enemy nations and people groups, not to mention exoplanetary life forms.

One wonders how much human dependence on a watchman who, from his space station or artificial satellite dictates the limits of all social orders through the militarization of space, is turning into the panopticon about which Michel Foucault warned his readers. In agreement, Macauley avers:

> The scheme for this haunting mechanism of utilitarian rationality organizes space so as to create a visual order that permits both inmates and guards (or anyone for that matter) to be watched and controlled anonymously, continuously, and methodologically through small cells or "theatres" viewed from a central tower.[60]

This watchman is one of the gods of modernity, and humans are bowing down to it, perhaps unknowingly, since it has taken centuries and multiple events of terror to fashion it. Drawing from Whitehead, this dependence began with the transformation of "the Galilean vision of humility" into the conquering might of the Caesars being granted divine status.[61] To this Caesar, he compares the search for and undue reliance upon empiricism.[62] For him, this search points to the evolution of a cherished Messiah being fashioned "in the image of the Egyptian, Persian, and Roman imperial rulers" such that the "church gave unto God the attributes which belonged exclusively to Caesar."[63] The divine imperialization of this kind of singular power (for example, totalitarianism) was personified in a "moral energy" and an "ultimate philosophical principle" that today represent "the most natural, obvious idolatrous theistic symbolism at all epochs and places."[64] An excellent statement captures this concept well: "[Evil] is the violence of strength against strength," which refers to the attempt at obliterating "the

---

(Intelsat) that the United States owns and that provides information to subscribing nations (274).

[60] Macauley, "Be-wildering Order," 124. To explore more on the concept of the panopticon, see Michel Foucault, *Discipline and Punish: The Birth of the Prison*, trans. Alan Sheridan (New York: Vintage Books, 1979).

[61] Whitehead, *Process and Reality*, 342.

[62] Ibid., 174.

[63] Ibid., 342.

[64] Ibid., 343.

clash of vivid feelings" that would otherwise fortify each other through their differences and as each would meet in the novel unity of adventure.[65]

As if reflecting on these views of Caesar, Mignolo calls this transcendental aspect of modernity the "imperial Other,"[66] for it holds the power to establish all limits even when floating free of the boundaries that it creates for others. It exerts dominance by force, for this Other authorizes the "one mode of being and one mode of thinking—that is, the imperial mode of being where one thinks."[67] In other words, a skewed sense of adventure, which today is scientific and technological, has ironically become akin to an assembly-line machine being run by an invisible hand. Rather than transcendent freedom and vivid feelings, its aim is to impose sameness and totality by manufacturing existence according to its prescribed pattern or mold being overseen from above. In other words, a scientific transcendence *devoid of wonder* has resulted in a universality to which everyone must submit. Are we entering an era of not being able to deviate from the totalitarianism of technological advancement?

Far Nobler Adventures

The photo of the earth taken from the moon has become a mandala, an icon of the new awareness of the delicate and sacred wonder of our planet floating in space and supporting our incredible life system. Cultivating that consciousness, remembering who we are in the larger scheme of things, is both amazing and humbling. It is a spiritual shift of *focus away from dreams of conquering space* [emphasis added] to grateful respect for Mother Earth—not a moralistic sermon, but a silent peace with strong ethical implications.[68]

How to curb the human thirst for absolute power when looking at the cosmos, pondering its infinity, and longing for transcendence? What other options can be collectively pursued when wanting to thwart efforts that use scientific discoveries on outer-space technology as weapons of blunt force in today's arms race? One option can be promoting what Macauley calls a "wild order" that reconfigures "the walls of the human house and

---

[65] Whitehead, *Adventures of Ideas*, 275.

[66] Mignolo, *Darker Side of Western Modernity*, 114.

[67] Ibid., 101.

[68] Bailey, *The Enchantments of Technology*, 154.

196   Wilding the Cosmos

household—and [social theory's] notions of order, power, and space—so as to be more receptive to the encompassing natural world."[69]

Similarly, for Whitehead, the actualization of such "wild order" would depend on an "essential relatedness" when exercising freedom. Relatedness is the bond that helps manifest a freedom that neither abrogates complex levels of individuality nor the individualized responsibility for the community.[70] For this, coordination is essential to perfecting individuality.[71] In particular, he is critical of how nature has been a "faint echo" when conceptualizing contemporary society.[72] Thus, Whitehead asserts:

> The whole concept of absolute individuals with absolute rights, and with a contractual power of forming fully defined external relations, has broken down. The human being is inseparable from its environment in each occasion of its existence. The environment which the occasion inherits is immanent in it, and conversely it is immanent in the environment which it helps to transmit.[73]

Subsequently, one can cultivate a sacred wonder, as stated above, in response to the *free* rhythms of nature and the cosmos and a spirituality that enables us to reach a level of awareness of our interconnectivity with the whole of reality. A renewed sense of "response-ability" carries the potential for making decisions in reference to this planetary and cosmic whole. Put differently, reflective wonder can also inspire us to build structures and systems that are, according to Macauley, "interdependent, coparticipatory, and symbiotic" rather than antidemocratic and homogenizing in the form "unecological technologies."[74] The quotation above, based on Bailey's reflections on the many mystical experiences of astronauts, steers the human sight in new directions: "away from dreams of conquering space" and toward unity.[75]

From the perspective of Whitehead's "philosophy of organism," there is another principle unlike the "ruling Caesars"[76] at work: the choice to actualize our erotic urge in freedom and in union with planetary beings and the whole universe. Thus, a path into new directions in outer space can be paved

---

[69] Macauley, "Be-wildering Order," 105–6.
[70] Whitehead, *Adventures of Ideas*, 41–42.
[71] Ibid., 67.
[72] Ibid., 63.
[73] Ibid.
[74] Macauley, "Be-wildering Order," 130.
[75] Bailey, *The Enchantments of Technology*, 154.
[76] Whitehead, *Process and Reality*, 343.

when abstaining from domestication by *force* or domination, by approaching change with the quiet gentleness of *persuasion*, and by being patiently guided by *love*. Whitehead, for instance, indicates that some forms of unrest characterize the best elements of civilization such as curiosity, *adventure*, and change, if unrest is guided by persuasion as a "nobler alternative" to force.[77] He then recommends that societies cultivate (among two other aspects) an "intellectual curiosity leading to the enjoyment in the exchange of ideas."[78] For this curiosity to serve as guide for "ideal ends," humans need to also develop a "greater bond of sympathy" and a "conscious discrimination of such ends," founded on *respect* for humans as humans, so that "liberty of thought and action, required for the upward *adventure* [emphasis added] of life on this Earth," can be secured.[79]

Adventure nourished by bonds of sympathy derive from the prehension of the universe that is modified by an earthly and cosmic complexity, and conversely, a universe that is modified by the self. Whitehead calls this interaction "mutual relatedness."[80] Transcendence of the "here-now," and for this reason adventure, can be the result of multiple interactions, from subatomic to macro cosmic, in an "interlocked community."[81] Here Whitehead also points to the value of individuality as it contributes to the whole and as it receives access to the grandeur of the whole.[82] Like the desire for further exploring the dark cosmos, life is enticed to higher and more complex forms of enjoying the fruit of being urged toward transcendence via *persuasive love*, therefore, via union or interconnectedness with all things equally seeking their own higher forms of complexity—a wildly free kind of love. This would be a Whiteheadian view of infinity attained each moment through mutual relatedness rather than individual and hermetic substances.

An excellent example of cultivating consciousness of a persuasive and adventurous form of wild ordering is the experience of self-transformation that Charles A. Lindbergh, the first man to fly solo and nonstop across the Atlantic Ocean, describes in his Pulitzer Prize–winning book *Spirit of St. Louis*. Lindbergh wondered about God, the universe, and his place in relation to the whole. As if drawing from American Indian wisdom, he

---

[77] Whitehead, *Adventures of Ideas*, 83. For various applications of this "nobler alternative," see Andrew M. Davis, *From Force to Persuasion: Process Relational Perspectives on Power and the God of Love* (Eugene, OR: Cascade, 2024).

[78] Whitehead, *Adventures of Ideas*, 86.

[79] Ibid.

[80] Whitehead, *Science and the Modern World*, 151.

[81] Ibid., 152.

[82] Whitehead, *Adventures of Ideas*, 282.

198 Wilding the Cosmos

describes how he felt connected to "vaporous, ethereal beings," and "universal emanations of age-old, powerful forces . . . spirits . . . like old family and friends of past incarnations."[83] He came to understand transcendence as expanding oneself "through the universe outside; a part of all existence, powerless but without need for power; immersed in solitude; yet in contact with all creation."[84]

Astronaut Edgar Mitchell, an MIT nautical engineer, details similar experiences in his book *The Way of the Explorer*. Mitchell felt overcome by the wonder of gazing through 240,000 miles of space and by the overwhelming experience of a "universal connectedness" and of a universe that is "an intelligent, harmonious, and loving system."[85] Mitchell mentally, emotionally, and bodily extended into the universe as his spaceship became the medium for "an incredible personal, ecstatic union with the vast creative cosmic process."[86]

Bailey beautifully muses:

> Following in the arc of Lindbergh's visionary experience, Mitchell was touched by a new cosmic awareness. We might expect this from an Indian yogi, but from an astronaut, a practical MIT engineer? The enchantment of technology took a new turn that day, for the very machinery that took earthlings to the moon enabled one to break out of the mental mold that had guided him there in the first place. Seeing the earth and the heavens from a new viewpoint can shift consciousness out of the one-sided utilitarian, materialistic philosophy that builds the rockets. This view opened the astronauts up into a broader, totally unexpected, and transforming spiritual vision.[87]

This sense of cosmic participation led to a *metanoia*, a turn in direction. For example, Mitchell began to struggle with materialistic philosophies that emphasized dualistic views of nature and to understand the crumbling edifice of the Cartesian separation of mind and matter. Mitchell embraced principles of quantum physics such as the *interconnectedness* and

---

[83] Bailey, *The Enchantments of Technology*, 134, citing Charles A. Lindbergh, *Spirit of St. Louis* (New York: Scribner's and Sons, 1953), 389–90.

[84] Ibid., citing Lindbergh, 353.

[85] Ibid., 149, citing Edgar Mitchell, *The Way of the Explorer* (New York: Putnam's, 1996), 3, 138.

[86] Ibid., 150, citing Mitchell, 58, 59.

[87] Bailey, *The Enchantments of Technology*, 149.

non-locality of wave particles that "behave as *fields*, filling all space."[88] He also began to understand the value of applying religion to scientific discoveries. Mitchell even pondered the meaning of transcendence in religious terms (for example, *nirvana, samadhi,* and *union with God*). He defined it as the eternal beings that all living things are and as the language and rhythms of the universe that pass through us as much as ours here on earth resonate "throughout the universe."[89] Such cosmic epiphanies, resulting in *metanoia,* Mitchell muses, can be experienced in "small, everyday ways."[90]

Not unlike this outer-space experience, in the "philosophy of organism," transcendence lies in the experience of the unity of adventure and *metanoia* results from discernment or discrimination of "ideal ends," thus from choosing to think and act nobly when being adventurous. For Whitehead, having no understanding of the world and not savoring the emotions being evoked in an event mean missing the vividness that adventures are meant to inspire. Vividness can be remembered, hence stimulating curiosity and desire for learning how to develop complex levels of consciousness. True social progress depends on vividness. A "living civilization requires learning" that lies beyond passive knowledge.[91]

Furthermore, active knowledge equals discernment, for *persuasive* power resides in the moment of "decision of the immediate subject-superject, constituting the modification of subjective aim."[92] This instance, according to Whitehead, is "the foundation of our experience of *responsibility,* of approbation or disapprobation, of self-approval or self-reproach, *of freedom,* of emphasis" [emphasis added].[93] Each actual entity must take the past into itself (must reach out and prehend other actual entities) and actualize eternal objects, thereby creating itself out of past events and future possibilities. Responsibility equals decision—a kind of "cutting off"—for oneself and for others that supersedes any decision being made. Actuality depends on discrimination, responsibility, or decision amid potentiality, the outcome of which is the enjoyment of the many entering a complex unity or becoming one, novel entity, "diverse from any entity in the 'many' which it unifies" and leaves.[94] As Whitehead summarizes: "The many become one,

---

[88] Ibid., 151, citing Mitchell, 107, 110.
[89] Ibid., 153, citing Michell, 213.
[90] Ibid., 151, citing Mitchell, 70.
[91] Whitehead, *Adventures of Ideas,* 279.
[92] Whitehead, *Process and Reality,* 47.
[93] Ibid.
[94] Ibid., 21.

200   Wilding the Cosmos

and are increased by one."[95] Therefore, each entity becomes the potentiality in processes of decision-making of other entities, which adds meaning beyond its actuality.

To me, this kind of adventure would be the *wild* element, or the element of cooperative freedom, of departure away from the blunt force of space conquest and toward respecting and honoring life both individually and collectively. Ultimately, freedom to choose a future that deviates from things destructive and violent can surpass our present utilization of outer-space technology. As such, the complex unity of a world-cosmos that is imbued with the divine element, the Eros of the universe, will continue to urge toward far more novel forms of existence that are universally beneficial.

To unpack this option for cultivating *metanoia* upon having developed an appreciation for a wildly ordered cosmos, one needs to understand how the antidote to blunt force, *persuasive love*,[96] can be practically employed through international diplomacy. As Vlasic astutely points out, in contemporary times, politics of outer space also remain a mirror image of earth's systems of cooperation.[97] For example, some domesticity of outer space has been positively the result of dialogue among nations for the establishment of monitoring systems on the development of space technology.

In 1958, the General Assembly of the United Nations adopted *A Resolution, the Question of the Peaceful Uses of Outer Space*,[98] which expressed a global desire for cooperation in the utilization of resources in outer space. Another resolution was adopted in 1961, stating that no nation could appropriate outer space and celestial bodies for its sole benefit. Also, by 1962, the Charter of the United Nations put in place a registry requiring information on all object-launchings into orbit. Other initiatives have been promoted and approved by the United Nations prescribing codes of conduct that promote international peace, security, and cooperation; requiring authorization and supervision; and calling for responsible use of outer space, among others.

Additionally, the Moscow Treaty Banning Nuclear Weapon Tests in the Atmosphere, in Outer Space, and Under Water, adopted in 1963 by more than one hundred nations (even as it was aimed for Russia and the United States), is still in effect. It was followed by another resolution (number 1884)

---

[95] Ibid.
[96] Ibid., 343.
[97] Vlasic, "The Relevance of International Law," 265.
[98] Ibid., 270.

that year which banned the orbiting of space objects with nuclear weapons or "any other kind of weapons of mass destruction," their installation on celestial bodies, or their stationing in any way.[99] Still, the arms race continues to catch the attention of many scientists who warn against the threat of anti-ballistic-missile (ABM) defenses that can be equally destructive. Furthermore, so that these resolutions can more fully attain ideal ends, they would need to abandon goals of exploration more pressingly as means of "*exploitation* of outer space for the benefit of mankind."[100] The presumption of an equality that is not yet existent among all nations, as already argued, remains too high a risk to ignore.

Thus, in considering the use of persuasive love as a practical solution to exploitation, intellectual curiosity needs to be perceived as potentially transformative of the past "into a new creation" in surpassing manner even to these diplomatic efforts.[101] Whitehead quips: "A race preserves its vigour so long as it harbours a real contrast between what has been and what may be; and so long as it is nerved by the vigour to adventure beyond the safeties of the past. Without adventure civilization is in full decay."[102] While these statements can be interpreted in various ways, as a limitless routing of novelty to benefit the powerful, for example, the spirit behind *vigorous* or resilient pursuit of alternatives is meant for counteracting the use of force. While the future is grounded in the past, it is also infinite in that eternal objects or numberless ideals are bequeathed to it while being limited or tempered by an already actualized world.

For this aspect of adventure to remain *vividly* manifested, prehensions or feelings that appear contrary or contrasting cannot be denied or anesthetized; rather, the clash must be a welcomed outcome that results in novel unity or a unity of adventure that makes room for peace or a harmony of contrasts. Otherwise, "violence of strength against strength" results and evil occurs.[103] The far nobler alternative to what has been already accomplished, in other words, is to expand spatial limits in the direction of intense contrasts or the welcome of difference in democratic ways. When absorbed by "a new unity with ideals and with anticipation," the decisions made can

---

[99] Ibid., 273; see also A. E. Gottlieb, "Nuclear Weapons in Outer Space," *Canadian Yearbook of International Law*, III (1965), 3.

[100] Ibid., 270; see also UN General Assembly, Resolution 1348 (XIII), December 13, 1958.

[101] Whitehead, *Adventures of Ideas*, 275.

[102] Ibid., 279.

[103] Ibid., 276.

202 *Wilding the Cosmos*

result in the transformation of the whole of reality, an ongoing process that Whitehead attributes to "the creative Eros" of the universe.[104]

In other words, the spirit of conquest that has ruled from past to present times can be overcome and society can move in the direction of mutually beneficial relatedness because of the awareness of "internal relatedness to the world," and hence the potential of developing *empathy* instead of egotism.[105] Such entanglements endure through time so the potential for actualization, even if not presently manifested, can be *"advent-ual."* We come full circle. A spirituality that cultivates awe awakens consciousness to one's interconnectedness with the whole and informs human decision for planetary and cosmic well-being. The ability to respond derives from the persuasive love of the Eros of the Universe that continuously beckons all creatures to actualize flourishing. What remains is a truly hospitable welcome of difference.

Ancient Wisdoms

> In beauty I walk
> With beauty before me, I walk.
> With beauty behind me, I walk.
> With beauty below me, I walk.
> With beauty above me, I walk.
> With beauty all around me, I walk.
> It is finished in beauty.[106]

So that adventure rides on the wings of persuasive love, one would need to further redirect Whitehead's concept of *respect* for humans as humans and of "upward *adventure* [emphasis added] of life on this Earth" even beyond his cosmic sights.[107] In other words, politics of outer space must focus on planetary well-being and foster peace on earth beyond Whitehead. For this, one needs to temper his optimism of European civilization. A critique based on the environmental racism now influencing the decisions made with respect to exoplanetary life in the use of space technology needs to be followed by an engagement of far more ancient wisdoms than those found in Whiteheadian philosophies. There is a certain hubris that prevails in the

---

[104] Ibid.

[105] Whitehead, *Science and the Modern World*, 151–52.

[106] Donald J. Hughes, *American Indian Ecology* (El Paso: Texas Western Press, 1987), 13, citing Washington Mathews, "Navajo Legends," *American Folklore Society Memoirs* 5 (1879): 273–75.

[107] Whitehead, *Adventures of Ideas*, 86.

field of philosophy, particularly when drawing from or focusing on science to address matters of technology, as if the ancient wisdoms of Indigenous cultures have very little to say about outer-space ethics. The opposite is the case.

A Whiteheadian self-critique can begin with the meaning of ideal ends when considering how the concept of an *ideal end* has commonly been equated with European and Anglo worldviews. To upward "lifts" in Platonic style have been attributed the redemptive, salvific, and heroic acts of the European race in its encounters with native others. Conversely, native others have been perceived as needing to be "lifted" away from their biography and geography, as needing an upward movement requiring the relinquishment of their worldviews. For example, Whitehead unexpectedly describes the voyage of Christopher Columbus in highly positive ways. This event illustrates human adventures that have led to the rise of new nations akin to European civilization. While factual and historical, he gives this example to support an understanding of civilization dependent on the "adventure of the imagination" and the human capacity "to anticipate the physical adventures of exploration," as a way for "dreaming of things to come" that are realized in due time even when aspects of it remain unactualized.[108]

With this kind of exploration Whitehead is not referring to the patient and tender effects of the divine lure, or to the persistence of eternal objects in actualizing eternal values like harmony, love, or peace at an opportune moment, but rather to how Columbus initially intended to find a new commercial route to the East yet arrived in lands not explored by Europeans until then. And look where we are now! See the grandeur of American civilization! Therefore, while Whitehead is critical of war and the use of force in civilizing humanity, and assumes that adventure rarely "reaches its predetermined end," he fails to specifically challenge the impetus of conquest associated with Columbus's voyage and other European sails across the Atlantic, adventures that resulted in the subjugation of numberless native populations of the Americas.

Whitehead even lauds the social evolution of European civilization here on American soil. He, for instance, equates it with the biology of fast growth by highlighting the success of organisms that "modify their environment" in ways that assist each other.[109] While there is much to unpack from this statement, he contrasts this kind of growth with the North American Indians, whose "population barely succeeded in maintaining themselves over the

---

[108] Whitehead, *Science and the Modern World*, 108–9.
[109] Ibid., 205.

204 *Wilding the Cosmos*

whole continent."[110] He then compares the Indigenous' lack of willingness to modify their environment in cooperation with one another (for example, lack of industry) to the European races who arrived at the continent much later and practiced contrary policies (for example, Protestant ethic). Concerning the Europeans, Whitehead surmises: "They at once cooperated in modifying their environment. The result is that a population more than twenty times that of the Indian population now occupies the same territory, and the continent is not yet full."[111]

Last, to the above two concepts one needs to add how for Whitehead commerce serves as an example of persuasive power in modern times. In defining civilization as the "maintenance of social order" by which persuasion would be the "nobler alternative," he acknowledges that "the recourse of force" can be unavoidable.[112] To illustrate, unrest can pave the way for societies to embrace some freshness of ideas that are commonly associated with "curiosity, adventure, and change."[113] Furthermore, so that civilized society thrives, it needs to keep alive its most humane principles as it also recognizes and surpasses its imperfections. It is in this context, as he is contrasting persuasion with the force of "war, slavery, and governmental compulsion" that he states: "Commerce is the great example of intercourse in the way of persuasion."[114] Today, and even in his lifetime, evidence has demonstrated that commerce is anything but persuasive. Its tentacles have reached across nations to impoverish Indigenous peoples of Latin America and across local territories to dispossess American Indians, not to mention how commerce has spearheaded environmental and exoplanetary exploitation since the start of modernity.

For these reasons the cosmos needs *rewilding*, not only in acknowledging the value of its galactic freedom—in itself and for itself—within the continuum of solidarity, but also because of the impact that freedom can have when opting for non-capitalistic ways of dealing with the earth and the cosmos, and when humbly welcoming so-called wild and savage alternatives to philosophical discourse. Again, one can acknowledge how exploration as an expression of adventure is innate to living beings' planetary existence and in outer space. The whole of life explores because of curiosity, creativity, and desire for physical well-being and intellective progress toward fuller

---

[110] Ibid.
[111] Ibid., 206.
[112] Whitehead, *Adventures of Ideas*, 83.
[113] Ibid.
[114] Ibid.

Elaine Padilla   205

expressions of a flourishing existence. But how about the element of surprise when encountering wild otherness? To further temper the idealization of Western civilization, one needs to also acknowledge how "diversity is the incurable but marvelous affliction" of Eurocentrism, as Highwater states in drawing from Antonio Machado-Ruiz.[115]

The hubris stemming from being civilized, technological, and scientifically rational, solely in Western terms, impoverishes everyone. For instance, in 2018, a group of Indigenous scholars was invited to attend a conversation on the search for extraterrestrial intelligence at the Berkeley SETI Research Center. These Indigenous scholars "challenged the language of expansion, frontiers, and conquest."[116] For them, when investigating the possibilities of encountering civilizations in outer space, the movement of "settlers taking Indigenous land and trying to eliminate Indigenous cultures" was recalled. These critiques, however, were not engaged in depth. Instead, "some of the SETI researchers were dismissive, even carrying on their own conversations during the scholars' presentation." The basis for this behavior among scientists starts much earlier in STEM programs that discourage students from applying Indigenous ways of thinking and knowing to scientific knowledge and training. Thus, another Indigenous scholar lamented:

> From a young age, Indigenous students are taught that their perspectives are not valid in classrooms. This, in turn, pushes them away from STEM fields. If education systems were to include some Indigenous knowledge, scientists from Indigenous groups might be better positioned to influence the conversation. Additionally, she said that the stories Western countries tell about the exploration of the Earth need to change.[117]

Hence, an inquiry into modern science needs to be voiced from the outer boundaries of the so-called savage, the primitive, the barbarian, the *wildling*. To them belong the silenced and emptied space of "being/not" human enough—the non-*Humanitas*. Their ancestral memories and ways of being human have been doomed to invisibility; they have been regarded as neither one nor many. From these contexts of wildness, to wonder then also means to ask questions about patterns of control established via scientism. As

---

[115] Highwater, *The Primal Mind*, 10.

[116] See Doug Johnson, "Decolonizing the Search for Extraterrestrial Life," *Undark* (April 4, 2022).

[117] Ibid.

206   *Wilding the Cosmos*

stated above, this global system of power—much of which is commercial and militaristic—assumes non-presence in the sense of being untouched by any cultural background, even as its effects are ever present. On this also, one would need to wonder about *ideal ends* that do not account for the philosophies and wisdoms of the very peoples against whom force has been bluntly exerted through a regime of sameness and ego-politics—the politics of the *one* conquering Caesar.

A Galilean humility can offer a path forward as one listens to seldom-heard stories of the past. Ancient wisdoms have walked in beauty, as expressed in the poem above, long before Whitehead and other Western philosophies of organism set foot on American soil. Their philosophies have always been ecological, as they have believed they are part of a sacred and internally related whole. Because of a deep awareness to their kinship to other living beings, this interrelational web is also highly democratic. For "every form of life has the right to live, perpetuate its species, and follow the way of its own being as a conscious fellow creature."[118] In addition, to the Indigenous, principles of relatedness are not mere ideas. They are a way of life, like breathing air. All natural elements on earth and the sky compose an interconnected and even ancestral reality. Chief Seattle delivered the following speech before the governor of the Washington territory in 1853:

> Our dead never forget the beautiful world that gave them being. They still love its verdant valleys, its murmuring rivers, its magnificent mountains, sequestered vales and verdant lined lakes and bays. . . .
>
> Every part of this soil is sacred in the estimation of my people. Every hillside, every valley, every plain and grove, has been hallowed by some sad and happy event in days long vanished. Even the rocks, which seem to be dumb, and dead as they swelter in the sun along the silent shore, thrill with memories of stirring events connected with the lives of my peoples.[119]

Their ethic is "protecting and life-preserving" in all spheres of life and all spaces on earth as well as the cosmos.[120] There is nothing living that is expendable. Each entity plays a unique role in sustaining life. To appreciate each contribution "requires intimate knowledge, familiarity" with how each

---

[118] Hughes, *American Indian Ecology*, 17.

[119] Ibid., 11; see W. C. Vanderwerth, ed., *Indian Oratory: Famous Speeches by Noted Indian Chieftains* (Norman: University of Oklahoma Press, 1971), 120–21.

[120] Ibid., 18.

completes the whole to avoid "inappropriate treatment" or responding in ways that hinder "its vital function."[121] Contrary to the spirit of conquest, for instance, life beyond earth cannot be exploited, but rather must be revered and loved for its intrinsic value. As J. Donald Hughes states: "The most powerful in the universe are not necessarily friendly or hostile to mankind, but rather indispensable parts of a carefully balanced whole, and therefore tend to sustain and preserve humanity along with everything else as long as the balance is not upset."[122] By powerful, American Indians do not mean technologically and militaristically advanced, because exoplanetary, conscious beings could be even less concerned than humans with such ideas of expansion.

For these reasons awareness of the problems of the racialization of the environment and the weaponization of outer space would not be enough; one needs to change behaviors, advocate for "holistic and systemic solutions," and develop networks and partnerships that integrate and give power to marginalized peoples and nations.[123] If many of the Indigenous beliefs and practices already recognize the sacred value of every space, earthly and cosmic, why not examine Western philosophical principles and heed the wisdoms integral to Indigenous worldviews? Nobler alternatives to human adventure can also be informed in dialog with these wild and novel ideals.

One noble alternative is already being posited regarding extraterrestrial intelligence by Indigenous scholars who have argued that one reason why humans have not encountered civilizations beyond earth is because of what they call the sustainability solution.[124] Differing from the Fermi solution, with emphasis on exponential population growth and resource depletion exacerbated by interstellar colonization (in the likes of human colonization), the sustainability solution focuses on intelligent life capable of interstellar travel and exponential growth, yet opting for far-more-sustainable solutions than humans. Some of these can be slow growth patterns, the maintenance of some planetary life such as undisturbed wildlife preserves (for example, the earth), and migratory patterns that do not exhaust the resources of the planets or enslave its inhabitants. A more sober reason can be that some exoplanetary life has undergone extinction due to unsustainable practices.

Sharing a similar sentiment, Bailey, insightfully asks:

---

[121] Whitt, et al., "Indigenous Perspectives," 13.

[122] Ibid., 15.

[123] Higgins-Freese and Tomhave, "Race, Sacrifice, and Native Lands," 719.

[124] Jacob D. Haqq-Misra and Seth D. Baum, "The Sustainability Solution to the Fermi Paradox," *American Indian Culture and Research Journal* 62 (2009): 47–51.

208   Wilding the Cosmos

But what if we did encounter aliens who told us that the universe is a caring, soulful place, that we are too obsessed with technology, too aggressive, greedy, domineering, and patriarchal, and that we should stop war and ecological disaster, spread wealth evenly, and give everyone full equality? Could we accept such meanings?[125]

Certainly, hope against hope remains vital when considering the need for higher levels of persuasive love. A grander adventure in outer-space exploration awaits us if humbly making room in the universe for otherness, especially, Indigenous wisdoms to resonate and vibrate within us. This would be a hospitable response to the enticing process of the divine eros by which philosophers can boldly welcome the yonder of one's limited perspectives to the table. An adventurous quest of knowing an other's ways of thinking and doing can halt the expansion of human narcissism to the outer limits of space and perhaps instead anticipate exoplanetary intelligence eager to engage human, noble adventures for its own enrichment and joy.

Closing Remarks

How, then, could the wild element of adventure be a force that can weaken the power of coloniality holding sway today? *When humans abstain from eradicating freedom* or, more optimistically put, when humans enable autonomy or the authentic and spontaneous expressions of the many, the wild element can have a positive impact on the emergence of new world orders. The value added can be in how wildness is beyond commodification and is that piece of the universe that my "I" cannot possess, the wild that escapes my grasp. Not only would we want to *temper* the devastation of our planet's resources, but also the impetus of conquest already informing solutions to the scarcities that we have created as we search for signs of a sustaining life in the universe.

Thus, we need to offer a counter-memory to "colonialism's violent erasure" and to the "devastation of the era of discovery" that novel perceptions of nature and the cosmos can furnish.[126] One way is to unearth buried wisdoms, such as those of American Indians, for whom kinship to the land and the cosmos is ancestral, so that our present time can be renewed.

---

[125] Bailey, *The Enchantments of Technology*, 142.
[126] George E. Handley, *New World Poetics: Nature and the Atlantic Imagination of Whitman, Neruda, and Walcott* (Athens: The University of Georgia Press, 2007), 6.

Ancestral memories, human *and beyond,* that have been cast to the darker side of Western modernity can come back to life within the complex web of relationships. There is not a facile dismissal of colonial history or neocolonial global power. Neither would it be a symptom of nostalgic yearning for purity and a return to innocence, but rather a counter-memory to a past that, as George Handley puts it, "might otherwise appear to be a 'virgin' landscape."[127]

For this wild principle to become pluriversal, one needs to welcome "the unexplored, unexpected, and inexplicably foreign dimension" of the cosmos to become a part of our "*material* imagination."[128] Between the cosmos as is and the cosmos as *created* lies the imaginary. The imagination mediates the world out there and creativity as it brings them together or puts them in relationship with divine novelty. When being seized by wildness, the randomness of lived experience and the expanse opening before it can actualize the kind of freedom of novelty in a complex unity at which the philosophy of organism aims. In some paradoxical form, wildness brings balance. Therefore, as the cosmos articulates its order and purposes, a "wild order" can inform the imagination.

Again, this wildness is not the antithesis of domestication or urban life. The intent is to minimize the domestication (from the term *domus,* which means "house") of world and cosmos, to abstain from taming it or civilizing it *according to one global power.* Awareness of creative evolution at a cosmic scale could deter confining wildness to a prescribed human order and dominant social norms. The discursive community can interpret and articulate planetary and intergalactic adventures as conducive for well-being and reflect on theories of the cosmos that reveal "a culture's cosmology" that both reflects space and time in terms of social action and vice versa as a social action that can reflect space and time.[129]

Now let us imagine ourselves once again resting flat on our backs with our legs bent and feet on the ground, peering upward toward the sky atop the Claremont Hills Wilderness Park. Whitehead's concept of a complex unity invites us to silence. Vastness turns microcosmic, shrinks in size, as the senses are finely attuned for an encounter with immensity. The world space and intimate space interconnect within a wildly free, persuasive, and loving unity of adventure. This is an ongoing world-cosmic dance that entices the

---

[127] Ibid., 9.

[128] Sean Miller, *Strung Together: The Cultural Currency of String Theory as a Scientific Imaginary* (Ann Arbor: University of Michigan Press, 2013), 35.

[129] Ibid., 199.

many to become one and then add to the satisfaction and enjoyment of numberless others. Vastness, the voluptuousness of the wild, envelops the event so that humanity can also become conscious of itself anew with and beyond humanity itself. May the wilding of the cosmos continue!

Cosmic Personalization

Teilhard's Omega and the Direction of Evolution

Ilia Delio

The whole future of the Earth, as of religion, seems to me to depend on the awakening of our faith in the future.
—Pierre Teilhard de Chardin

What is the direction of evolution? Does evolution have a direction? These are interesting questions to reconsider today in light of complexity science and systems biology. Until recently, most scientists rejected orthogenesis, which posits that organisms evolve in a particular direction due to some internal mechanism or driving force and are not merely sporadic or fortuitous. They argued instead that evolution is based only on natural selection, adaptation, and random mutations, principles that undergird survival but not necessarily direction. Recently, however, scientists such as evolutionary biologist David Sloan Wilson and cyberneticist Francis Heylighen, among others, have revisited the question of direction in evolution, turning to the ideas of Pierre Teilhard de Chardin and his notion of the noosphere. Teilhard was a scientist, naturalist, geologist, and Catholic priest who sought a comprehensive understanding of human nature, in both interior and exterior dimensions. His work anticipated developments in evolutionary biology not realized until the latter half of the twentieth century, including the rise of the noosphere, a level of thought now enhanced by the internet and artificial intelligence.

This chapter aims to explicate Teilhard's ideas on Omega and the noosphere in terms of cosmic personalization and emergence of a personalized

212   *Cosmic Personalization*

holism expressed in thought and action. The story of directed evolution supported by Wilson and his colleagues becomes even more engaging when Teilhard's ideas on the Omega principle are illuminated. This chapter suggests that a new synthesis of science and religion will better support us as architects of the future.

Teilhard's Cosmic Holism

Teilhard was a Catholic priest who did not hold to a doctrine of creation or an explicit theological anthropology and rejected original sin as a straitjacket that side-tracked the human person as a phenomenon of nature and ignored the basic elements of evolution. His methodology was unique. To understand it, I begin with the introduction of his *Human Phenomenon* by Sarah Appleton-Weber and the reason she re-translated the title and text from the 1959 translation by Bernard Wall.

The subject of the human phenomenon was developed by Teilhard in three earlier essays of 1925, 1928 and 1930. He wrote *The Human Phenomenon* at a time of war, "from a sense of organic crisis in evolution, to free humanity from fear and despair so as to give new hope and heart for life."[1] This work frames his comprehensive vision of science and religion; its stated purpose is to introduce the reader to the "epic and drama of space-time."[2] He composed it not as a work of metaphysics, still less as a theological essay, but simply as a scientific treatise.[3]

In the revised edition of *The Human Phenomenon*, Appleton-Weber writes that the title of the 1959 translation, *The Phenomenon of Man*, is incorrect because Teilhard's subject of this work is not the phenomenon of man as one among other species, but the ever-evolving human phenomenon, as it is developing in and around us at this very moment. According to Appleton-Weber, the 1959 translation seemed blind to the biological reality of collective unity in *The Human Phenomenon*. The older text distorted the cosmic whole by mispresenting the relationship of the part or "element" within the whole. It failed to recognize that the human phenomenon is a

---

[1] Sarah Appleton-Weber, "Introduction," Pierre Teilhard de Chardin, *The Human Phenomenon* (Brighton: Sussex Academic Press, 1999), xxi.

[2] Ibid.

[3] Pierre Teilhard de Chardin, *The Phenomenon of Man*, trans. Bernard Wall (New York: Harper and Row, 1959), 29.

unique biological, collective, and global phenomenon whose past, present, and future are intimately bound up with the formation, life, and ultimate transformation of the earth. The magnitude of the human phenomenon is on the level of matter's first forming of the planet earth; the human phenomenon represents a new zone in the universe, independent, yet somehow born of the entire maturation of the earth. Humanity is the earth (we can even say nature) "hominized."[4]

In the opening pages of *The Human Phenomenon* Teilhard states: "Nothing but the phenomenon. Do not look in these pages for an explanation of the world, but only an introduction to an explanation."[5] The purpose of the work is not to discover a system of ontological and causal relations among the elements of the universe but an *experimental law of recurrence* that operates at different levels of successive appearance in the course of time. The human phenomenon is basically experiential, and the work seeks to recognize the whole in movement, which neither science alone nor philosophy or theology alone can explain:

Just like meridians as they approach the pole, so science, philosophy and religion necessarily converge in the vicinity of the whole. They converge without merging and never ceasing to know the real from different angles.[6]

The "whole" is an irreducible presence that is relational and contingent, yet distinct. Appleton-Weber writes: "It [the whole] has a mysterious unity and active power in itself—a birth, unfolding, and a passing. Humanity belongs to this category."[7] The whole signifies that collective reality is more than the sum total of its parts. Each part is a whole, and each whole is more than the sum of the parts. Teilhard indicates that "the more we cleave and pulverize matter, the more we can see its fundamental unity. . . . There are no isolated things in the world. There are only elements of a whole in process."[8] Those who see are those who have the sense of the world as a unified whole. Those who do not see, do not see beyond the multiple. They perceive the world as fragmented and ultimately absurd [or fallen]. If the

---

[4] Appleton-Weber, "Introduction," xviii.
[5] Teilhard, *The Human Phenomenon*, 1.
[6] Ibid., 2.
[7] Appleton-Weber, "Introduction," xix.
[8] Ibid.

214 *Cosmic Personalization*

human is a fragment of the whole (comparable to a fossil), what is the whole of human existence? Albert Einstein captured the human phenomenon when he wrote:

> A human being is a spatially and temporally limited piece of the whole, what we call the "Universe." He experiences himself and his feelings as separate from the rest, an optical illusion of his consciousness. The quest for liberation from this bondage [or illusion] is the only object of true religion.[9]

Similarly, Teilhard wrote in 1942 that in studying the history of the cosmos and of all forms of life,

> we have gradually come to understand that no elemental thread in the Universe is wholly independent in its growth of its neighboring threads. Each forms part of a sheaf; and the sheaf in turn represents a higher order of thread in a still larger sheaf—and so on indefinitely. . . . This is the organic whole of which today we find ourselves to be a part, without being able to escape from it. . . . In countless subtle ways, the concept of Evolution has been weaving its web around us. We believed that we did not change; but now . . . we are becoming aware of the world in which neo-Time, organizing and conferring a dynamic upon Space, is endowing the totality of our knowledge and beliefs with a new structure and a new direction.[10]

Teilhard created a developmental narrative in *The Human Phenomenon* based on the relationship of part to whole so that in each section:
- first the element is presented;
- then the whole of which it is a part; and
- then the whole is set within its context of the global evolution of the earth.

Teilhard rejects metaphor but uses language of analogy, reflecting the idea that the human phenomenon is part of nature; he strives for language that expresses the developmental patterns of nature. For example, terms like

---

[9] Albert Einstein, "Letter of 1950," *New York Times*, March 29, 1972, quoted in Bryce Haymond, "Einstein's Misquote on the Illusion of Feeling Separate from the Whole," blog.

[10] Pierre Teilhard de Chardin, *The Future of Man*, trans. Norman Denny (New York: Image Books, 2004), 74–89.

grow or *develop* become more inclusive in their application as the world progresses. "A term may embrace more than one domain, and the terms from one domain may be applied to another, expressing a fundamental difference yet continuity of development."[11] For example, Teilhard uses the term *aggregate* to describe the loose form of grouping at the level of the cell or isolated groups of cells but goes on to use the same term to describe the collective reality of humanity as a super-aggregation.[12] Or, extending back in time from the human being, in a descending direction, Teilhard integrates the human's inner dimension within the parameters of physics and biology so that terms like *consciousness* or *spontaneity* are found within the primordial dust and within the pre-life particles of the juvenile earth.

Appleton-Weber affirms that his use of a term, isolated from the whole, may appear to be metaphorical, but in reality these apparently metaphorical comparisons are the expression of physical and biological structural realities. Because of the biological quality and properties of thought that make the human both center of perspective and center of construction of the universe, metaphor is virtually eliminated from Teilhard's text, which develops by structural analogy, connoting a deep natural bond between humans and cosmos.[13] Appleton-Weber warns that *if Teilhard's terms are not translated consistently within their space–time dimensions, the coherence which is the source of the work's transforming power and truth, is lost.*[14]

Teilhard's method is like a hologram in movement and requires the capacity to see. His method calls for a new type of holistic consciousness where things are *first seen together* and then as distinct within this togetherness. By *vision* Teilhard means something more than mere physical sight. He writes: "To see is to develop a homogenous and coherent perspective of our general experience as it extends to the human being; that is, to see a whole that unfolds."[15] To see is not only to know, it is to unite: "One can say that the whole of life lies in seeing—if not ultimate, at least essentially. . . . Unity grows . . . only if it is supported by an increase of consciousness, of vision."[16] He goes on to say, "If we lack these qualities of sight, no matter what anyone does to show us, the human being will indefinitely remain for

---

[11] Appleton-Weber, "Introduction," xix.
[12] Ibid., xx.
[13] Ibid., xx, 71.
[14] Ibid., xx.
[15] Teilhard, *The Human Phenomenon*, 6.
[16] Ibid., 3.

216   Cosmic Personalization

us . . . an erratic object in a disconnected world."[17] Those who see have the sense of the world as a unified whole in movement. We are linked organically and psychically with all that surrounds us. "We realize," he writes, "that which is emerging in us is the great cosmos."[18] Those who do not see, do not see beyond the multiple. They perceive the world as fragmented and ultimately absurd.[19]

Matter and Consciousness

Teilhard was highly attuned to the revolution in physics brought about by quantum mechanics. In a provocative article entitled "The Spirit of Einstein and Teilhard in the 21st Century," Ervin Lazlo writes that "Einstein's general relativity gave us the relativistically interlinked universe . . . and Teilhard laid the foundations of a unified theory where life and mind emerge consistently out of the physical world."[20] In the early twentieth century physicist Max Planck wrote of consciousness as fundamental to matter, indicating that we cannot consider matter apart from consciousness:

> All matter originates and exists only by virtue of a force which brings the particle of an atom to vibration and holds this most minute solar system of the atom together. We must assume behind this force the existence of a conscious and intelligent mind. This mind is the matrix of all matter.[21]

Like Planck, Erwin Schrödinger thought that consciousness is fundamental to matter and always experienced in the singular; everything begins with consciousness, which itself is immaterial.[22] The philosopher Bertrand Russell wrote, "[W]e know nothing about the intrinsic quality of physical events

---

[17] Ibid., 5.

[18] Pierre Teilhard de Chardin, *Science and Christ*, trans. René Hague (New York: Harper and Row, 1968), 27.

[19] Appleton-Weber, "Introduction," xix.

[20] Ervin Laszlo, "The Spirit of Einstein and Teilhard in 21st Century Science: The Emergence of Transdisciplinary Unified Theory," *Revista Portuguesa de Filosophia* 61 (2005): 136.

[21] Max Planck, as quoted in Susan Borowski, "Quantum Mechanics and the Consciousness Connection," *AAAS* (July 16, 2012).

[22] Erwin Schrödinger, *What Is Life?*, trans. Verena Schrödinger (Cambridge: Cambridge University Press, 2012, reprint edition), 93–95.

except when these are mental events that we directly experience."[23] Also in the 1950s astrophysicist James Jeans wrote: "The universe looks more like a great thought than a great machine. Mind no longer appears as an accident intruder into the realm of matter. . . . The quantum phenomena make it possible to propose that the background of the universe is mindlike."[24]

Although no one really knows what consciousness is, we know that consciousness is fundamental to life itself. Without mind, matter would not exist, or, to put it this way, we could not know if matter exists apart from the mind. Nothing can be said about anything apart from consciousness. Philosopher Gaylen Strawson describes this as the "hard problem of matter."[25] "Consciousness is not the fundamental mystery," he states, "matter is."[26] He goes on to say: "The ultimate intrinsic nature of the stuff of the universe is unknown to us—except insofar as it is consciousness."[27] David Bohm said that consciousness is part of a higher dimension of reality of implicate order, but it is difficult to say what this could mean, scientifically, apart from consciousness. In their book *The Conscious Universe*, Menas Kafatos and Robert Nadeau argued that, if the universe is an indivisible wholeness, then everything comes out of this wholeness and everything belongs to it, including our own consciousness. In this respect consciousness is a cosmic property.[28]

Dual-Aspect Monism

Teilhard was a disciple of the new physics and held to a dual-aspect monist position to explain evolution. Dual-aspect monism means that the mental and the material are different aspects or attributes of a unitary reality, which itself is neither mental nor material. Dual-aspect monism gives greater emphasis to matter, compared to panpsychism, which states that all matter has some degree of consciousness.[29] Teilhard's views on

---

[23] Bertrand Russell, "Mind and Matter" (1950).

[24] James Jeans, *The Mysterious Universe* (New York: Macmillan, 1931), 158.

[25] Gaylen Strawson, "Consciousness Isn't a Mystery. It's Matter," *New York Times*, May 16, 2016.

[26] Ibid.

[27] Ibid.

[28] Menas Kafatos and Robert Nadeau, *The Conscious Universe: Parts and Wholes in Physical Reality* (New York: Springer, 1990).

[29] See Philip Goff, *Consciousness and Fundamental Reality* (New York: Oxford University Press, 2017).

218   Cosmic Personalization

mind and matter fall between dual-aspect monism and panpsychism, but one can detect a development in his thought toward panpsychism. He described matter as bifacial, indicating that mind and matter are part of the same cosmic face:. He wrote: "For me, matter was the matrix of consciousness; and wherever we looked, consciousness, born of matter, was always advancing towards some ultra-human."[30] Life is a specific effect of matter turned complex; a property that is present in the entire cosmic stuff.[31] Matter and consciousness are not two substances or two different modes of existence, but two aspects of the same cosmic stuff.[32] Matter is united in ever greater patterns of physical complexity, supporting greater consciousness and ultimately self-consciousness. Life is an emergence of mind and matter.

The mutuality of matter and energy led Teilhard to state that matter has a withinness and a withoutness.[33] The withinness of matter is a psychic quality or dimension, a type of radial energy that escapes scientific measurement, whereas matter's withoutness is a capacity to aggregate through tangential energy or energy of attraction.[34] These two dimensions of the material world reflect an evolutionary process of interiorization and subjectivity that begins on the simplest levels of life and develops into complex organisms and species on higher levels.

Based on the unified relationship of mind and matter, Teilhard posited a fundamental principle, the law of complexity-consciousness. He spoke of complexification as an all-pervading tendency, involving the universe in all its parts in an *enroulement organique sur soi-même*, or as a *reploiement sur soi-même*. Thus, he envisaged the world-stuff as being rolled up or folded in upon itself, creating an increase in energetic tension in the increased organized complexity. Matter is always in the process of greater physical organization as consciousness increases, and the increase in conscious matter entails a higher level of energized relationship or spirit. Spirit is the higher state of matter.[35] There is only one real evolution, he said, the evolution

---

[30] Pierre Teilhard de Chardin, *The Heart of Matter*, trans. René Hague (New York: Harcourt Brace Jovanovich, 1979), 45.

[31] Pierre Teilhard de Chardin, *Man's Place in Nature*, trans. René Hague (New York: Harper and Row, 1966), 34.

[32] Teilhard, *The Phenomenon of Man*, 56–64.

[33] Ibid., 45.

[34] Ibid.

[35] Ibid., 35.

of convergence, because it alone is positive and creative.[36] The universe is oriented toward conscious, intelligent life.

The Whole of the Whole: Omega

The magnitude of the human phenomenon begins on the level of matter's first forming of the planet earth, encompassing the human future within its globe and motion. Tracing the composite human back to its source in the stuff of the universe, Teilhard identifies the three major pillars of life as matter, energy, and plurality, and positions the human phenomenon within the unfolding of space-time. He begins with the stuff of the universe: "Moving an object back into the past is equivalent to reducing it to its simplest elements; followed as far as possible in the direction of their origins, the last fibers of the human composite are going to merge in our sight with the very stuff of the universe."[37] By tracing the human back to its origin in the universe, Teilhard finds a collective, the *totum* or whole which he calls Omega, a principle of wholeness and centricity that influences the bottoms-up activity.

Teilhard introduced the Omega principle as a fundamental principle of centration in evolution. He called this principle Omega because it is the point of unity within the evolutionary process and yet more than the process itself. The basis of Omega is not mechanistic but *experiential*. It emerges from seeing that the universe is psychically convergent, a phenomenon that cannot be accounted for by the increasing entropy of emergent life. Teilhard was aware that science cannot prove the existence of Omega; what is needed is faith in the existence of an organized whole seeking greater wholeness. It is both a scientific principle and a religious one not subject to scientific materialism or reductionism. He writes:

> The universe has no complete reality except in the movement which causes all its elements to converge upon a number of higher centres of cohesion (in other words, which spiritualizes them); nothing holds together absolutely except through the Whole; and the Whole itself holds together only through this its future fulfilment.[38]

---

[36] Pierre Teilhard de Chardin, *Christianity and Evolution*, trans. René Hague (New York: William Collins & Sons, 1971), 87.

[37] Teilhard, *The Human Phenomenon*, 11.

[38] Teilhard, *Christianity and Evolution*, 71.

220 Cosmic Personalization

Teilhard described Omega as a universal center that "causes conscious particles of the universe to converge upon itself in order to ultra-synthesize them."[39] It is independent of the collapse of forces with which evolution is woven. Omega is not merely the point that would eventually be reached by the process of evolution itself; rather, Omega is "already in existence and operative at the very core" of evolution.[40] That is, Omega is both a final cause of the evolutionary process and a formal cause. It is the energetic (or informational) presence that undergirds the unitive nature of evolution toward more complexified wholeness. It is supremely present and supremely personal, a universal center that influences individually centered human personalities without annihilating those centers.[41] It is a principle of centricity within each entity yet independent of the entity. It is within the cosmic order and yet not subject to the laws of physics; in nature but not subject to the forces of nature; distinct yet intrinsic; autonomous and independent. Patrick Byrne states: "What is deepest in the center of every human being is the very thrust of evolution toward ultimate fulfillment that produces every evolved being."[42] This immanent impulse is Omega, the dynamic impulse in cosmic life.

For Teilhard, evolution is not merely a process of natural selection or survivability; evolution is the ascent toward the maximization of consciousness.[43] While mechanisms of evolution can account for the features of evolution, they do not entirely explain the direction of evolution toward greater wholeness. Evolution proceeds toward more consciousness because something in the cosmos escapes entropy and does so increasingly. The Omega principle is the principle of wholeness open to future fulfillment.[44] Omega is that which centrates the evolution of consciousness. Teilhard writes:

> The conclusion is inevitable that the concentration of a conscious universe would be unthinkable if it did not reassemble in itself all consciousnesses as well as all the conscious; each particular consciousness remaining conscious of itself at the end of the operation and each

---

[39] Ibid., 143–44.

[40] Teilhard, *The Phenomenon of Man*, 289.

[41] Ibid., 261–62.

[42] Patrick H. Byrne, "The Integral Visions of Teilhard and Lonergan: Science, the Universe, Humanity, and God," in *From Teilhard to Omega: Co-Creating an Unfinished Universe*, ed. Ilia Delio (Maryknoll, NY: Orbis Books, 2014), 88.

[43] Ibid., 258.

[44] Teilhard, *The Phenomenon of Man*, 257–60.

particular consciousness becoming still more itself and thus more clearly distinct from others the closer it gets to them in Omega.[45]

Scientifically, we could think of Omega as a factor of complexity, but Teilhard also sees Omega operating as a principle of personalization.[46] Omega is a principle of centration energized by love, that is, Omega is the presence of love energy. Love is the energy of differentiation, and differentiation is the outcome of union. In *The Human Phenomenon* he writes that "union differentiates." The more parts unite, "the more they accentuate the depths and incommunicability of their *ego*," because it is the core "self" that is the basis of union. On the human level, "the only way we can find our person is by uniting with one another."[47] Omega is the most intensely personal center that makes each entity personal and centered. We might think of it as the attractive center of love that empowers every center to love.[48] He writes: "In any domain—whether it be the cells of a body, the members of a society or the elements of a spiritual synthesis—union differentiates."[49] Love orients matter toward fullness because love is unitive energy. The openness of love to more being-in-love drives conscious material life toward greater complexity. Omega, therefore, accounts for the "*more* in the cell than in the molecule, *more* in society than in the individual, and *more* in mathematical construction than in calculations or theorems."[50] As a fundamental aspect of evolution, Omega is operative from the beginning, acting on pre-living cosmic elements, even though they are without individualized centers, by setting them in motion as a single impulse of energy.[51] Teilhard states that the force of love-energy is present from the Big Bang onward, which leads him to posit that "the physical structure of the universe is love."[52] Omega is brought into the field of consciousness, as it emerges from the organic totality of evolution, and it is the goal toward which evolution tends.[53]

---

[45] Ibid., 261.

[46] Ibid., 262–63.

[47] Teilhard, *The Human Phenomenon*, 186–87.

[48] Pierre Teilhard de Chardin, *Activation of Energy*, trans. René Hague (New York: Harcourt Brace Jovanovich, 1970), 112.

[49] Teilhard, *The Phenomenon of Man*, 262.

[50] Teilhard, *The Human Phenomenon*, 191.

[51] Teilhard, *The Phenomenon of Man*, 262.

[52] Pierre Teilhard de Chardin, *Human Energy*, trans. J. M. Cohen (New York: William Collins & Sons, 1969), 72.

[53] Teilhard, *The Phenomenon of Man*, 114.

222 *Cosmic Personalization*

The Human Phenomenon:
Thought

The unfolding of the human story begins on the level of matter's first forming of the planet earth, encompassing the human future within its globe and
motion. Teilhard looks for structural patterns throughout the development
of life by which he can understand the construction of the universe and the
properties of thought that distinguish the human. He tells us at the end
of the prologue of *The Human Phenomenon* that he particularly chose the
expression "human phenomenon" to affirm that "the human" is authentically
a fact in nature, falling (at least partly) within the province of the requirements and methods of science.[54]

Teilhard's subject is the ever-evolving human phenomenon, as it is developing in and around us at this very moment, a unique biological, collective, and global phenomenon whose past, present, and future is intimately
bound up with the formation, life, and ultimate transformation of the earth.
The law of complexity-consciousness works as the principal law of human
emergence, as well as the future of human evolution, so that the "option for
the evolving future of the earth and her thinking layer (ourselves) lies in our
own hands."[55] With the emergence of the self-reflective mind, humankind
enters a new age where a new spirit of the earth is born.

To trace the emergence of thought, Teilhard states that at all known
levels of the universe, there are units or "grains" that include stars, atoms,
molecules, cells, people, and so forth. Sometimes the particles are gathered
together in aggregations (for example, a pile of sand or a galaxy of stars);
sometimes they are linked together to form a crystal. While a crystal builds
up through indefinitely repeating the same molecular pattern, life builds up
by uniting into ever more complex and intricate structures of relatedness.

This center-to-center bonding of complexity, which is characteristic of all
living things, captured Teilhard's attention. His paradigm can be described
in three stages of evolution: increasing organization, convergence, and the
radiation of consciousness throughout the whole. The first stage sees evolution as following an axis of increasing organization. When we consider
the age of the universe (13.8 billion years), there came a point where inert
elements merged and formed the first living cell. All the separate elements
were there before the cell appeared, but the union of these elements caused

---

[54] Teilhard, *The Human Phenomenon*, 6.
[55] Appleton-Weber, "Introduction," xxvii.

a new entity to emerge that was more than the sum of its parts. "True unity does not fuse the elements it brings together," Teilhard wrote, "rather by mutual fertilization" it "renews them; union differentiates."[56] The movement toward greater complexity means that each individual cell continues to reach beyond itself to find new elements and incorporate them into its unity. Evolution is the story of "plus one." "The many become one and are increased by one."[57] Unfolding life is an incredible confluence of processes working together, testing new relationships, picking up and moving on when the time is right. In Teilhard's view "life has constructed organisms of ever greater complexity, and with this increased complexity the organism has also shown an increase in consciousness, that is, an increase of intention, of acting with a goal."[58]

The second stage of human evolution is one of convergence toward a projected point of maximum human organization and consciousness. In the course of evolution the human person emerges from a general searching of the world; thought is born. Teilhard sees consciousness as intrinsic to the process of evolution and states that evolution is fundamentally the rise of consciousness. He did not see the human person lost or insignificant in view of evolution; rather, he saw the human person as truly unique; not a chance arrival, but an integral element of the physical world.

The third stage is the maximization of thought whereby consciousness radiates throughout the whole, in every aspect of the cosmos, as the cosmos is recapitulated on the level of the human person. With self-reflective consciousness, the human person can stand apart from the world and reflect on it. Evolution proceeds through the spheres of matter, life, and consciousness and gives rise to thinking creatures.

How Teilhard positions the human in the overall scheme of cosmic life is significant. Once the whole of the human is integrated—the "inside" as well as the "outside"—into a coherent representation of the world, the human comes to be seen as the very axis and arrow pointing the direction of evolution itself. If we are to see ourselves completely and survive, it must be as part of humanity, with humanity as part of life, and life as part of the universe.[59]

---

[56] Quoted in Thomas M. King, *Teilhard's Mysticism of Knowing* (New York: Seabury, 1981), 32.

[57] Alfred North Whitehead, *Process and Reality: An Essay in Cosmology*, corrected ed., ed. David Ray Griffin and Donald Sherburne (New York: The Free Press, 1978), 21.

[58] King, *Mysticism of Knowing*, 33.

[59] Teilhard, *The Human Phenomenon*, 5.

224   Cosmic Personalization

In light of evolution Teilhard describes human distinction in three ways: (1) the extreme physical complexity of the human brain, indicating that the human person is the most highly synthesized form of matter known in the universe; (2) the most perfectly and deeply centered of all cosmic particles within the field of our experience; and (3) the high degree of mental development (reflection, thought) places the human person above all other conscious beings known to us, not in an ontological sense but as the *recapitulation* of all cosmic life.[60]

The human person is integrally part of evolution in that we rise from the process, but in reflecting on the process, we stand apart from it. The human phenomenon is the cosmic phenomenon on the level of thought: "We discover we are not an element lost in the cosmic solitudes but that within us a universal will to live converges and is hominized."[61] Julian Huxley writes: "Once he had grasped and faced the fact of man as an evolutionary phenomenon, the way was open towards *a new and comprehensive system of thought*."[62] We are the thinking portion of the universe.

The human phenomenon, therefore, represents a new zone in the universe, independent, yet somehow born of the entire maturation of the earth. Hence, the human is not the static center of the world . . . but the axis and arrow of evolution," which, Teilhard adds, "is much more beautiful" than being a mere center.[63] The human person is "evolution become conscious of itself." To this idea he adds, "The consciousness of each of us is evolution looking at itself and reflecting upon itself."[64] Each of us is "the point of emergence in nature, at which this deep cosmic evolution culminates and declares itself."[65] Evolution itself is so fully reducible and identifiable with the advance toward thought that the movement of our soul expresses and measures the very progression of evolution.[66]

---

[60] Pierre Teilhard de Chardin, *The Future of Man*, trans. Norman Denny (New York: Harper and Row, 1964), 90. For Teilhard, the human person is everything the universe is, but the human is distinguished by the capacity for self-consciousness. In this respect the human stands apart from the universe as one who can reflect on it; yet, as part of the universe, the human person can shape its future direction.

[61] Teilhard, *The Phenomenon of Man*, 36.

[62] Julian Huxley, "Introduction," *The Phenomenon of Man*, trans. Bernard Wall (New York: Harper, 1959), 21.

[63] Teilhard, *The Human Phenomenon*, 7.

[64] Teilhard, *The Phenomenon of Man*, 221.

[65] Teilhard, *Human Energy*, 23.

[66] Teilhard, *The Human Phenomenon*, 154.

Direction in Evolution:
Complexity-Consciousness

The question of whether or not evolution has direction has been a controversial one among scientists. Most scientists reject evolutionary teleology because the Darwinian mechanisms of biological evolution do not support such a claim affirmed by religion. However, a turn in the road was made recently by the eminent evolutionary biologist David Sloan Wilson. Turning to Teilhard's *The Future of Man*, Wilson claims that Teilhard's scientific insights are reasonable and emphasizes that Teilhard's noosphere of self-reflective thought is a necessary stage in human *cultural evolution*. Science has not paid attention to the impact of cultural evolution; however, as Wilson points out, mathematical modeling of complex systems shows otherwise.[67] The social integration of people around the globe into some kind of "super-humanity" presupposes the further self-evolution of the whole human species toward a higher order. While lower species fan out in evolution, humans are continuously coalescing into superspecies.

Wilson identifies the Omega Point as a single global super-organism on the level of the noosphere. He sees Teilhard's law of complexity-consciousness as a basis to describe major evolutionary transitions in which mechanisms evolve to suppress the potential for disruptive within-group selection, whereby between-group selection becomes the dominant evolutionary force and the group becomes so cooperative that it qualifies as a higher-level organism. Wilson's support of Teilhard's orthogenic evolution is echoed by systems scientist Francis Heyligen, who sees direction in evolution based on Teilhard's law of complexity-consciousness. Systems evolve to become simultaneously more complex and more conscious. For example, in the development of multicellularity, where the cooperation between cells makes them more dependent on others [integration], complexity allows for greater degrees of specialization. Complexity and cooperativity support greater resilience in view of environmental forces, and greater differentiation in terms of specialization. Hence complexity is a significant factor in the overall development of organisms toward more wholeness.

---

[67] David Sloan Wilson, "Reintroducing Pierre Teilhard de Chardin to Modern Evolutionary Science," *Brain, Religion and Behavior* 13, no. 4 (2021): 10.

226   Cosmic Personalization

Collective Movements

Teilhard took it for granted that a basic mutation had already taken place in modern post-Darwinian, post-Marxian, and post-Freudian consciousness, but he postulated yet another necessary mutation: a greater awareness of humanity's necessary collectivity and the emergence of a higher collective consciousness to form a higher, new collaborative reality. In this respect he was attracted to movements that promised greater coherence, because evolution always moves in the direction of greater organization. In his own day he was interested in totalitarian movements such as Fascism and Communism. The personalizing direction of evolution meant that the process cannot terminate in the human person who is still in need of improvement; rather evolution is in the direction of the "New Person," which is why Teilhard thought that modern totalitarian regimes could be potentially the next level of cosmic evolution. John Passmore writes: "It was much easier for Teilhard to sympathize with Fascism or with Communism than with some of his fellow-Christians who were suspicious of new social orders or saw no reason for expecting that the future would be brighter and better than the past."[68] However, while he saw the potential for collective energy within these movements, he also saw their horror, crushing the human spirit into termites, instead of building up fraternity. In his *The Human Phenomenon* he writes:

> At no other age in history has humanity been so well-equipped and made so many efforts to create some kind of order out of its multitudes . . . [yet] with Communism and National Socialism, all this has only ended up in the most appalling linkage in chains! In the crystal instead of the cell. The termitary instead of the fraternity. Instead of the expected upsurge of consciousness, what we have is the mechanization that inevitably seems to emerge from totalization.[69]

While these horrific movements have perverted the rules of noogenesis, according to Teilhard, they also show signs of a potential to collectivize into a greater unity. In his words: "As monstrous as it seems, must not modern totalitarianism be the distortion of something very magnificent and very

---

[68] John Arthur Passmore, *The Perfectability of Man* (London: Duckworth, 1972, reprint edition), 167.

[69] Teilhard, *The Human Phenomenon*, 182.

close to the truth? There can be no doubt about it, the great human machine was made to work—and it *must* work by producing a superabundance of spirit."[70] However, anything that strips matter of spirit fails the movement and derails evolution. Teilhard saw the totalitarian movements as dangerous forms of mechanization: "Everything that turns us into termites is wrong and under sentence of death."[71] If life develops in the direction of a greater union, then the new level of humanity must be on the order of love. "Society will inevitably become a machine if its successive growths do not . . . culminate in Someone," that is, in a deeply personal center of love.[72] The sign of growing personalization is the actualization of love in all forms of life. "One single thing is loved in the end, the loving center of all convergence."[73] Omega emerges from totality of love.

The Power of Matter

As an evolutionary biologist whose work brought him into intimate contact with the earth, Teilhard recognized the power of matter: "In the beginning was *Power*, intelligent, loving, emerging . . . there was the *Fire*."[74] This power of matter was the ultimate real for him, an indestructible presence not subject to the forces of entropy. He experienced this power in rocks and minerals, as well as within himself. Because of this power of matter within all things, "each human ego is co-extensive with the entire universe."[75] Teilhard blesses matter, not for what it tells us about itself, but because we would remain ignorant both of ourselves and of God without it.[76] In his "Hymn to Matter" he poetically writes:

> I bless you, matter . . . in your totality and your true nature. You I acclaim as the inexhaustible potentiality for existence and transformation. . . . I acclaim you as the universal power which brings together and unites. . . . I acclaim you as the divine milieu, charged with

---

[70] Ibid., 182.

[71] Teilhard, *Human Energy*, 81.

[72] Ibid.

[73] Ibid., 84.

[74] Teilhard, *The Heart of Matter*, 121–22.

[75] Teilhard, *Activation of Energy*, 218.

[76] Pierre Teilhard de Chardin, *Hymn of the Universe*, trans. Gerald Vann, OP (New York: Harper and Row, 1965), 69.

228   *Cosmic Personalization*

creative power. . . . Raise me up then, matter . . . until, at long last, it becomes possible for me in perfect chastity to embrace the universe.[77]

Matter is neither fallen nor profane. Rather, through matter we enter the world, and the world enters us. The observer is part of what she or he observes. Teilhard says that the more we try to break down matter into isolated entities, the more we can see its fundamental unity. He writes: "There are no isolated things in the world. There are only elements of a whole in process."[78] We live in a participatory universe of inseparability where everything is connected to everything else.

A careful reading of his essay "The Heart of Matter" clearly shows his deep insights, namely, that the physical cosmos emerges out of and is integral to a cosmic plenum or wholeness. This Jesuit priest writes about the power of rocks and metal to convey the profound truth of existence; faith begins with matter itself. He tells us how he was first attracted to the world of rocks, which, he claimed, helped him broaden *the foundations of my interior life.*[79] When he discovered minerals, he was set "on the road towards the 'planetary.'"[80] He woke up to "the stuff of things." This stuff began to emerge in the direction of a fundamental basis of everything, so that matter ultimately became for Teilhard the place of the Absolute.[81] "The truth is that even at the peak of my spiritual trajectory I was never to feel at home unless immersed in an Ocean of Matter."[82] He felt himself to be in contact "with the Cosmic 'in the solid state.'"[83] When he discovered physics, he realized that on either side of matter stood life and energy: "There gradually grew in me, as a *presence* much more than an abstract notion, the consciousness of a deep-running, ontological, total current which embraced the whole universe in which I moved; and this consciousness continued to grow until it filled the whole horizon of my inner being."[84]

In short, Teilhard discovered a new and vital presence of God, not a God draping the world with power, but God integral to the world's becoming. Matter is God-bearing. There is an inextricable relationship between God and matter; "I see in the world a mysterious product of completion and

---

[77] Ibid., 69–70.
[78] Appleton-Weber, "Introduction," xix.
[79] Teilhard, *The Heart of Matter*, 20.
[80] Ibid.
[81] Ibid.
[82] Ibid.
[83] Ibid., 22.
[84] Ibid., 25.

fulfillment for the Absolute Being himself."[85] We do not go to God directly; we go to God in and through matter. "Matter puts us in touch with the energies of earth and together with the earth we find ourselves looking to the 'Unknown God' who is to come."[86] Without matter, God would have no form, and without God, matter would have no direction. Matter matters to God.

Pantheism and the God of Evolution

Teilhard's relational holism governed by the principle of Omega is the basis of his theogenesis. In the essay "The God of Evolution" he writes, "Only a God who is functionally and totally 'Omega' can satisfy us," which led him to ask, "who will at last give evolution *its own* God?"[87] His efforts on reformatting theology to fit the contours of evolution were bold, daring, and brilliant. His new insights on God began not with scripture or tradition, but from the experience of matter. Thomas King writes: "In the direct experience of the cosmos, Teilhard believed he found an Absolute that drew him and yet remained in hidden. . . . He seems to sink down into matter—the primordial essence from which all emerges and to which all returns."[88]

Teilhard's God is divinely personal and relational. God is the immanent presence of the transcendent power of love. He writes: "God is not conceivable (either structurally or dynamically) except in so far as he coincides with (as a sort of 'formal' cause) but without being lost in, the center of convergence of cosmogenesis."[89] God acts upon the whole at once and each element individually. He writes: "God acts from within, at the core of each element, by animating the sphere of being from within. Where God is operating, it is always possible for us to see only the work of nature because God is the formal cause, the intrinsic principle of being, although God is not identical with being itself."[90] Teilhard opts for a new type of theology, or what he calls a "second form of pantheism" informed by Omega,[91] which

---

[85] Ibid., 54.

[86] Thomas M. King, "Teilhard and the Environment," in *Teilhard de Chardin on People and Planet*, ed. Celia Deane-Drummond (New York: Routledge, 2006), 185.

[87] Teilhard, *Christianity and Evolution*, 240.

[88] King, "Teilhard and the Environment," 181.

[89] Teilhard, *Christianity and Evolution*, 26–27.

[90] Ibid., 27.

[91] Ibid., 137.

230   Cosmic Personalization

is neither supernatural nor natural, but a new type of holism that resonates with contemporary ideas on quantum holism.

Pantheism is problematic for Christianity because it can strip God of divine distinction. Here I distinguish between ontological pantheism reflective of pre-quantum philosophy and experiential pantheism, which builds on panpsychism.[92] Ontological pantheism connotes one substance, either divine or material, whereas experiential or deep pantheism undergirds the experience of matter's depth and ineffable quality. Whereas ontological pantheism is identifiable as unitive substance, deep pantheism is the presence of energy seeking form.

Teilhard is an experiential pantheist. He invites us to think in terms of *energy* and *presence,* two words that support his metaphysics of union or hyperphysics.[93] God is Spirit, the energy of divine love, not a thing in relation to other things. The divine energy of love is the centrating presence of Omega, present to everything and to each particular entity in a way that we can say God is entangled. Entanglement is born from the strangeness of quantum physics and undergirds reality as an unbroken whole. It refers to the inseparability of phenomena, so that relationship is primary to that which is related.

Entanglement is a helpful concept to understand the relational holism of mind and matter, and correspondingly, the relationship between God and matter. Teilhard writes, "What comes first in the world for our thought is not 'being' but 'the union which produces this being.'" Raimon Panikkar's term *cosmotheandrism* is helpful to understand divinity, humanity, and cosmos as entangled realities, a holographic unity or a "cosmotheandric reality."[94]

The terms *entanglement* and *cosmotheandrism* refer to the inextricable relationships between God and conscious matter as these are recapitulated in the human person. If Christian pantheism is the entanglement of God and matter, then the unitive nature of these entangled realities is the basis of monism or the formation of the universe into a personal form, following the law of complexity-consciousness. Teilhard writes:

---

[92] On the various types of panpsychism, see Joanna Leidenhag, "Panpsychism and God," *Philosophy Compass* (November 2022).

[93] See Ilia Delio, "Trinitizing the Universe: Theogenesis and the Dynamism of Love," *Open Theology* 4 (2018): 158–69.

[94] For a discussion on Christ as the Cosmotheandric Mystery, see Raimon Panikkar, *Christophany: The Fullness of Man* (Maryknoll, NY: Orbis Books, 2004), 180–84; and Cheriyan Menacherry, *Christ: The Mystery in History: A Critical Study on the Christology of Raymond Panikkar* (Frankfurt am Main: Peter Lang, 1996), 117–20.

Only to the Christian is it given to be able to locate at the summit of space-time not merely a vague, cold something but a warm and well-defined someone; and so hic et nunc only . . . is one in a position to believe utterly in evolution—evolution that is no longer simply personalizing (that is giving rise to human persons) but is personalized—and (what is psychologically even more important) to dedicate himself to it with love.[95]

Ian Barbour, in his essay on Teilhard's process metaphysics, states that "Teilhard falls into the Scylla of a well-known mythology. According to it, God fulfills Himself in creating the world. God engages in a struggle with the Many (the ancient chaos) in order to find Himself again, richer and pacified, at the terminus of this world. This is an old gnostic idea which is found in Boehme, Hegel and Schelling."[96] But this is not exactly what Teilhard posits. He writes: "Christianity is pre-eminently a faith in the progressive unification of the world in God; it is essentially universalist, organic and monist."[97] God is the center of energetic life, the Whole of every whole element, daring to risk in love, to enjoin the adventure of evolution to which God is committed unreservedly.[98] Scholars avoid describing Teilhard's system as "pantheism" or "pantheistic" because it evokes what Mary Jane Rubenstein calls the "panic of theism";[99] however, without understanding his unique description of Christian pantheism, we cannot appreciate the full scope of his personalizing universe.

Teilhard rejected any type of dissolution or absorption of God into materiality; on the other hand, he saw that without matter God is unknown. The key to Teilhard's pantheism is in his principle, *union differentiates*. Pantheism can lead to the cult of a great All "in which individuals are merged like a drop in the ocean or like a dissolving grain of salt."[100] However, he sees within matter an indestructible presence not subject to the forces of entropy. He clearly tried to convey the idea that divinity and materiality are inseparable and united in such a way that something or Someone is in evolution. He states: "No spirit (not even God within the limits of our

---

[95] Teilhard, *Christianity and Evolution*, 156.

[96] Ian Barbour, "Teilhard's Process Metaphysics," *The Journal of Religion* 49, no. 2 (1969): 152. Refer to Appendix A in the current volume.

[97] Teilhard, *Christianity and Evolution*, 171.

[98] Ibid., 85.

[99] Mary Jane Rubenstein, *Pantheologies: Gods, Worlds, Monsters* (New York: Columbia University Press, 2018), 30.

[100] Teilhard, *The Phenomenon of Man*, 262.

232   Cosmic Personalization

experience) exists . . . without an associated multiple. All that exists is matter becoming spirit. There is neither spirit nor matter in the world; the stuff of the universe is spirit-matter."[101] God is not that which is; God is that which is coming to be.

The word *pantheism* undergirds a doctrine that essentially states that All (*pan*) is God and God (*theos*) is All; however, there are many different types of pantheism, as Dean Inge notes. It is interesting that Teilhard did not uses the word *panentheism*, which affirms God *in* all things and all things *in* God. The preposition *in* undergirds an ontology of relationship whereby the intimacy of relationship retains distinction of that which is related. However, this is *not* what Teilhard proposes. God is not only *in* all things, he states, but *as* all things, and there is an absolute Oneness of all. Teilhard's God is entangled in such a way that God can be conceived as the great entangler or the field of entanglement, a fundamental energetic presence in which the terms *God* and *world* are derived from the relationship. Rather than a distinction of entities in relationship, Teilhard proposes a new entity emerging in evolution from the complexity of energies, in which God is the entangled whole of the Whole. He states: "God can only be defined as a center of centers. In this complexity lies the perfection of his unity, the only final goal logically attributable to the developments of spirit-matter."[102] He asks: "What name should we give to this physico-moral energy of personalization to which all activities are reduced? Love. The physical structure of the universe is love."[103] What Teilhard proposes as pantheistic Christianity cannot be understood from a philosophy of the new materialisms.

Teilhard's pantheism is based on the eternal deepening of consciousness upon itself, due to complexification and the personalizing principle of Omega. Evolution proceeds morphologically with an increasing personalized form. By "personalizing," Teilhard means increased thought, action, and being, driven by the energies of love toward more consciousness. Love unites and differentiates and undergirds the personalizing form of evolution:

> Many a system of pantheism has led us astray to the cult of a great ALL. . . . The law of union rids us of this perilous and recurrent illusion. . . . The grains of consciousness do not tend to lose their outlines and blend, but, on the contrary, to accentuate the depth and incommunicability of their egos. The more other they become in

---

[101] Teilhard, *Human Energy*, 58.
[102] Ibid., 68.
[103] Ibid., 72.

conjunction, the more they find themselves as "self." How could it be otherwise if they are steeped in Omega?[104]

In a 1944 essay, he defines Christian pantheism as unification and differentiation:

> Since, from the Christian point of view, the universe is finally and permanently unified only through personal relations (that is, under the influence of love) the unification of beings in God cannot be conceived as being effected by fusion, with God being born from the welding together of the elements of the world or on the contrary by absorbing them in himself. It must be effected by differentiating synthesis, with the elements of the world becoming more themselves, the more they converge on God. For it is the specific effect of love to accentuate the individuality of the beings it associates more closely. Ultimately, God is not alone in the totalized Christian universe (in the pleroma, to use St. Paul's word); but he is all in all of us ("en pasi panta theos"): unity in plurality.[105]

Ontological pantheism is problematic when it flattens God into matter without distinction. Teilhard, however, invites us to think in terms of energy and presence, two words that support his metaphysics of love or hyperphysics.[106] God is the energy of divine love, not a thing in relation to other things but the relational energy itself by which everything diffracts in its relatedness, including God. For Teilhard, love is the energy of unitive growth. God is not only persuasive love; God is self-involving love, and the enfoldment of divine love drawing matter into greater complexity and consciousness *is* the emergence of God.

Divine energy and created energy are entangled in the development of cosmic personal form, which is the Christ. Hence, the form of the personal impels Teilhard to identify pantheism as the basis of true unity:

> It is only in fact the "pantheism" of love or Christian "pantheism" (that in which each being is super-personalized, super-centered, by union with Christ, the divine super-center)—it is only that pantheism which correctly interprets and fully satisfies the religious aspirations

---

[104] Teilhard, *The Phenomenon of Man*, 262.
[105] Teilhard, *Christianity and Evolution*, 171.
[106] Delio, "Trinitizing the Universe," 158–69.

of man, whose dream is ultimately to lose self-consciously in unity. That pantheism alone agrees with experience, which shows us that in every instance union differentiates. And finally, it alone legitimately continues the curve of evolution, on which the centration of the universe upon itself advances only through organic complexity.[107]

Teilhard's Christian pantheism is the basis of a personalistic universe because true union differentiates. Love does not absorb the other but differentiates personalities; love is the unitive energy of personal differentiation. If the universe is an experiential process according to Whitehead, for Teilhard it is a process of personalization. Love unites and unitive love differentiates in a way that complexity increases, and consciousness rises. Hence Teilhard states, "Driven by the forces of love, the fragments of the world seek each other so that the world may come to being."[108]

Pantheism, therefore, is key to Teilhard's personalistic universe. God is not only in all things but *as* all things, which means God emerges with complexified matter.[109] Society will inevitably become a machine if its successive growths do not culminate in a cosmic, personal Someone.[110] As love draws separate entities into unitive existence, God emerges as the horizon of wholeness, dawning in evolution through higher levels of conscious love and the actualization of love. "Only one single thing is loved in the end, the loving center of all convergence."[111]

Evolution, Pantheism, and Personalization

In his essay "Sketch of a Personalistic Universe," Teilhard describes a cosmic synthesis in which plurality manifests itself in increasingly complex and organic forms. Spirit and matter are two aspects of the same reality: "There is not matter and spirit. All that exists is matter becoming spirit. The stuff of the universe is spirit-matter."[112]

---

[107] Teilhard, *Christianity and Evolution*, 171.

[108] Teilhard, *The Phenomenon of Man*, 264.

[109] Matthew Segall proposes a similar argument for Whitehead, although Whitehead argues for a panentheistic God-world relationship. See Matthew David Segall, *Physics of World-Soul: Alfred North Whitehead's Adventure in Cosmology* (Grasmere, ID: SacraSage Press, 2021), 129.

[110] Teilhard, *Human Energy*, 81.

[111] Ibid., 84.

[112] Ibid., 57–58.

For Teilhard, growth in consciousness and growth in complexity are mutually reinforcing and give rise to greater overall unity. Once the universe is ordered along its axis of increasing centro-complexity, it is not only centered in its totality, moved along by a stream of centration, which is what Teilhard means by "convergence," but it is vitalized by an attractive energy of love.[113] His law of creative union corresponds to this movement of convergence. Love alone is capable of drawing together and uniting in such a way that the elements of union are more integrally themselves. Love transforms because love unites. The union of love differentiates, and differentiation is the basis of true union. Without this reality of love as the core of evolution, the fibers of the world-stuff recoil in on themselves leading to shriveled egos and eventually termination of the evolution process.[114] "It is egoism that hardens and neutralizes the human stuff."[115] "The way out of early cosmic termination is by yielding to the power of love, because what we really love is always 'another' ahead of us."[116]

Teilhard's personalistic universe is governed by three laws: (1) the law of complexity-consciousness; (2) the law of creative union; and (3) the law of recurrence, by which life emerges like fractals, recurring patterns of order increasing over time. These architectonics of evolution, he states, have exactly the same characteristics of universality and faith that are distinctive of religion, particularly Christianity. However, the reformatted version of Christianity that Teilhard sees is based on personalism and pantheism: "The essence of Christianity is . . . a belief in the unification of the world in God by the incarnation. All the rest is secondary." Hence "Christianity is essentially the religion of personality."[117]

Teilhard saw the divine activity of creation, incarnation, and redemption as three aspects of the same divine process operative within the inextricable realities of divinity, materiality, and consciousness. This cosmotheandric reality led him to describe creative union as a *fourth* divine mystery: "the mystery of the creative union of the world in God or pleromization."[118] Pleromization is a *fourth mystery* because it is not merely the union of divinity and materiality as the distinction of natures (cf. Chalcedon), but the ongoing evolution of God and matter in an emergent union of personal

---

[113] Teilhard, *Activation of Energy*, 103.

[114] Teilhard, *Human Energy*, 62.

[115] Ibid., 63.

[116] Ibid., 62.

[117] Ibid., 91.

[118] Teilhard, *Christianity and Evolution*, 183.

236   Cosmic Personalization

formation in which something new emerges, that is, a *tertium quid*. Evolution is the emergence of the New Person, symbolized by the Christ.

Teilhard used the term *Christogenesis* to indicate that the biological and cosmological genesis of creation—cosmogenesis—is from the point of faith, Christogenesis, the birthing of Christ [Someone] in evolution. God's involvement in evolution is not for the sake of matter alone but for the sake of divine pleroma. God becomes the fullness of divine life in evolution.[119] He writes: "Not only theoretically but experientially our modern cosmogony is taking the form of a cosmogenesis (or rather a psycho or noo-genesis) at the term of which we can distinguish a supreme focus of personalizing personality."[120] By saying that cosmogenesis is now Christogenesis, Teilhard indicated that the very being of the world is being personalized. He sums up his ideas in a creed:

> I believe that the universe is in evolution
> I believe that evolution proceeds towards spirit
> I believe that spirit is fully realized in a form of personality
> I believe that the supremely personal is the universal
>   Christ.[121]

The ongoing unification of divine and human energies emerges in a third energy of personal form—the Christic—a new type of person in creation symbolized by the Christ; more God than "God" and more human than "human." He writes: "There is more in the total Christ than Man and God. There is also He who, in his 'theandric' being, gathers up the whole of creation: *in quo omnia constant.*"[122] Christ is the whole space-time-matter evolution in a personal union of entangled divine love. Christ symbolizes the future fullness of the whole evolutionary process, the "centrating principle," the "pleroma" and "Omega Point" whereby the individual and collective adventure of humanity finds its end and fulfillment.

Teilhard spoke of a third nature of Christ, indicating that divinity, humanity, and cosmos are three interlocking realities united in a single reality. He describes this nature as follows: "Between the Word on the one side and Man-Jesus on the other, a kind of 'third Christic nature' (if I may dare

---

[119] Ibid., 178–79.
[120] Ibid., 180.
[121] Ibid., 96.
[122] Ibid., 93.

to say so) emerges . . . that of the total and totalizing Christ."[123] This third aspect or nature of the theandric (divine-human) complex is "the *cosmic nature*," which, in Teilhard's view, has not been sufficiently distinguished from the other two natures (divine and human). The apprehension of a third nature of Christ means that the whole physical world has a spiritual nature that attains its full consciousness and openness to God in the person of Jesus Christ.

By using the term *third nature*, Teilhard suggests that Christ is related organically not simply juridically to the whole cosmos. The third nature of Christ reflects the entangled God-world relationship; it is cosmotheandric wholeness in evolution. James Lyons states that Christ, in his third nature, is the organizing principle in Teilhard's evolving universe.[124] God and world are in the process of becoming *something more* together because the universe is grounded in a personal *center* of divine love. Thus, Teilhard writes, "there is only one real evolution, the evolution of convergence, because it alone is positive and creative."[125] God and humanity are in an entangled state and the individuation of each is inextricably bound with the other. *The evolution of God and the evolution of humanity cannot be separated.*

Teilhard's personalistic universe is like a vast trans-human body in the process of formation. Individuals are like partially separable cells that make up the cosmic Body, the great Being that is coming to be. The universe tends toward the hyperpersonal, the emerging New Person. The Christic symbolizes the collective whole in formation unified by love. God emerges in evolution, as matter complexifies and consciousness rises. Such a position does not diminish God; rather, matter "contributes something that is vitally necessary to God."[126] This dynamic unitive becoming is Omega in

---

[123] Ibid., 179; J. A. Lyons, *The Cosmic Christ in Origen and Teilhard de Chardin: A Comparative Study* (Oxford: Oxford University Press, 1982), 183–96. The concept of a "third nature" is difficult to grasp if we conceive of nature as substantial being. Although Teilhard's insight is more mystical than scientific, we can describe this third nature along the lines of what science is telling us today about matter, namely, it is thoroughly relational. There is no part that is not related to other parts and every part is the result of its relationships. Hence, the whole is in every part and every part represents the whole. If Christ is the divine Word truly incarnate, then every aspect of matter is truly Christ, and Christ is every aspect of matter. The humanity of Christ symbolizes not only the meaning of Christ for humanity but for the entire creation. In short, the cosmic or third nature that Teilhard describes is not a figurative description but a literal one.

[124] Lyons, *The Cosmic Christ in Origen and Teilhard de Chardin*, 183–96.

[125] Teilhard, *Christianity and Evolution*, 87.

[126] Ibid., 177.

238 Cosmic Personalization

evolution, the pleromizing energy of love toward fullness (*pleroma*). We live in an entangled universe of inseparability where everything is connected to everything else, including God. As Teilhard states: "I see in the world a mysterious product of completion and fulfillment for the Absolute Being himself."[127]

Knowing the Whole Through Science and Religion

Teilhard reframed religion as a natural part of evolution. His religious spirit was deeply connected to his love of the earth. "By upbringing I am a child of heaven," he writes. "By temperament and intellect I am a child of the earth."[128] This coincidence of matter and spirit influenced his paradigm of faith and evolution: "After thirty years devoted to the pursuit of interior unity [between these two currents] I have the feeling that a synthesis has been effected naturally between the two currents that claim my allegiance. The one has not destroyed but reinforced the other."[129] This unity of religion and evolution was so strong in his life that he writes: "If I were to lose my faith in Christ, my faith in a personal God and my faith in spirit, I would continue to believe invincibly in the world."[130]

For Teilhard, religion is not a supernatural phenomenon but a phenomenon integral to evolution; religion is faith in the whole: "Religion, born of the earth's need for the disclosing of a god is related and coextensive with *not the individual man but the whole of humankind* [emphasis added]."[131] Science now tells us that the cosmos has become a cosmogenesis, and this fact alone "must lead to the profound modification of the whole structure not only of our thought but of our beliefs."[132] What is needed is a new religious consciousness that can utilize all the "free energy" of the earth to build humankind into greater unity. The relationship between religion and evolution is so fundamental that in 1916 Teilhard wrote:

> Religion and evolution should neither be confused nor divorced. They are destined to form one single continuous organism, in which their respective lives prolong, are dependent on, and complete one another,

---

[127] Teilhard, *The Heart of Matter*, 54.
[128] Ibid., 96–97.
[129] Ibid., 97.
[130] Ibid., 99.
[131] Ibid., 119.
[132] Teilhard, *The Future of Man*, 261.

without being identified or lost. . . . Since it is in our age that the duality has become so markedly apparent, it is for us to effect this synthesis.[133]

In view of evolution, religion is integral to the future of the earth; its purpose is "to sustain and spur on the progress of life." The emergence and growth of religion corresponds to the evolution of the human *in nature* and the rise of a divine pole through complexified-consciousness, as one is drawn up ahead. However, the human person is not the *terminus ad quem*; evolution passes *through* the human personality without staying there, which means the goal of evolution is infinitely beyond the human, as Teilhard states, the "ocean of an immense future in which there is no possible stopping-place before the appearance of a single center of the noosphere."[134]

It is because religion is the transcendent energy of evolution that any religion which focuses on the human person alone or a supernatural heaven opposes the dynamism of evolution. "People are looking for a religion of mankind and of the earth which gives meaning to human achievements, a religion that enkindles cosmic and human evolution and a deep sense of commitment to the earth."[135] On the human level religion is primarily "on the level of consciousness and human action, rather than on the level of institutions or belief systems, except insofar as these systems manifest and give direction to the former."[136] Thought, creativity, and engagement are all salvific means to participate in the evolutionary movement toward Omega. As Teilhard puts it: "One cannot be saved except through the universe and as a continuation of the universe."[137]

While Teilhard found axial religions stifled by old philosophies and static metaphysics, he equally lamented the suffocation of materiality brought about by modern science. The purpose of science is to extend and complete the ongoing process of hominized evolution; hence it has a sacred duty charged with futurity.[138] However, science has failed to live up to its noble purpose by seeking to control and manipulate nature rather than advance its wholeness. Scientific progress has now fallen into an intellectual and moral

---

[133] King, *Teilhard de Chardin and Eastern Religions*, 179–80.

[134] Teilhard, *Human Energy*, 44, 65.

[135] Ursula King, *The Spirit of One Earth: Reflections on Teilhard de Chardin and Global Spirituality* (St. Paul, MN: Paragon House, 1998), 109.

[136] Teilhard, *Activation of Energy*, 240–42.

[137] Ibid.

[138] Teilhard, *Human Energy*, 171.

240   Cosmic Personalization

crisis, the crisis of scientism.[139] We are no longer certain whether it is possible or good to attempt further scientific advances toward the building of a future for humanity. Teilhard said that science can depersonalize us into a faceless organism, a diffuse and impersonal humanity, thus vitiating the whole progress of evolution.[140] He was clearly aware of the perils of scientific materialism with regard to eugenics and transhumanism: "The servants of material progress or of racial entities may try their hardest to emerge into freedom, but they are fatally sucked in and assimilated by the determinisms they construct. Their own machinery turns them into machines."[141] Science is not fruitful without some religion to animate it. "Religion is the soul biologically necessary for the future of science," Teilhard claims.[142] In *The Human Phenomenon* he describes religion and science as "two conjugated faces or phases of one and the same complete act of knowledge, the only one which can embrace the past and future of evolution and so contemplate, measure and fulfil them."[143]

Christianity is a religion of evolution, according to Teilhard, because it posits the union of divinity and materiality and has a narrative of personalization that reflects the direction of evolution. In this respect the Christian claim "humanization by redemption" and the scientific claim "humanization by evolution" are essentially the same. Religion is an essential aspect of evolution, and so too is science. Together they advance a wholeness of evolution toward greater unity and consciousness. This emerging wholeness is God-Omega, the vital power of a world in movement.

Toward the Future

Teilhard's insights on a personalizing universe are comprehensive of his vision of evolution toward Omega. Four ideas emerge from his scheme:

1. The human is not the end of the cosmotheandric process of evolution because the universe is still in formation. However, Teilhard was not entirely clear as to the finality of evolution, seeing it as an immense and dynamic process of evolving consciousness.[144]

---

[139] Ibid., 175.
[140] Ibid., 151.
[141] Ibid.
[142] Ibid., 180.
[143] Teilhard, *The Human Phenomenon*, 204.
[144] Teilhard, *Human Energy*, 65.

2. Personalization is the internal deepening of consciousness on itself, which begins on the level of the individual but continues on the level of the collective and super-collective as identified in the noosphere.[145]

3. God is emerging as the complexified whole of evolution. God is being born from within by the convergence of the many into one. While God is the complexified wholeness emerging within, God is always ahead. Hence, God is the name given by the human to the consummated being.[146]

4. Because the human person is not the end of evolution, the fullness of personality lies ahead, in the ongoing complexification of conscious-loving life, a point Teilhard expands by his extension of the noosphere into extraterrestrial life.[147]

Teilhard argues for a greater wholeness of society infused by mutual love in which human life advances toward more life. He emphasizes that the success of humanity's evolution will not be determined by the survival of the fittest but by our own capacity to creatively converge and unify. To this extent, computer technology can be vital to the process of personalization, creating a new type of inter-thinking humanity into a new type of organism, the ultra-human, whose destiny it is to realize new possibilities for evolving life on this planet.

Humanity is moving into a new environment, into a world that is *being born* instead of a world that *is*, with a new relationship between matter and spirit, a new humanism, and a new understanding of God—complementary movements that mark the beginning of a new era for humankind. Ursula King grasped the import of Teilhard when she wrote:

> He expressed with clarity and forcefulness that we are *one* humanity, with *one* origin, and *one* destiny. We are also a group of humans that have not yet reached maturity in terms of our possibilities. Our immense problems somehow resemble the turmoils of youth.[148]

We find ourselves today on the threshold of a new age, one that impels us to ask, "How can we be 'architects of the future'"?[149] How can we develop

---

[145] Teilhard, *The Human Phenomenon*, 185.

[146] Teilhard, *Human Energy*, 67.

[147] Teilhard, *Christianity and Evolution*, 229–34.

[148] Ursula King, "Teilhard de Chardin's Vision of Science, Religion, and Planetary Humanity: A Challenge to the Contemporary World," *Journal for the Study of Religion* 31, no. 1 (2018): 143.

[149] Ibid., 144.

242   *Cosmic Personalization*

a better, higher life for planetary life? He reflected on the conditions and criteria by which human beings might become more united—economically, politically, and spiritually. How will the human species evolve further?

His book *The Future of Man* carries the motto: "The whole future of the Earth, as of religion, seems to me to depend on the awakening of our faith in the future."[150] He combined his faith in the future with his faith in the world, as well as faith in the further development of human beings and in the greater global collaboration, and unity among the peoples of the earth.[151] He spoke of a new threshold in the development of human consciousness and organization, not simply to survive but to creatively thrive. Life must continue to develop into a higher form of life, a more unified humanity. King summarizes the Teilhardian moment in this way:

> The problem of the future is paramount for the present. Will humanity survive or will it be annihilated? Will it progress or stagnate? Teilhard thought we have no decisive evidence for either hope or despair, but one thing is certain: we need to find the right road, make the right choices and put our will into effective action to create the right world for humanity today. He was convinced that despair cannot provide the necessary energy for action, but hope can.[152]

Humanity now bears full responsibility for its own future; both education and scientific research play a great role in this task. It is also an immense challenge—the kind of future we will get depends to a large extent on the quality of people who shape it.

Teilhard emphasized the need for a *homo progressivus*,[153] future-affirming beings with a wide, open awareness who have the energy of thought, vision, and perception to recognize the problems of the future and find their solutions—and who possess the necessary energy and will to action for putting them into practice. He never tired of pointing out that our understanding of science is too narrow, too particularistic and fragmentary. Its power of analysis must now be matched by attempts at synthesis, by a more holistic and global way of thinking. Scientists have analyzed the physical-biological, as well as the mental and psychic aspects of the human being; now we need

---

[150] Ibid.

[151] Teilhard, *Christianity and Evolution*, 121, 175.

[152] King, "Teilhard de Chardin's Vision of Science, Religion and Planetary Humanity," 144.

[153] Teilhard, *The Future of Man*, 130.

new methods of seeing the world as an emergent complex whole. We are to think, act, and live differently—not simply to live but to "superlive," to live a fuller, better, more rewarding life shared with one's fellow human beings, all earthly creatures, and planetary life.

The science and religion dialogue must give way to a new synthesis because either discipline, by itself, is insufficient to bring about a higher level of thought on the level of interconnected, planetary life.[154] To contribute to the overall development of terrestrial life, science needs to acknowledge the essential role of spirituality in the search for true knowledge. The mind can push evolution onward toward greater complexity, but love draws the stuff of life into greater unity. Love is not a determinant force but a gift that must be actualized through receptivity and shared life. All of nature knows this secret.

Nature also knows that love is unyielding. We are moving because we are driven by an irresistible power of love on every level of cosmic life. The sheer fact that we are moving means that humans are not the end of evolution; rather, evolution is oriented toward Omega. It may take billions of years of cosmic complexity and intergalactic life for love to be fully realized. But what is time in this vast, unfolding universe? For, in truth, the end is in the beginning, and life is always beginning.

---

[154] Ibid., 75; W. Henry Kenny, *A Path through Teilhard's Phenomenon* (Dayton: Pflaum Press, 1970), 138.

The God of Creative Union

*Renewing the Biblical Portrait of Divine Love
in Teilhard and Whitehead*

Robert Nicastro

Few philosophers and theologians would likely disagree that the doctrine of divine love is *the* starting point for any meaningful and reliable discussion about the nature of God. Lutheran theologian Eberhard Jungel, for instance, insisted that a theology of divine love must be the ground and grammar of all our knowledge of God.[1] While the Abrahamic religions—Judaism, Christianity, and Islam—have long prided themselves on the scholarly use of biblical testimony as a critical component of the "ground and grammar" of their theological proposals, much of our Western discourse about God has become unmoored from its scriptural foundations. In its persistent attempts to reconcile inconsistent biblical imagery with Greek philosophical categories, classical theism has described a God who dwells outside the spoils of space and time, essentially unaffected by the world's events and experiences. To allow for a degree of relationality, this influential approach ultimately places limits on divine love by assuring us of God's unconditional fidelity and concern, on the one hand, but from a safe and serene distance, on the other. Rather than a real relationship that makes real demands on us, we are left instead with sterile concepts of love that breed little more than attitudes of sentimentality and individualism.

Contrary to popular assumption, the biblical writers implicitly grasped that theology is the process of *faith seeking understanding*. They recognized

---

[1] See Eberhard Jungel, *God as the Mystery of the World*, trans. Darrell L. Guder (Grand Rapids, MI: Eerdmans, 1983).

245

246   *The God of Creative Union*

that the truth about creation is not generated simply by theological reflection alone and used the culturally available "prescientific" knowledge of the world to speak about God's relationship to creation in ways that were reasonable and substantive.[2] Much like the methodology employed in the ancient world, the principal task of contemporary theology is likewise to integrate materials from multiple disciplines into an intellectually coherent and biblically consistent system of thought. With no little support from the central biblical portrait of God as open and internally receptive to the world, Jesuit scientist Pierre Teilhard de Chardin and philosopher Alfred North Whitehead enjoin us to embrace a new theological horizon: one that transcends inherited metaphysical categories and outgrows the dualistic split between the sacred and secular. Theirs is a metaphysics of creative union that is consonant with the primacy of love as envisioned in the Hebrew Bible.[3] This chapter briefly highlights this consonance and concludes with a few remarks about how this pearl of great price heretofore largely hidden in the work of Teilhard and Whitehead helps us renew the kind of love necessary for the successful continuance of our world.

The Power of Metaphor

In their groundbreaking book *Metaphors We Live By*, George Lakoff and Mark Johnson discuss the fundamental role that metaphors play in interpreting our experience and creating meaning of the world around us. In an unavoidable way metaphors provide the framework for helping us make sense of who we are, how we act, and what type of purpose and value we ascribe to reality. Lakoff and Johnson explain: "In all aspects of life . . . we define our reality in terms of metaphors and then proceed to act on the basis of the metaphors. We draw inferences, set goals, make commitments, and execute plans, all on the basis of how we in part structure our experience,

---

[2] See Terence E. Fretheim, *God and World in the Old Testament: A Relational Theology of Creation* (Nashville, TN: Abingdon Press, 2005).

[3] While love is the preeminent metaphor that most fully and vividly discloses the inner reality of divine life in both the Hebrew and Christian scriptures, I choose to engage only with the Hebrew Bible for three reasons: (1) The entire mission and ministry of Jesus was decisively formed by his reading of the Torah; (2) without diminishing the core importance of the Christ event, the Old Testament bears witness in numerous ways to the pervasive presence of divine love prior to the historical person of Jesus; and (3) by focusing on the Hebrew Scriptures, this chapter can take a more manageable and hopefully readable scope.

consciously and unconsciously, by means of metaphor."[4] Metaphors are our principal vehicles for determining what is true in our daily lives.

By extension, the metaphors we use in terms of our thinking and speaking of God are immensely important, as those metaphors will condition our experiences of the divine in significant ways and will necessarily affect how we negotiate our immediate and larger contexts.[5] According to Hebrew Bible scholar Terence Fretheim, our biblical ancestors deployed a rich panoply of metaphoric images to describe their experiences of the sacred. Deeply connected to the land, the biblical writers used metaphors grounded in their experiences of the natural world.[6] They experienced themselves as living in a world in which the realm of the sacred was immediate and intimate. James Kugel explains:

> There are not two realms in the Bible, this world and the other, the spiritual and the material—or rather, these two realms are not neatly segregated but intersect constantly. God turns up and around the street corner, dressed like an ordinary person. . . . He appears in actual brushfire at the foot of the mountain. And it is not even that, on such occasions, He enters the world as we conceive of it from somewhere else. Rather, it seems that the world itself as we conceive it (at least the biblical world) has little cracks in it here and there. . . . The spiritual is not something tidy and distant, another order of being. Instead, it is perfectly capable of intruding into everyday reality, as if part of this world.[7]

---

[4] George Lakoff and Mark Johnson, *Metaphors We Live By* (Chicago: University of Chicago Press, 1980), 158.

[5] Ibid., 158.

[6] See Terence Fretheim, *The Suffering of God: An Old Testament Perspective* (Philadelphia: Fortress Press, 1984). In addition to Fretheim, Old Testament scholar J. Gerald Janzen is clear that though the utilization of metaphors is not literal in a strict sense, there is literalness intended in the relationship to which the metaphor has reference. He explains: "For all their manifold richness and overtone and symbolic expression, metaphors at their center do imply one thing and not another; and the most natural procedure is to take the metaphor as adumbrating an essential character which is equivalent to the metaphoric vehicle, and not contrary to it. . . . Metaphors do reveal an essential continuity with the reality of God and therefore are certainly reality depicting." For more information on metaphorical language in the Old Testament, specifically in terms of how metaphors are applied to the relationship between God and the prophets, see J. Gerald Janzen, "Metaphor and Reality in Hosea 11," *Semeia* 24 (1982): 1–26.

[7] James L. Kugel, *The God of Old: Inside the Lost World of the Bible* (New York: The Free Press, 2003), 35–36.

248   *The God of Creative Union*

To access this realm of the sacred was not a matter of departing the world but of fully immersing oneself *in* the world. It was contingent upon one's ability to see and experience the godly in one's midst.[8] The biblical narratives are "reports" that use metaphors to impart an experience of an encounter with the divine that is ultimately beyond the ability of language to express fully and completely.[9]

Given the vast and often complex metaphors for God in the history of biblical interpretation, one of the persistent dangers is to think that all metaphors have the same value or revelatory capacity. If some of the metaphors for God are neglected, subordinated, abstracted, or not kept in proper relation to one another, God's story becomes incoherent and fails to capture and communicate our experience and understanding of God in each new time, place, and circumstance. The central issue then is how exactly persons should go about discerning a reliable metaphorical pattern throughout the Bible, one whose continuity has a considerable capacity to reveal what kind of God it is who is involved in the life of the world.

Love as the Preeminent Metaphor

The Hebrew Bible brims over with metaphorical images of the divine, and several of these images have had an appreciable influence on how we conceive of God in Western culture. With the copious metaphors for the divine at hand, such as God as rock, king, shepherd, ruler of justice, human parent, and so forth, it is quite reasonable to wonder whether there is an overarching metaphor that furnishes us with a first and last word account of the biblical portrait of God. This question has been thoroughly addressed by Terence Fretheim. He notes that within the broad spectrum of biblical images and language of God, *love* is the preeminent metaphor. Love is the "controlling metaphor" that bears the strongest resemblance to the divine reality and therefore plays an indispensable role within the overall biblical account of God. Fretheim writes: "[Love] brings coherence to a range of biblical thinking about God. It provides a hermeneutical key for interpreting the whole."[10] Love is the *concrete reality* that unifies and manifests all the divine attributes.

---

[8]   Kugel, *The God of Old*, 37–70.

[9]   Ibid., 64. Like Kugel, Fretheim makes plain that the issue for the ancients, and so for us, is not whether we *believe* in the existence of God, but what *kind* of God in whom we believe. Fretheim, *The Suffering of God*, 1. Repeatedly, the emphasis is on coming to appreciate the divine as not an abstract concept but as an experience of something more in the world. The spiritual is a presence, an energy, a longing.

[10]   Fretheim, *The Suffering of God*, 11.

As such, love is not something God has; love is what God *is*—God's very essence. To say "God is love" is to affirm a God who stands in passionate relationship with the world. Hoping to convey a substantive sense of this relationship of reciprocity, Abraham Heschel summarizes the essential meaning of love in terms of divine pathos: "The divine pathos is the unity of the eternal and the temporal, of meaning and mystery, of the metaphysical and the historical. It is the real basis of the relation between God and man, of the correlation of Creator and creation, of the dialogue between the Holy One of Israel and His people."[11] Similar to Kugel's elucidation of the material and spiritual realms as constantly co-mingling, Heschel's commentary on divine love lends considerable credence to the words of Psalm 33:5: "The earth is full of divine presence." It supports the idea that God's presence to and relationship with creation is more than external; there is an inwardness or interiority of the world and its creatures such that a genuine relationship with God exists. Moreover, the belief in divine love as the lifeblood of the world logically presupposes that "God's presence is neither static nor passive but an active presence that is integral to the world, profoundly grounded in and shaped by steadfast love for the good of all creation."[12] The prophet Jeremiah resounds: "I have loved you with an everlasting love" (31:3). To fully appreciate the extent of this interconnectedness, however, we will need to examine briefly the relational model of divine love and creation in the imagination of Old Testament writers.

The Openness of God[13]

Much like our world, the category of relationship is central to Israel's theological reflection on God. In the Hebrew Bible, relationships constitute life

---

[11] Abraham Heschel, *The Prophets* (New York: Harper & Row, 1982), 298. While Heschel does state that the "prophets never identify God's pathos with His essence because for them pathos is not something absolute, but a form of relation" (*Prophets*, 298), biblical theologian Michael Chester contends that by doing so Heschel was trying to preserve the unfathomable mystery of God's love, namely, the inexhaustible and inexpressible depth of divine relatedness that could not be fully absorbed by their consciousness at any one moment of interaction. To delve more deeply into this perspective, see Michael A. Chester, *Divine Pathos and Human Beings: The Theology of Abraham Joshua Heschel* (Elstree: Vallentine Mitchel, 2005).

[12] Fretheim, *God and World in the Old Testament*, 24.

[13] This section title is not to be confused with the ideas underscored by Clark Pinnock et al. in *The Openness of God: A Biblical Challenge to the Traditional Understanding of God* (Downers Grove, IL: InterVarsity Press, 1994), in which the authors to a great extent critique rather than endorse process theism's reinterpretation of divine power as

250 *The God of Creative Union*

itself. Fretheim writes: "Interrelatedness is a basic characteristic not only of the relationship between God and people (and between God and the world) but also of the very nature of the created order. To live in a genuinely relational world inevitably means that every creature will be affected by the activity of every other; each creature is caught up in the interconnected life of all."[14] Above all, God so relates to this interrelated world that every movement in the web of life affects God just as it affects the world; God too gets caught up in these interconnections and works within them as a power of creative transformation for the sake of the future fulfillment of both God and world.[15] As God's relationship with the world is constituted *from within* the fabric of space and time, and not on the world from without, "everything said about Yahweh is said about Yahweh in relation to the world and its creatures."[16] Divine love, therefore, manifests as the ultimate source of the world's creativity and union.

The language of creativity is indeed significant not only for appreciating the reality of divine love but for appreciating that God's relationship with the world is ongoing and requires a comprehensive and universal frame of reference. The verb *bara*, "to create," is not restricted to the origination of the cosmos but refers to God's continuing activity of sustaining life, ordering creation, and holding everything together in unfathomable intimacy.[17] Creation is a ceaseless act of divine steadfast love whereby heaven and earth are constantly being brought into explicit manifestation and arrangement.[18] Such ordering activity is not simply working with a "rearrangement" of what already has been created, a sort of preservation that connotes a finished product; rather, it results in something genuinely new, and hence properly receives the designation "new creation."

---

inherently persuasive, a constitutive element in this system of thought that is ironically more reflective of the God of the Bible and so is foregrounded in this piece.

[14] Terence E. Fretheim, *God So Enters into Relationships That . . . A Biblical View* (Minneapolis: Fortress Press, 2020), 4.

[15] Fretheim, *God and World in the Old Testament*, 20.

[16] Tod Linafelt and Timothy K. Beal, eds., *God Is the Fray: A Tribute to Walter Brueggemann* (Minneapolis: Fortress Press, 1998), 312.

[17] Bernhard W. Anderson, *From Creation to New Creation: Old Testament Perspectives* (Minneapolis: Fortress Press, 1994), 89. See also Brevard S. Childs, *Biblical Theology of the Old and New Testaments: Theological Reflection on the Christian Bible* (Minneapolis: Fortress Press, 1993), 397, in which he explicitly states that nowhere is "God depicted as a static being but is engaged in constant creative activity."

[18] Northrop Frye, *The Great Code: The Bible and Literature* (New York: HarperOne, 1982), 106–14.

This biblical picture is certainly in agreement with contemporary scientific and theological discussions. For instance, the commonly held assumption of a fully formed cosmos is shattered by the relatively recent theory of strong emergentism, namely, the continued birth of new and more sophisticated forms of reality at various stages in the history and development of nature.[19] To claim that something is "new" is to speak of an irreversible process by which a more complex, intelligent, and distinctive entity arises out of the previously existing material, and the language of "new creation" effectively captures these novelties.[20] As God is involved in the gradual maturation of life, it is in effect reasonable and important to speak of something *genuinely* new coming into existence through space-time.[21] As the divine wellspring of love, God works creatively with already existing realities to advance the creative process. This understanding similarly suggests the idea that the present and future are not wholly determined by the events of the past. By being related to the world in the flow of events, God does not know the future, but rather God and the world co-creatively construct the events that give rise to today and tomorrow.

The awareness of the continual development of the God-world relationship also has unique implications for the human person. Despite public opinion, the human is not a fixed entity but, along with the rest of creation, is in the process of becoming. The human is not exempted from the novelty taking place in the larger creative enterprise. Rather, creation as a single organic process is open to a future in which the authentically new can be actualized, and humans are invited to play a pivotal role in the becoming of both God and world. Fretheim expounds:

> The co-creative process shared by God and world is intensified at the level of the human person. The command to be fruitful and multiply is another way of saying, "Be creative and innovative in ways that make

---

[19] For a strong defense of a new paradigm that integrates the science of emergentism, consciousness, and religion in a coherent and meaningful way, see Philip Clayton, *Mind and Emergence: From Quantum to Consciousness* (Oxford: Oxford University Press, 2006).

[20] Ted Peters, ed., *Cosmos as Creation: Theology and Science in Consonance* (Nashville, TN: Abingdon Press, 1989), 85.

[21] The language of God's desire for "new things" is peppered throughout scripture. In the Hebrew Bible, see specifically, Isa 42:9; 43:19; 48:6; see also Jer 31:22: "[God] has created a new thing on the earth." According to Stefan Paas, the use of the preposition *on* (i.e., "on the earth") assumes that God is working with the preexisting material. For more detail on this point, see Stefan Paas, *Creation and Judgement: Creation Texts in Some Eighth Century Prophets* (Netherlands: Brill Academic Publishing, 2003), 71–72.

252 *The God of Creative Union*

the sheer intimacy of my [God's] love real and true." This command indicates a decisive sharing of creative powers with the human. Every birth, every appearance of life, testifies to God's loving participation in the continuing creative process; and this from *within* the created order.[22]

To the biblical mind, divine love necessitates a mutual sharing of creative powers between God and world, and the creative activity of the human person, who is gifted with the advanced capacities of reflection and relationships, has the potential of significantly enhancing (or diminishing) the web of cosmotheandric life, ultimately bringing into being that which is genuinely new. To slightly paraphrase Rabbi Toba Spitzer: God's love is a cosmic flow that seduces us in the direction of more life, love, and creativity. It is up to us whether we will swim in harmony with the flowing steam and advance godly life.[23] Since the first moment of consciousness, God's life is forever entangled with the life of the world.[24] To unleash the energies of love is to enrich the quality and depth of all life; it is to make life for God more complex and *real*.

Before moving forward, a brief recapitulation of the main points of this section might be helpful for the sake of clarity. First, for Israel, there exists a relationship of reciprocity between God and the world: the world is not only dependent on God; God is also dependent on the world. God is always lovingly working from within the vast depths of the world and not on it from some supernatural vantage point. Walther Zimmerli affirms: "The whole thrust of the Old Testament proclamation of divine love guards against any flight into a beyond which is turned away from the world."[25] Second, the world is not only affected by God; God is affected by the world in both positive and negative ways. Third, transcendence is not compromised by the reality of relationship. Fretheim captures the point best: "We should not think of God as transcendent *and* in relationship, but God is transcendent *in* relationship. God is not less than God in relationships, rather God is the

---

[22] Fretheim, *Suffering of God*, 74.

[23] Toba Spitzer, *God Is Here: Reimaging the Divine* (New York: St. Martin's Essentials, 2022), 57–59.

[24] In Jeremiah 22:1–5, for example, the response of human persons to "divine empowerment" concerning issues of social justice affect the future of God as well as the future of the world.

[25] Walther Zimmerli, *The Old Testament and the World*, trans. John J. Scullion (London: SPCK, 1976), 13–14.

Holy One in the midst of Israel (e.g., Isa 12:6; Hos 11:8–9)."[26] Fourth, God knows all there is to be known about the world, but there is a future that does not yet exist and so is not known even to God. Finally, God is absolute with respect to love: love that is not private, sentimental, or emotional, but that draws together and unites.

As agreement with scripture is a necessarily important test for any theological proposal, the crucial question is whether current developments in conventional theology are congruent with the biblical witness of divine love. Do they reflect a doctrine of God that is social, dynamic, mutual, holistic, and genuinely relational, or are they a departure from this fundamental mooring? Put another way, do our metaphors for theologizing God incorporate reality as we now understand and experience it?

The Folly of Divine Imperiality

In our modern era the image of the universe as a machine has been transcended by the alternative perception of an indivisible, dynamic, and developmental whole whose parts are essentially interrelated and can only be comprehended as patterns of a great cosmic process. Like many discoveries since Charles Darwin proposed his theory of evolution, it took notable time before the new quantum awareness began to break down radical atomism. Thanks to the revolutions in scientific thought, psychology, and historical studies, we are now beginning to understand reality as more holistic and relational. We have been influenced by Georg Hegel, Karl Marx, Charles Darwin, Sigmund Freud, Albert Einstein, Niels Bohr, David Bohm, and other significant contributors to the modern worldview in the last two centuries in ways that we can no longer recognize. What we call commonsense ways of looking at reality have been affected tremendously by these individuals.

Much of our conventional theological discussion in the West, however, lags considerably behind this brave new world. While many today no longer resonate with the abstract and idealistic categories that were the hallmark of intellectual discourse inspired by Greek philosophy, classical theism persists in thinking and speaking about God from one of two extremes. On the one hand, God is imaged as eternal, unchanging, and aloof, ultimately

---

[26] Fretheim, *God and World in the Old Testament*, 16. For a more comprehensive treatment of this notion, see Jon D. Levenson, *Love of God: Divine Gift, Human Gratitude, and Mutual Faithfulness in Judaism* (Princeton, NJ: Princeton University Press, 2016).

254　*The God of Creative Union*

removed from any real or meaningful contact with the world. On the other hand, God is imaged as a "Big Person" who is in absolute control of the world such that the reality of human choice is effectively erased. If one or the other image is the primary metaphor by which we understand God's "relationship" to us, then we human persons, created in the image of God, are encouraged to be either passive spectators or rigid micromanagers in control of the created order.[27] Surely, our most basic metaphors for God will shape our lives, including how we think about the larger ecological and environmental contexts in which we find ourselves.

In its attempts to marry Greek philosophy with biblical theology, Heschel observes that classical theism commits a great folly: it shifts its focus

> from the primary metaphor of divine love to divine imperiality. He writes: The notion of God as a perfect being or ruler is not of biblical extraction. It is the product not of prophetic religion but of Greek philosophy; a postulate of reason rather than a direct, compelling, experiential answer of man to His reality.[28] . . . A God of abstraction . . . a high and imperial First Cause . . . dwelling in the lonely splendor of eternity is a far cry from the God of love experienced by the prophets, involved in history and affected by the world.[29] . . . The God of Israel is a God who loves, a God who is deeply known to, and concerned with the world.[30]

In the conventional model God is a divine power that somehow operates outside of, or over against, the natural laws of physics and biology, "a Supreme Being, apathetic and indifferent to [the world]."[31] Even if God is conceived of as the ultimate source of those natural laws, the implicit meaning of the image of God as divine ruler rather than divine lover is that God can suspend those laws on a whim. Furthermore, to argue that an all-powerful God "chooses" to limit divine power willy-nilly leaves us with a divinity that is at best capricious and at worst malevolent.

---

[27] Fretheim, *God and World in the Old Testament*, 14.

[28] Abraham Joshua Heschel, *Man Is Not Alone: A Philosophy of Religion* (New York: Farrar, Straus, and Giroux, 1976), 101.

[29] Heschel, *The Prophets*, 39.

[30] Ibid., 4.

[31] Ibid., 15.

In a trenchant analysis of this system of thought, Rabbi Bradley Shavit Artson concludes that the principal problem we face is not so much with God but with our limited and mischaracterized notions of power. We project our human fantasies of omnipotence onto God and turn power into the ability to control rather than that which enables our capacity for freedom and animates a *living soul*. From the perspective of the Hebrew Bible, God's power is not coercive or all-powerful; God cannot break the rules of nature or unilaterally dictate our choices. Having ordered and partnered with the cosmos, "[divine] power is a persuasive and transforming love that makes God vulnerable to the choices that each of us makes as co-creators."[32] Divine love is the engine that drives the expansion of life toward greater complexity and consciousness. Artson writes: "The God of Israel works in, with, and through creation as it is. Divine love is that which is persistently, tirelessly luring creation toward its optimal expression—greater love, greater union, greater engagement."[33] In his own way theologian Vincent Brummer confirms and then offers an admonishment to present-day philosophers and theologians alike:

God's love, God's essence, is inextricably interwoven with the cosmos. This love, like all love, is reciprocal and has integrity. . . . A great deal of our grasp of love, however, has generally been taken to be an attitude of one person toward another—a sentiment—rather than as a real relation between persons. This thinking about love is in large part due to the fact that western thought has suffered from a philosophical blind spot for relations.[34]

In the final analysis the point of these biblical and biblically minded scholars is simple and sure: the philosophical overlay of Hellenistic thought on contemporary theological speculation renders God a predominately sentimental Unmoved Mover. We need a metaphysics that seeks to renew the biblical portrait of divine love and that more comprehensively and

---

[32] Rabbi Bradley Shavit Artson, *God of Becoming and Relationship: The Dynamic Nature of Process Theology* (Woodstock, VT: Jewish Lights, 2016), 13. For another sound and detailed discussion on the biblical portrait of divine power as persuasive, see also Fretheim, *God So Enters into Relationships That*, 91–104.

[33] Artson, *God of Becoming and Relationship*, 158.

[34] Vincent Brummer, *The Model of Love: A Study in Philosophical Theology* (Cambridge: Cambridge University Press, 1993), 33. See also Thomas C. Oden, *The Living God* (San Francisco: Harper & Row, 1987), 121.

256   *The God of Creative Union*

systematically focuses on relationality and becoming, the concrete and real, as the central mode of conversation for both creation *and* Creator.

The God of Creative Union

Over the course of the last generation several major biblical-theological developments have recovered the relational model of divine love and have enabled such a frame of interpretation to receive a place of greater prominence in Old Testament scholarship. Terence Fretheim, Jon Levenson, Ronald Simkins, Norman Habel, William Brown, Erich Zenger, Rabbi Bradley Shavit Artson, and others affirm the need for a theological (and philosophical) understanding of the God-world relationship that takes seriously the metaphor and implications of divine love captured by biblical literature and perspectives. These texts give testimony to a God who does not stand at an untouchable remove from the world but is understood to be in the total universal process, thoroughly and completely immersed in every facet of history, nature, and human consciousness. Divine love, therefore, certainly can be conceived of as a creative energy that draws, entices, persuades, and lures the entire evolutionary enterprise toward more complex relationalities. Such was the existing imagery of divine love in the writings of two foremost pioneers of process thought, namely, the philosopher Alfred North Whitehead and the Jesuit scientist Pierre Teilhard de Chardin. In their own ways they each held that love "orders" and "unifies" existing matter.

While Teilhard was neither a trained theologian, nor do his writings formally engage with biblical texts or citations from the Hebrew Bible, his philosophy of love is thoroughly consonant with our interconnected universe and with how the metaphor of love serves to characterize the God-world relationship for the ancient Israelites. Teilhard's God-world relationship is one of "creative union."[35] He posited a genuine complementarity between God and the world, in which they formed an interrelated and complementary pair. God is more than the world but personally linked to

---

[35] Teilhard's doctrine of creative union was never intended to be a metaphysical doctrine in the classical sense of the term. He explains: "[Creative Union] is much more a sort of empirical and pragmatic explanation of the universe; I have developed it to meet the need to reconcile, in a solidly coherent system, scientific views on evolution (now definitely accepted in their essence) with the innate tendency that urges me to seek the divine, not by breaking away from the physical world, but through matter and, and in some way, in union with it." Pierre Teilhard de Chardin, *Writings in Time of War*, trans. René Hague (New York: Harper & Row, 1968), 152.

it in a relationship of integrity and mutuality.[36] The heart of creative union *is* divine love. Consistent with the concerns of biblical theologians, Ursula King highlights: "Teilhard criticized the traditional concept of love as too static, too abstract, too spiritualized, too divorced from its cosmic roots and from natural passion, in which all love, including the love of God, has its starting point."[37] He instead saw love as a cosmic energy, a mysterious force working toward the attraction and unification of divergent elements into more complex and deeply personal configurations, from the lowest to the highest level of life.[38] For him, love is the core energy of evolution and is intrinsically relational. It is "the most universal, the most tremendous and the most mysterious of the cosmic forces."[39]

Similar to the doctrine of continuing creation in the Hebrew scriptures, Teilhard maintained that we are an integral dimension of a world "that is *being born* rather than that *is*."[40] As "the spearheads of evolution," those who recapitulate and advance cosmic wholeness on the level of self-consciousness, God neither abandons creation nor retains all power, but rather permeates, grounds, and unifies all becoming by working with us to fulfill our optimal potentialities (new creation).[41] In an effort to juxtapose his position with a classical metaphysical stance he states: "We must remember, union does more than transform things and add to them. It *produces*. Every new union to be effected increases the absolute quantity of being existing in the universe."[42] Steeped in the energy of divine love, creative union sets up a direct and genuine relationship between the evolution of Spirit and the complexity of matter.[43] Therefore, God's creating is not one of *ex nihilo* from without, but rather a unitive process of galvanizing continuous self-creativity from within. From the growth of complexity and an increase in consciousness, the contours of divine love expand, and God is realized in evolution. The slightly adapted words of Jeremiah ring true, God's love

---

[36] Pierre Teilhard de Chardin, *Christianity and Evolution: Reflections on Science and Religion*, trans. René Hague (New York: Harcourt, 1971), 227.

[37] Ursula King, "Theories of Love: Sorokin, Teilhard and Tillich," *Zygon* 39, no. 1 (March 2004): 85.

[38] Pierre Teilhard de Chardin, *Human Energy*, trans. J. M. Cohen (New York: Harcourt Brace Jovanovich, 1969), 23, 72.

[39] Ibid., 32.

[40] Pierre Teilhard de Chardin, *The Future of Man*, trans. Norman Denny (New York: Image Books, 1959), 88.

[41] Ursula King, *The Spirit of One Earth: Reflections on Teilhard de Chardin and Global Spirituality* (New York: Paragon House, 1989), 30.

[42] Teilhard, *Writings in Time of War*, 163.

[43] Ibid., 165.

258   *The God of Creative Union*

slowly "fills" heaven and earth (23:23–24). We and everything in the cosmos are not only co-creators with God but co-revealers.

In this paradigm God is the everlasting, uncreated member of the cosmic community who is being constantly created through the infinite potential of new interpersonal unions. At the same time, God is the one who fully absorbs and is affected by all the world's choices and vicissitudes. When tragedy strikes, our sorrows are not lost; they become a permanent part of the fabric of divine love. Our joys and our lives are not forgotten, but rather they are eternally experienced and preserved in the divine mind. Teilhard assures us: "[God is the energy that] sustains and animates and holds together [all things]. . . . He is . . . the growth and final term of all things. Everything lives, and everything is raised up—everything in consequence is one—in Him and through Him."[44] As he likewise believed that true union differentiates, the world will never cease to retain its integrity as world, even while filled with the presence of divine love. Similarly, as the overflow of love, God will never cease to be transcendent. Ilia Delio clarifies: "For Teilhard, the world is not God and God is not the world, yet God is the unlimited depth of love, the center, of all that is: a love that endlessly overflows onto new life. God is not a supernatural being hovering above the earth but the supra-personal whole, the Omega, who exists in all and through all."[45] There will always be more to fill in an emerging universe.

Although references to the Hebrew Bible can be found in Whitehead's philosophical corpus, he does betray a lack of critical study of these texts. He writes, for example, "It was a mistake, as the Hebrews tried, to conceive of God as creating the world from the outside, at one go. An all-foreseeing Creator, who could have made the world as we find it now—what could we think of such a being?"[46] Despite this oversight, Whitehead's thought in general and his outlook on love in particular are strikingly in sync with Old Testament theology as well.

In his system God is not a supernatural deity but an essential part of the relational process: the chief exemplar of goodness and love in creation.[47] As in the biblical texts, "the divine," as the highest form of reality, "is caught up

---

[44] Ibid., 47.

[45] Ilia Delio, "Evolution and the Rise of the Secular God," in *From Teilhard to Omega: Co-Creating an Unfinished Universe*, ed. Ilia Delio (Maryknoll, NY: Orbis Books, 2014), 45.

[46] As recorded by Lucien Price, *Dialogues by Alfred North Whitehead* (Boston: Nonpareil, 1954), 366.

[47] Alfred North Whitehead, *Process and Reality: An Essay in Cosmology*, corrected ed., ed. David Ray Griffin and Donald Sherburne (New York: The Free Press, 1978), 343.

in the always ongoing adventure of all that was, is, and will be."[48] Comparable to Teilhard, according to Segall, Whitehead's God-world relationship was also one of creative union, in which divine love, or what he called "eros," unendingly brings the world out of primordial chaos into new and richer instantiations of union. God shares in the creative process as the erotic energy permeating every entity and lures all onward toward possibilities that generate novel intensities of relatedness.[49] Reflective of the biblical worldview, divine love is not a power of coercion or omnipotence but is completely relational. "Under the relational concept of power," Bernard Loomer explains, "the true good of divine love is not a function of controlling or dominating influence. The true good is an emergent from deeply mutual relationships."[50] The divine lure of love, in other words, has an unquenchable desire for fuller cosmic identification but can only do so if we seek to unite ever more deeply in love with one another and the entire planet. In biblical parlance godly power *is* persuasive power and described with terms like *chesed* and *tzedek*, understood as a dynamic and persistent invitation of divine love that human persons can either ignore or embrace.[51] Life lived in harmony with these powers or principles brings abundance; refusing or revoking them inevitably leads to both ecological and social disaster.

Certainly, such mutual and meaningful interaction between God and world also implies some kind of change on the part of both parties to the interaction. According to Whitehead, all life, whether subatomic particles or human persons, are in process in that they interact with the environment around them, are affected by their environment, and assimilate this experience into the next moment of becoming.[52] In accord with biblical theology,

---

[48] Roland Faber, "De-ontologizing God: Levinas, Deleuze, and Whitehead," in *Process and Difference: Between Cosmological and Poststructuralist Postmodernisms*, ed. Catherine Keller and Anne Daniell (Albany: State University of New York Press, 2002), 222–23; quoted in Matthew David Segall, *Physics of the World-Soul: Whitehead's Adventure in Cosmology* (Grasmere, ID: SacraSage, 2021), 147.

[49] Segall, *Physics of the World-Soul*, 146.

[50] Bernard Loomer, "Two Conceptions of Power," *Criterion* 15, no.1 (Winter 1976): 7–29. For different perspectives consistent with Loomer's emphasis on relational power, see Andrew M. Davis, ed., *From Force to Persuasion: Process-Relational Perspectives on Power and the God of Love* (Eugene, OR: Cascade, 2024).

[51] Artson, *God of Becoming and Relationship*, 95–99.

[52] See C. Robert Mesle, *Process-Relational Philosophy: An Introduction to Alfred North Whitehead* (West Conshohocken: Templeton Press, 2008), 43, in which he explains: "It is impossible for experience to exist independently: Experience arises out of that which is lived. That which is experienced from 'outside' us becomes 'inside' us, or, better, becomes part of us because it is taken into our self as experiencer. Every drop of experience is a novel weaving of the world of preceding experiences out of which that drop arises."

260   *The God of Creative Union*

he maintained that God is likewise inextricably intertwined with the world and thus is becoming something more with the world. Far from diminishing God, this inherent relationality is at the very foundation of what it means for God to truly "love and need" us. Rabbi Artson remarks:

> A God who learns is a God who teaches, and a God who teaches is one who is able to invite us to make the best decisions, to perceive right from wrong because of what we intuit inside, because of the messages that God constantly allows to spill out of our hearts and minds when we align ourselves with his wealth of increasing knowledge.[53]

Process philosopher Robert Mesle lends support to this claim:

> God is good because God is love, and divine love shares the experience of every creature and every drop of becoming—every pain, joy, hope, despair, failure, and triumph. . . . God is the only one who has the strength, the ability, to be open to every single experience in the world. God is the only one who can take everything in, integrate it with God's own infinitely ancient wisdom, and create God's self out of that relationship in each moment. God is the only one who can then feed back to every creature in the world a lure and call toward those possibilities that are best for it. All the possibilities are there, good and bad, but they come to us with God's tender call toward the better.[54]

In this sense, Whitehead affirms: "God is the great companion—the fellow-sufferer who understands."[55] In God, there is no loss of value, no obstruction. God's experience of the world is one in which the creative advance is preserved in everlasting immediacy.[56]

Renewing the Biblical Portrait of Divine Love

Without a compelling way of talking about how the God so profoundly experienced by our biblical ancestors is still active in our lives and in the world

---

[53] Artson, *God of Becoming and Relationship*, 179.
[54] Mesle, *Process-Relational Philosophy*, 86, 87.
[55] Whitehead, *Process and Reality*, 351.
[56] Ibid., 346.

around us, our theological story threatens to become little more than wistful nostalgia or fantastical folklore. Without a way to frame our understanding of God that is intellectually coherent and biblically consistent—that is, the imagery we choose to employ stirs the waters of thought and ensnares the senses—religion surrenders its power to shape our individual and collective lives, as well as the future direction of the world, in any positive, meaningful, and lasting way. Both Teilhard and Whitehead knew this well and, as a result, their philosophical theologies effectively renew our appreciation of the relational paradigm of divine love as envisioned in the Hebrew Bible. They do so in four notable respects.[57]

First, where the conventional theological guiding conceptions focus on division and hierarchical arrangement between God and world, Teilhard and Whitehead emphasize interdependency and interrelatedness of God and the ongoing creative activity of the world. As in the biblical texts, they do not so much sharply differentiate between the transcendent and immanent dimensions of God but rather view them holistically as a unified testimony to the presence of divine love in the universe. The realm of the divine and the realm of the world are seen not as disconnected from each other; there are coinciding powers, roles, and responsibilities to which the metaphor of divine love attests.[58] God's relationship with the world is not a vague outpouring of impersonal goodness, but rather the genuine relatedness of a personalizing love.

Second, in light of this relational perspective, the God of the Torah and of our lived experience of the world is not an abstract, omnipotent, unchanging, and immutable Unmoved Mover, but that which lovingly enables the universe to unfold in all its extraordinary complexity. In a similar way Teilhard and Whitehead remind us that true love qualifies power and really requires the existence of the other, not merely the idea of the other. They, too, speak of God as one who is inherently persuasive rather than coercive, respecting the freedom and creativity of universal life and itself affected by the ever-changing dynamics of creation at large. God is envisioned as a transpersonal energy through which creation is forever coming into existence and co-evolving with all other creatures that inhabit the universe. This is a God who is not "a cosmic watchmaker," as Lewis Ford quips, "but

---

[57] While their philosophical formulations of divine love certainly offer many more principles, I chose only to indicate and explain four for the sake of concision.

[58] Fretheim, *God and World in the Old Testament*, 271–72.

262   *The God of Creative Union*

a fellow gardener in the vineyard who nurtures and preserves the best possible growth in all life."[59]

Third, while there is only one reality, it is not one-dimensional and on one level but is rich in layers. The transcendent layer of reality is not more real or valuable than the terrestrial. As Rabbi Spitzer warns: "It is only by taking very seriously our physical experience of this material world that we can access divine Presence at all."[60] Teilhard and Whitehead challenge us to realize that the only spiritual task worthy of our efforts is to *see* the godliness slowly rising up within material reality, and that ultimately all perceived separateness—between people, between other living organisms, and between the world at large—is artificial and illusory. In the truest sense, the divine oneness spoken about in the Bible is tantamount to the cosmotheandric wholeness experienced by the mystics and reaffirmed by the relational philosophies of Teilhard and Whitehead.

Finally, scripture considers love to be a universal vocation. We all have a special responsibility to cultivate a world in which the love of God is primary. Therefore, divine love gives us a direction, if not a moral imperative, in terms of our choices. Whitehead refers to this impulse as the "adventure of the spirit," in which we respond to the inviting power to surpass ourselves and move toward growth and innovation; and Teilhard describes it as the "zest for life," in which we acknowledge and activate the transformative energy of evolution necessary for building the world anew.[61] This certainly demands renewed attention and reflection. It teaches us that if we love what is best in ourselves, if we love our potentials for growth, development, creative ability, and communion with others, then this love, which is our essential nature, urges us to live a life of higher quality. This love is then never again a purely sentimental or passive obstacle to loving others and the world in the same way, but rather is a powerful impetus for doing so and the promise of hope for a better future. In the end, we and the world become what we are meant to be by our courage to love indiscriminately and without reservation.

---

[59] Lewis S. Ford, *The Lure of God: A Biblical Background for Process Theism* (Philadelphia: Fortress Press, 1978), 21.

[60] Spitzer, *God Is Here*, 246.

[61] Ursula King, *Christ in All Things: Evolving Spirituality with Pierre Teilhard de Chardin* (Maryknoll, NY: Orbis Books, 2016), 74.

Part III

Possibilities and Perils of the Future

The Unsatisfied Theists

Pierre Teilhard de Chardin, Alfred North Whitehead,
and the Future of Religion

JOHN BECKER

In *The Phenomenon of Man*, Pierre Teilhard de Chardin surveys the attitude of the nineteenth-century religious landscape and laments about its sad state of affairs. The human condition is riddled with existential angst or apathy because Christianity, and religion more generally, has lost its ability to offer an optimistic vision. It no longer speaks to the human spirit. Yet, he intuits something important; namely, that a genuine atheistic vision is not the dominant response to this particular predicament. Rather, Teilhard prophetically suggests that those struggling with the religious sentiment of his day are better characterized as "unsatisfied" theists.[1] His is an era of unsatisfied theism. He wrote these words about a century ago.

While much has changed between the centuries, I cannot think of a better description for our contemporary indifference toward religiosity. Teilhard wrote this within a Christian context, but the pattern holds throughout notions of religious affiliation, particularly in America. An updated and more inclusive term may be *unsatisfied religionist*. Today, the rise of the "nones" and the "spiritual but not religious" (SBNR) is a testament to Teilhard's observation. This demographic is opaque and indeterminate, but it is telling that the SBNR still find spirituality a central concern. For me, this suggests that religion is still vitally important for many within this group, yet the way religious traditions have and continue to engage modernity is

---

[1] Pierre Teilhard de Chardin, *The Activation of Energy: Enlightening Reflections on Spiritual Energy*, trans. René Hague (New York: HarperOne, 2002), 239–41.

265

266 *The Unsatisfied Theists*

deemed too uninspiring and in need of change. Christianity needs a new story, a new metaphysic to meet the "dis-ease" of the *sensus fidelium* (the sense of the faithful).

Teilhard and Alfred North Whitehead were both acutely aware of "unsatisfied theists" because they were both, in their own ways, part of this crowd. Teilhard and Whitehead were both unsatisfied theists, and in response they advanced radical new visions of not only Christianity, but religion as well. The story, however, does not end there. Paradoxically, they were also "unsatisfied scientists," and as before, they proffered an alternative to scientific materialism by incorporating other experiential dimensions. Despite responding to two different concerns, their solutions shared an overarching conviction. They were committed to a solution that was able to frame a cosmic vision. Approaches to reality must be holistic, navigating both terrains without relegating one in favor for the other.

A new universe reveals itself by upholding such a cosmic vision, and this chapter attempts to delineate some of these novel trajectories for religions and their future. The first section develops Teilhard's evolutionary vision as he negotiates between his scientific orientation and Catholic faith. One's faith, church, and scientific progress cannot be separated from one another in this cosmic becoming. Next, Whitehead's philosophy of organism is presented, with particular attention to the dynamism of religion. As with Teilhard, religiosity cannot be an exception to cosmic rules but flourishes or deteriorates under its universal principles. Central to the process is humanity, the fulcrum that decides its religion and the world's fate. The concluding section constructively brings together their cosmic visions to suggest what the future of the religion and religiosity may bring.

The Unsatisfied Teilhard

Teilhard famously stated that "evolution is a light illuminating all facts, a line that all lines must follow."[2] Despite materialist assumptions, for him, evolution did not exclude the spiritual dimension. In fact, while he certainly upheld this evolutionary approach to religion, he simultaneously provided the inverse: a groundbreaking religious approach to evolution theory. It is no easy task to balance insightfully the requirements each discourse expects while still providing important contributions. Teilhard's ideas about the

---

[2] Pierre Teilhard de Chardin, *The Phenomenon of Man*, trans. Bernard Wall (New York: Harper Perennial Modern Classics, 2008), 219.

future of religion begin not with the current state of religiosity today or their respective histories, but with the formation of the universe itself. Hence, to understand the future of religion, we must go back, all the way back, to the inception of the universe itself.

In *The Phenomenon of Man* Teilhard provides such a cosmic story (Big History), starting from the material foundation of the universe to the present. In this task he describes the various demarcated eras that the universe has perceptively undergone. He describes three different transitional periods that correspond to the first three sections, called books, of *The Phenomenon of Man*, each one building off the previous: the geosphere (*Before Life Came*), biosphere (*Life*), and the noosphere (*Thought*). With each respective period the emergence of higher forms of complexity provides the foundation upon which the preceding sphere is built. The cosmic dance of continuity and discontinuity provides the creative advance of evolution.

According to Teilhard, whether we examine the dynamics of the geosphere or the currently fomenting noosphere, there is a distinct universal pattern: evolution. He identifies two defining features to this process: first, there is a cosmic impetus for greater complexity, from atoms coalescing into tangible matter to single-celled organisms slowly emerging into intricate multicell organisms. What is dispersed naturally gravitates into a collective that gives rise to new modes of togetherness. While hundreds of millions of years make this model discernible, it is a pattern that holds universally.

Second, the movement toward complexity is not merely the reshuffling of matter but leads to pressurization and propels the cosmic story into novel dimensions. Something new is introduced into the universe through complexification. This is the only way to explain the emergence of life from pure matter. A leap in the geosphere miraculously gave rise to a living, single-celled organism, just as planetary life hit a threshold whereby human consciousness arose. Consciousness is the new area of evolutionary progress. He writes, "After the grain of matter, the grain of life; and now at last we see constituted the grain of thought. . . . From now onwards it was not merely animated grains which the pressure of evolution pumped up the living stem, but grains of thought."[3] These two aspects point to an ongoing process of complexity and novelty.

We may pause to ask what exactly propels or drives the creative impetus for these natural movements toward complexity and the creation of new evolutionary "spheres." Is the creative force from within or without? This

---

[3] Teilhard, *The Phenomenon of Man*, 173–74.

268   The Unsatisfied Theists

question leads us to one of the contested ideas of Teilhard's evolutionary theory: radial energy. This concept spiritualizes the evolutionary process by maintaining there are innate energies that animate the universe. Teilhard writes that "beneath the 'tangential' we find the 'radial.' The impetus of the world, glimpsed in the great drive of consciousness, can only have its ultimate source in some inner principle, which alone could explain its irreversible advance towards higher psychisms."[4] Elsewhere he writes: "By their very nature, and at every level of complexity, the elements of the world are able to influence and mutually penetrate each other by their within, so as to combine their 'radial energies' in 'bundles.'"[5] Evolution is not only a material movement, but more important, a spiritual process. He even suggests that the evolutionary process is moving toward spiritualization, and it is it within the spiritual dimension that the new frontier of the cosmic story will continue.

This is an admittedly simplified version of Teilhard's theory of evolution, yet it is an important working framework in which religions and their future find meaning. The energy of evolution is now localized on the spiritualization of the cosmos through humankind. As Ilia Delio rightly states, "Religion is not a human phenomenon but a cosmic one."[6] Yet, unlike the previous evolutionary spheres, the noosphere is qualitatively different due to the human element. While Teilhard is assured that the Omega Point will be reached, human anxiety hinders the evolutionary process.[7] "We are evolution," he emphatically states, and we must now fulfill our spiritual evolutionary task.[8] But exactly how this fulfillment will transpire is unclear, as he acknowledges.

The religion of the future is an "unknown form of religion," yet Teilhard proffers thoughts on how the spiritual realm advances.[9] As Delio and Ursula King have noted,[10] he developed a stance of genuine interreligious dialogue and advocated for a unitary vision characterized as "a harmonized complexity."[11] Accordingly, religions and communities must engage one

---

[4] Ibid., 149.

[5] Ibid., 239.

[6] Ilia Delio, "Teilhard de Chardin and World Religions," *Journal of Ecumenical Studies* 54, no. 3 (Summer 2019): 306–27, 309.

[7] Teilhard, *The Phenomenon of Man*, 276.

[8] Ibid., 234.

[9] Teilhard, *The Activation of Energy*, 383.

[10] For example, see Ursula King, "Religion and the Future: Teilhard de Chardin's Analysis of Religion as a Contribution to Inter-Religious Dialogue," *Religious Studies* 7, no. 4 (1971): 307–23; Delio, "Teilhard de Chardin and World Religions."

[11] Teilhard, *The Phenomenon of Man*, 262.

another in love and authenticity. Teilhard warns that "contact is still superficial, involving danger of the yet another servitude. . . . Love alone is capable of uniting living beings in such a way as to complete and fulfill them, for it alone takes them and joins them by what is deepest in itself."[12] He envisions world religions as points in a polycentric format, slowly gravitating toward one another and the Omega Point, where each religious tradition becomes more distinct in themselves. In its various manifestations religion in the future does not become an amorphous unity but a "comm-unity." It is here that love flourishes.

His distinction between tangential and radial energy is paramount to appreciate his assessment here. Tangential conveys an external quality and is an inferior type of energy. For example, this room has a tangential togetherness insofar as we are a collection of entities. Yet this tangential togetherness is arguably superficial. It lacks genuine concern for the other—it does not stir our innermost nature, our radial energy. Put differently, tangential energy is like those popular *Coexist* stickers where religions merely coexist with one another (tangential). Radial energy goes beyond existence to mutual or co-flourishing, where there is a genuine concern for one another from the innermost parts of humanity.

Behind these energies and their evolutionary movements is God. Not a transcendent overseer, but, as Teilhard brilliantly puts it, a "Prime Mover ahead."[13] The world's religions are not just gravitating toward one another, but also into the future, toward the center of evolution, the Omega Point (which is already operative in the universe). This point is the distinct center "radiating at the core of a system of centers."[14] The closer religions come to the Omega Point, the more they become distinct in themselves. Whereas religions historically developed separately, the religions of the future will grow together.

In *Toward the Future* Teilhard provides imagery of this togetherness as several rivers converging into a single flow, finding a shared way forward.[15] Of importance here is that Christianity alone cannot bring about this cosmic fulfillment. Different religiosities have a role to play in the cosmic story. Delio notes that Western religions emphasize a personal element to the universe and Eastern religions emphasize an expanse consciousness, but

---

[12] Ibid., 265.

[13] Ibid., 271.

[14] Ibid., 262.

[15] Pierre Teilhard de Chardin, *Toward the Future*, trans. René Hague (New York: HarperOne, 2002), 209–11.

270   The Unsatisfied Theists

"no one religion can satisfy the religious spirit of the earth."[16] In a sense, we are all in this together, and this has important implications for the future of religion. But before exploring Teilhard's vision further, I now turn to Whitehead's processual worldview and role of religion in the future.

The Unsatisfied Whitehead

Like Teilhard, Whitehead emphasized the need to shift our fundamental orientations toward the world, including religions. As he explained, the process of truth, religious or otherwise, is the continual process of framing concepts "in evolving notions which strike more deeply into the root of reality."[17] The explanatory power of the evolutionary perspectives clearly meant that processes and change are the guiding principles of the universe, and all areas of knowledge must take note.

In a chapter entitled "Religion and Science" in *Science in the Modern World*, Whitehead brilliantly illustrates this point through "Roman Catholic writers." Here, he references a work by Father Dionysius Petavius, a seventeenth-century French Jesuit, who wrote about historical movements of theological discernment. Without going into details, Whitehead remarks that Father Petavius "showed that the theologians of the first three centuries of Christianity made use of phrases and statements which since the fifth century would be condemned as heretical."[18] The language of the past required greater judgements to fit the growing convictions of the church.

This example, as he notes, is not a characteristic reserved for religion alone, but a universal law. All knowledge requires vigilance and continual modification. He continues: "Science is even more changeable than theology. No man of science could subscribe without qualification to Galileo's beliefs, or to Newton's beliefs, or to all his own scientific beliefs of ten years ago."[19] For Whitehead, to be malleable is a sign of vitality, authenticity, and maturity.

The above pattern of processual discernment is fleshed out more critically in *Religion in the Making*, where Whitehead proffers the dynamism of

---

[16] Ilia Delio, *The Not-Yet God: Carl Jung, Teilhard de Chardin, and the Relational Whole* (Maryknoll, NY: Orbis Books, 2023), 41.

[17] Alfred North Whitehead, *Religion in the Making* (New York: Cambridge University Press, 2011), 117.

[18] Alfred North Whitehead, *Science and the Modern World* (New York: The Free Press, 1967), 183.

[19] Ibid., 183.

progressive and regressive forms of religiosity. He identifies a notable shift in religiosity during the so-called Axial Age. During this era individuals became aware of themselves through a newly forming, yet obscure, world consciousness. Whitehead explains this as a shift from "tribal religion" to "rational religion," where individuals are able to disengage themselves from their particular socio-religious context and entertain new possibilities. A defining feature of rational religion is rational criticism. Being critical of a group dynamic meant that individuals were to play a greater role in the future of religion. To this point, he speaks of the great prophets as exemplars in this respect, and "in this way the religions evolved towards more individualistic forms, shedding their exclusively communal aspect."[20]

With a new critical eye toward tribal forms of religiosity, Whitehead states that the old religions "could no longer contain the new ideas, and the modern religions of civilization are traceable to definite crises in this development process." This shift toward rational religious consciousness is not the spiritual finale but religion's most effective arrangement to date. For each new generation, for each new revolutionary discovery, religions should continually acquire "more suitable forms of self-expression."[21] These "suitable forms of expression" entail a cosmic awareness where religion must be open to modify, not discard, religious dogmas and practices in purview of "the complete circle of our knowledge."[22]

Crossing the threshold into a rational religion, however, is not a permanent feature. Once this critical spirit is lost, reversal is possible. This reversion, Whitehead argues, "is partly due to the fact that each religion has unduly sheltered itself from the other." He laments at the end of chapter one in *Religion in the Making* that Christianity and Buddhism, and religions more generally, "are in decay" because they have lost the ability of "constructive criticism."[23] Over the past few centuries the contemporary religious landscape has slipped back into the patterns of tribalism, albeit in new forms. This trend is not surprising, according to Whitehead, since the promise offered by other religions or spheres of knowledge can be misconstrued as threatening, thereby creating walls of nationalism and tribal superiority. This is in direct contrast to rational religion's porous, attentive walls to the cosmos.

---

[20] Whitehead, *Religion in the Making*, 25.
[21] Ibid., 22.
[22] Ibid., 69.
[23] Ibid., 33.

272   *The Unsatisfied Theists*

While Whitehead maintains the importance of solitariness for religiosity, he does not understand it as a form of solipsism or isolationism. Rational religion is individualistic to the extent that one can critically and creatively approach one's immediate environment with an extended notion of valuation. Solitariness for Whitehead includes:

1. The value of the individual for itself.
2. The value of the diverse individuals of the world for each other.
3. The value of the objective world which is a community derivative from the interrelations of its component individuals, and also necessary for the existence of each of these individuals.[24]

Put more directly, religion "is the wider conscious reaction of men to the universe in which they find themselves."[25] This new awareness of one's environment produces the necessary vitality that propels religion into new dynamic forms. Whitehead acknowledges that rational religions display a "world-loyalty."[26] This is the function of religion at its finest.

The discussion between tribal and rational religions elucidates an important Whiteheadian concept: contrasts. As with Teilhard, the cosmic advance depends on differences, and outright rejects bland unity. Contrastive intensities between what is (actuality) and what may be (potentiality) give rise to an aesthetic experience that depends on two elements: First, the novel consequent must be graded in relevance so as to preserve some identity of character with the ground. Second, the novel consequent must be graded in relevance so as to preserve some contrast with the ground with respect to that same identity of character.[27] Here, we see Whitehead's cosmic dance between stability and becoming, each being integral to effective change. When obsessed with preserving religious identity, stagnate tribalism transpires. When obsessed with radically breaking from the past, it fails to honor the continuity needed to inspire the respective community.

However, when religions are open to the creative process and balance the extremes, "religion can be, and has been, the main instrument for progress."[28] Within the context of the future of religions, they must continue providing their unique perspective to provide a catalyst for the movement into

---

[24] Ibid., 48.
[25] Ibid., 31.
[26] Ibid., 49.
[27] Ibid., 101.
[28] Ibid., 20.

the future. As Whitehead movingly noted, "The whole world conspires to produce a new creation."[29] God is intimately tied to this process, for God provides values that lure creation into novel patterns. There is a symbolic dynamism at play here. Humanity materializes God's lures and guides the creative advance into the future, only for God to provide new lures to becoming. God and the world unceasingly constitute one another.

Famously, Whitehead has termed God as "the poet of the world."[30] He acknowledges that God is "the binding element in the world. The consciousness, which is individual in us, is universal in him: the love which is partial in us, is all-embracing in him."[31] God's purpose in the world is quality of attainment. As with Teilhard, God is simultaneously transcendent and immanent in the cosmic process. When an individual is able to synthesizes felt contrastive intensities (what Whitehead terms concrescence), satisfaction or value is obtained. Such contrast for our purpose could be the creative tension felt between science and religion or doctrinal differences between religious traditions.

To reconcile such experiences is a providential act, a commitment to world loyalty, as Whitehead would retort. The derivative value is not instrumental but one imbued with aesthetic qualities of emotive and spiritual importance. God's incessant lures require individuals and their communities, religious or otherwise, to strive for greater sympathy and relationally. In the end, we are left with an unfinished cosmic story that aspires for great conviviality but is not assured of it.

Contrasting Patterns of Hope

Admittedly, both Teilhard and Whitehead do not supply concrete perspectives on the future of religion, but some comparative observations can be made. First, love and hope are indispensable for the future. Second, the God of a processual or evolutionary world is modified into a dynamic, interdependent God. Each observation is taken in turn.

The success of the future religion depends on the awareness of a relational whole imbued with love. Teilhard notes that "the noosphere tends to constitute a single closed system in which each element sees, feels, desires,

---

[29] Ibid., 99.

[30] Alfred North Whitehead, *Process and Reality: An Essay in Cosmology*, corrected ed., ed. David Ray Griffin and Donald Sherburne (New York: The Free Press, 1978), 346.

[31] Whitehead, *Religion in the Making*, 143.

274   *The Unsatisfied Theists*

and suffers for itself the same things as all others at the same time."[32] Similarly, Whitehead holds that God is an all-embracing love of our finite love. Love operates on the distinction between the lover and the loved, and as such, religions must embrace the other precisely as the other. This is not the selfish love of narcissism but rather a sympathetic love that recognizes the happiness of one is dependent upon others.

Our unsatisfied theists also recognize that which is applied to creation must be equally applied to all facets of the universe, including God. As noted, a sympathetic love cannot be forced, self-serving, or unrequited. Traditional God-talk must be revised. God cannot be unmoved or wholly transcendent. No. God's transcendence is modified to the future. For Teilhard, the God of the not yet, and for Whitehead, the God of the becoming. This aspect of the future alludes to something crucial. Creation cannot be forced into this love but instead requires a divine invitation. This God persuades rather than coerces, and lures the radial energies toward God's self in the evolutionary process.[33]

What is apparent from the first point and central to the second point is that God and creation have a dynamic relationship. This point is more contentious within Teilhard's Catholic world than Whitehead's. The end of *Process and Reality* highlights this point among five others: "It is as true to say that God creates the World, as that the World creates God."[34] There is a real reciprocity between creation and God for Whitehead. They require one another in the process of becoming.

Teilhard, from my reading, teeters back and forth on this cosmic dynamic. On the one hand, Teilhard's evolutionary account speaks of the noosphere as involving a unique facet that did not figure previously in the cosmic story: human consciousness. Whereas the geo- and biosphere operated under uniformed laws with limited forms of consciousness, the highly developed consciousness of the noosphere is essentially stubborn because this "thinking layer" has choices. The evolutionary progress of the noosphere seems optional.[35] Collectively, humankind must decide between an "absurd universe" and a "universe to which we can unhesitatingly entrust ourselves."[36] As Ursula King notes, responsibility for further self-evolution

---

[32] Teilhard, *The Phenomenon of Man*, 251.

[33] For an excellent work on this topic, see Dan Dombrowski, *Whitehead's Religious Thought: From Mechanism to Organism, From Force to Persuasion* (Albany: State University of New York Press, 2017).

[34] Whitehead, *Process and Reality*, 348.

[35] Teilhard, *The Phenomenon of Man*, 250–75.

[36] Ibid., 233.

lies now with humans themselves rather than with external factors."[37] In this sense God and the cosmos depend upon one another for their ultimate fulfillment. Through this reading, Teilhard and Whitehead share a common cosmic vision.

On the other hand, Teilhard is also firm in his conviction that the Omega Point will unquestionably be realized. He states, "However improbable it might seem, we must reach the goal, not necessarily, doubtless, but infallibly."[38] For Teilhard, the entire cosmos is moving toward the God of the future in an imperfect, non-linear way. Such conviction is inspiring, but Whitehead holds no such conviction. This appears to be the fundamental difference between Teilhard and Whitehead: a teleological eschaton. Despite humanity's central role in the future via the noosphere, it appears it is not a matter of *if* but *when*. In other words, humanity's intellectual anxiety may delay the fulfillment of the cosmos in Christ, but not indefinitely. Whitehead and Teilhard part ways in this reading.

There is an end goal to the ever-growing complexity of the universe that results in the amassing of Christ, the Christogenesis in realizing the Omega Point. Whitehead's universe will always be incomplete, searching for ever-greater modes of togetherness, complexity, tragedy, and beauty. However, despite their divergent views concerning teleological ends, their overarching evolutionary approaches share striking similarities and offer a new cosmic story. Yet another reading of Teilhard is possible, one entertained by the prominent Teilhardian scholar Ilia Delio.

According to Delio, common interpretations pertaining to the actualization of the Omega Point erroneously assume a cosmic stop point, a reached state of divine inertia. That is, once it has been achieved, the cosmic story ceases to continue. Delio holds that there is no definable conclusion to the cosmic story. She writes that our universe will incessantly drive and actualize this point and yet "perhaps this will be the end of our Big Bang universe, but I am sure there will be others."[39] The problematic rendering fails to take seriously Teilhard's cosmic vision. The coalescing of mind and matter in the Omega Point is surely an astonishing feat, yet must we assume that this concludes the story?

One way to move beyond this position is to hold to the evolutionary pattern outlined by Teilhard. He theorizes about the emergence of distinct

---

[37] Ursula King, *Teilhard de Chardin and Eastern Religions: Spirituality and Mysticism in an Evolutionary World* (Mahwah, NJ: Paulist Press, 2011), 182.

[38] Teilhard, *The Phenomenon of Man*, 276.

[39] Delio, *The Not-Yet God*, 212.

276   The Unsatisfied Theists

epochs, each having new complex and defining elements. When a certain threshold or pressurization is met during a specific era, a new one is initiated. Following this pattern, what if the Omega Point is not a hard stop or end to the evolutionary story, but rather serves as an era-specific placeholder for the next dynamic era's actualization? In this way the Omega Point is a constantly recurring actualization for each new era, leading to ever-higher forms of complexity of the cosmic story. The God of the future is a moving divine target, and once actualized, a new target is revealed with greater possibilities of fulfillment in the future. If this was Teilhard's intent, then his affinity with Whitehead's processual schemata deserves further study.

The worldviews put forth by these "unsatisfied theists" provide startling new cosmological visions. They offer a universal vision that is characterized by radical entanglement. This process is not limited to certain facets of reality but its defining principle, and being open to this dynamic is the hallmark of flourishing. These cosmic principles suggest novel ramifications for religious identity, religions, and their engagement with one another.

A Satisfying Religious Future?

What can these prophetic voices tell us about religion and its future? As noted in my opening paragraphs, Teilhard's and Whitehead's dissatisfaction is now recognized as a growing religious phenomenon: the nones and the spiritual but not religious. In fact, this demographic recently usurped Protestantism as the single largest "religious" group in America.[40] Religious dissatisfaction is palpable, and while the reasons for the rise of the nones is multifaceted, it is clear that religion has lost its vitality to inspire. A new vision is needed. Teilhard and Whitehead offer such a vision. In this concluding section I offer opportunities gleaned from these cosmic stories.

The future of religiosity can be characterized as a radical openness to otherness and difference. In a sense this captures our unsatisfied theists core contention: the complex layers of existence and its derivative knowledge demand a togetherness, a dynamic entanglement. Our modern patterns of thought have compartmentalized our world and distorted it as a relational whole. As the saying goes, *Don't lose the forest for the trees.* Spheres of knowledge and experience must be reconciled into higher forms of awareness.

---

[40] Jason DeRose, "Religious 'Nones' Are Now the Largest Single Group in the US," *NPR*, January 24, 2024.

This cosmic openness presents interesting possibilities for religions and the religious, including the SBNR.

The first point pertains to the institutional side of religions. What is clear from the investigation above is that meaningful religions of the future can no longer resort to intellectual isolationism. They must be open to the evolutionary process, a process that brings disparate forms of knowledge and experiences into constructive contact. Such interactions will reveal new opportunities of development both within and without of a respective religious tradition. The core difference in this vision is that various religious and spiritual traditions develop together in a spirit of cosmic entanglement. This is the difference between being a religion in the world and being a cosmic religion. This paradigm holds that different traditions must faithfully respond and be open to reenvisioning themselves in relation to all forms of secular and spiritual knowledge. I personally feel that this was the spirit and hope of the Second Vatican Council. It was rejecting its historical patterns of isolationism and redefining what it meant to be the universal church in diverse global context. The hope of this message is still being played out today.

Second, the authentic coalescing of religious and spiritual traditions will undoubtedly lead to novel forms of personal spirituality. When cosmic entanglement is genuinely practiced, not just entertained as a conceptual necessity, those spiritual gray areas will find a legitimate grounding. Here, the contentious embodiment of "dual belonging" becomes a genuine option for future forms of spirituality. King notes that "perhaps we need a new kind of 'world believer' who can meaningfully relate to the perspectives of more than one religious tradition and thereby find a deep enrichment through what has been called a 'double' or even 'multiple' religious belonging."[41] Interestingly, Teilhard's personal writings show a keen interest in Shiva, the Hindu God who is understood within the Shaivite tradition to be the protector and sustainer of the universe.[42]

A point of caution is necessary here: such hybridity cannot become uncritical syncretism or superficial universal religion. Both Teilhard and Whitehead would find such an approach untenable. There is a natural process to evolutionary becoming that demands recognition. New religious movements cannot be formulated from the outside but must build upon the old. There are no hard breaks in evolution, and the same applies to forms of religiosity. Furthermore, if religious traditions embrace the evolutionary

---

[41] King, *Teilhard de Chardin and Eastern Religions*, 246.
[42] Ibid., 229.

278 The Unsatisfied Theists

process, the identities that constitute the faithful will have greater fluidity. This grey area will be novel, but it can never be a naive syncretism.

Teilhard wrote that the future entails an "unknown form of religion," and Whitehead penned that "religion is the vision of something which stands beyond, behind, and within, the passing flux of immediate things, something which is real, and yet waiting to be realized."[43] The future of religion and its various manifestations of faith is surely unknown. Yet the visions presented here offer hope. In the end it seems that Teilhard and Whitehead are prophetic in their perspectives: On the one side, we are witnessing greater engagement between religions as never seen before. The other side reveals that the earlier barbaric and nationalistic-infused forms of religion are still alive and well. It seems our current era is one of pressurization and on the threshold of change. Despite this, one thing is clear for both Teilhard and Whitehead: humanity is the current engine of evolution, and we have a responsibility to make choices that determine the cosmic story to come.

---

[43] Teilhard, *The Activation of Energy*, 383; Whitehead, *Science in the Modern World*, 191.

Cultivating Noosphere Evolution in the Spirit of Teilhard and Whitehead

STEVE MCINTOSH

For the last forty years I have been continuously inspired by the writing of both Pierre Teilhard de Chardin and Alfred North Whitehead. But unlike most of the distinguished academics who are writing in this volume, I am not a professional scholar of either Teilhard's or Whitehead's philosophy. Nevertheless, what we might recognize as the combined spirit of Teilhard and Whitehead serves as a foundation for my work as an author and social entrepreneur. For me, this combined spirit is found in their shared focus on the universal process of becoming, together with their insights into the spiritual significance of the scientific facts of evolution.

In this chapter I consider how this generalized spirit of Teilhard and Whitehead points to a positive future for the evolution of the noosphere. Despite the dire threats and challenges faced by humanity in our present historical moment, I remain hopeful that the culture of the developed world, and American culture in particular, can and will grow into a better version of itself. And I believe that the project of working to advance the evolution of human culture can be beneficially guided (or should I say "lured"?) by the combined wisdom of these two great thinkers.

Indeed, we might expect that a transcendent vision of noosphere evolution, which Teilhard and Whitehead each expresses in his own way, can help bring about the further evolution of our culture. Although the genius of Teilhard and Whitehead may not be adequately appreciated in our time, as I argue below, the combined spirit of these visionaries constitutes a politically potent philosophy, the revival of which can help us overcome the daunting global challenges that we now face.

280 *Cultivating Noosphere Evolution*

Insights from the Structure of Evolutionary Emergence

Beginning in my twenties, the teaching of Teilhard that first captured my attention was his elegant description of the structure of evolutionary emergence: physiosphere-biosphere-noosphere. Although the unfolding of human history has been the focus of myriad thinkers before and after Teilhard, his situation of history within a larger evolutionary context pointed to the deeper meanings behind our universe of becoming. Then later, when I began reading Whitehead and his interpreters, I could see how process philosophy, like Teilhard's philosophy, was similarly moved by what I eventually came to see as the "spiritual teachings of evolution."

Among the numerous teachings of evolution, the aspect of universal becoming that has intrigued me most is the structural sequence of evolutionary emergence. As Teilhard understood, evolution moves toward complexity and consciousness at both micro and macro scales of development. He summed this up in his brilliant observation that "the Universal and Personal . . . grow in the same direction and culminate simultaneously in each other."[1]

Although the patterned *structure* of emergence serves as the foundation for the thesis in this chapter, we know from Whitehead that the course of evolutionary growth is first and foremost a dynamic *process*, rather than merely a built-up structure. But this large-scale process of "creative advance," like the vital process of an ecosystem, also includes evident structural elements. In fact, there is no development that lacks a structure. Whitehead envisioned the structure of emergence as a sequence of occasions of experience, while Teilhard characterized this structure as the series of enveloping spheres mentioned above. Evolution's process of emergent becoming is, of course, multifaceted, and a variety of valid ways describe its structure. But among the features that seem most significant is how, at the micro level, each of us embodies and uses this structure within our own bodies and minds—from the hydrogen atoms in our cells to the great realizations of history that uphold our modern form of consciousness. And the way this systemic structure of emergence lives within each of us suggests how this same structure is also alive at the macro level within the "organism" of the universe as a whole.

The structural sequence of evolutionary emergence has recently become the focus of popular culture through what is loosely called Big History.

---

[1] Pierre Teilhard de Chardin, *The Phenomenon of Man* (New York: Harper & Row, 1959), 285.

Prominent writers such as Yuval Harari and David Christian have helped make grand narratives of universal evolution fashionable. Yet when I read these popular descriptions of the story of our origins, which are explicitly advanced as a secular substitute for religious notions of our transcendent provenance, I can't help but cringe at the flatness and vacuity of their strictly physical account of how we came to be.

This purely physical account of emergence may seem adequately to describe the trajectory of cosmological evolution through the periodic table of elements, as well as the unfolding of biological evolution through the phylogenetic tree of life (although Teilhard and Whitehead both dispute the adequacy of strictly physical explanations). But when it comes to noosphere evolution, the materialistic story becomes particularly thin and implausible. As history professor Ian Hesketh observes: "Big History reduces the vicissitudes of human history to processes that are ultimately beyond human control. What this means is that Big History necessarily privileges the cosmic at the expense of the human, the natural at the expense of the political."[2]

Big History's description of the evolution of human societies focuses almost exclusively on technology and energy flows, not only because it wants to avoid complicating its scientific pretenses with political contingencies, but also because many academics in the social sciences and humanities reject the basic idea that culture evolves. Academia's aversion to the notion of a structure of emergence in cultural evolution is well articulated by academic philosopher William Wimsatt, who writes, "[cultural evolution] conjures up shadows of an older anthropological tradition in which diverse peoples, groups, and societies were fitted—in procrustean fashion—onto a template of evolutionary progress with Western categories and social organization presumed as the apotheosis of cultural development."[3]

While I acknowledge that early attempts to chart the course of cultural evolution were problematically Eurocentric, I think it is a mistake to abandon all attempts to identify the overall structure of evolutionary emergence in the noosphere. Gaining a better understanding of this structure is crucial, because it is by recognizing its trajectory that we can begin to see, and effectively work for, the next step of our own cultural development.

---

[2] Ian Hesketh, "What Big History Misses," *Aeon Magazine,* December 16, 2021.

[3] Alan C. Love and William C. Wimsatt, "Explaining Cultural Evolution," in *Beyond the Meme: Development and Structure in Cultural Evolution* (Minneapolis: University of Minnesota Press, 2019), vii.

Integral Philosophy

The school of thought to which I belong, generally known as integral philosophy, goes against the grain of contemporary social science discourse. Integral philosophy strongly affirms that the nested structure of transcendence and inclusion that is evident in cosmological and biological evolution can also be found in the domain of cultural evolution. Integral philosophy also goes beyond Big History by recognizing what Teilhard called "the within of things"—the interior dimensions of the coevolution of consciousness and culture. Integral philosophy is one of several schools of thought that have grown out of, and attempted to build on, the spirit of Teilhard and Whitehead. Although some may associate integral philosophy primarily with the theories of Ken Wilber, this branch of philosophy also includes writers like me who are not "Wilberians." Although I owe much to Wilber's thinking, my interpretation of integral philosophy differs from his on numerous points.

Wilber and I agree, however, that the unfolding of noosphere evolution evinces structural stages of development. In fact, growth by stages is a ubiquitous feature of almost all developing systems, and the "ecosystem" of human cultural evolution is no exception. Within the wider subculture of integral thinking there are a variety of overlapping yet competing stage theories. And most of these stage theories (including Wilber's) point to the findings of developmental psychology as their primary source of evidence. Yet while I acknowledge the important contributions of developmental psychologists such as Robert Kegan and Clare Graves, I remain skeptical of the excessive linearity and empirical claims of this branch of psychology.

So, rather than basing my arguments for stages of noosphere evolution on the evidence of adult psychological development, I focus on the historical record. As discussed below, this record provides abundant evidence for the sequential emergence of large-scale cultural worldviews within the timeline of human history. I define the concept of a worldview as a coherent system of values, beliefs, and ideals that persists across multiple generations. Worldviews are widely held cultural agreements about what is good, true, and beautiful. They provide personal identity and political solidarity. As I argue in my 2020 book, *Developmental Politics*, worldviews are the basic units of cultural analysis and interpretation—the most fundamental structures of emergence within cultural evolution.[4]

---

[4] Steve McIntosh, *Developmental Politics: How America Can Grow into a Better Version of Itself* (St. Paul, MN: Paragon House, 2020), 8.

Even those who reject the idea that noosphere evolution advances primarily through the sequential emergence of worldviews must nevertheless acknowledge the monumental significance of what Whitehead called "the modern world." Indeed, I think the emergence of what is now widely recognized as modernity provides Exhibit A for the argument that worldviews constitute the primary structures of evolutionary emergence in the noosphere.

The Emergence of Modernity

As we consider the development of the noosphere over the last ten-thousand years of cultural evolution, we have to acknowledge what has been called the "Great Fact." In the places where the culture of modernity has been successfully adopted, material conditions have been immensely improved. The rise of the modern world has created unprecedented "revolutions" in science, industry, agriculture, and human rights. The advent of scientific medicine alone can be credited as having materially benefited humanity more than any other single factor in history.

Of course, many sensitive thinkers now take a dim view of modernity, characterizing it as a brutal form of neoliberal capitalism. But even if we feel the world would be better off if modernism had never arisen, this Great Fact is nevertheless a world-historical event of cultural emergence that must be reckoned with by those who feel called to work for the further evolution of the noosphere overall.

So what is modernity? Although it can be framed in numerous ways, I think the best characterization is that modernity is a distinct worldview— a coherent set of secular-rational values that brings about significant scientific and economic progress and also results in negative externalities such as environmental degradation, nuclear proliferation, and gross inequality.

Yet whether we focus on modernity's dignities or its disasters, it is hard to avoid the conclusion that modernity constitutes a *stage of cultural development*—a frame of values that can be compared and contrasted with the great religious worldviews that precede modernity in the timeline of history. The idea that history can be roughly divided into "modern" and "premodern" forms of culture is a well-established idea within many academic disciplines. And by accepting that the distinction between modern and premodern culture represents a valid interpretation of an actual turning point, or "hinge of history," even those who reject the idea of stages of development are nevertheless working with a two-stage model.

Once this two-stage model of historical development is acknowledged (even with reservations), one doesn't have to agree with any of the stage theories posited by developmental psychology to see the potential for a stage of cultural development beyond modernity. Adding a third "postmodern" stage to this basic model of historical development is therefore not much of a stretch. As is now apparent to even casual observers, in the last sixty years or so a new worldview has in fact emerged beyond modernity in many parts of the developed world. This is the rise of what is perhaps best termed the *progressive postmodern worldview.*

The Emergence of Progressive Postmodernity

Like the word *postmodern,* which remains a battleground of meaning, the word *progressive* is also subject to a variety of interpretations. The mainstream media has only recently begun to distinguish "progressives" from "liberals," thereby acknowledging a meaningful difference between center-left modernists and far-left progressives. This difference, however, is much more than merely a matter of political preference. Like traditional religious worldviews, the contemporary worldview of progressive postmodernism constitutes a coherent set of values that frames almost every aspect of what it means to live a good life. As it has come of age during this century, progressive postmodern culture can now be recognized as a historically significant worldview in its own right, one which can be compared and contrasted with the previous but still extant worldviews of secular modernism and religious traditionalism.

As with modernism and traditionalism, progressive postmodern culture also contains both dignities and disasters. The positive values of postmodernism include a heightened interest in equality and social justice, an expanded concern for the welfare of animals and the environment, and an emergent form of world-centric morality that expands our circle of care to include everyone. If we are going to build a better world, values like these are indispensable. The rise of progressive postmodernism, however, has also brought negatives. Following the pattern of previous forms of noosphere emergence, postmodernism has made its advance by pushing off against the problems and shortcomings of the culture that precedes it in history, which in this case is modernism. Modernity's evident unsustainability, both environmentally and culturally, has shaped and charged the values of progressive postmodernism from the beginning. Ongoing animosity toward the modernist worldview can accordingly be seen as the binding element that ties together the wide diversity of views that are embraced within progressive culture. And it is in progressive postmodernism's often intense anti-modernism that we can recognize its accompanying pathologies.

Pointing out progressive postmodernism's negatives—such as its illiberalism, its performative contradictions, and its militant rejectionism—can be an unwelcome exercise within contemporary intellectual culture. But in order to understand our current state of cultural evolution with the hope of fostering further evolution, we need to view it as Teilhard did, from a *planetary perspective*. To gain an accurate understanding of the overall structure of noosphere evolution in which we are embedded, we need to perceive this structure not as partisans for our cultural team, but as would-be agents of evolution overall. Which means we need to recognize clearly the positives and negatives of each emergent layer within this larger structure. Seeing the whole sympathetically from "outside and above" begins to show how the values of all three of these major stages of cultural development—traditional, modern, and postmodern—are actually interdependent.[5]

This planetary view, however, also reveals how the conflicts and tensions among these three major worldview structures are an important part of the larger cultural ecosystem in which they live. That is, to appreciate the dynamism, and thus the evolutionary potential for further growth inherent in the noosphere's overall cultural ecosystem, we need to recognize its dialectical process of development.

Cultural Evolution's Dialectical Process of Development

Although it can't be conflated with biological or cosmological evolution, cultural evolution is real evolution, and as such it partakes in universal patterns of development—habits of growth—that are common to all forms of evolution. While we can identify many common patterns and processes that have shaped evolution's overarching structure, perhaps the most fundamental process is dialectical development. Recognizing the outworking of this

---

[5] Ibid., chaps. 2 and 4.

286   Cultivating Noosphere Evolution

dialectical evolutionary process in our current historical moment provides the key to cultivating the further evolution we need.

The process of dialectical development has been framed in numerous ways. But I define it as the universal process through which tension between differentiated entities can cause transformation into more complex forms of integration. This ubiquitous evolutionary process of differentiation and integration—transcendence and inclusion—is how evolution unfolds at every level; it cannot be reduced to merely "Hegel's dialectic." Moreover, despite its association with Marxist materialism, dialectical development cannot be accurately equated with strict determinism. As Whitehead understood, the process by which "the many enter into complex unity"[6] is compatible with the idea of freedom, especially in the realm of cultural evolution.

The extent to which Whitehead's thought can be considered dialectical is open to debate.[7] But I think I can safely claim that Teilhard's philosophy is firmly dialectical, even though he appears not to have read much of Hegel. According to historian Richard Tarnas, for Teilhard, "cosmogenesis is a dialectical unfolding."[8] So without arguing the point further, I trust readers will allow me to say that recognizing the dialectical character of evolutionary development is compatible with the general spirit of Teilhard and Whitehead.

Recognizing the pattern of dialectical development in our present historical circumstances allows us to better understand the intersubjective value commitments of progressive postmodern worldview. This worldview embraces many positive and hopeful values, but it has made its advance primarily by questioning, and in many cases militantly rejecting, the "establishment" values of modernism and traditionalism. In short, progressive postmodernism stands in *antithesis* to much of Western civilization.

Although it has been criticized as an oversimplification, the construct of *thesis-antithesis-synthesis* does reveal important features of the dialectical process. Applying this construct to our current time in history shows how postmodernity exemplifies the antithesis phase of this universal pattern. Even though each major worldview evinces aspects of all three "moments" of the dialectic within itself, the rejectionistic spirit of the progressive

---

[6] Alfred North Whitehead, *Process and Reality: An Essay in Cosmology*, corrected edition., ed. David Ray Griffin and Donald Sherburne (New York: The Free Press 1978), 21.

[7] See, for example, Charles Nussbaum, "Logic and the Metaphysics of Hegel and Whitehead," *Process Studies* 15, no. 1 (Spring 1986): 32–52.

[8] Richard Tarnas, *The Passion of the Western Mind* (New York: Ballentine Books, 1991), quoted in Hub Zwart, "Pierre Teilhard de Chardin's Phenomenology of the Noosphere," in *Continental Philosophy of Technoscience* (Cham, Switzerland: Springer, 2021), 207–27.

postmodernism points to its center of cultural gravity in the dialectical sequence. Indeed, postmodernity's antithetical stance toward the modernist-traditionalist "thesis" is apparent in nearly all of its cultural expressions.

Therefore, if we are willing to accept the proposition that progressive postmodernism represents a kind of antithesis, this points to the next potential step in the structural sequence of noosphere emergence—a transcendent yet inclusive *synthesis*.

The Next Step in Noosphere Evolution: A Post-Postmodern Cultural Synthesis

The logic is simple: the progressive postmodern worldview is not the end of history. In the same way that postmodernity has emerged beyond modernity, we can reasonably anticipate that another historically significant worldview will in turn eventually emerge beyond postmodernism. And just as postmodernism arose to remedy the negative externalities of modernity, the next major worldview in the structure of noosphere emergence can find its opportunities for advance within the limitations of postmodern culture.

As with each of the worldviews we are considering, postmodernism's limitations are tied directly to its strengths. Among progressive postmodernism's numerous strengths is its commitment to inclusivity. Postmodernism's expanded scope of moral concern transcends modernity's value of "equal opportunity" by attempting to uplift those who have been previously marginalized and oppressed. Inclusivity can therefore be recognized as an important line of evolutionary growth—a line that has been followed by each major worldview in its distinct contribution to history. Traditional worldviews make their advance by going beyond kinship affiliation to include all those who believe in the same religion. Modernism's democratic forms of government go further by including multiple religions and ethnicities within a single nation-state. And as noted, postmodern culture goes further still by including previously oppressed groups within its circle of care.

But despite its caring values, the limits of progressive postmodernism's inclusivity can be seen in its inability to appreciate and integrate the values of modernism and traditionalism, upon which postmodern culture ultimately depends. The opportunity for further growth in inclusivity can thus be seen in a move toward integration—a higher-level synthesis—which the postmodern value frame cannot achieve due to its inherent character of antithesis. In other words, postmodern culture is not able to include

288   Cultivating Noosphere Evolution

adequately the full diversity of valid values and viewpoints represented by the developed world's contemporary spectrum of cultural evolution. Recognizing the limits of progressive postmodernism accordingly illuminates the path ahead for further noosphere evolution.

A detailed description of the process through which evolutionary growth moves from antithesis to synthesis is beyond the scope of this chapter. But in some ways the process is deceptively simple. As Whitehead realized, evolution can be understood as growth in the ability to experience intrinsic value. He saw this as evolution's higher purpose. In *Religion in the Making* Whitehead writes, "The purpose of God is the attainment of value in the temporal world."[9] Eminent process philosopher David Ray Griffin elaborates on this idea, writing: "This Whiteheadian criterion for judging evolutionary progress—greater capacity for experience that is intrinsically valuable—is positively correlated with greater capacity to include more feelings and objective data from the environment in one's experience."[10]

The idea that we can evolve by expanding the scope of what we can value is elegantly simple yet politically powerful. This is what a synthesis does; it expands the scope of what can be valued by moderating the preceding antithesis so as to reinclude the lost values of the original thesis, which the antithesis negated in its move toward transcendence. Hegel famously described the process of synthesis as a "negation of the negation."[11]

As with modernism and traditionalism, progressive postmodernism still has important work to do. So I am not suggesting that it should be vilified, discarded, or otherwise completely negated. However, America's ongoing culture war, coupled with progressive postmodernism's inability to build electoral majorities, points to the need for further noosphere evolution. While all three of these major worldviews may continue to evolve on their own terms, here in America we need to find a way to regain the minimal level of social solidarity necessary for a functional democracy. Yet because of its totalizing critiques and rejectionistic stance toward modernism and traditionalism, the postmodern value frame is not capable of restoring our culture's social solidarity. Which is why we need to work for a cultural synthesis that can effectively transcend postmodernism while simultaneously

---

[9] Alfred North Whitehead, *Religion in the Making* (Cambridge: Macmillan, 1927), 100.

[10] David Ray Griffin, *Religion and Scientific Naturalism: Overcoming the Conflicts* (Albany: State University of New York Press, 2000), 301.

[11] G. W. F. Hegel, *Science of Logic*, trans. A. V. Miller (London: Allen & Unwin, 1969), 837.

carrying forward its important values, together with the values of modernism and traditionalism, in a more inclusive new whole.

Those who understand noosphere evolution, even if partially, are called to become advocates for our culture's next evolutionary step. And as I'm arguing, if this next step is to achieve the higher-level synthesis we need, it must be effectively *post-postmodern*. This post-postmodern worldview, referred to within my school of thought as the *integral worldview*, seeks to advance noosphere evolution by integrating the values of all three major worldviews within a larger circle of inclusion. Indeed, in the interdependent process of dialectical development, wherein each level builds on its predecessor, the degree of our transcendence is ultimately determined by the scope of our inclusion.

As a consequence of their time in history, both Teilhard and Whitehead were culturally modernist. Yet their combined spirit transcends modernist culture by offering insights that every worldview can appreciate. In fact, Teilhard and Whitehead can both be recognized as early proponents of the integral worldview, not only because they integrated science and religion, but also because they both affirmed ongoing progress in the evolution of consciousness and culture.

By building on the combined philosophy of Teilhard and Whitehead, integral philosophy is able to see more clearly than ever before how the distinct worldviews that now compete for dominance within our contemporary political milieu actually form a larger cultural ecosystem. Once we recognize this larger system as a whole, this very recognition empowers us to undertake the crucial project of championing a new cultural synthesis. The integral philosophy behind this project accordingly aims to help the partisans of each major worldview to better appreciate the values of their political opponents, together with the larger interdependent system of values to which these worldviews belong. It is thus by working to bring about a next-level synthesis that "the many" can "become one," and "increase by one," and thereby forward the creative advance of noosphere evolution.[12]

---

[12] Alfred North Whitehead, *Process and Reality: An Essay in Cosmology*, corrected ed., ed. David Ray Griffin and Donald Sherburne (New York: The Free Press, 1978), 21.

Open Universe, Closing Window

Climate Conversation
with Teilhard and Whitehead

CATHERINE KELLER

In my intellectual formation, Teilhard plays more the role of Alpha than of Omega.

I happened upon *The Future of Man* when I was sixteen or seventeen. The book was just lying there. I vividly remember reading the opening. I was startled to hear that our species can look forward to a promising future. "We are moving! We are going forward!" It got to me in a way that even the hippie hymn—"this is the dawning of the Age of Aquarius"—never quite had. This was also the first work of such breadth, philosophical or theological, that I had encountered. I went other ways, finding voice and future especially through feminism. But it seems now non-accidental that I later morphed into a process theologian.[1] The version of process I encountered, given my (loosely) Protestant context, was Whiteheadian. John Cobb's *Christ in a Pluralistic Age* called me to Claremont to study with him. But it is only in writing this chapter that I became conscious that Teilhard is sprinkled all through that work, and those references were surely part of my decision to do doctoral work in theology.

---

[1] Let me dedicate this paper in gratitude to Roger Haight, SJ; Alfred Pach III; and Amanda Avila Kaminski, for their edited work *Spirituality of Creation, Evolution, and Work: Catherine Keller and Pierre Teilhard de Chardin* (New York: Fordham University Press, 2023). They sum up the indirect connection of my work to Teilhard's in three points: "the basic premise of process or becoming, the understanding that the idea of creation should not be understood as an act that happened in the past but as an ongoing process, and the strong bond between matter and spirit" (5).

292   Open Universe, Closing Window

The timing of this fresh conversation between Whiteheadians and Teilhardians feels synchronistic in a more than personal, in an actually planetary, sense. Most thinking people at this point in history struggle to find grounds for collective hope. In the face of dire threats to democracy, or to any just and sustainable governance, around the earth, and at the same time to the life of the planet itself—the literal ground for any social and political future—hope, feeling forced or false, dwindles. So it may well be that we need Teilhard's help, more direct and confident in its forward gaze than Whitehead's, in order to nurture hope for a "future of man," for a future of our species and of our shared becoming. His Omega opens our terrestrial future into an endlessness of fulfillment. So it would seem to promise to draw us humans through and beyond the destructive cycle—even if barely apparent in Teilhard's time, let alone Whitehead's—of laissez-faire capitalism and climate change.

With Whitehead we surely envision a radically open universe. This is the openness of a radical indeterminacy—certainly more hopeful than any mere closure. But such an indeterminate future offers no assurance that we will overcome the causes of global warming in time to save our planetary habitat. It does offer that *possibility*, indeed manifold, divergent, and relevant possibilities at every moment. But Teilhard offers optimism. Whitehead is no pessimist. He also recognizes evolutionary ongoingness, human and otherwise. But he expresses no exceptionalist faith in the ultimate terrestrial, let alone the specifically human, future. From this point of view, the universe will remain open even if our species' window slams shut.

So the questions can only persist: Is Teilhard's Omega Point overly confident? Does its eschatological optimism contribute to a futurist version of providential complacency? And at the same time, might the unmistakable anthropocentrism of that becoming noosphere foster detachment from both the mass of nonhuman earthlings and from the material future of the human? For in Teilhard's vision, does materiality itself, as instrumental means to the end, ultimately cease to matter?

The question presses back, however, from the other side: does Whitehead's endless world, with indeterminacy characterizing every actual occasion of becoming, leave the future too radically open—so uncertain as to undermine the hope we earthlings now need, the hope without which we can hardly expect to motivate collective transformation?

How do these two quite different openings to the future work in relation to, say, current climate examples—the summer heat, as I write, apparently the hottest on record? Or the devastating forest fires in Canada, Europe,

Hawaii, heating up the already vicious circle adding CO_2 in the atmosphere while taking out the trees we need to suck down and store the carbon? Or the unthinkable losses through the flood in Libya, based on a megastorm that climate change apparently intensified? Fresh present examples of fire and flood, of toxicity, drought, and species' extinctions, do—and will continue to—present.

Then which is it that can better help us to respond—us theologians, us earthlings—responsibly? The Omega optimism or the process indeterminacy? Another way to put the question: might the latter's radically open end, by allowing for a possibly tragic closure of our habitat, actually make it more likely? While the Omega Point can encourage and empower more confident collective action? But if so, why has Whitehead inspired such a deep tradition of ecological theology, with extensive and growing activist actualizations?[2]

A series of questions fold out from that big one, that capital "O" Omega question. First—rather than (as is our wont) quietly rejecting the Omega Point, might Whiteheadians instead help to reinforce its open-endedness? If so, might Teilhardians at the same time help to strengthen the Whiteheadian sense of the divine lure? Not by conceptually endowing it with interventionist force, or with a more determinate eschaton, but by intensifying its attractive energy? Such an energy arises from the *within* of matter itself, in its radical—indeed in Teilhard's sense "radial"—interdependence? And next: may we discern the (or an) Omega at work in every actual occasion? Perhaps also an Alpha? And third, theologically speaking: how might the Whiteheadian construct of the two natures of God figure here in the current comparison? And if then Teilhard's noosphere resembles the communion of saints in a profoundly Christian sense, indeed in the sense of Teilhard's "Christogenesis"—how does it work with a globe of multiple religions, of manifold Ways, and so with the pluralism so key to process theology? What about the risks of the Christocentrism, as it centers an apparent anthropocentrism, in Teilhard? Neither pose a threat in Whitehead. But perhaps the risk does arise—as in my Alpha text from the seventies, *Christ in a Pluralistic Age*[3]—in John Cobb's Christology of the creatively transformative Logos at work in all things. And finally, how

---

[2] John B. Cobb, Jr., *Is It Too Late? A Theology of Ecology*, Faith and Life Series (Beverly Hills, CA: Bruce, 1972) marks the beginning of the explicit application of Whiteheadian metaphysics to ecological theology and action. A 50th anniversary edition was released by Fortress Press in 2021.

[3] John B. Cobb, *Christ in a Pluralistic Age* (Philadelphia: Westminster Press, 1975).

294   *Open Universe, Closing Window*

should pan*en*theists deal with Teilhard's avowed pantheism? In both cases we have to do with a counter-traditional God, one not just of being, but *in* becoming, in and through the interrelated becomings of all things—*en pasi panta theos.* Perhaps Teilhard would welcome the *en* of panentheism, suggestive of his own deep "within" of love. And the *pan* might, can, keep us returning to the question of specifically *earthly* eco-catastrophe. So then, which version of the God in all—either that of an optimism of the ultimate Omega or that of the indeterminacy of the endless creation—can now best serve collective human responsibility for our future?

Not surprisingly, I hope for an answer that can refuse all versions of this either/or. It would do so by way of the Whiteheadian unity of a novel "contrast"[4] coupled with the Teilhardian sense that "union differentiates."[5] That latter phrase will now stay with me. Its discourse of union does not homogenize, nor merely protect difference—it actively differentiates. So in terms of this conversation's aim, the Whiteheadian contrast with Teilhard can mean neither fusion nor separation. But an obstacle—even to a differential union—remains. The Omega of Christogenesis still appears to operate in its optimism rather close to an infallible telos or eschaton. And its confidence seems to feed on its indubitable anthropocentrism, and this not just as the honest self-reflection of a human perspective, but as an ultimate disinterest in the inherent value of all the nonhumans making up the world. They have already served their main evolutionary purpose: to prepare the way for our big-brained species. That the other species continue to experience life in their wildly distinctive ways is a matter of past significance, instrumental rather than inherent in value. Only *we* have the reflexive consciousness of thought.

Yet the terms of my question already underplay an attractive dimension of Teilhard's work, one that actually ties him closely to Whitehead: "the within to things." It is this concept that lets him discover "the universal hidden beneath the exceptional"—a phrase that surely cuts against his apparent anthropic exceptionalism. "Co-extensive with the Without," he claims, "there is a Within to things." And so "life inevitably assumes a 'pre-life' for as far back before it as the eye can see."[6] Therefore, even so-called

---

[4] Alfred North Whitehead, *Process and Reality*, 2nd ed. (New York: The Free Press, 1979), 24.

[5] Pierre Teilhard de Chardin, *The Phenomenon of Man*, 1st ed. (Harper Perennial Modern Classics, 2008), 262. First published in French as *Le Phénomène Humain* (Paris: Éditions du Seuil, 1955).

[6] Teilhard, *The Phenomenon of Man*, 56.

inert matter has a within. And this of course keeps his cosmology congenial with Whitehead's, even at the elemental level. That within resonates with Whitehead's "Nature Alive,"[7] and so with the concrescence by which every actual entity, every atom, internalizes its world, and does so by feeling it. Very much a pre-life before organic life. That for Teilhard both within and without have the property of atomicity also corresponds to Whitehead's microcosmic occasions. Teilhard holds the within and the without in anti-dualistic coherence with his notion of "the interdependence of energy."[8] That binary emerged from his earlier distinction of tangential and radial energy—which one might relate to the mental and physical poles of an actual occasion.

With Teilhard that radial energy is drawing each thing toward "ever greater complexity and centricity—in other words forwards."[9] In that microcosmic or atomic unit of evolution, if I read it correctly, the Omega is actually always already at work, not at all postponed until the culmination of the world. So in that way a kind of entelechy similar to Whitehead's "initial aim" works at every scale and level of creature. In other words, I may be letting go of a ready misunderstanding, one that places the Omega, as the quite *literal* last letter, at the end of the alphabet of creation. It is called "a superior pole to the world"[10]—but is in no way simply abstracted from or dualistically transcendent of the world.

Of course, an insight crucially in common with Whiteheadians is that of the radical interrelation not just of energy as such, but of all actual entities. So with Whitehead "we must say that every actual entity is present in every other actual entity"; or "in a sense, every entity pervades the whole world."[11] Nothing can be extracted from the rest of the universe. And Teilhard insists, powerfully, that the more we learn about the facts of matter, "the more we are confounded by the interdependence of its parts. Each element of the cosmos is positively woven from all the others: from beneath itself by the mysterious phenomenon of composition." And he adds: "the mesh of the universe is the universe itself."[12] These beautifully process-relational elements exhibit the textured composition of Teilhard's thinking. He then infers from the common spatiality of all atoms that "the volume of each of

---

[7] "Nature Alive" names the culminating chapter of Alfred North Whitehead's *Modes of Thought* (New York: The Macmillan Company, 1938).

[8] Teilhard, *The Phenomenon of Man*, 64.

[9] Ibid., 64–65.

[10] Ibid., 66.

[11] Whitehead, *Process and Reality*, 50, 28.

[12] Teilhard, *The Phenomenon of Man*, 44.

296   Open Universe, Closing Window

them is the volume of the universe. . . . It [each] is the infinitesimal center of the world itself."[13]

Within this omnicentrism I can no longer presume any simple anthropocentrism. Nor will I belabor the concern that the Omega somehow degrades matter itself. Somehow all the relations composing matter fold—in the Omega—into the noosphere. And that energetic interdependence of all does surely constitute its own cosmic ecology, in which every element—albeit infinitesimal—does in its moment have its inherent value and experience. Process theology can surely embrace and supplement such a vision without yielding to any anthropocentric tendencies. If each bit of matter materializes "the infinitesimal center of the world itself"[14]—it can hardly be read as insignificant.

What of the theologies in play here? Of the material micro unit of the universe Whitehead avers: "The quantum is that standpoint in the extensive continuum which is consonant with the subjective aim in its original derivation from God."[15] That original derivation of creaturely purpose by way of the initial aim hardly seems alien to the operation of the Omega at every moment and scale. Grace of the primordial nature, the Whiteheadian deity tickles every actual occasion with possibility—a possibility for bringing the without *within* in some freshly felt, somehow novel way. And whatever becomes, then comes to be objectively immortal—and is felt as such in the *consequent* nature, that growing, ever becoming within of God. That deity somehow spirals through the next moment of the *primordial* nature, in its aim, as sheer possibility, at the origin of every becoming. The creaturely creativity, minimal or immense, obstructed or attuned, actualizes something of that divine possibility, and is felt in, felt into, the divine becoming. So might one discern something comparable in the consequent nature to what Teilhard calls noogenesis? I am tempted here to dub the primordial aim the *Alpha*, and the consequent reception the *Omega*. But, of course, both divine poles in Whitehead express what for Teilhard would be that "superior pole," "the mysterious centre of our centres which I have called Omega."[16] And the noosphere, the realization toward which the Omega points, suggests—not unlike the consequent nature of God in process—the realization not of God alone, but of the world in God. *Panentheos.*

---

[13] Ibid., 45–46.

[14] Ibid.

[15] Whitehead, *Process and Reality*, 283.

[16] Teilhard, *The Phenomenon of Man*, 66, 268.

Nonetheless, as we question the solely human consciousness of the noosphere, process theologians may worry about another difference. The consequent nature is enfolding in itself the entire universe at every moment, in its utter polycentrism of becomings: each materialization somehow mattering, however significant the human role—or not. As process thinker Andrew M. Davis suggests in his adventurous *Metaphysics of Exo-Life*, we can barely imagine what other forms of reflective consciousness might have evolved far beyond or merely other than ours. So if each becoming perishes into the consequent nature, "this is not only the case for our species, but any and all extraterrestrial species across an evolutionary cosmos."[17] Might we then consider that the noosphere, as it delicately surrounds the planet in a soul-filled skin of differentiated unity, of love energy, though it is not identical with the consequent nature of God, reveals a specifically *earth-centered portion* of it? Whatever other worlds and intelligences there may be, the noosphere might then name something mystically specific to us anthropoids—yet surely not cut off from exo-life—something inspiring, not escaping from matter, but stimulating greater attention to the mattering earth that this noetic skin envelopes.

In the spiral back to each emergent creature (keeping the anthropoid in the spotlight for this discussion), the question of Christogenesis arises. For, indeed, Teilhard's Christ occupies the center of his convergent world. As Ilia Delio writes, "Christ is the universal and the Evolver, the one who brings to the world the phylum of love which provides the true direction for the convergence of the human community around its center."[18] In the materiality of love as phylum, a classification of species, she illumines how with Teilhard's "science charged with faith" he offers "not a naive optimism but a call to wake up and to see the core of religion—love, truth, goodness, and beauty—written into the very fabric of the cosmos."[19] That fabric, that mesh of the universe, reveals its center in the Christ-event. Of course, one has reason to worry about the triumphalism of such a high—and deep, and broad—cosmic Christology regarding other world religions. But it may be

---

[17] Andrew M. Davis, *Metaphysics of Exo-Life: Toward a Constructive Whiteheadian Cosmotheology* (Grasmere: SacraSage, 2023), 90. See also Andrew M. Davis, ed., *From Force to Persuasion: Process-Relational Perspectives on Power and the God of Love* (Eugene, OR: Cascade, 2024). I am grateful to have participated in both volumes and the conferences that prepared their way—and for Andrew Davis's brilliant leadership in both cases.

[18] Ilia Delio, "Introduction," in *From Teilhard to Omega: Co-Creating an Unfinished Universe*, ed. Ilia Delio (Maryknoll, NY: Orbis Books, 2014), 2.

[19] Ibid., 3.

298   *Open Universe, Closing Window*

quite kin, if not to Whitehead's Jesus, to John Cobb's Christ, as Logos of the universe itself, identified with the initial aim, and so as the call to the creative transformation of every creature. Cobb's solution to the dilemma posed to Christianity by other traditions is disarming. In *Christ in a Pluralistic Age*, it is Christ himself calling Christians to interreligious exchange, and so to self-criticism and transformation. Indeed, that Logos is heard calling some—such as Cobb himself—to welcome a "Christianized Buddhism and a Buddhized Christianity."[20] This Christology has fostered immense global dialogue with Buddhists. Might Teilhard appreciate such a deep pluralism?

I have raised the question of the ecological implications of anthropocentric thought patterns. It happens that in the above 1975 Christology, Cobb offers an ecologically important chapter called "The City of God." He unfolds there the concrete example of the visionary Paulo Soleri's architectural ecology, condensed by Soleri into "arcology." With a few of Cobb's other students, I traveled around 1980 from Claremont to the Arizona desert. Soleri worked there with a community of architectural followers, where he had built the base of one of these cities designed as a solution to earth's ecological crisis. The architect died without any of his manifold plans for arcologies being funded and built, beyond that start at Arcosanti. But consider here his summary of arcology:

> The Arcological Commitment is indispensable because it advocates a physical system that consents to the high compression of things, energies, logistics, information and performances, thus fostering the thinking, doing, living, learning phenomenon of life at its most lively and compassionate state of grace (esthetogenesis) possible for a socially and individually healthy man on ecologically healthy earth.[21]

Catch the hint of Teilhard? Soleri, resolutely not a Christian, was a deep disciple of Teilhardian principles. Arcology, therefore, serves Cobb as an exemplification of the City of God. So what about belief in Christ? "Soleri," writes Cobb, "is but another example of the mystery that frequently, where the Christian discerns Christ most clearly, the agent of Christ refuses to identify herself or himself as a Christian."[22] But Soleri does not deny his discipleship to Teilhard. He writes: "We, the humankind, are

---

[20] John B. Cobb, Jr., *Becoming a Thinking Christian: If We Want Church Renewal, We Will Have to Renew Thinking in the Church* (Nashville, TN: Abingdon Press, 1993).

[21] Paulo Soleri, quoted in Cobb, *Christ in a Pluralistic Age*, 198.

[22] Cobb, *Christ in a Pluralistic Age*.

matter transcended into spirit: a raw, dark violent excess-prone spirit as yet."[23] Soleri certainly belies any stereotype of Teilhardian optimism. And Cobb ends the chapter carefully as follows: "Soleri understands himself as a servant of those energies that Teilhard named Christ. If with Teilhard we strip from Christ all that does not belong to him, we will not falsify Soleri's faith by naming what he serves in our Christian way."[24] In the Teilhard/Whitehead forcefield of the present conversation, I am also ceasing to hear any triumphalism. Both discourses are capable of spiraling between their Christocentric cosmologies and an ecumenical pluralism. To grow planetary coalitions that confront climate change (to return to my driving concern) requires the help of an ecumenism that reads also as *eco*-menism.

I realize, however, that I am still concerned about the problem of Teilhard's avowed optimism in the face—the anachronistic face—of global warming. So I suggest as a general practice replacing optimism, so flattened at this point by presumptions of American capitalist progress, with hope, which carries ancient prophetic shadows. Yet in that connection I do still worry about the implicit determinism of Teilhard's Omega. And whether a subtle omnipotence guarantees its triumph after all.

Whitehead's initial aim helps here to interpret what Teilhard calls the "supremely attractive centre which has personality."[25] If in process theology the divine aim operates at the center of any personality, indeed as the initial aim of every moment of becoming, we recognize its supremacy not as omnipotent control but precisely as attractive force—the force of the divine *lure*, the call of a deity also imagined as personality. That primordial nature would effect an *Alpha*, while the consequent nature delivers the *Omega*. Such an interplay of Alpha and Omega can be read into this bipolarity perhaps only if we let Teilhard's divine matrix enhance our intuition of the way the consequent nature spirals not just from the objective immortality of the world at the moment—but spirals forward into the primordial nature, accounting for a selection among pure possibilities. Such a reading works toward a conjunction of the sheerly open universe of Whitehead with a stronger aim for our collective future, not just as objectively immortal, but as somehow intersubjectively evolving. Cobb moves in that direction, with his development of subjective immortality.

In the meantime, this meaner time, regarding our collective material process, ecotheology returns emphasis always to the mattering future—as

---

[23] Soleri, in ibid., 202.

[24] Cobb, *Christ in a Pluralistic Age*, 201–2.

[25] Teilhard, *The Phenomenon of Man*, 284.

300   Open Universe, Closing Window

it emerges now—of our inescapable planetary life. I am recognizing that the materiality of the earth is not demeaned by a responsible reading of Teilhardian eschatology. Otherwise, one could make no sense of Teilhard's profound influence on important ecological thinkers like Thomas Berry and Mary Evelyn Tucker[26]—let alone Soleri. And as the prolific Teilhardian scholar of science and religion John F. Haught puts it, "Nothing could be more foundational to Christian ecological ethics than rejoicing in the inseparable connection among my story, your story, and the story of the universe." But the question persists of the demotivating effect of the assurance of "the ultimate earth." Thus Haught brings his book on Teilhard's cosmic vision to its conclusion by insisting upon "the ecological implications of Teilhard's awareness of our living in a world that is still in the making."[27] A world in the making surely suggests radical open-endedness. But then when will the "final convergence" happen? More important, is it for Teilhard in some christogenic sense guaranteed? It is surely more assured than is "real potentiality" in Whitehead.

The answer comes down to what Teilhard renders thus: "We must reach the goal . . . not necessarily, doubtless, but infallibly."[28] That is a subtle distinction. *Infallibly*, but *not necessarily*, cannot mean deterministic certainty. So is it a matter of an unquestionable providential aim? An Omega that we *must* reach, not because we are incapable of failing or betraying it, but because we are evolved for it, because its ultimacy is not relativized by our fallibility? "Must reach the goal" then carries more of an ethical imperative than an evolutionary certainty; the Omega reads not as a simple matter of telic necessity, but as direction, not as predestination but as destiny. Destiny, which can be betrayed, lacks the power of predetermination. So we can then rely on Teilhard's "not necessarily." It allows the more Whiteheadian reader to relativize a now unconvincing language of progress and optimism

---

[26] Mary Evelyn Tucker, John Grim, and Andrew Angyal, *Thomas Berry: A Biography*, illustrated ed. (New York: Columbia University Press, 2019); Brian Thomas Swimme and Mary Evelyn Tucker, *Journey of the Universe*, reprint ed. (New Haven, CT: Yale University Press, 2014); John Grim and Mary Evelyn Tucker, *Ecology and Religion*, illustrated ed. (Washington: Island Press, 2014); Mary Evelyn Tucker and John H. Berthrong, eds., *Confucianism and Ecology: The Interrelation of Heaven, Earth, and Humans*, Religions of the World and Ecology (Cambridge: Distributed by Harvard University Press for the Harvard University Center for the Study of World Religions, 1998).

[27] John F. Haught, *The Cosmic Vision of Teilhard de Chardin* (Maryknoll, NY: Orbis Books, 2021), 225.

[28] Teilhard, *The Phenomenon of Man*, 296.

Catherine Keller   *301*

without defeating the *hope* for—and the genuine possibility of—collective transformation.

At the end of *The Phenomenon of Man* we are left with two reverberating possibilities for our planet. First, that being "conquered by the sense of the earth and human sense, hatred and internecine struggles [as well as disease and hunger] will have disappeared in the ever-warmer radiance of Omega. . . . The final convergence will take place in peace." (Though not without extreme tension, he clarifies in a note.) But he acknowledges another possibility: "Evil may go on growing alongside good, and may attain its paroxysm at the end in some specifically new form." Now we might add: as in the form of the heating planet, in opposition to the radiance of Omega. In the second case, "universal love," he writes, "would only vivify and detach finally a fraction of the noosphere so as to consummate it." This is more like, as he admits, traditional apocalyptic thinking. But some percentage will enter into the culminating ecstasy, whether in concord or discord, but either way "by excess of interior tension."[29] That tension may be likened to the tension of contrast as it plays out—creatively or destructively—in the Whiteheadian "discordant multiplicity of things."[30] So I am just about over my worry about a Teilhardian determinism, an Omega guarantee stamped upon evolutionary and now ecological struggle.

Perhaps the tensive attraction between Teilhardian and Whiteheadian forcefields—a tension creatively enacted in this very conversation—adds in some small but significant way to the terrestrial work we have to do. If so, it is work mindfully done with and within the God who shall be, with Teilhard's Paulinism, all in all. *Pan en pasi.* So might what Teilhard—for his context riskily—names "a superior form of 'pantheism'"[31] find in panentheism a more apt and useable name? The process theological *panentheos*, without any certitude of an end point of arrival for the creation, can and does also work with nondeterministically eschatological, sometimes apocalyptic, frameworks.[32] So we Whiteheadians can, I think, embrace the Teilhardian vision of God "unifying" the world "organically with himself."[33] For union

---

[29] Ibid., 288–89.

[30] Whitehead, *Process and Reality*, 349.

[31] Teihard, *The Phenomenon of Man*, 294.

[32] Catherine Keller, *Apocalypse Now and Then: A Feminist Guide to the End of the World* (Boston: Beacon Press, 1996); *Facing Apocalypse: Climate, Democracy, and Other Last Chances* (Maryknoll, NY: Orbis Books, 2021); Joseph A. Bracken, ed., *World without End: Christian Eschatology from a Process Perspective* (Grand Rapids, MI: Eerdmans, 2005).

[33] Teilhard, *The Phenomenon of Man*, 293–94.

302 *Open Universe, Closing Window*

differentiates. Indeed, the organicism of Teilhardian language well serves the possibility of the becoming of an ecologically healthy earth in which our species actually does exchange materialist greed for material care.

The open universe does not foreclose the Omega Point; nor does the closing window of time, our earth time, shut out the continuing attraction, the lure, of the Omega at the Alpha of every occasion. So the only constructive move here will be a mutual supplementation of Whiteheadian and Teilhardian visions—very much for the sake of all earthlings. Indeed, for the whole—*kath-holos*. As Ilia Delio puts it, by "bringing together evolution and Christianity in a single vision, Teilhard restored catholicity to its original meaning: consciousness of belonging to a whole and making new wholes by thinking and acting toward wholeness."[34] Delio thus theologically strengthens the wholemakers involved in greening the earth, in environmental sustainability in relation to every manner of social justice. Even the most Protestant of process thinkers must find such deep catholicity irresistible.

What I cannot resist now is to repeat the cosmic exuberance that concludes *The Divine Milieu*:

> Now the earth can certainly clasp me in her giant arms. She can swell me with her life, or take me back into her dust. She can deck herself out for me with every charm, with every horror, with every mystery. She can intoxicate me with her perfume of tangibility and unity. She can cast me to my knees in expectation of what is maturing in her breast. . . .
>
> But her enchantments can no longer do me harm, she has become for me, over and above herself, the body of the one who is and of the one who is coming.
>
> The *divine* milieu.[35]

That is one gorgeously earthy, earthbound revelation of what some process theologians call the body of God—a God who can be read as the soul of the world.[36] In that soulfully terrestrial milieu, ecological struggle, far from demotivated, can be hypermotivated. Time is limited. But the open universe itself resists the slamming shut of earth's window of hope.

---

[34] Ilia Delio, *Making All Things New* (Maryknoll, NY: Orbis Books, 2015), 193.

[35] Pierre Teilhard de Chardin, *The Divine Milieu* (New York: Harper Perennial Modern Classics, 2001), 134.

[36] Matt Segall offers a profound meditation on the trope of the world soul in Whitehead in *Physics of the World-Soul: Alfred North Whitehead's Adventure in Cosmology* (Grasmere: SacraSage Press, 2021).

For the sake of the *oikos*, ecumenical and ecological, which is the earth home, the Whiteheadian cosmology can surely embrace the Teilhardian hope as a visionary alternative both to progress optimism and to paralyzing pessimism. We might together deconstruct any determinist projection of "The End." And we can do so in the transformative spirit that for Teilhard signifies Christian love. May that spirit indefinitely unfold this particular conversation, this adventure of ideas—which we owe especially to Ilia Delio—with its earth-spiriting catholicity and in its divine milieu.

Teilhard, Whitehead, and the Reasons for Hope

JOHN F. HAUGHT

What exhilarates us human creatures more than freedom, more than the glory of achievement, is the joy of finding and surrendering to a Beauty greater than man, the rapture of being possessed.
—PIERRE TEILHARD DE CHARDIN, *HYMN OF THE UNIVERSE*

The teleology of the Universe is directed toward the production of Beauty. Thus any system of things which in any wide sense is beautiful is to that extent justified in its existence.
—ALFRED NORTH WHITEHEAD, *ADVENTURES OF IDEAS*

At the end, we will find ourselves face to face with the infinite beauty of God (cf. 1 Cor 13:12), and be able to read with admiration and happiness the mystery of the universe, which with us will share in unending plenitude.

—POPE FRANCIS, *LAUDATO SI'*

Recently, Dennis Overbye, a widely known science writer, posted an article in the *New York Times*[1] expressing his sadness that when the universe runs out of usable energy billions or trillions of years from now, all thoughts will also come to an end—forever. Somewhere and sometime in the universe's

---

[1] Dennis Overbye, "Who Will Have the Last Word on the Universe?" *New York Times,* May 2, 2023.

306   *Teilhard, Whitehead, and the Reasons for Hope*

future, he laments, there will be a *final thought*. Overbye cites the words of Janna Levin, a cosmologist at Barnard College, who remarked: "There will be a last sentient being, there will be a last thought." "When I heard that statement recently," Overbye confesses, "it broke my heart. It was the saddest, loneliest idea I had ever contemplated. I thought I was aware and knowledgeable about our shared cosmic predicament—namely, that if what we think we know about physics and cosmology is true, life and intelligence are doomed." He goes on:

> The universe as we know it is now 14 billion years old, which seems like a long time but is only an infinitesimal sliver of the trillions and quadrillions of years of darkness to come. It will mean that everything interesting in our universe happened in a brief flash, at the very beginning. A promising start, and then an eternal abyss. The finality and futility of it all!

In his article Overbye then adds: "I thought I had made some kind of intellectual peace with that." But "this was an angle that I hadn't thought of before. In the distant future, somewhere in the universe there will be a last sentient being." And so, there will be a last thought, and it "will vanish into silence." How do we know? "Because thinking takes energy, eventually there will not be enough energy in the universe to hold a thought. In the end there will only be subatomic particles dancing intergalactic distances away from each other in a dark silence."[2]

Overbye is expressing here the opinion, if not necessarily the emotional tone, of most scientific thinkers today; namely, that both life and consciousness will end tragically. As I was reading Overbye's article, what struck me immediately, and not for the first time, was the unquestioning way in which most respected intellectuals now take for granted the original, as well as the final, mindlessness of our universe. Overbye's article made me think right away of how Teilhard de Chardin, the now famous Jesuit geologist and evolutionist, reacted when he heard his fellow scientists talking about the eventual death of the cosmos and consciousness. Teilhard writes:

> Promise the earth [we may now say "the universe"] a hundred million [we may now say, "trillions"] more years of continued growth. If, at the end of that period, it is evident that the whole of consciousness must revert to zero, without its secret essence being garnered anywhere at

_____

  [2] Ibid.

all, then, I insist, we shall lay down our arms—and mankind will be on strike. The prospect of a total death (and that is a word to which we should devote much thought if we are to gauge its destructive effect on our souls) will, I warn you, when it has become part of our consciousness, immediately dry up in us the springs from which our efforts are drawn.[3]

Alfred North Whitehead thought similarly about the alleged finality of perishing. Apart from a vision of something "which stands beyond, behind, and within, the passing flux of immediate things . . . and yet is beyond all reach," every loss would be final.[4] Whitehead believed, however, that a preservative principle accompanies the cosmic process, a "tender care" that nothing be "lost." This vein of caringness in the universe includes and preserves—in association with all things going on in space-time—not only each thought but also each event, each pulse of feeling, and each life, gathering all of them into an ever-intensifying and indestructible beauty. Both Whitehead and Teilhard refer to this preservative principle as God. They link the whole universe and human consciousness to a divine indestructibility.[5]

Predictions of the eventual death of thought, as Overbye exemplifies, are inseparable from the modern picture of a lifeless and mindless universe. Before the age of science the universe was not generally thought of this way. Philosopher Hans Jonas tidily summarizes how the notion of a lifeless and mindless universe came to be taken for granted in modern intellectual history: "From the physical sciences there spread over the conception of all existence an ontology whose model entity is pure matter, stripped of all features of life. This means that the lifeless has become the knowable par excellence and is for that reason also considered the true and only foundation of reality. It is the 'natural' as well as the original state of things."[6] The thought that being is essentially lifeless makes the universe measurable and mathematically intelligible to science, but it also sentences life and thought to death.

---

[3] Pierre Teilhard de Chardin, *How I Believe*, trans. René Hague (New York: Harper & Row, 1969), 42–44.

[4] Alfred North Whitehead, *Science and the Modern World* (New York: The Free Press, 1925), 191–92. The term *hopeless* in this excerpt does not mean "despairing" but rather "endless" in the sense of never fully exhausted.

[5] Alfred North Whitehead, *Process and Reality,* corrected ed., ed. David Ray Griffin and Donald W. Sherburne (New York: The Free Press, 1978), 346.

[6] Hans Jonas, *The Phenomenon of Life* (New York: Harper & Row, 1966), 9–10.

308   Teilhard, Whitehead, and the Reasons for Hope

Modern philosophies of nature in which "death is the knowable par excellence" have no intellectual room for anything so lively as intelligent subjectivity. Hence, to make the universe stand still long enough to be measured and rendered geometrically understandable, scientific naturalists assume that it must be cleansed of any contamination by the slipperiness of subjectivity. Once it is assumed that vitality, beauty, and value are not real, then thought too must be tossed into the burgeoning bin of epiphenomena, of things that are "not really real."

I am dwelling here on Overbye's poignant article because it gives me the opportunity to reflect on what originally brought the contributors of this volume together in Philadelphia. At least many of us came to that conference because we had heard or learned that both Teilhard and Whitehead do *not* believe that a right reading of the universe requires the absolute death of thought.

Teilhard, among his fellow scientists, is controversial mostly because he finds a place for hope in the universe. Whitehead also implicitly makes room for hope by locating tragedy within a cosmos of ever-widening beauty. But are these great thinkers not leading us astray, and doesn't the pursuit of scientific objectivity require a vision of the universe that brings in what Matthew Arnold, in "Dover Beach," called "the eternal note of sadness"?

Both Teilhard and Whitehead place mental events—and hence the phenomenon of thought, or intelligent subjectivity—squarely *within* the natural world. Unfortunately, scientific thinkers like Overbye still understand thought as having no intelligible place in nature. The most eminent philosophers of mind still assume that the universe, in order to be scientifically intelligible, must be stripped bare of sentient or intelligent subjects.[7] In a mindless universe, they assume, thought is somewhat of a misfit. They casually allow thought to disappear from nature because they assume it never really belonged there in the first place. Recently the philosopher Thomas Nagel was widely scorned for expressing doubts about the modern materialist expulsion of mind from the cosmos.[8] He doubts now that mind

---

[7] I am referring here, for example, to John R. Searle, *Mind: A Brief Introduction* (Oxford: Oxford University Press, 2004), 135–36; Steven Pinker, *The Blank Slate: The Modern Denial of Human Nature* (New York: Penguin Books, 2002); Owen Flanagan, *The Problem of the Soul: Two Visions of Mind and How to Reconcile Them* (New York: Basic Books, 2002); and Daniel C. Dennett, *Consciousness Explained* (New York: Little Brown, 1991).

[8] Thomas Nagel, *Mind and Cosmos: Why the Materialist Neo-Darwinian Conception of Nature Is Almost Certainly False* (New York: Oxford University Press, 2012).

is a misfit in the universe, and his reward for doing so is that he is now considered a misfit to his fellow philosophers.[9]

Overbye seems to take for granted the materialist consensus of most scientific thinkers that thought has stumbled blindly into the universe with no prospect of outlasting its cosmic host. Many others also, including some environmental philosophers, assume that thought is a disposable appendage to life. In his recent book *The Revolt against Humanity*, Adam Kirsch, for example, wonders whether, in view of rapid anthropogenic climate change and other threats that humans have posed to the flourishing of life, the thinking species can any longer justify its presence on earth, the only place in the universe where we know for sure that thought is active.[10]

In his survey of recent antihumanist environmentalism, Kirsch brings up an uncomfortable thought: maybe now is the right time to let our species, along with its strange capacity for thought, perish completely from the natural world for the sake of the survival of the rest of life. Out of respect for the precarious but precious nonhuman species of life that contribute much more than we humans to the earth's ecological well-being, should we not consent, starting right now, to the elimination of the dysfunctional human presence in terrestrial history, even if it means letting go of the phenomenon of thought for good? Should we not allow the only species of life that "knows that it knows" to be cleansed from the cosmos? And should lovers of ecological integrity be sad about that loss?

Scientists and philosophers of mind have yet to find a comfortable place in the cosmos even for their own thoughts. Since many of them agree that the phenomenon of thought has never *essentially* belonged to nature, it is not a big deal for them to just let this dispensable interloper escape from the cosmos fully, finally, and forever. If mind does not belong to the natural world by definition, its final loss would not rise to the level of a cosmic catastrophe, even if in the short run it saddens a few sensitive human souls.

Furthermore, we must observe that the opinion that thought does not really belong to nature is not unprecedented. The separation of thought from nature is central to the modern creed that Whitehead called scientific materialism, but before that it was part of cosmic myths that existed long before the age of science. Before science came along, myths, religions, and philosophies often placed thought in a supernatural sphere of being outside

---

[9] See Michael Chorost, "Where Thomas Nagel Went Wrong," *Chronicle of Higher Education*, May 13, 2013.

[10] Adam Kirsch, *The Revolt against Humanity: Imagining a Future without Us* (New York: Columbia Global Reports, 2023).

310   *Teilhard, Whitehead, and the Reasons for Hope*

of, or only loosely connected, to nature. The traditional mythic separation of mind from matter prepared the way for modern materialists to expel thought (including their own?) from the whole house of being.

The Awakening Universe

The post-Einsteinian idea that the universe is an awakening places the whole topic of cosmos and thought in a new light. It is significant that Teilhard realized that the universe is a drama of awakening, and that Whitehead came to view the natural world as an adventure aiming toward the intensifying of beauty. The metaphors of awakening and adventure were not intended to replace scientifically essential mathematical and geometric models of the universe, but science itself in the twentieth century led to a new "narrative" way of understanding the universe that could not be represented in the language of geometry. Soon after Albert Einstein had published his theory of general relativity (1916), several mathematical physicists noticed that beneath the surface of his equations lurked a long and previously unknown cosmic drama. Teilhard, once he became aware of this discovery, realized that in addition to Einstein's search for geometric coherence, understanding the universe must also mean the quest for its narrative coherence. And since the story is still going on, understanding the universe requires that we keep looking toward the future to find out what the story is all about.

Does the cosmic story carry meaning? If we follow it all the way, a story can gather the unintelligible fragments and contingencies of its early episodes into a surprising coherence later on. So, as we read the new scientific cosmic story, full intelligibility may at present be partially or even mostly out of range. The universe is not a state but a dramatically ordered sequence of moments, episodes, and epochs that may anticipate a dramatic coherence, a kind of meaning we can presently encounter not by geometry alone (as Einstein assumed), but mostly by *anticipation*. Anticipation is not daydreaming, but a joining of our minds (and perhaps our lives) to the forward flow of time and then waiting patiently to make out what is happening up ahead. In a similar way Whitehead's idea of the universe as an adventure in effect turns our thoughts about nature not toward present or past forms of order but, more adventurously, toward new and richer forms of ordered novelty arriving from up ahead.

To both Teilhard and Whitehead the restlessness of human thought is not due to the human mind's being a strange intruder from outside of nature, but to the universe's being an adventurous and dramatic awakening. The human mind's constant fidgeting, in this cosmic perspective, is not due to its being exiled from a timeless world of eternal perfection and hence nostalgically longing to "get back home." Rather, thought's restlessness is a signal that the universe to which life, thought, *and faith* belong has always been a drama or an adventure of awakening. Ironically, Overbye's provocative *New York's Times* essay is itself an instance and expression of this restlessness.

Generally speaking, human mental and religious uneasiness is not a signal that the cosmos was not made for minds. Rather, our mental fragility and instability are signs that the *universe* to which we humans belong is stirring within us, coming into the light after a dark and immense dormancy. As they burst open, our minds are often uneasy—and hence may sometimes seem not to fit the cosmos. But fundamentally the universe itself is a restless adventure, an unsettled and unsettling drama of awakening.

Unaware that our thoughts *are* the universe in the throes of an awakening, many scientists and philosophers have tried to bring intellectual closure to their cosmologies by denying that mind and thought are really part of the natural world. This exclusion may have been more tenable when the machine was our main metaphor for the universe. Formerly it was tempting to picture thought as something extraneous to the world-machine. Thought, the human capacity to experience, think, judge, and decide, still seems so different from other things in nature. So we are easily inclined to place it outside of nature. And since the universe got along quite well without actual human minds for billions of years prior to human evolution, can it not get along without them again?

It is not just lonely human minds, but the whole universe that is undergoing a dramatic and disturbing adventure of awakening. Awakening to what? To being, meaning, goodness, truth and beauty, that is, to what philosophers used to call the *transcendentals*. These ideals, as Einstein would have agreed, are real, timeless, and immortal. So, when thought occurs in the universe (at least on earth), it is because our minds have been grasped by the imperishable ideals of being, meaning, goodness, truth, and beauty—which, taken together, may be called *Indestructible Rightness*. Thought can never be separated from the timeless ideals that are awakening it. Thinkers may die, but the transcendentals to which a mind awakens are imperishable. By virtue of its being taken captive by the transcendentals, I suggest, each mind and each thought participates in what is imperishable.

312   Teilhard, Whitehead, and the Reasons for Hope

I believe, though I cannot prove, that thought is always being quietly taken up irreversibly into what is indestructible. Its restlessness is not simply a matter of humans trying to adapt to, or escape from, a universe that is inherently inhospitable to thought. Thought, instead, *is* the universe, now in the mode of awakening to a Rightness rising on the horizon of what is Not-Yet. The only universe we know of has always been a drama of awakening. From the beginning it has carried the promise of becoming more. The story of a universe now awakening to Indestructible Rightness (to boundless being, meaning, truth, goodness, and beauty) can, by virtue of its linkage to the transcendentals, never be reduced to nothingness. Contrary to Overbye, there can be no absolutely final thought.

Consequently, we cannot speak meaningfully and truthfully about the cosmos, if, when telling its story, we leave out the adventure and drama of its awakening. The phenomenon of thought is essential and not incidental to an awakening universe. By belittling thought scientists and philosophers are shrinking our universe. Moreover, apart from the temporal irreversibility made possible by the cosmic drift toward thermodynamic equilibrium, the universe could not have been a story at all. The very same entropic cosmic slope that makes Overbye sad is also what enables the cosmos to be an irreversible story of awakening. And, again, the thing about a story is that it can carry meaning. Still, the universe's narrative coherence remains mostly hidden until the whole story has been told. For this reason, cosmic meaning cannot be grasped but only anticipated.

Overbye, in the very act of trusting his own mind as he writes his article, implicitly attributes great value to the phenomenon of thought. And it can only be because of his tacit love of thought that he is filled with sadness at the prospect of its death. Yet no less distressing than a cosmic story that ends with a final thought is the modern materialist idea of a universe that allows no real room for thought in the first place.

In Overbye's universe the cleansing of thought from nature has already taken place in principle, long before the evolution of mind has begun. What makes the cosmic story meaningful, even as the forces of nature steer it toward thermodynamic collapse, is its openness to what is Not-Yet. The cosmos has always had a narrative constitution, one that allows it to become new each moment. As it awakens, the universe always follows the arrow of time forward in the direction of a new future, a state of being that has not yet become fully actual. Anticipation looks for the world's meaning neither by going back to the cosmic past, following atomist and materialist instincts, nor by following the supernaturalist escapism into a timeless haven of perfection. Rather, the meaning of time is to open the universe to *more* consciousness, *more* being—and to an ever-intensifying Beauty that is both Not-Yet and everlasting.

Our minds cannot live or function in the absence of anticipation. Anticipation seeks indestructibility not by geometry but by putting on the virtue of hope. It refuses to follow Einstein's goal of getting out of time by clinging to the timelessness of geometry. Instead, anticipation looks forward in hope to the *fulfillment* of time. The ancient figure most representative of the anticipatory vision is Abraham. Biblical stories about this historically obscure character have been recited over and over by followers of Judaism, Christianity, and Islam. Their effect has been to give people a sense that time is filled with promise. As long as the cosmic story is not over, realism requires that we be patient enough to stay in touch with its narrative drift. This means that we may have to wait, perhaps intergenerationally, if we really care to understand the universe in depth.[11] Even if the universe is "running down" thermodynamically in the direction of a far-off energy collapse, nothing can ever undo the fact that a cosmic story has taken place, and that the story is one of awakening and not just a roundabout tale of physical determinism and decay. You may find direct evidence of our awakening universe in your own attempt right now to experience, understand, and judge the claims I have been making in this chapter. Your mind has not just dropped into the universe from outside. Your mind *is* the universe now awakening to a meaning arriving from the direction of the Not-Yet.

Consequently, I want to ask (with Teilhard) whether it is reasonable for us ever to trust the human mind's claims to right understanding, including in the sphere of scientific knowing, if every thought (including scientific thought) is destined to be totally dissolved in the bath of final nothingness? Can scientists, for example, rightly claim—even here and now—to be authoritative and trustworthy if the whole phenomenon of thought is going to perish utterly along with the cosmos? If at heart the destiny of thought is pure nothingness, then why should we pay any attention to Overbye's sad thoughts about thought since, like all other thoughts they too are finally reducible to—nothing?

The intelligibility—or meaning—that we may look for in the universe story is not already rounded off or eternally unchanging. It is not waiting to be disclosed fully by either mathematics or meditation. Instead, we may assume with Teilhard that the universe's narrative meaning is still unclear

---

[11] Pierre Teilhard de Chardin, *The Heart of Matter*, trans. René Hague (New York: Harcourt Brace Jovanovich, 1978).

314 Teilhard, Whitehead, and the Reasons for Hope

by necessity. Cosmic meaning is not lurking passively beneath our surface impressions, as though it were a geometric form ready to flash before our eyes in full immediacy. Rather, meaning is somehow always still arriving, and it can be encountered only by way of anticipation. It is coming from up ahead, from a realm of possibilities not yet actualized. Meaning, at least from a terrestrial perspective, is always somehow incomplete, and this is why we can see its products only "through a glass darkly" (1 Cor 13:12). Mostly, we have to wait for it, not passively but *actively*, by contributing our own lives and struggles to the drama of its arrival. We encounter it only because in each new moment of our lives, the cosmos, from which we hope never to be separated, is still awakening, still being drawn into the mystery of an inexhaustible and surprising future. A good name for the ground of this never fully accessible Future is God. A good name for our allowing ourselves to be taken into this Future is hope.

Conclusion and Summary

It is unthinkable, then, that thought—a phenomenon inseparable from the whole cosmic story of emerging physical complexity—could ever perish utterly. This is because the imperishable transcendental ideals that are now awakening the universe can never let go of our minds. The imperishability of thought is a gift given in advance to anticipatory minds that are just now awakening to an indestructible horizon of Rightness—that is, to indestructible being, meaning, goodness, truth, and beauty. Since God's will is the maximizing of beauty, as Whitehead puts it, we may conclude that our own "doing God's will" must take the form of beautifying the world, keeping it from lapsing into a desert of monotony, on the one hand, and the abyss of disorder, on the other. We may do God's will not only in grand ways but also by undertaking the most ordinary obligations. In doing so, we shall be following the message of Pope Francis's encyclical *Laudato Si'*, trusting that the meaning and goal of our lives is not only to contemplate or be swept away by beauty but also to participate here and now in the adventure of saving and bringing it about.

I would like to add that an understanding of the universe as a drama of awakening, or as an adventure toward beauty, is wide enough to embrace a multiverse—if it exists. Metaphysically speaking, there is a oneness or togetherness of the many universes, should they exist, inasmuch as they all share in the arrival of Rightness. Altogether they would share the trait of futurity or of Not-Yetness. Theologically, then, there is only one universe with many dimensions, epochs, laws, and so forth. So, the real questions are: why is there being and not nothing, and why does the universe (or multiverse) unfold as a story following what we may call the *narrative cosmological principle*? It is significant that our search for the intelligibility of a multiverse is a search *for a unifying principle* that we do not yet have, but that somehow has us. We cannot help anticipating it because our minds have already been grasped by it.

The Christic

Teilhard's Last Will and Testament

Kathleen Duffy

Teilhard wrote many religious essays during his lifetime. Now available in thirteen volumes, these essays represent his attempt to refine and clarify his emerging synthesis of Christ and the evolution of the world. His essay "The Christic"[1] is therefore a particularly important one for two reasons. First, because it is his last essay, it contains the final statement of his deepest and most precious spiritual experience of the Christic. And second, it is an essay he wanted so desperately to write. In fact, in a 1950 letter to his friend Jeanne Mortier he writes: "I want to live long enough to have time to express [this extraordinary Christic] more or less as I now see it taking shape, with an ever-increasing sense of wonder."[2] Having arrived in New York City in 1951 for the final phase of his many years of exile from Paris, he knew his end was near. This was his last chance. And so, he resolved to end well, which meant, among other things, that he would at the very least write this final essay. Convinced of the coherence of his synthesis as well as its implications for action in the world and for the life of the church, he felt great urgency.

The essay would not be totally new. It would include material from his earlier work, *The Divine Milieu*,[3] and "The Mass on the World."[4] However,

---

[1] Pierre Teilhard de Chardin, "The Christic," in *The Heart of Matter*, trans. René Hague (New York: Harcourt Brace Jovanovich, 1978), 82–102.

[2] Pierre Teilhard de Chardin, letter to Jeanne Mortier, August 19, 1950, in *Lettres à Jeanne Mortier* (Paris: Éditions de Seuil, 1984), 66.

[3] Pierre Teilhard de Chardin, *The Divine Milieu: An Essay on the Interior Life* (New York: Harper Row, 1960).

[4] Pierre Teilhard de Chardin, "The Mass on the World," in *The Heart of Matter*, 119–34.

317

318   The Christic

it would be a matured version, a version he had recently attempted to share in his spiritual autobiography, "The Heart of Matter."[5] But now he would describe for the last time, and in words that are usually impossible even for a mystic, a key piece of his synthesis, a version that had occurred to him only later in life. He now had a clearer and deeper idea of how to represent his experience of his ever-growing sense of the influence and presence of Christ and the evolution of the world, "the union of the pleromizing-Christ of Revelation and the emergent Evolutive of Science."[6] This would be his parting gift to the world. When, in March 1955, a month before he died, he finally completed the essay, he must have felt relieved.

As usual, Teilhard relies on imagery from a variety of fields of study, particularly from science, to attempt to convey meaning that is deeper than words. This essay is typical, with images from physics (space-time diagrams, radiation, magnetism, and chain reactions), from geometry (cones, spheres, and circles), from thermodynamics (currents and vortices), as well as evolutionary processes (cosmic currents), all attempting to describe the indescribable. In this chapter I make use of his images from geometry, radiation, and evolution.

Overview

Teilhard opens the "The Christic" by sharing the two burning passions of his life and imaging them as dynamic and directed currents.[7] Because these passions emerged from very different sources, he initially experienced them as disconnected. Yet, as we will see, both currents were all the while flowing toward the same endpoint, waiting patiently to be seen as two sides of a single phenomenon. Teilhard's awareness of the first current, which he calls cosmic convergence, traces his growing passion for Earth and was sparked during his frequent nature walks through the countryside and among the volcanic hills of the Auvergne with his father. The second, which he calls Christic emergence, focuses on his ever-expanding love for God and arose spontaneously from the influence of his mother's deep devotion to the Sacred Heart. As these currents made their way through the stream of his life, continually moving him toward something yet to be discovered, they

---

[5] Pierre Teilhard de Chardin, "The Heart of Matter," in *The Heart of Matter*, 15–79.

[6] Pierre Teilhard de Chardin, letter to Jeanne Mortier, September 22, 1954, in *Lettres à Jeanne Mortier*, 162.

[7] Teilhard, "The Heart of Matter," 2–79.

sometimes encountered a smooth landscape and a flow that was unobstructed. But often, the contour of the terrain through which these currents were flowing was rough and their forward movement was obstructed by turbulence and eddies. Yet Teilhard still followed their lead as they propelled him to explore the cosmos in what seemed at first two very different directions. But, by listening attentively and responding wholeheartedly to forces within these streams, he found that, little by little, he was compiling the data that would inform a profound synthesis of science and religion. Eventually, he was able to gather enough evidence to begin to formulate that synthesis, one that would set his world on fire. And because Teilhard the scientist believed in revealing both his data and the sources of his inspiration, many with intuitive or mystical roots, in his essay "The Christic" he carefully charts for us not only his results, but also their development along this pair of deep-running, psychic currents.[8]

Current One: Cosmic Convergence

Although Teilhard always experienced Something shining at the heart of matter, his journey along the first current, cosmic convergence, seemed anything but religious. Even as a child, he found the countryside alive and filled with a numinous presence. The solidity of the rocks in his collection gave him an inward sense of security. However, during his days as a Jesuit seminarian, his focus on collecting specimens of rock was enhanced by excitement with the theory of evolution, delight at unearthing Earth's long history, and concern for mapping the structure of Earth's crust. Over many years as a brilliant practicing paleontologist and geologist, he experienced at an intimate level the stages of Earth's struggle to diversify. The energy and dynamism of the evolutionary perspective delighted him. And his approach to evolution is unique. Unlike most scientists at the time, he focused not only on evolution's physical processes. The psychic aspects of evolution, its meaning and direction, were integral. Eventually he was able to reject the dualistic notion that matter and spirit are separate entities, seeing them instead as two sides of a single coin, sharing a single identity. His passion for Earth continued to grow. It was Earth that he loved, evolution that he believed in.

Although its endpoint was still unclear, Teilhard sensed that this first current was leading him somewhere. Intense field work gave him plenty

---

[8] Ibid., 25.

320   *The Christic*

of time to observe and reflect on the data he was amassing and to recognize the patterns governing the evolutionary process. As he assembled the details of the cosmic story, he noticed that these patterns demonstrate a clear direction forward. He found union everywhere, even from the very beginning. Protons and neutrons join to form nuclei; nuclei fuse to form atoms; atoms join to form molecules; molecules to form cells; cells to form organisms. His conclusion: diversity and complexity arise from union, and the product of each union is more conscious than the individuals that constitute it. This pattern is present at every level of the evolving world. It convinced him that the cosmos as a whole is not only directed; it is also moving toward ever greater union and ever greater consciousness. He renamed the evolutionary process as a Cosmogenesis and formalized these insights in two laws: the *law of creative union*, which states that when two or more entities cede their sense of individualism but not their identity and unite, they are capable of becoming more, of becoming something new, and the *law of complexity-consciousness*, which states that as matter complexifies, it becomes capable of generating and sustaining more developed forms of consciousness and encourages still greater complexity. He experienced the implications on these laws on the psychic level as well. With the members of his troop during the war, he came to realize the deep bonding that occurs when a project greater than oneself is fully embraced, and in his relationship with his cousin Marguerite, he sensed both the power of the feminine and the power of love.

As Teilhard began investigating how Creative Union has been operating throughout the ages, how the consequence of its influence has been determining the fourteen-billion-year history of the cosmos, and how complexification and diversification continue to develop even to this day, he was filled with awe. However, the coming of the human stood out for him as a unique and somewhat astonishing critical point in this long and creative evolutionary process. The emergence of the human with its capacity for co-reflection introduced a totally new phase in evolutionary history. Co-reflection provides the human with ways to engage in total human acts such as thinking with the other and co-conscientizing,[9] sharing thought and passion with every other thinking being, weaving our learnings into coherent wholes, and most of all, preserving them. This gift allows the human community to discover where we've come from and to project into the future.

With the dawn of human co-reflection, the universe began converging upon itself, becoming collectively more conscious, extending itself with

---

[9] Ibid.

increasing speed beyond insignificant individual centers in the direction of a complexity-consciousness of planetary dimensions.[10] Not only is matter complexifying; thought itself is becoming ever more complex, and evolution is developing a common psychogenic concentration of the world upon itself. In fact, because of this, there is no limit to what Teilhard sees as the onset of ultra-hominization, that is, the union of humanity with Christ.

In conversation with philosopher and mathematician Édouard Le Roy, Teilhard coined the term *noosphere* for the spherical shell of thought that surrounds Earth's surface. In this ethereal space cosmogenesis continues the work of complexification as a noogenesis, a process that causes the universe to converge on itself and to personalize what it unites. Whether we realize it or not and whether we contribute to its forward movement or impede its progress, we are being swept away in its flux, a flux that made it clear to Teilhard that humanity will continue to evolve and to converge onto an ultra-human stage. The dynamics of the current of cosmic convergence convinced him that this process is irreversible.

Noogenesis also gave geometrical shape to Teilhard's world. To help visualize its nature, he suggests plotting a complexity-time diagram in which he represents phases of ever-increasing awareness and knowledge as sectors of a cone.[11] As time elapses and the complexity of the cosmos increases, the radius of each new sector of the cone decreases and the cosmos moves ever closer toward the peak, the omega point of evolution, the ultra-center of thought and action. This evolving cone is clearly convergent (see Figure 15-1 below).

It took twenty years of research and reflection for Teilhard to develop the details of the evolutionary story that he relates so meticulously in *The Human Phenomenon*.[12] But, even then, he had not discovered the Christic. This would still take time.

Current Two: Christic Emergence

Teilhard's immersion in the second cosmic current, Christic emergence, began with his childhood devotion to the Sacred Heart, a devotion that persisted throughout his life, albeit with variations. Each evening after dinner

---

[10] Ibid., 86.

[11] Laura Eloe, "Teilhard's Mathematical Analogies and the Tradition of the Church," *Teilhard Studies* 87 (Fall 2023): 1–23.

[12] Pierre Teilhard de Chardin, *The Human Phenomenon*, trans. Sarah Appleton-Weber (Portland, OR: Sussex Academic Press, 1999).

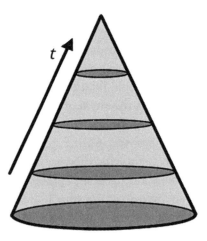

Figure 15-1. Complexity-Time Diagram

his family would gather for prayer around the statue of the Sacred Heart. At first, because of his propensity to suffer anxiety regarding the fragility of living things, focus on a human heart caused him great discomfort. To calm his anxiety, he would concentrate on the crimson and gold metallic piece that surrounds the all-too-real heart, finding within it a place of comfort and safety. This impulse to find a way to materialize the spiritual continued, as did his devotion to the Sacred Heart. One day while serving as a stretcher bearer during World War I, he had a particularly moving mystical experience. As he stood at the back of a local church gazing at an all-too-stylized picture of the Sacred Heart, a totally new vision of Christ came over him. Christ's garment suddenly began expanding into the cosmos while Christ emerged as a person of great warmth and empathy. This moment provided Teilhard with both a dynamic experience and a tangible image of the Cosmic Christ.[13]

In Jesus of Nazareth, Teilhard also found a tangible God, one he could see and touch. Jesus who was born into the very process of evolution to encourage its positive direction. After suffering and dying a brutal death, he rose from the dead to exhibit the cosmic dimension of the Christ, a capacity that relates Christ to the entire universe. Throughout the years the example of the life of Jesus has empowered acts of great love by persons with amazing courage and altruism. Teilhard also found Christianity

---

[13] An account of this vision can be found in Teilhard's essay "The Picture," in Teilhard, *The Heart of Matter*, 61–65.

organic. Emboldened by the inspiration apparent in the life of Jesus and its faith in the resurrection, the church has, over the years, been capable of tremendous growth and change, of bringing people from many areas of the world together into a single body, and of spreading love throughout the world. These aspects provided Teilhard with evidence for a process he called Christogenesis, "the rise of a *certain universal Presence* which is at once *immortalizing* and *unifying*."[14] Christ became for him the Omega of evolution, its endpoint.

Along this second current, Christic emergence, Teilhard's relationship with God deepened. He experienced an ever-expanding and ever-evolving image of God. Yet he was never completely satisfied. He longed to know an ever-greater God, a God more vast, more immense, more dazzling than the world, a God beautiful enough to adore. His devotions became more cosmic, more universalized. Yet, more than ever, he yearned for a reformed church that would universalize the static Christian God of his youth, the God he called the God of the Above, and that would allow the God of evolution, whom he called the God of the Ahead, its rightful place in the scheme of things.

The Conjunction

Two currents—dynamic and directed—evolved and transformed Teilhard's unconscious drives into deep and effective passions. By responding to their movements over a lifetime, Teilhard's cosmic sense became ever more intimate and his Christic sense ever more certain. His journey along the current of cosmic convergence revealed a noogenesis capable of personalizing the cosmos. And his journey along the current of Christic emergence revealed an incarnate God capable of amorizing the world, of filling the world with the energy of love. As he observed humanity complexifying and extending ever deeper and wider, while at the same time converging upon itself, he realized that the cosmos is actively seeking a Center. On the other hand, along the second current, he found a Christian Center searching for a Sphere, for a God who is large enough to adore.[15]

When astronomers study a celestial body, they collect information coming from the object using several different types of telescope. Some are Earth-bound, while others orbit Earth, bypassing interference from Earth's

---

[14] Teilhard, *The Heart of Matter*, 90.
[15] Ibid.

324   The Christic

atmosphere. Each telescope is designed to collect radiation within a limited region of the electromagnetic spectrum. By analyzing this light, astronomers determine important information such as the object's chemical composition, its temperature, its age, its distance, and the speed with which it moves. For instance, a radio telescope collects the object's long wave spectrum and reveals more than what can be learned from the spectrum of radiation available from an optical telescope, which collects light in the visible range only. And an infrared telescope, such as the James Webb Space Telescope, reveals even further detail, data that complements what is already known. To obtain a more complete picture of the object, astronomers superpose details gathered from their many observations.

Teilhard's experience of coming to know the cosmos is similar to that of the astronomers. Like the data of the astronomers, Teilhard's data seemed to be coming from different sources, different directions. Yet over time, the results of his study and the contemplation of the data provided him with rich and complementary details. And just as astronomers must bring together information obtained from different parts of the electromagnetic spectrum, all Teilhard needed to do was to conjoin the data that he had gathered from his two currents. Once he did this, a subtle harmony appeared. His Cosmic sense and his Christic sense became one, and as is always the case with Creative Union, his understanding of both Christ and the universe became ever greater.

The Christic

By assuming that the Omega of evolution, Teilhard's God of the Ahead, coincides with the Christ of Revelation, his God of the Above, Christ came to be known as Christ the Prime Mover of Complexity-Consciousness, the force who is alluring the cosmos toward ultimate union.[16] In their conjunction the world finds its Center and Christ finds its Sphere. What is more, an ever-greater Christ appears. No longer simply human and divine, Christ acquires a cosmic nature, a theandric nature, in which the human and the divine cooperate to do the task at hand, which, according to St. Paul, is to hold all things together. In Christ, the divine, the human, and the cosmic are one. And, as the world continues to evolve and as Christ continues to relate to the world, Christ becomes more vast and more beautiful. Christ

---

[16] Ibid., 94.

becomes an ever-larger God, the ultimate phase of evolution into which all preliminary phases converge.

In the conjunction, cosmogenesis reaches its mystical stage, which is Christogenesis. The peak (Omega) of the converging cone of evolution that, while traveling along his first current, Teilhard plotted to illustrate the trajectory of growing consciousness, merges with the Christ of Revelation, the ever-greater Christ, the Center (Omega) of the Christosphere, whom Teilhard came to know deeply along the second current (see Figure 15-2).

Figure 15-2: The Christic: The Conjunction of the Omega of Evolution and the Omega of Revelation

This sphere surrounds the entire cone, encompassing and embracing the total history of the world. From this Center and in touch with the whole cosmos, Christ amorizes matter, Christ radiates the energy of Love throughout the entire volume of the converging complexity-time cone and, in the process, fills the cosmos with the energy of Love. In contact with the Center, matter becomes Christified and, as a result, ever more personal, ever more loving. Radiation coming from Point Omega, that privileged evolutive summit, reflects from matter and scatters throughout the sphere. The intensity of love energy is building up throughout, causing the cosmos eventually to catch fire, to become incandescent. In this super theo-cosmic dimension, Christ, who is present at all levels of the universe driving evolution toward ultimate union, is universalized through radiation, while the Christified universe reveals an ever-more-loving countenance. As is always the case with Creative Union, Christ does not subordinate, fuse, or dissolve

326   *The Christic*

what is brought together but rather amorizes it. And as the cosmos expands, humanity is further amorized by Christ. This Christ is a God Teilhard can trust, an indestructible Center he can love.

In this final stage of evolution a supernatural ultra-human milieu appears, a final realization and incorporation of the human, and through the human, the whole universe, into Christ Omega. Opposition between universal and personal is eradicated. Love of God and love of Earth now become a single act. Christ becomes diaphanous, transparent, as crimson gleams of matter glide into the gold of Spirit, transforming the cosmos into a universe that is Person and surrounded always by the Feminine.[17] Teilhard has found a God he can love, a God with whom relationship is now on a cosmic scale. As the Heart of the universalized Christ coincides with the heart of amorized matter, Teilhard realizes that "the Heart of Matter [is] A World Heart, The Heart of a God,"[18] a God who is growing ever greater, ever more beautiful. The metal patch of crimson and gold that Teilhard worshiped as a child has finally become a glowing core of Fire. Teilhard's cosmos has been set aflame.

Postscript

Yet several serious questions continued to haunt Teilhard: how to activate the spiritual energy that is available to the human community so that the Christic can be effective; how to increase humanity's response to Omega, the driving force of evolution; and how to intensify humanity's "eagerness to act, to seek, to create."[19] Inspired in part by the attention being given at the time to the huge amounts of nuclear energy released by the newly discovered nuclear processes of fission and fusion, Teilhard hoped to find a complementary way to generate huge amounts of energy in the noosphere. He looked to religion, a religion that would stimulate humanity, activate humanity with a willingness to contribute to a project greater than itself. However, the religion of Teilhard's day was definitely not the answer. Given the enormous task that humanity faces, a religion based on a static view of the world, and one with a theology that retains a separation between spiritual activity and work in the world, could never provide the impetus needed to encourage faith in the future. But the major components for such

---

[17] Ibid., 16.
[18] Ibid., 15.
[19] Ibid., 97.

a religion as love of God, faith in the world, and hope in the future were not yet strong enough in Christianity.

Instead, Teilhard longs for what he calls the Religion of Tomorrow,[20] one with a more integrated approach to spirituality, one in which his image of the Christic would call forth a worthy response from humanity to the problems that beset our world, one that would encourage a vision of the future that promotes a better world not only as a good but rather as a supreme necessity. Such a religion would have the power to attract, to organize, and to activate. But most of all, it would motivate humanity not only to work to survive, but more than that, to super-live. And living within Earth's evolutionary paradigm would influence our approach to the world, as it did for Teilhard.

Having spent his whole life searching for an evolutionary spirituality while at the same time living the best of the Christian tradition to the full, Teilhard found potential for an evolved Christianity, but only if it were a renewed and evolved Christianity whose context and vision would be based on an understanding of the theory of evolution. Several of its characteristics also encouraged him: its tangible and Immanent God of the Gospels, the one born of Mary whose life, death, and resurrection give both solace and examples of how to contribute to a world longing to be one, to engage in a project greater than oneself; the Transcendent Christ of Paul, who holds all things together and whose cosmic nature opens up a much greater view of cosmic processes; and the Christian understanding of the double power of the cross and resurrection that encourages humanity to bear the weight of a world in evolution and to be willing to take on the sufferings entailed in a commitment to the Religion of the Future. For Teilhard, Christianity's greatest asset is its personal God. These characteristics gave him hope that an evolved religion could be effective.

The cosmic, the human, and the Christic—the successive heralding of a universe that is Person, of a God who is both tangible and ubiquitous. Despite the beauty and the coherence of Teilhard's vision of the Christic, his vision has not yet become widespread and has not yet been able to motivate the action needed to work toward union. However, the vision has its time. One day the Omega of human experience, whom Teilhard perceived through his scientific inquiry along the current of cosmic convergence, will conjoin with the Omega of faith in the Incarnate Word whom Teilhard came to know along the current of Christic emergence. One day Teilhard's

---

[20] Ibid., 96.

328 *The Christic*

vision will erupt and a powerful faith in the future will allow humanity to be drawn toward the Transcendent and opened to the Imminent. One day, the Omega of evolution will join with the Omega of revelation to become the driving force of action in the world. On that day, engulfed in the spiritual energy released in the conjunction of a personal God with an amorized universe, the cosmos will finally burst into flames.

Part IV

Appendix

Marcel Brion et le Père Teilhard de Chardin, par Roger Wild

Meeting with
Father Teilhard de Chardin

Interview by Marcel Brion (1951)

TRANSLATED BY DONALD WAYNE VINEY

What follows is my English translation of Marcel Brion's interview with Teilhard de Chardin, preceded by my commentary on the historical context of the interview. Brion's interview is accompanied by a sketch of the two men in conversation drawn by the Swiss artist Roger Wild (1894–1987), which is on the facing page. It would seem to be a rare piece of Teilhardiana as it is not reproduced in the most well-known works by and about Teilhard, including the major biographies as well as the *Teilhard de Chardin Album*, designed and edited by Jeanne Mortier and Marie-Louise Aboux.[1]

The Context of Teilhard's Interview
with Marcel Brion

In a letter dated January 28, 1951, Pierre Teilhard de Chardin (1881–1955) wrote to his fellow priest and close friend Pierre Leroy (1900–1992):

> In a long interview ("A Meeting with") which appeared in the *Nouvelles Littéraires* of January 11, I arranged with Marcel Brion (in a text I wrote up myself and [René] d'Ouince reviewed) to say that I

---

[1] Jeanne Mortier and Marie-Louise Aboux, *Teilhard de Chardin Album* (London: Collins, 1966).

332   *Meeting with Father Teilhard de Chardin*

want to make my real intellectual position public and to address the false interpretations (millennialism and "Hinduism") which are too often given.[2]

In view of this testimony, it is a fair guess that Teilhard presented Brion with a text that he used as a basis for questions. Brion seems familiar with parts of "Le Coeur de la Matière" ("The Heart of Matter"), Teilhard's autobiographical essay, completed in October 1950. In fact, Teilhard's answers concerning his childhood fascination with iron and stone are almost verbatim excerpts from the early part of that essay, published only after Teilhard's death. Indeed, apart from more focused scientific studies, *all* the writings that most clearly express what Teilhard here calls his "real intellectual position" appeared posthumously. Yet, he was already enough of a celebrity to merit a front-page interview in a major French literary newspaper. The situation invites comment.

Teilhard's work as a geologist and paleontologist (highlighted in the interview) made him famous, but from his earliest essays written during the First World War he strove to express his ideas about the fertile interconnections between science and religion. It is a vision in which the cosmos is reframed as a cosmogenesis, an evolutionary process of ever more complex forms of life and mentality, animated by a divine spirit, consummated in a personalized center he called Omega. The latest stage in the process—characteristic of "the human phenomenon"—is where the threshold of reflective thought has been crossed. As for the relationship between God and creatures, Teilhard says that God does not so much *make things* as to *make things make themselves.*[3] Teilhard's religious superiors always prohibited him from publishing the works in which he promoted these (and other) bold

---

[2] Pierre Leroy, SJ, *Lettres Familières de Pierre Teilhard de Chardin Mon Ami, Les Dernières Années: 1948–1955* (Vendôme: Éditions Centurion, 1976), 93–94. See also *Letters from My Friend Teilhard de Chardin 1948–1955*, trans. Mary Lukas (New York: Paulist Press, 1980), 85. Mary Lukas and Ellen Lukas indicate that "all of d'Ouince's persuasiveness" was needed to secure Teilhard's right of censorship over the interview. Mary Lukas and Ellen Lukas, *Teilhard: The Man, the Priest, the Scientist* (Garden City, NY: Doubleday and Company), 293.

[3] In early 1920, Teilhard wrote: "Properly speaking, God *does not make*. He *makes things make themselves.*" Pierre Teilhard de Chardin, *Christianity and Evolution*, trans. René Hague (New York: Harcourt Brace Jovanovich, 1971), 28. A year and a half later he expressed the same thought: "God, as one might say, does not so much 'make' things as 'make them make themselves.'" Pierre Teilhard de Chardin, *The Vision of the Past*, trans. J. M. Cohen (New York: Harper and Row, 1966), 25.

ideas. Indeed, at times, the preservation of these writings was precarious, as church authorities sometimes ordered them destroyed.[4]

Three women were especially important in preserving and disseminating Teilhard's wider corpus of writings: first, during World War I, his cousin Marguerite Teillard-Chambon (1880–1959) (who wrote pseudonymously as Claude Aragonnès); second, his longtime friend Simone Bégouën (1897–1960); and finally, Jeanne Mortier (1892–1982). In 1928, Bégouën proposed to type Teilhard's manuscripts; she effectively served as his archivist as his cousin had done during the war years. In February 1933, Bégouën suggested duplicating his writings (using a renotype machine) for distribution to the increasingly large network of his friends who were both in agreement with Catholic thought and largely open to the modern world.[5] With a certain rebellious irony, Teilhard called these copies of his works *clandestins*.[6] The project was a considerable "underground" venture, as hundreds of copies were printed and sent out. In a May 1937 letter to Lucille Swan (1887–1965), Teilhard spoke of "a real clandestine shop" at Simone Bégouën's residence in Paris.[7] Bégouën mastered the practice of compiling and distributing the clandestins, but when she and her husband (Max) left Paris in 1940 to live in Casablanca, she passed the torch to Mortier. In a 1946 letter to Mortier, Teilhard suggested that she preserve "the Bégouën system."[8] Mortier became Teilhard's literary executor, and it was she who, immediately after Teilhard's death, shepherded his works to publication, freed from the oversight of religious censors.

It is a mistake to think of the distribution of the clandestins as a case of disloyalty on Teilhard's part. To be sure, in order to become a Jesuit, Teilhard

---

[4] For example, Gérard-Henry Baudry notes: "Between 1940 and 1944, the order was given to the Jesuit houses to destroy all of Teilhard's writings." See Gérard-Henry Baudry, *Dictionnaire des Correspondants de Teilhard de Chardin* (Lille: Chez l'Auteur, 1974), 93. This must be an exaggeration since Teilhard's strictly scientific works were not prohibited.

[5] Pierre Teilhard de Chardin, *Le Rayonnement d'une Amitié, Correspondance avec la Famille Bégouën (1922–1955)*, ed. Michel Hermans and Pierre Sauvage (Bruxelles: Lessius, 2011), 6, 34, 63.

[6] Baudry, *Dictionnaire*, 25. Patrice Boudignon points out that "clandestine" is pejorative, for the writings were not anonymous. They bore Teilhard's name and the date of composition, and they were known to his superiors. See Boudignon, *Pierre Teilhard de Chardin: Sa Vie, Son Oeuvre, Sa Réflexion* (Paris: Éditions du Cerf, 2008), 162.

[7] *The Letters of Teilhard de Chardin and Lucile Swan*, ed. Thomas M. King, SJ, and Mary Wood Gilbert (Scranton, PA: University of Scranton Press, 2001), 86.

[8] Pierre Teilhard de Chardin, *Lettres à Jeanne Mortier* (Paris: Éditions du Seuil, 1984), 28.

334 Meeting with Father Teilhard de Chardin

took a vow of obedience. It is a vow he respected, although, where the publication of his works was concerned, there was some leeway and the situation was not always under his control. Nothing prevented him from distributing lecture notes to students, and he was not prohibited from sharing lengthy essays and manuscripts with fellow scholars. Teilhard referred to these works as his "scientifico-philosophico-religious writings." They circulated widely, especially when he returned to Paris from China, where he had been stranded by the events of the Second World War. René d'Ouince recalls:

> [Teilhard] was received as a prophet by a crowd of those he did not even know. . . . Not simply a Parisian personality, he was a sort of movie star in the intellectual world, especially among students. Suddenly, as if by magic, his unpublished work proliferated.[9]

Rome was not pleased. At the beginning of 1947, he received an order from his superior general to put an end to the circulation of texts that had not been submitted to the official censor. Teilhard's best intentions notwithstanding, the situation was out of hand. D'Ouince, as Teilhard's immediate superior, was obliged to enforce the order, despite his support for Teilhard's cause. He says that he collected two- or three-hundred notebooks from a little dispensary and paid those who were distributing them for the cost of printing them. D'Ouince says that he destroyed a certain number but sheltered the rest in the hope that the order would be lifted. D'Ouince asked and received permission from the father general to keep a complete set; he avers that he was not the only Jesuit to do so.[10]

After 1947, it became increasingly difficult to obtain the clandestins.[11] Teilhard did not make it easy on anyone eager to broadcast his views. He refused an offer to issue a privately published edition of *Le Milieu Divin*. In addition, he discouraged anyone wishing to author a book on his thought,

---

[9] René d'Ouince, *Un Prophète en Procès: Teilhard de Chardin dans l'Église de son Temps* (Paris: Aubier-Montaigne, 1970), 149.

[10] Ibid., 150. From 1935 until 1973, D'Ouince (1896–1973) was the superior at the Jesuit house in Paris, home of the periodical *Études*. He and Teilhard had a warm relationship. D'Ouince's actions cannot be interpreted as an effort to silence Teilhard, for he was in deep sympathy with his project. He sought, rather, to moderate his friend's pronouncements and to protect him from a more serious censure from Rome that others had experienced. His book *Un Prophète en Procès* (A Prophet on Trial) is perhaps the finest source on Teilhard's relations with the church written by one who was in the thick of the controversy. For more on D'Ouince, see Baudry, *Dictionnaire des Correspondants de Teilhard de Chardin*, 101–3.

[11] Exceptions are mentioned in *Lettres à Jeanne Mortier*, 60, 67, 69, 71, 176.

and he refused permission to quote longer extracts from *Le phénomène humain*. Finally, he declined an offer to be feted during his brief return to Paris in 1954.[12] Until the very end, Teilhard cautioned Mortier to be discrete so as not to contravene the formal directions from Rome. In a letter of October 20, 1954, he counseled to continue working within the church: "Nothing to do, I fear, except continue the old (and expensive) tactic. Keeping the fire under the cinders, patiently waiting for the regime to change."[13] The flame, however, was not so easily contained, for the clandestins had made him a *cause célèbre* with the liberal-leaning press, especially in France. In an August 1950 edition of *Le Figaro Littéraire*, André Billy of the Academy Goncourt referred to Teilhard as "our greatest prose poet."[14] Teilhard's nervous superiors might at least have been happy to learn that Billy indicated the difficulty in obtaining Teilhard's works. Be that as it may, Teilhard's popularity was not so well received among conservative Catholic outlets.[15] The founder of *Pensée Catholique*, L'Abbé Luc Lefèvre, published a critique of Teilhard and his thought titled *L'Evolution Rédemptrice du P. Teilhard de Chardin* (The Redemptive Evolution of Father Teilhard de Chardin).[16] This was the first book-length treatment of Teilhard of any sort, issued fully five years *before* the works Lefèvre is criticizing began to be published; Teilhard indicated that he did not recognize his thought in Lefèvre's book.[17]

Teilhard welcomed the *Nouvelles Littéraire* interview as an opportunity to clarify his thought and to counteract the misunderstandings of it. However, it is notable that, notwithstanding his strong convictions about what he called a metaphysics of union, the evolutionary significance of Christ, and his belief in an Omega Point of the evolutionary process, none of these

---

[12] D'Ouince, *Un Prophète en Procès*, 179–81.

[13] Ibid., 164.

[14] André Billy, "Un grand poète à demi clandestin," *Le Figaro Littéraire*, August 5, 1950.

[15] Teilhard's notoriety extended beyond France. For example, there is a story in the March 27, 1937, edition of *Newsweek* (30–31) concerning Teilhard that includes a photograph of him. Both *Newsweek* (April 25, 1955), 73, and *Time* (April 25, 1955), 104, carried notices of Teilhard's death.

[16] *L'Evolution Rédemptrice du P. Teilhard de Chardin* (Paris: Librairie du Cèdre, 1950). No one is listed as the author of the book, but Mlle. Mortier learned that it was Lefèvre. See *Lettres à Jeanne Mortier*, 64.

[17] Pierre Teilhard de Chardin, "Review of *L'Evolution Rédemptrice du P. Teilhard de Chardin*," in *L'Oeuvre Scientifique* 10, ed. Nichol and Karl Schmitz-Moorman (Olten/ Freiburg-im-Breisgau: Walter Verlag, 1971), 4290. A second book critical of Teilhardism appeared two years later: Louis Cognet, *Le Père Teilhard de Chardin et la Pensée Contemporaine* (Paris: Au Portulan, chez Flammarion, 1952). For Teilhard's comments on this book, see Lukas, *Letters from My Friend Teilhard de Chardin*, 131.

336 *Meeting with Father Teilhard de Chardin*

ideas are specifically mentioned. In a word, he endeavored to express himself in purely scientific terms without wandering into the realms of philosophy and theology. In the last thing he wrote before his death, he spoke of this endeavor as "psychologically unviable" and even "directly contrary . . . to the greater glory of God."[18]

Teilhard's unabashed public mention of Piltdown as one of two great opportunities in his career carries special interest. Almost three years after the interview, Piltdown Man was revealed as a hoax. Stephen Jay Gould (1941–2002) thought that Teilhard was complicit. Part of his case against Teilhard was how rarely he mentioned Piltdown in his scientific works. Gould considered this lacuna "inexplicable to the point of perversity."[19] In light of the Brion interview, this argument carries much less, if any, weight. Teilhard's comments to Brion dovetail with what he had said to others. In a letter dated April 8, 1930, to Max Bégouën, Teilhard spoke fondly of his experiences at Piltdown and his role in working with the discoverers of Peking Man: "I love to see in these two opportunities of my life the smile of the Savior proving to me that my effort to reincarnate Christ in our modern views of the world is wanted by Him."[20]

Teilhard's attitude did not prevent him from realizing how difficult it was to fit Piltdown into a coherent evolutionary development. In his first comment on the revelation that Piltdown was a fake, he wrote in response to an inquiry from K. P. Oakley:

> I congratulate you most sincerely on your solution of the Piltdown problem. Anatomically speaking, *"Eoanthropus"* was a kind of monster. And, from a paleontological point of view, it was equally shocking that a "dawn-Man" could occur in England. Therefore, I am fundamentally pleased by your conclusions, in spite of the fact that, sentimentally speaking, it spoils one of my brightest and earliest paleontological memories.[21]

---

[18] "Recherche, Travail et Adoration," in Pierre Teilhard de Chardin, *Science et Christ* (Paris: Éditions du Seuil, 1965), 283; "Research, Work and Adoration," in *Science and Christ* (New York: Harper & Row, 1968), 214. Teilhard explained to Mme. Mortier that this paper was "the reaction to the last 'direction' sent to me by the Father General. The lines were written to and for the Company's [the Jesuits'] use. But they have a general relevance which may interest whomever." Teilhard, *Lettres à Jeanne Mortier*, 179.

[19] Stephen Jay Gould, *Hen's Teeth and Horse's Toes: Further Reflections in Natural History* (New York: W. W. Norton & Company, 1983), 216.

[20] Teilhard, *Le Rayonnement d'une Amitié*, 53.

[21] *L'Oeuvre Scientifique 10*, 4561.

With other scientists, Teilhard could not reconcile the mandibles of the Piltdown skull with the jaw and its teeth. In a letter dated April 27, 1929, to Bégouën he said, "I wrote at length to Boule about the pieces already unearthed: two mandibles, with entirely human dentition and an almost chimpanzoid shape. It's very curious."[22] It was later discovered that the jaw was that of an orangutan. Teilhard was ever reluctant to suspect Charles Dawson of fraud, although subsequent investigations show that he was almost certainly the perpetrator and that he acted alone.[23]

In the translation that follows, I include a few annotations in the form of footnotes that provide some further clarification.

---

[22] *Le Rayonnement d'une Amitié*, 44–45.

[23] For a narrative account of the Piltdown affair, including Teilhard's unwitting role in "discovering" the canine tooth that seemed to confirm that the bones were genuine, see John Evangelist Walsh, *The Science Fraud of the Century and Its Solution: Unraveling Piltdown* (New York: Random House, 1996). Walsh effectively refutes Gould's energetic case for the prosecution that Teilhard was complicit. See also Thomas M. King, SJ, "Teilhard and Piltdown," in *Teilhard and the Unity of Knowledge*, ed. Thomas M. King, SJ, and James F. Salmon, SJ (Mahwah, NJ: Paulist Press, 1983), 159–69.

Meeting with Father Teilhard de Chardin[1]

Les Nouvelles Littéraires

Tuesday
January 11, 1951

Thirty years ago, Frédéric Lefèvre began, under the title An hour with, *that was to become so famous, a vast investigation which constitutes a veritable panorama of the French intellectual movement between the two wars. We wanted to mark this important anniversary in the life of our newspaper by undertaking a new series, entitled* Meeting with, *which will not only be a series of interviews with eminent personalities, but also critical studies of their work and an evocation of their life. Our collaborators Marcel Brion and Gabriel d'Aubarède will carry out these consultations by addressing writers, philosophers, historians, scholars, artists at the height of their careers, as well as men who already occupy a place of prominence, but who are still being debated. Thus it is that Gabriel d'Aubarède will soon give us* Meeting with Jean-Paul Sartre.[2]

We wanted to inaugurate this series with a personality who established himself before the war, in the fields of geology and paleontology and, today, in that of philosophy and metaphysics. There is no need to emphasize the importance of the interview that you are about to read. Let us confine ourselves to recalling that this is the first time that Father Teilhard de Chardin has agreed to allow declarations of this importance to be published and that they constitute a synthesis—which has never been attempted before—of the doctrines of the one whom the Institute de France recently called upon to join its ranks.[3]

---

[1] Originally published as "Rencontre Avec le Père Teilhard de Chardin," *Les Nouvelles Littéraires*, January 11, 1951.

[2] A chaplain of students told René d'Ouince: "If you want to pack a room full at the risk of seeing some chairs broken, just invite Jean-Paul Sartre or Father Teilhard." D'Ouince, *Un Prophète en Procès*, 149.

[3] On May 22, 1950, Teilhard was elected as a non-resident member of the Institut de France. Teilhard interpreted his election not only as a recognition of his scientific achievements, but also as "a gesture of approval for freer 'religious' thought." Claude Cuénot, *Teilhard de Chardin: A Biographical Study*, trans. Vincent Colimore and ed. René Hague (Baltimore: Helicon, 1965), 276. Translated from Cuénot, *Pierre Teilhard de Chardn: Les Grandes Étapes de son Évolution* (Paris: Librairie Plon, 1958), 334.

Translated by Donald Wayne Viney   *339*

Marcel Brion

Each time I met Father Teilhard de Chardin, I was struck by this "climate" of high spirituality and pure science that he carries with him everywhere. He is, in his cell in the rue Monsieur, as he is on the excavations of China or in the laboratory of the Museum, with this amiable and ironic grace, this acute finesse, benevolent at the same time, and this Oxfordian distinction that makes one think of some English scholar, who would be both Darwin and Newman. He is happy and worried at the same time to see that his doctrine—it must be called that, because *theory* or *system* would be insufficient—reaches an increasingly vast public, increasingly attentive, and I would say, myself, more and more enthusiastic and convinced, in spite of the obstacles which the dissemination of his thought has sometimes encountered up to now. Happy, because this scientist brings to humanity a message of confidence, of hope, of vital dynamism, of an invitation to a higher awareness of the possibilities of progress that are offered to it and of the increase in responsibilities that is also the consequence. Worried, since this recently explicitly formulated doctrine has already found itself disfigured, deformed, falsely interpreted, in certain scientific and other circles, and since, as a result, many misunderstandings have arisen and controversies have begun even before that the works in which Father Teilhard de Chardin exposes, in an overview, the results of his scientific work and his reflections have been published.

How was he led to the discoveries which made his name popular and led him to formulate a whole new theory of man and the universe? This is what I had the inquisitiveness to ask him, and I think that the readers of *Nouvelles Littéraires* will also be happy to listen to the confidences he was kind enough to share with me.

Teilhard: My early childhood was spent among the stones, in the mountains of Auvergne, with a naturalist father who gave me a taste for nature and guided my budding passion for geology. My walks among the rocks inspired me with the desire to know this mineral world, so mysterious and so fascinating, which already exerted a powerful and tenacious attraction on my child's mind. Then, I studied at the Collège de Mongré, near Lyons, and no doubt having breathed the atmosphere of this holy house, I entered the Society of Jesus at the end of my studies. You know, those of you in Aix, the calm and silent rue Lacépède, you who have lived in Aix-en-Provence for a long time? This is where my time [was]

340   *Meeting with Father Teilhard de Chardin*

spent in the novitiate, enhanced by holidays and vacations at our country house in Tholonet.

Brion: In this intensely geological landscape of the Sainte-Victoire mountain, of which Cézanne made a kind of cosmic myth, of original divinity, of primary element, raised in the mineral vehemence of metamorphoses?

Teilhard: Yes, but it wasn't long before I left France for the Channel Islands; at that time, indeed, the congregations were driven out of the country and forced to seek refuge abroad.[4] There, while pursuing my philosophy studies in Jersey, I was lucky enough to find on this island a veritable mineralogical garden where I could initiate myself scientifically to the study of matter, an object that had always fascinated me.

Brion: You have written, I remember: "Through the rocks, I found myself engaged in the direction of the *planetary*."[5] Instinctively, in the mineral, you were looking at the same time for the durable, the incorruptible. As a child, you were sorry when you discovered that iron was perishable and rusted.

Teilhard: Yes, so much so that, to comfort myself, I looked for equivalents elsewhere. Sometimes in a blue flame floating (at once so material, so elusive and so pure) on the logs of the hearth. More often in some more transparent or better colored stone: crystals of quartz or amethyst, and especially shiny fragments of chalcedony, such as I could pick up in my country of Auvergne. In the latter case the cherished substance naturally had to be resistant, unassailable and *hard*.

And that's how, little by little, I woke up to the notion of the *stuff of things*. Gradually and subtly, this famous *consistency*, which I had hitherto pursued in the solid and the dense, was revealed to me in the direction of *something fundamental* everywhere widespread—whose very ubiquity formed its incorruptibility.

---

[4] The year 1901 saw the *lois d'exception* in France restricting the activities of religious orders. In 1902, when the antireligious ex-seminarian Émile Combes became premier, the law was enforced and the Jesuits and other religious orders were expelled from France. On this subject the Lukas sisters speak of the "periodic anticlerical nervous breakdowns" of the French Republic. *Teilhard: the Man, the Priest, the Scientist*, 26.

[5] Pierre Teilhard de Chardin, *Le Coeur de la Matière* (Paris: Éditions du Seuil, 1976), 28; *The Heart of Matter*, trans. René Hague (New York: Harcourt Brace Jovanovich, 1978), 20.

Later, when I would do geology, one might think that I was simply exploring, with conviction and success, the chances of a scientific career. But, in reality, what would invincibly bring me back for a lifetime (even at the expense of paleontology) to the study of large eruptive masses and continental bases, is nothing other than an insatiable need to maintain contact with some sort of universal root or matrix of beings. Curious thing, I admit, this axial place invariably held by the passion and science of *stones* throughout my spiritual embryogenesis!

Brion: You left Jersey, I believe, at the end of this mineralogical initiation, around 1905?

Teilhard: Yes, because at that time I was appointed professor of physics in Egypt. A real godsend, since it is in this Nile valley where a prodigious civilization was born and developed over the millennia [and where] the study of the fossils exposed on the surface of the desert made me drift toward paleontology.

Brion: Which is, I know, your great specialty.

Teilhard: In fact, my scientific interest has always been and remains divided between human paleontology and questions of continental geology, a bit, if you will, like Darwin between fossils and crystals. In this competition, however, it was ultimately the study of the human phenomenon that ended up taking over my tastes. And this by virtue of a series of events that I could call the great opportunities of my career: the first of these being (just after my time in Egypt) to have found myself involved, around 1910, in the discovery of the famous Piltdown Man (*Eoanthropus*) in the Quaternary gravels of southern England.

Brion: By chance?

Teilhard: Yes, by chance. One day when I was hunting for dinosaur fossils around Hastings, I met another geologist engaged in the same research. But this competitor was Charles Dawson himself (the discoverer of *Eoanthropus*), who invited me right away to come and participate in his excavations, then just in progress. And so it was that, alongside Sir Arthur Smith-Woodward (then director of the British Museum), I was able, soon after, to assist and collaborate in the discovery of one of the

342   *Meeting with Father Teilhard de Chardin*

most enigmatic and discussed fossil men of the world. This with, for me, an important practical result, since it is my participation in the affair (in addition to my quality of being from Auvergne) that earned me, a little later, the sympathy of Marcellin Boule and my admission to his museum laboratory in 1912.

Brion: The adventure of *Eoanthropus*, so decisive for your orientation in paleontology—it was a fine start—was it not accompanied for you, at about the same time, by another discovery, of an entirely different genre, but also important for your career?

Teilhard: Yes, in the realm of scientific thought, the discovery, the realization, I mean, of the idea of evolution—biological evolution, I mean—which allowed me to connect, in the field of experience, the two notions of material energy and psychic energy.

Brion: And then you had to leave the museum in 1914, for the front, with the Zouaves and the skirmishers. But was it not at the front that the notion, so original and fruitful, of a noosphere around the earth germinated in you? And would you like to define, for our readers, what you mean by this word *noosphere*?

Teilhard: I used this word, for the first time, in one of my first essays on the human phenomenon, around 1927.[6] But the idea was actually born in me, in the trenches, of a human spiritual community extending to the organic: the idea, I mean, of a kind of special biological "mega-unit" constituting the *thinking envelope of the earth*. This, for me, is the noosphere.

---

[6] Teilhard first used *noosphere* in his essay "Hominization," finished in Paris and dated May 6, 1925. Pierre Teilhard de Chardin, *La Vision du Passé* (1957), 89–90. The English translation, *The Vision of the Past* (1966), incorrectly marks the date as May 6, 1923 (see p. 79), but Teilhard was in China at that time. While he was in Paris in the 1920s, Teilhard worked closely with Édouard Le Roy (1870–1954), whose ideas often mirrored his own, and who eventually wrote about the noosphere. Teilhard also saw Vladamir Vernadsky (1863–1945) in Paris at this time, another thinker who wrote on the noosphere (Cuénot, *Pierre Teilhard de Chardin*, 80). Teilhard remembered coining the term *noosphere*, but he added, "sait-on jamais" (one never knows). See *Lettres Intimes de Teilhard de Chardin à Auguste Valensin, Bruno de Solages, Henri du Lubac, André Ravier: 1919–1955*, intro. and notes Henri de Lubac (Paris: Aubier Montaigne, 1974), 151.

Translated by Donald Wayne Viney   *343*

Brion: At the end of the war, did you immediately resume your work in the field and in the laboratory?

Teilhard: Not immediately. My dear friend Jean Boussac, the son-in-law of the great Termier and like him a geologist, having died in Verdun, did me the honor of thinking of me for the chair of geology at the Catholic Institute of Paris. However, I didn't stay there long, for, no sooner had I set foot there, than the second great opportunity of my life occurred unexpectedly. Fr. Emile Licent, the explorer of Northern China and the founder of the Tientsin Museum, was looking for a geologist to accompany him. Thanks to the protection of my master Boule and the late Lacroix, one of the pillars of the Academy of Sciences, I found myself in charge of a mission in China, by the museum, in 1923. And it was then that Fr. Licent and I had the chance, in the loess of the Yellow River basin, to get our hands on the first known traces of a paleolithic period in China. An important find, but soon to be eclipsed by an even more sensational discovery: that (by Dr. Anderson, Dr. Davidson Black and the Geological Survey of China) of Peking Man, or *Sinanthropus*, a close relative of the *Pithecanthropus* of Java—both representing perhaps the oldest and most primitive fossil men yet known.[7]

Brion: I also know (another opportunity of your life!) that you were led to collaborate very closely in this discovery, which earned science six *Sinanthropus* skulls, a good half-dozen mandibles, and several scores of isolated teeth, all of this during ten years of research, from 1927 to 1937. Is this not so?

Teilhard: These human remains, belonging to about thirty individuals, were collected, during important and prolonged excavations, in a vast pocket (virtually fifty meters) representing the contents of an old cave filled and leveled. [There were also] many associated stone tools, and an enormous number of fossilized bones of deer, elephant, rhinoceros, camels, buffaloes, antelopes and various carnivores, almost all representing species long extinct. It is of course still difficult to date this distant cousin of modern man in years. But what we can affirm is that, when he lived, the mantle of yellow earth had not yet been deposited on the soil of China.

---

[7] *Sinanthropus* and *Pithecanthropus* are now classified by paleontologists as specimens of *Homo erectus*.

344   *Meeting with Father Teilhard de Chardin*

Which throws us very far, very far back. A matter, at the very least, of a hundred millennia.

Brion: At that time, hadn't you become adviser to the National Geological Survey of China?

Teilhard: Yes, and theoretically I still am. A good part of my heart stayed there. And it would be with joy that, if conditions allowed, I would resume there a work interrupted by the war of 1940.

At that time, I had had the good fortune to follow many scientific expeditions to the Far East: Roy Chapman Andrews Expedition, Gobi (1930); Hardt-Citroën Trans-Asian Expedition (1931); Yale-Cambridge Expedition, North and Central India (1935); Carnegie Expedition, Burma and Java (1938). So many high peaks used or chosen for a vast triangulation making it possible to determine, as a first approximation, in central, eastern and southern Asia, the main phases of human expansion during Pleistocene times. A last and important campaign was planned for the summer of 1940, in the Hundes Basin (between the two Himalayas), intended to bridge the gap between the quaternary of India and that of Chinese Turkestan. And it was then that events stopped everything.

Brion: I know the general conclusions to which your long career as a scientist has led you. Would you like to summarize them for our readers? It is not a question, of course, of going into the details of the problems, but only of glimpsing this "ultra-human" that scientifically, according to you, takes shape at the end of the evolution of *Homo sapiens*, as paleontology makes it known to us and invites us to extend it?

Teilhard: Specifically, please note, I am neither a philosopher nor a theologian, but a student of "phenomenon" (a physicist, in the old Greek sense). However, at this modest level of knowledge, what dominates my vision of things is the metamorphosis that the human phenomenon [l'homme] obliges us to subject the universe around us from the moment when (in accordance with the imperious invitations of science) one decides to consider it as forming an integral, native part of the rest of life. As a result, in fact, of this effort of incorporation, two capital observations emerge, if I am not mistaken, in our experimental perception of things. The first being that the universe, much more than by an "entropy" (bringing it back to *the most probable* physical states), is characterized by a preferential

Translated by Donald Wayne Viney 345

drift of part of its fabric toward more and more complicated states, and underpinned by ever-increasing intensities of "consciousness." From this strictly experimental point of view, life is no longer an exception in the world; it appears as a characteristic product—the most characteristic—of the universal physico-chemical drift. And the human, at the same time, becomes, in the field of our observation, the provisionally extreme term of the whole movement. The human: a goal of the world.

This being said, the second observation to which one finds oneself led, in my opinion, by an integral scientific acceptance of the "human phenomenon," is that the current of complexity-consciousness, of which the reflective psychism (that is to say, thought) is experimentally derived, is not yet settled, but that, through the biological totalization of the human mass, it continues to function—carrying us, by biological effect of socialization, toward certain still unrepresentable states of collective reflection—in other words, as I say, toward some "ultra-human."

All this, I repeat, by simple extrapolation of a law of recurrence positively observable over the entire extent of the past, that is to say, outside of all sentimentality and all metaphysics.

Now it is this strictly objective position that, misunderstood, has given rise to and spread, on my account, a certain number of legends, the most harmful of which can be reduced to the following two:

First, I was seen as a blissful optimist or utopian, dreaming of human euphoria or comfortable millennialism. As if the human *maturation* that the facts seem to me to announce did not present itself, in my perspectives, not as a rest, but well and truly as a *crisis of tension*—a crisis paid for by an immense trail of disorders and suffering; a crisis laden with risks and therefore more dramatic still, owing to the enormity of the interest involved (the success of a universe, no less!), than all the self-absorbed and morbid imaginations of contemporary existentialism.

Worse still, people go on repeating that I am the prophet of a universe that destroys individual values, since, in my eyes, it is toward a *synthetic* state that, according to me, experimentally, the world is moving. But, in truth, my great concern has always been to affirm, in the name of facts, that *true union* does not confuse, but *differentiates*; and even that, in the case of thinking and loving beings (such as man), far from mechanizing, it *personalizes*, and this doubly: intellectually, first, by super-reflection, and then affectively, by unanimization.

Thus, despite the primacy that I technically grant to the whole in relation to the element, I find myself, by the very structure of my scientific thought, at the antipodes either of a social totalitarianism leading to the termite mound, or of a Hindu pantheism seeking the outcome and the ultimate figure of the spiritual in the direction of an identification of beings with a common background underlying the variety of events and things. Not mechanization, therefore, or identification by fusion and loss of consciousness, but unification by laborious ultra-determination and love.

Admittedly, these *biological* views may have some implications for our appreciation of human values. They incline us to a certain humanism of a renewed type, based, no longer as in the sixteenth century, on a rediscovery of the past, but on unexpected possibilities held in reserve for us by the future.

But isn't the birth, around us, of such a "neo-humanism" (linked in my religious thought to the progress of "charity") quite precisely one of the distinctive characteristics of the times we are going through?

Teilhard's Process Metaphysics (1969)

IAN BARBOUR

The writings of Teilhard de Chardin can be read in a variety of ways: as evolutionary science, as poetry and mysticism, as natural theology, and as Christian theology. There is, however, one aspect of his thought to which little attention has been given, namely, his undeveloped process metaphysics, which, I have suggested, plays a crucial role in his synthesis of scientific and religious ideas.[1] In this paper I will explore some of Teilhard's metaphysical categories which reflect both evolutionary and biblical assumptions. Successive sections will be devoted to: (1) reality as temporal process, (2) the "within," (3) freedom and determinism, (4) continuing creation, (5) God and time, (6) the problem of evil, and (7) the future of the world.

Teilhard's thought can be illuminated by comparing it with that of Alfred North Whitehead, the most systematic exponent of a philosophy of process. The striking similarities may help to show the character of Teilhard's ideas. The significant differences may make more evident the points at which his contribution is distinctive, or in some cases may suggest ambiguities or limitations in his approach. I will not deal directly with his Christology, which is a major point of divergence from Whitehead; but by showing the influence of Teilhard's temporalistic metaphysics on his interpretation of a number of biblical themes, I hope to point the way to a subsequent study of his *process theology*. By concentrating on his conceptual thought, I will of course be neglecting many aspects of his complex personality, including the profound spirituality and mysticism which were his most impressive characteristics.

---

[1] Ian G. Barbour, "Five Ways of Reading Teilhard," *Soundings* 1, no. 2 (Spring, 1968): 115–45; reprinted in *The Teilhard Review* 3, no. 1 (Summer, 1968): 3–20. In Section V of "Five Ways" I discuss the treatment of Teilhard's metaphysics by several of his recent interpreters.

348   Teilhard's Process Metaphysics (1969)

Teilhard's style is very different from Whitehead's. He was not a philosopher; he used vivid analogies and poetic images where Whitehead used carefully defined philosophical abstractions. Yet their underlying insights were often very similar. I will not dwell on the historical reasons for these parallels. Neither man was familiar with the work of the other, but both acknowledge great indebtedness to Henri Bergson.[2] Both were deeply impressed by the status of time in modern science—primarily in evolutionary biology in Teilhard's case and in relativity and quantum physics in Whitehead's. Our task, however, will be to examine the content rather than the genesis of their ideas. Let us start from their reflections on the general structure of the world.

Reality as Temporal Process

Teilhard and Whitehead both adopt a radically temporalistic outlook in place of the static viewpoint which has dominated most of Western thought. For Teilhard, "the universe is no longer a State but a Process."[3] "Taken at this degree of generalization (in other words where all experimental reality in the universe forms part of a *process*, that is to say, is born) evolution has long ago ceased to be a hypothesis and become a *general condition of knowledge* (an additional *dimension*) which henceforth all hypotheses must satisfy."[4] Teilhard asserts, in a variety of contexts, that "this new perception of time" alters all our ways of looking at things. We live in "a world that is *being born* instead of a world that is."[5] Ours is an embryonic and incomplete universe; change and development are its pervasive features.

Teilhard suggests that we have usually thought of *time* as a kind of neutral container in which self-sufficient objects could be rearranged without being affected, "a sort of vast vessel in which things were suspended side by side." But now one must acknowledge that "duration permeates the

---

[2] See M. Barthélemy-Maudale, *Bergson et Teilhard de Chardin* (Paris: Éditions du Seuil, 1963). Cuénot says that in 1945 Teilhard "songe à lire Whitehead, *La science et le monde moderne*"—which may mean that he actually read it; see Claude Cuénot, *Pierre Teilhard de Chardin* (Paris: Libraire Plon, 1958), 292.

[3] Pierre Teilhard de Chardin, *The Future of Man* (New York: Harper & Row, 1964), 261.

[4] Pierre Teilhard de Chardin, *The Appearance of Man* (New York: Harper & Row, 1965), 211n.1; cf. Pierre Teilhard de Chardin, *The Vision of the Past* (New York: Harper & Row, 1966), 246.

[5] Teilhard, *The Future of Man*, 88.

essence of every being." Reality does not consist of inert objects moving through successive instants, but of processes having temporal extension. "Every particle of reality, instead of constituting an approximate point in itself, extends from the previous fragment to the next in an invisible thread running back to infinity."[6] For Whitehead also the world is made up of events and processes. He rejects both the scholastic view of unchanging substances with changing attributes and the Newtonian picture of unchanging particles which are rearranged but never altered in themselves. Whitehead and Teilhard both employ categories of becoming and activity rather than of being and substance.[7]

Teilhard refers frequently to the organic interdependence of all entities. The world is not a collection of self-contained objects related only externally to each other, but a network of mutual influences spread through time and space. Every entity is constituted by its relationships; "every element of the cosmos is woven from all others." "However narrowly the 'heart' of an atom is circumscribed, its realm is coextensive at least potentially with that of every other atom."[8] The "web of life" is a fabric of interactions, "a single process without interruption." A close parallel is Whitehead's rejection of "Simple Location," the mechanistic assumption that independent particles can be completely described "apart from any essential reference of the relations of that bit of matter to other regions of space and to other durations of time."[9] Whitehead proposes "a social view of reality" as a community of interacting temporal events.

Despite this emphasis on interdependence, neither author ends with a *monism* in which the parts are less real than the total process. Every entity is a center of spontaneity and self-creation contributing distinctively to the future. But in Whitehead this *pluralism*, which counterbalances the idea of unity, is carried much further. He starts from a plurality of beings whose individuality and integrity are always preserved. Whitehead wants us to look at the world from the point of view of each entity itself—considered as a moment of experience which inherits its data from previous events, yet is radically on its own during the moment it responds: Each occasion or "concrescence" is a unique synthesis of the influences on it, a new unity

---

[6] Ibid., 84; Teilhard, *The Vision of the Past*, 129.

[7] Alfred North Whitehead, *Science and the Modern World* (New York: the Macmillan Co., 1925), 71–77, 157ff., 188–89; Alfred North Whitehead, *Process and Reality* (New York: Macmillan Co., 1929), 122–23, 317–22.

[8] Pierre Teilhard de Chardin, *The Phenomenon of Man* (New York: Harper & Row, 1959), 41; cf. *The Future of Man*, 85.

[9] Whitehead, *Science and the Modern World*, 84.

350   *Teilhard's Process Metaphysics (1969)*

formed from diversity. Only as it perishes does it influence other events.[10] Whitehead thus envisages not a continuous process but an interconnected series of discrete events. Continuity is accounted for by the succession of individual units of becoming, each of which is completed and then superseded by other units.[11] There is no agency except that of a multiplicity of actual occasions, including God. Whitehead has none of Teilhard's "temporal threads running back to infinity," but only a network of threads connecting each event with its immediate predecessors. This greater pluralism in Whitehead's scheme has repercussions which we will note in his treatment of mind and matter, freedom and determinism, and God's relation to the world.

In Teilhard, the balance between pluralism and monism is tipped in the opposite direction. "Everything forms a single whole," an integral cosmic process.[12] We will find that in some passages the whole of cosmic history seems to have a unified structure not unlike that of a single Whiteheadian concrescence; Teilhard predicts the "convergence," "centration," and "involution" of the universe. Where Whitehead is concerned to give a generalized account of the growth of all particular entities, Teilhard tries to delineate the patterns of universal history. While these two tasks overlap considerably, they tend to encourage differing emphases. At a later point, we will see that Teilhard's belief in the unity of creation was strengthened by his own mystical sense of experienced oneness and by the biblical hope of a single eschatological goal of history.

Both authors portray *continuity* as well as *discontinuity* between the levels of reality, but Teilhard puts somewhat greater stress on continuity. There are no sharp lines between the non-living and the living, or between life and mind. Each level has its roots in earlier levels and represents the flowering of what was potentially present all along, though these roots are "lost in darkness as we trace them back." The higher was already present in the lower in rudimentary form: *"In the world, nothing could ever burst forth as final across the different thresholds successively traversed by evolution (however critical they be) which had not already existed in an obscure and primordial way. . . .* Everything, in some extremely attenuated version of itself, has existed from the very first."[13] Yet within this continuity there were thresholds and critical points. These "crises" were not gaps or absolute discontinuities, but

---

[10] Whitehead, *Process and Reality*, 95, 188.

[11] Ibid., 53.

[12] Pierre Teilhard de Chardin, *The Divine Milieu* (New York: Harper & Row, 1960), 30.

[13] Teilhard, *The Phenomenon of Man*, 71, 78.

each marked a major breakthrough. There was real novelty at each new level (life, thought, society), even though each was anticipated in previous levels. Teilhard gives the analogy of a gradually heated liquid which reaches a critical temperature, a boiling point at which a change of state suddenly occurs.[14] He uses the words "metamorphosis" and "transformation" to describe these changes in which new properties emerged.[15]

Whitehead shares Teilhard's assumptions concerning the historical continuity of the past, though his attention is directed to the ontological similarities among differing types of entities today. For him also the higher is present in the lower in rudimentary form. Since he takes metaphysics to be the search for interpretive categories of the widest generality, these categories must be applicable to all entities. Yet the modes in which they are exemplified may vary widely; "there are gradations of importance and diversities of function." Whitehead makes greater allowance than Teilhard for the diversity of events which occur at different levels of reality.[16] Let us look in particular at their views of mental life.

The "Within"

In Teilhard's philosophy every entity has a "within." Even among atoms there was a tendency to build up molecules and then cells of more highly centered complexity; he attributes this to a "radial energy" which produced and maintained very improbable systems in violation of the law of entropy. Next there was an elementary responsiveness which was a forerunner of mental life. He does not, of course, ascribe self-awareness or reflection to simple organisms; their "psychic life" was infinitesimal, a rudimentary beginning of perception, anticipation, and spontaneity "in extremely attenuated versions."[17]

We have seen that Teilhard mentions "critical points" at which novel phenomena occurred for the first time; there were "metamorphoses" of the "within" to new forms, which were "quite different." But his terminology tends to blur any such distinctions. With the exception of reflective thought (which is imputed to man alone), Teilhard's various terms are used interchangeably all the way down the scale from man to cell: the "within,"

---

[14] Ibid., 78, 168; Teilhard, *The Vision of the Past*, 180.
[15] Teilhard, *The Phenomenon of Man*, 79, 88.
[16] Whitehead, *Process and Reality*, 127–67.
[17] Teilhard, *The Vision of the Past*, 235; *The Phenomenon of Man*, 54ff.

352   Teilhard's Process Metaphysics (1969)

interiority, psychic life, mentality, consciousness, etc. He sometimes says that in simple organisms these are all *potentially* present (though he provides no specific analysis of the concept of potentiality). More often he says they are *actually* present in infinitesimal degree. At higher levels, consciousness is said to be proportional to the development of the nervous system and brain; at lower levels, it is said to be proportional to complexity, even in the total absence of a nervous system.[18]

Whitehead's "subjective pole" resembles Teilhard's "within." In general, every entity takes account of previous events, responds to them, and makes a creative selection from alternative potentialities. But Whitehead's basic categories characterizing all events have very diverse exemplifications. A stone has no organization beyond the physical cohesion of its parts and hence it has no "subjective pole" at all; it is a "corpuscular society" which is not the locus of any unified events. A cell has only an incipient psychism, which is so vanishingly small that for all practical purposes it may be considered absent; its response to changing stimuli testifies at most to an exceedingly attenuated form of aim or purpose. Only with animals is there a single "dominant occasion" of awareness. Whitehead holds that there is no consciousness, even in a rudimentary form, in lower animate beings, much less in inanimate ones.[19]

Clearly, both Teilhard and Whitehead do use human experience, with various qualifications, as a model for the interpretation of other entities. Why do they make this generalization from man? Their reasons appear to be similar:

(1) *The Unity of Man with Nature.* Man is part of nature; he is a product of the evolutionary process. "The roots of our being," says Teilhard, "are in the first cell." Human experience is a fact within nature. We cannot be content with a physical description "which leaves out thought, the most remarkable phenomenon which nature has produced." "The apparent restriction of the phenomenon of consciousness to the higher forms of life has long served science as an excuse for eliminating it from its models of the universe. A queer exception, an aberrant function, an epiphenomenon—thought was classed under one or other of these heads in order to get rid

---

[18] Teilhard, *The Phenomenon of Man*, 53–66, 71, 88, 149–52; *The Vision of the Past*, 227–28; Pierre Teilhard de Chardin, *Man's Place in Nature* (New York: Harper & Row, 1966), 32–33.

[19] Whitehead, *Process and Reality*, 164–67; Alfred North Whitehead, *Modes of Thought* (New York: Macmillan Co., 1938), 38; Alfred North Whitehead, *Adventures of Ideas* (New York: Macmillan Co., 1933), 164.

of it."[20] Whitehead likewise defends man's unity with nature and shows the inadequacy of accounts which omit the most distinctive features of human experience. A world of particles-in-motion would be a world to which man's purposes and feelings would be totally alien.[21] We must not ignore the part of the universe we know most directly—our own experience.

(2) *The Continuity of the World.* We have seen that in spite of the occurrence of thresholds Teilhard traces a continuous evolutionary development. There was an unbroken spectrum of complexity from cell to man; one can set no absolute limits at which the basic features of human experience may have been present. Nature is an integral process: "Since the stuff of the universe has an inner aspect at one point of itself, there is necessarily *a double aspect to its structure*, that is to say in every region of space and time. . . . *In a coherent perspective of the world, life inevitably assumes a 'pre-life' for as far back before it as the eye can see.*"[22] Teilhard gives another analogy: Just as we assume (in relativity theory) that a change-in-mass too small to detect occurs in objects moving at low velocity, since a detectable change-in-mass is found at high velocities, so also can we assume a "within" in beings of low complexity, since its effects are noticeable in those of high complexity.[23] The force of the analogy depends on the assumption that the "within" is, despite its "metamorphoses" into differing forms, a single continuous function of complexity. Whitehead likewise defends the continuity of historical development, but we have noted that he gives greater prominence to the emergence of genuinely new phenomena at higher levels of organization.

(3) *The Coherence of Interpretive Categories.* The search for a coherent metaphysics presupposes the unity of the world, but it directs attention to the consistency and generality of one's conceptual system. Whitehead holds that metaphysical categories should be applicable to all events, including our awareness as experiencing subjects; human experience is taken to exhibit the generic features of all experience. "An occasion of experience which includes a human mentality is an extreme instance, at one end of the scale, of those happenings which constitute nature."[24] In order to give a unified account of the world, he seems in effect to employ concepts most appropriate to a "middle range" of organisms; these concepts can in very attenuated form be applied to lower entities, and yet they are capable of

---

[20] Teilhard, *The Phenomenon of Man*, 55; *The Vision of the Past*, 162.

[21] Whitehead, *Science and the Modern World*, 78ff.

[22] Teilhard, *The Phenomenon of Man*, 56–57.

[23] Ibid., 54, 301.

[24] Whitehead, *Adventures of Ideas*, 237.

354 Teilhard's Process Metaphysics (1969)

further development when applied to human experience. A similar concern for intellectual coherence in our understanding of the world seems to have been one of Teilhard's motives.

(4) *The Inadequacy of Mind-Matter Dualism.* Both authors want to overcome the dualism which has been prominent in Western thought since Descartes. They seek a unitary ontology, not by reducing mind to matter (materialism) or matter to mind (idealism), but by making organic process primary. "Mind" and "matter" are not two distinct substances, but two aspects of a single complex process. Whitehead finds them inseparably interwoven in human experience—for instance, in the bodily reference of feeling and perception. Teilhard reacts not only against mind-matter dualism, but against the dichotomy of matter and spirit which Christian thinkers have supported. Here he adopts a biblical view of the unity of man as a whole being and rejects the assumption that matter and spirit are separate substances or antagonistic principles.

The two authors differ considerably, however, in their representations of the relationship between the "within" and the "without." In Whitehead's system, subjectivity and objectivity occur in distinct phases of the concrescence of an event. Every momentary subject first inherits objective data from its past. It is then on its own in subjective immediacy, appropriating this data from its unique perspective, selecting among alternative possibilities, and producing a novel synthesis. The resulting outcome is then available as objective data to be appropriated by subsequent moments of experience. Efficient causality characterizes the transition between such events, while final causality dominates the internal growth within the concrescence as it actualizes its own synthesis. Teilhard pictures no such successive phases; for him every entity is simultaneously subjective and objective.[25] He stresses the continuity of experience, whereas Whitehead stresses its fragmentary character.

This difference has a significant methodological consequence. Whitehead claims that the scientist, relying on sense perception, can deal directly only with the outcome of a past event; the isolated moment of present subjectivity is inaccessible to him: "Science can find no individual enjoyment in nature; science can find no aim in nature; science can find no creativity in nature; it finds mere rules of succession. These negations are true of natural science; they are inherent in its methodology."[26] Teilhard agrees that the

---

[25] Cf. Richard Overman, *Evolution and the Christian Doctrine of Creation* (Philadelphia: Westminster Press, 1967), 227.

[26] Whitehead, *Modes of Thought*, 221.

"within" of another being is not itself directly observable; but he seems to think that its effects are among the "phenomena" which a more open-minded science will in the future be able to analyze. But he has perhaps given insufficient consideration to the epistemological problem of how an inherently private mental life expresses itself in the public world.

Freedom and Determinism

For Teilhard, then, all beings are temporal, interdependent, and characterized by a "within." But is their activity free or determined? In many contexts, Teilhard seems to reject determination by either natural laws or divine omnipotence. In discussing evolution, he repeatedly mentions "random mutations," "blind chance," and "billionfold trial and error." Particular combinations of atoms or configurations of species were "accidental," "fortuitous," and "unrepeatable." "Even if there were only one solution to the main physical and physiological problem of life on earth, that general solution would necessarily leave undecided a host of accidental and particular questions, and it does not seem thinkable that they would have been decided *twice in the same way*. . . . The genesis of life on earth belongs to the category of absolutely unique events that, once happened, are never repeated."[27] Whereas the scholastics interpreted the actualization of potentiality as the unfolding of what was there all along, Teilhard speaks of *alternative potentialities* not all of which are actualized. He gives the example of a molecule which could exist in either of two forms (mirror images of each other); it is today found in all living organisms in only one of these forms—which presumably represents the way in which the atoms happened to collide in the primeval molecule from which all the samples today are descended. The present world "exhausts *only a part of what might have been*."[28]

With the advent of simple organisms there was novelty and spontaneity, according to Teilhard. With reflective consciousness came moral choice and responsibility. Man's destiny is now in his own hands; he can "grasp the tiller of evolution" and steer his own course. Teilhard makes frequent reference to the "choices," "options," and "crossroads" which we face. His political philosophy indorses individual freedom and diversity despite the

---

[27] Teilhard, *The Phenomenon of Man*, 100; cf. *The Future of Man*, 74, 307.

[28] Ibid., 95; cf. *The Future of Man*, 220.

356 Teilhard's Process Metaphysics (1969)

need for collectivization and global unity.[29] He grants that in the future, man's free decisions may thwart the progress of the universe toward union; final success "is not necessary, inevitable or certain." Some men may fail to co-operate, for man has the power to refuse to love.[30]

On the other hand, many of Teilhard's statements sound completely deterministic. Various stages of past evolution were "inevitable," "inexorable," or "necessary." The future convergence of the cosmos is "inescapable." There is an "over-riding super-determinism which irresistibly impels Mankind to converge upon itself."[31] He even suggests that it would be futile for anyone to try to oppose global socialization, since it is inevitable. The total process is one of "sure ascent" and "irreversible movement." How can one reconcile Teilhard's apparently contradictory declarations of freedom and determinism? There seem to be three ways in which he attempts a reconciliation:

(1) *The Law of Large Numbers.* Events such as the tossing of a coin can be individually random yet statistically lawful; the individual case is unpredictable but the group can be accurately predicted. Teilhard applies this principle to chance in evolution and extends it to human freedom. He holds that each person considered separately may fail, but "by a sort of 'infallibility of large numbers,' Mankind, the present crest of the evolutionary wave, cannot fail."[32] "It is statistically necessary that in any large number of letters there will regularly be mistakes: stamps forgotten, addresses incompleted, etc. Yet each sender is free not to make mistakes."[33] Teilhard makes the rather dubious assumption that chance and freedom are subject to the same kind of statistical consideration. There are, he says, "two uncertainties related to the double play—the chance at the bottom and freedom at the top. Let me add, however, that in the case of very large numbers (such, for instance, as the human population) the process tends to 'infallibilise' itself, inasmuch as the likelihood of success grows on the lower side (chance) while that of rejection and error diminishes on the other side (freedom) with the multiplication of the elements engaged."[34]

---

[29] Teilhard, *The Future of Man*, 194, 241.

[30] Teilhard, *The Phenomenon of Man*, 288, 306; *The Future of Man*, 232.

[31] Ibid., 128; cf. *The Future of Man*, 71.

[32] Teilhard, *The Future of Man*, 237.

[33] See Christopher Mooney, *Teilhard and the Mystery of Christ* (New York: Harper & Row, 1966), 127.

[34] Teilhard, *The Phenomenon of Man*, 307.

(2) *The Universe as a Unified Power.* Teilhard sometimes speaks of the cosmos as a single agency which will prevail in its purposes regardless of the vagaries of individuals. In the past, evolution has won over all obstacles and found a way out of all impasses; it would be absurd for it to abort now after it has gotten this far. The subject of the following propositions is "the world": "To bring us into existence it has from the beginning juggled miraculously with too many improbabilities for there to be any risk whatever in committing ourselves further and following it right to the end. If it undertook the task, it is because it can finish it, following the same methods and with the same infallibility with which it began."[35] Teilhard's confidence undoubtedly rests ultimately in the power of God, but he often writes as if the cosmic process is itself a trustworthy and purposeful agency which will determine the outcome:

> No doubt it is true that up to a point we are free as *individuals* to resist the trends and demands of Life. But does this mean (it is a very different matter) that we can escape collectively from the fundamental set of the tide? . . . The earth is more likely to stop turning than is Mankind, as a whole, likely to stop organising and unifying itself. For if this interior movement were to stop, it is the Universe itself, embodied in Man, that would fail to curve inwards and achieve totalisation. And nothing, as it seems, can prevent the Universe from succeeding—nothing, not even our human liberties, whose essential tendency to union may fail in detail but cannot (without "cosmic": contradiction) err "statistically."[36]

(3) *God's Control of the World.* Teilhard's conviction of the inevitable convergence of the world rests finally on his Christian belief in the omnipotence of God. "Only Omega can guarantee the outcome." To the Christian, "the eventual biological success of Man on Earth is not merely a probability but a certainty, since Christ (and in Him virtually the World) is already risen."[37] In later sections we will examine Teilhard's views of evil, progress, and eschatology. At the moment, we may note that in his doctrine of providence he faces the difficulty with which so many theologians of the

---

[35] Ibid., 232; cf. 276.
[36] Teilhard, *The Future of Man,* 152.
[37] Ibid., 232.

358   Teilhard's Process Metaphysics (1969)

past wrestled: How can one consistently believe in both human freedom and divine determination? On this problem he throws little new light.

Whitehead, by contrast, is specific in rejecting all forms of determinism. He holds that the existence of genuinely alternative potentialities is incompatible with predestination. God radically qualifies but does not determine the action of each actual entity. "It derives from God its basic conceptual aim, relevant to its actual world, yet with indeterminations awaiting its own decisions."[38] God provides a cosmic order within which there is self-determination by each being. Whitehead attacks the idea of a predetermined and fixed divine plan; God has unchanging general purposes, but his goals for particular events are modified as individual entities take their own actions in response to his initiative. Whitehead thus departs further than Teilhard from the traditional doctrine of divine omnipotence.

Teilhard has been accused of adopting pantheism, which in the past has often taken deterministic forms. But the accusation is unjust. Teilhard is critical of the Eastern "mysticism of identification," in which the individual seeks absorption in the All, hoping to merge "like a drop in the ocean." He adheres to the Western "mysticism of union," in which individuality and personality are not lost.[39] Convergence will be achieved "not by identification (God becoming all) but by the differentiating and communicating action of love (God all in everyone)."[40] Ultimate reality is neither an undifferentiated unity nor an impersonal structure, but a supreme person. Nevertheless, the reader may easily forget, amid Teilhard's frequent references to "the All" and "the whole," that God is to be distinguished from the cosmos. In Whitehead's writing, on the other hand, it is always clear that God is one among a plurality of entities. Each occasion retains its individuality and self-determination, even in relation to God.[41]

Continuing Creation

For Teilhard, as for Whitehead, the understanding of the world as temporal process outlined in the preceding sections has important implications for

---

[38] Whitehead, *Process and Reality*, 343.

[39] Teilhard, *The Divine Milieu*, 94.

[40] Teilhard, *The Phenomenon of Man*, 308; cf. 262, and *The Future of Man*, 207; see Henri de Lubac, *The Religion of Teilhard de Chardin* (New York: Desclee, 1967), 143–60.

[41] See William Christian, *An Interpretation of Whitehead's Metaphysics* (New Haven, CT: Yale University Press, 1959), 403–9.

the representation of God's relation to the world. God is not the external fabricator of an essentially static system but a creative influence immanent in an evolutionary development. Teilhard urges us to think of creation not "as an instantaneous act, but in the manner of a process or synthesizing action."[42] "Creation has never ceased. Its act is a great continuous movement spread out over the totality of time. It is still going on."[43]

Teilhard proposes that creation consists in the *unification of the multiple*. Whereas Bergson conceived of an original unity which differentiates and diverges into multiplicity, Teilhard assumes a primeval multiplicity which converges toward a final unity. In several of his early writings, he speaks of creation as "a struggle against the many," but he maintains that in its disunity "the many" represents only a potentiality for being rather than an independent reality over against God.[44] In an essay written in 1948, he imagines four "moments" in which the world originated. Initially there was only a self-sufficient First Being. Second, according to revelation, there was a movement of internal diversity and union in the divine life understood as "trinitization" rather than static unity. I quote in full his speculation concerning the third and fourth "moments," since it is controversial and not yet published:

> By the very fact that he unifies himself interiorly, the First Being ipso facto causes another type of opposition to arise, not within himself but at his antipodes (and here we have our third moment). At the pole of being there is self-subsistent Unity, and all around at the periphery, as a necessary consequence, there is multiplicity: *pure* multiplicity, be it understood, a "creatable void" which is simply nothing—yet which, because of its passive potency for arrangement (i.e. for union), constitutes a possibility, an appeal for being. Now everything takes place as if God had not been able to resist this appeal, for at such depths our intelligence can no longer distinguish at all between supreme necessity and supreme freedom.
>
> In classical philosophy or theology, creation or participation (which constitutes our fourth moment) always tends to be presented as an

---

[42] Teilhard de Chardin, "Christologie et évolution" (1933), quoted in Robert L. Faricy, "Teilhard de Chardin on Creation and the Christian Life," *Theology Today* 24, no. 3 (January 1967): 510.

[43] Teilhard de Chardin, "Le milieu mystique," in *Écrits du temps de la guerre* (1916–19) (Paris: Éditions Bernard Grasset, 1965), 149.

[44] Teilhard de Chardin, "L'union créatrice," "Les noms de la matière," and "La lutte contre la multitude," in *Ecrits du temps de la guerre*; also, "Mon univers," in *Oeuvres de Teilhard de Chardin*, vol. 9 (Paris: Éditions du Seuil, 1965).

360 Teilhard's Process Metaphysics (1969)

almost arbitrary gesture on the part of the First Cause, executed by a causality analogous to "efficient" and according to a mechanism that is completely indeterminate: truly an "act of God" in the pejorative sense. In a metaphysics of union, on the contrary—although the self-sufficiency and self-determination of the Absolute Being remain inviolate (since pure, antipodal multiplicity, is, I insist, nothing but pure passivity and potentiality)—in such a metaphysics, I say, the creative act takes on a very well defined significance and structure. . . . To create is to unite.[45]

This idea of "creative union" is not in itself incompatible with the idea of "creation out of nothing." Teilhard says that God is "self-sufficing" and initially "stood alone." He denies the need for a "preexisting substratum" on which God operated and holds that matter is not eternal. As North points out,[46] the multiple is little more than potential-for-being; union is equated with being and disunion with non-being. De Lubac argues that Teilhard's "creative union" takes place moment by moment *within* the process and that one can still consider the whole process as created *ex nihilo*.[47] But Teilhard does treat the ongoing process (the fourth moment) rather than an instantaneous beginning as the really creative stage of God's work. In effect he seems to assume that the cosmic process has a convergent and unifying character; therefore, he extrapolates to a primeval state of "pure multiplicity," whose relation to the prior unity of God remains problematical.[48]

Whitehead shares Teilhard's themes of continuing creation and unification, but he explicitly rejects "creation out of nothing." He holds that time

---

[45] Teilhard de Chardin, "Comment je vois" (1948), quoted in Mooney, *Teilhard and the Mystery of Christ*, 172–73. Alternative renditions in Faricy, "Teilhard de Chardin on Creation and the Christian Life," 510–11; and Piet Smulders, *The Design of Teilhard de Chardin* (Westminster: Newman Press, 1967), 79–81. A letter from Teilhard to my father accompanying a copy of this essay and commenting on it is given in George B. Barbour, *In the Field with Teilhard de Chardin* (New York: Herder & Herder, 1965), 125–26.

[46] Robert North, *Teilhard and the Creation of the Soul* (Milwaukee: Bruce Publishing Co., 1967), 88–91.

[47] De Lubac, *The Religion of Teilhard de Chardin*, 195–200. See also Smulders, *The Design of Teilhard de Chardin*, 77–85.

[48] In *Teilhard and the Creation of the Soul*, 116, North claims that, without intending to, Teilhard adopts an implicit emanationism in which the world is made from the substance of God. He argues that if there is a temporal symmetry between Alpha and Omega, and if Omega involves "absorption in divinity," then creation must have arisen "by a sort of sifting out of divinity." However, he never shows that Teilhard's thought entails such an assumption of symmetry. See also Robert North, "Teilhard and the Problem of Creation," *Theological Studies* 24 (1963): 577–601.

is infinite. There was no first day, no initial act of origination, but only a continuing bringing-into-being in which past, present, and future are structurally similar. God has a priority in ontological status but no temporal priority over the world. God "is not *before* all creation but *with* all creation."[49] However, no ready-made materials were given to God from some other source, and nothing can exist apart from him; he is the ground of order as well as novelty in the world. As Cobb suggests, Whitehead attributes to God a fundamental role in the birth of each new event, though there is no event which he alone determines absolutely.[50]

I would submit that even though Whitehead rejects and Teilhard qualifies the idea of "creation out of nothing," both men share the *motives* which led the church fathers to the formulation of the traditional doctrine. The formula is not of course itself scriptural; Genesis does not open with "nothing" but with the primeval chaos of a watery deep prior to God's acts of creation. *Ex nihilo* was first propounded in the intertestamental period and was later elaborated by such theologians as Irenaeus and Augustine, in order to exclude the Hellenistic idea that matter on which God imposed form existed independently of him and constituted the source of evil in the world.[51] But Teilhard and Whitehead are as insistent as the church fathers that matter is in itself basically good rather than evil.[52] An additional motive in the *ex nihilo* doctrine was the assertion of the total sovereignty and freedom of God. Teilhard and Whitehead do limit God's omnipotence, but neither of them adopts an ultimate dualism or imagines a Platonic demiurge struggling to introduce order into recalcitrant matter; this is no cosmic carpenter who must use the materials on hand. Even Whitehead agrees that nothing has ever existed in independence of God.

In regard to creation as a continuing process, it is not altogether clear how Teilhard thinks of divine activity in relation to the order of nature. He avoids claims of God's intervention at specific points; he advocates "a creation of evolutionary type (*God making things make themselves*)."[53] Such passages would be consistent with the assumption that evolution is in principle scientifically explicable in terms of natural forces. In such a framework God's functions would be (1) to design and effect a set of natural

---

[49] Whitehead, *Process and Reality*, 531.

[50] John B. Cobb, *A Christian Natural Theology* (Philadelphia: Westminster Press, 1965), 211–12.

[51] Langdon Gilkey, *Maker of Heaven and Earth* (Garden City, NY: Doubleday & Co., 1959), chap. 3; Bernhard W. Anderson, *Creation versus Chaos* (New York: Association Press, 1967).

[52] See, for example, Teilhard, *The Divine Milieu*, 81–84.

[53] Teilhard, *The Vision of the Past*, 154.

362   Teilhard's Process Metaphysics (1969)

laws which would of themselves gradually produce the foreordained cosmic progression and (2) to preserve and sustain this natural system in operation and concur in its results. If this is Teilhard's view, it would be essentially the scholastic notion that God as *primary cause* works through the operation of law-abiding *secondary causes*.

However, Teilhard's terminology frequently suggests that God's role is more active than this. He says that God "animates" and "vivifies" the world, "controls" and "leads" it to fulfilment. There are passages in which God is invoked to explain phenomena held to be scientifically inexplicable: "In Omega we have in the first place the principle we needed to explain both the persistent march of things toward greater consciousness, and the paradoxical solidity of what is most fragile."[54] God's action is not simply that of an Aristotelian "final cause" which is built into the functioning of all beings as they follow their inherent natures. Teilhard seems to believe that the "within" is a more effective vehicle of divine influence than the "without," but he does not clarify the modes of causality involved.

Whitehead, on the other hand, does assign to his equivalent of the "within" the crucial role in God's action on the world. He gives a detailed analysis of causation which includes the influence of past causes, present initiative, and divine purpose in the coming-to-be of each event.[55] Briefly stated, every new event is in part the product of the *efficient causation* of previous events, which in large measure—though never completely—determine it. There is always an element of *self-causation* or self-creation as an entity appropriates and responds to its past in its own way. In the creative selection from among alternatives in terms of goals and aims, there is *final causation*. By structuring these potentialities, God is the ground of both order and novelty, but the final decision is always made by the entity itself; at the human level this means that man is free to reject the ideals which God holds up to him. Whitehead thus works out in much greater detail than Teilhard a set of categories which allow for lawfulness, spontaneity, and divine influence in the "continuous creation" of the world.

God and Time

Teilhard, like Whitehead, holds that there is reciprocal interaction between God and the world. Both men criticize traditional thought for making

---

[54] Teilhard, *The Phenomenon of Man*, 271.

[55] See, for example, Ivor Leclerc, *Whitehead's Metaphysics* (New York: Macmillan Co., 1958), 170–74.

creation too arbitrary and the world too "useless" and "ontologically super-fluous" to God.[56] In place of what he calls the "paternalism" of the classical view, Teilhard substitutes "a functional completing of the One and the Multiple."[57] He maintains that the idea of the complete self-sufficiency of God makes him seem indifferent and leads to a deprecation of the value of the world and human endeavor in it. "Truly it is not the notion of the contingency of the created but the sense of the mutual completion of God and the world that makes Christianity live. . . . God, the eternal being in himself, is everywhere, we might say, in process of formation for us."[58]

Does Teilhard imply that God experiences change? There are a number of texts which speak of "the fulfilment of God," who "consummates himself only in uniting." "God is entirely self-sufficient, and nevertheless creation brings to him something vitally necessary."[59]

> In the world viewed as the object of "creation," classical metaphys-
> ics accustoms us to see a sort of extrinsic production, issuing from
> the supreme *efficiency* of God through an overflow of benevolence.
> *Invincibly*—and *precisely* in order to be able to act and to love fully at
> one and the same time—I am now led to see therein (in conformity
> with the spirit of St. Paul) a mysterious product of completion and
> fulfilment for the Absolute Being Himself.[60]

Teilhard has received considerable criticism for this idea. Thus, Tres-montant comments:

---

[56] See, for example, Teilhard de Chardin, "Contingence de l'univers et goût humain de survivre" (1954), in *Oeuvres de Teilhard de Chardin*, vol. 10. Whitehead uses almost identical terms, e.g., *Adventures of Ideas*, 213ff.

[57] Teilhard de Chardin, "L'étoffe de l'univers," in *Oeuvres de Teilhard de Chardin*, vol. 7, 405.

[58] Teilhard, "Contingence de l'univers et goût humain de survivre"; "Three Stories in the Style of Benson," in Teilhard de Chardin, *Hymn of the Universe* (New York: Harper & Row, 1965).

[59] Teilhard, "Comment je vois," quoted in Smulders, *The Design of Teilhard de Chardin*, 276; "Christianisme et évolution" (1945), in *Oeuvres de Teilhard de Chardin*, vol. 11.

[60] Teilhard de Chardin, "Le coeur de la matière" (1950), in *Oeuvres de Teilhard de Chardin*, vol. 13; quoted in Claude Tresmontant, *Pierre Teilhard de Chardin: His Thought* (Baltimore: Helicon Press, 1959), 93. On page 30 of the mimeographed version given by Teilhard to George Barbour, the phrase "a mysterious product of *completion* and *fulfillment* for the Absolute Being Himself" is replaced by "a mysterious product of *satisfaction* for the Absolute Being Himself" (italics added). Smulders, *The Design of Teilhard de Chardin*, 276n.17, mentions this difference between the two versions of the essay and considers the latter "less shocking."

364   Teilhard's Process Metaphysics (1969)

In order to avoid the Charybdis of a universe created in a purely contingent and arbitrary way, Teilhard falls into the Scylla of a well-known mythology. According to it, God fulfills Himself in creating the world. God engages in a struggle with the Many (the ancient chaos) in order to find Himself again, richer and pacified, at the terminus of this world. This is an old gnostic idea which is found in Boehme, Hegel and Schelling.[61]

Mooney suggests that Teilhard's statements are less objectionable if one notes that God's "need of the world" and "dependence on man" are the results of his own sovereign decision and free self-limitation rather than of a necessity imposed on him. He also points out that some of the statements about the world as "completing" God can be interpreted as referring to man's co-operation in building up the Body of Christ in the world. I would submit, however, that Teilhard's ideas do entail a revision of the traditional understanding of God's relation to temporality.

Whitehead goes further than Teilhard in modifying the classical assertion that God is timeless and immutable. God's purposes and character are eternal, but his knowledge of events changes as those events take place in their own spontaneity; he cannot know the future if his creatures have genuine freedom. God contributes to the world and is in turn affected by it (Whitehead calls this the "consequent nature" of God). Yet in his "primordial nature" he is independent of events, unchanging in character and aim; his timeless envisagement of pure possibilities is unaffected by the world. Of all actual entities, he alone is everlasting, without perishing, without beginning or end. He is omniscient in that he knows all that is to be known, all ideal potentialities, and a past which is preserved without loss.[62]

Whitehead's idea of God's "primordial nature," like Teilhard's Alpha, refers to God's eternal purposes for the world; the "consequent nature," like Teilhard's Omega, includes the world's contribution to God. For Teilhard, however, Omega is primarily in the future, though it exerts an attraction on the present. For Whitehead, the two aspects represent two continuing roles of God which are abstractions from his unity:

But God, as well as being primordial, is also consequent. He is the beginning and the end. He is not the beginning in the sense of being

---

[61] Tresmontant, *Pierre Teilhard de Chardin*, 94. For Mooney's comments, see Mooney, *Teilhard and the Mystery of Christ*, 127.

[62] See Christian, *An Interpretation of Whitehead's Metaphysics*, 364–403.

in the past of all members. He is the presupposed actuality of conceptual operation, in unison of becoming with every other creative act. Thus by reason of the relativity of all things, there is a reaction of the world on God. . . . God's conceptual nature is unchanged, by reason of its final completeness. But the derivative nature is consequent upon the creative advance of the world.[63]

Whitehead holds that there is successiveness and becoming within God, since he prehends worldly events which come into being successively. But God is a non-temporal single occasion who does not perish and lose immediacy as every temporal entity does. Thus, creatures in the world are *temporal*, and God's "primordial nature" is *eternal* (unaffected by time), but his "consequent nature" is neither temporal nor eternal but *everlasting*, in Whitehead's terminology. One wonders whether Teilhard might not have found such a formulation acceptable.

The Problem of Evil

Let us consider next Teilhard's assertion that evil is an inevitable byproduct of an evolutionary process. There can be "no order in process of formation that does not, at all its stages, involve disorder."[64] The pain of growth and the presence of failure and death are structural concomitants of evolutive development; in any advance, much must be left behind. Ours is "a particular type of cosmos in which evil appears necessarily and as abundantly as you like in the course of evolution—not by accident (which would not matter) but through the very structure of the system." "Pure unorganized multiplicity is not bad in itself; but because it is multiple, i.e. essentially subject in its arrangement to the play of chance, it is absolutely impossible for it to progress towards unity without producing evil in its wake through statistical necessity."[65]

Teilhard is particularly concerned to show that suffering is an integral part of any evolutionary system. "The world is an immense groping, an immense attack; it can only progress at the cost of many failures and much

[63] Whitehead, *Process and Reality*, 523–24.

[64] Pierre Teilhard de Chardin, "Le Christ évoluteur" (1942), in *Cahiers* (Paris: Éditions du Seuil, 1965); in *Oeuvres de Teilhard de Chardin*, vol. 10; cf. *The Divine Milieu*, 58n.1.

[65] Teilhard, "Comment je vois," quoted in Mooney, *Teilhard and the Mystery of Christ*, 108.

366   Teilhard's Process Metaphysics (1969)

pain."[66] Suffering and death are not in themselves products of human sin or means to its expiation:

> Following the classical view, suffering is above all a punishment, an expiation; it is efficacious as a sacrifice; it originates from sin and makes reparation for sin. Suffering is good as a means of self-mastery, self-conquest, self-liberation. In contrast, following the ideas and tendencies of a truly cosmic outlook, suffering is above all the consequence and price of a labor of development. It is efficacious as effort. Physical and moral evil originate from a process of becoming; everything which evolves experiences suffering and moral failure. . . . The Cross is the symbol of the pain and toil of evolution, rather than the symbol of expiation.[67]

In answer to the charge that his interpretation limits God's power, Teilhard replies that a world in evolution and a world without disorder are simply contradictory concepts:

> We often represent God to ourselves as being able to draw a world out of nothingness without pain, defects, risks, without "breakage." This is conceptual fantasy which makes the problem of evil unsolvable. No, it is necessary instead to say that God, despite His power, *cannot* obtain a creature united to Him without necessarily entering into struggle with some evil; because evil appears *inevitably* with the first atom. . . . Nobody has ever been astonished because God could not make a square circle or set aside an evil act. Why restrict the domain of impossible contradiction to these single cases?[68]

Teilhard holds that evil is intrinsic to an evolutionary cosmos as it would not be in an instantaneously produced one; like Whitehead, he claims that this insight exonerates God from responsibility for evil. He points out also that the failure and death of individuals contribute to the advance of the total process. God can make use of patterns which entail evil; he "transfigures them by integrating them into a better plan."[69] Sin is one more form of a universal and inevitable imperfection. Original sin is a result of structural

---

[66] Pierre Teilhard de Chardin, "La signification et la valeur constructrice de la souffrance," in *Oeuvres de Teilhard de Chardin*, vol. 6, 63.

[67] Pierre Teilhard de Chardin, "La vie cosmique," in *Écrits du temps de la guerre*.

[68] Teilhard, de Chardin, "Note sur les modes de l'action divine dans l'univers" (1920), quoted in Tresmontant, *Pierre Teilhard de Chardin*, 96.

[69] Teilhard, *The Divine Milieu*, 27.

conditions, not of an accidental act on the part of Adam and Eve. I cannot at this point discuss the theological adequacy of this view of sin; it is considered here only as a form of the wider phenomenon of evil—concerning which, his position is summed up in the following sentence: "Evil, in all its forms—injustice, inequality, suffering, death itself—ceases theoretically to be outrageous from the moment when, *Evolution becoming a Genesis*, the immense travail of the world displays itself as the inevitable reverse side—or better, the condition—or better still, the price—of an immense triumph."[70]

For Whitehead, too, evil is an inescapable concomitant of temporal process. "The nature of evil is that the characters of things are mutually obstructive."[71] But he sees evil as arising not simply from the incompatibility of alternative potentialities or the unavoidable conflict among a multiplicity of beings; it also stems from the choice of less valuable alternatives by individual beings. Whitehead's stress on the freedom of each creature in choosing evil seems more compatible with the traditional idea of sin than Teilhard's ideas of statistical necessity. But has Whitehead exonerated God from responsibility for evil at the cost of leaving him powerless to do anything about it? Whitehead's God cannot ensure that what is chosen will be the ideal or even the best of the options open, but he can hold out the higher option as a possibility, and he can achieve some positive value from every event. He shows how evil can be turned to good account by integration into a wider pattern of harmony which is everlastingly preserved in his memory. He "loses nothing that can be saved."[72]

Here again Whitehead limits God's power more drastically than Teilhard. Both men object to the idea of arbitrary divine acts. But Whitehead reacts more vehemently to the image of the "absolute monarch" which he sees in much Christian thinking.[73] His assumption of a pluralism of actual occasions leads him to a greater emphasis on the world's freedom. "The divine element in the world is to be conceived as a persuasive and not a coercive agency."[74] God lures every being toward co-operation in the production of value; he is a transforming influence in the world without determining it omnipotently. But he is ultimately in control through the power of a love which respects the integrity and freedom of his creatures;

---

[70] Teilhard, *The Future of Man*, 90.

[71] Whitehead, *Process and Reality*, 517; cf. *Adventures of Ideas*, 333.

[72] Whitehead, *Process and Reality*, 525.

[73] Whitehead, *Process and Reality*, 146, 519; *Religion in the Making* (New York: Macmillan Co., 1926), 55, 74–75; *Science and the Modern World*, 266.

[74] Whitehead, *Adventures of Ideas*, 213.

368   Teilhard's Process Metaphysics (1969)

like human love, it influences by the response it evokes. Even more than in Teilhard's writing, the future actualization of the divine ideal is understood to be dependent on the world's activity.

The Future of the World

Consider, finally, Teilhard's expectations of the future. Evolution continues; its next stage will be the convergence of mankind into an interthinking network, the "noosphere." The new level of planetary consciousness will require global unification and the interpenetration of cultures.[75] Teilhard is confident that such a "social organism" will not submerge individuality and diversity in totalitarian uniformity. He seems to base this vision of the future on three kinds of assumptions:

(1) *Extrapolation from the Convergent Past.* He projects into the future the previous trend toward greater complexity, consciousness, and personalization. This trend will now continue at the level of culture, which is the extension of biology; man's past is today transmitted by education more than by genes. Man has not followed the pattern of most creatures, namely, divergence into separate species. Moreover, convergence is now aided by the "planetary compression" imposed by the globe's limited surface and by improved intercommunication. Teilhard also introduces a more pragmatic argument: Faith in a convergent future and in human solidarity is a condition of mankind's continued survival. Teilhard's apologetic interest in addressing the unbeliever leads him to seek grounds for hope independent of revelation, even though it would appear that his own optimism had primarily Christian roots.

(2) *The Unity of the World Process.* Teilhard's belief in interdependence and unity is expressed in his portrayal of a convergent cosmos. Whitehead, by contrast, visualizes *each* event as converging from multiplicity toward a new unity, which serves in turn as part of the multiple data inherited by its successors. Teilhard sees the *whole* cosmic process as one slowly culminating event with a single goal. Here, as elsewhere, the monistic elements in his thought predominate over pluralistic ones, whereas in Whitehead the relative balance is reversed. (If space permitted, we could explore how their differing assumptions concerning pluralism are reflected in their political philosophies—e.g., their views of the relation between the individual and the collective.)

---

[75] Teilhard, *The Future of Man*, 119, 167, 228 *et passim.*

(3) *The Unity of All Things in Christ.* Teilhard's idea of the "cosmic Christ" combines his conviction of the organic interdependence of the world and his biblical belief in the centrality of Christ. Redemption is not the rescue of individuals from the world but the fulfilment of the world's potentialities; the corporate salvation of the cosmos is integral with the activity of continuing creation. The world converges to a spiritual union with God in Christ, whose relation to the world is organic and not merely juridical and extrinsic. The incarnation reveals God's participation in matter and his universal involvement in cosmic history. The mystical side of Teilhard is expressed in his extension of the imagery of the Mass; the sacramental transformation of matter which occurs in the Eucharist is the paradigm of the universal "Christification" of matter. In a prayer written in Asia on an occasion when he had neither bread nor wine, he offers the whole creation as "the all-embracing Host."[76]

Teilhard's vision of the culmination of cosmic history in the Parousia shows once more the influence of his process thought on his reinterpretation of biblical doctrines. One change, of course, is the time scale; no imminent end is expected, and Teilhard speculates that we may have "millions of years" ahead of us. Again, he is more concerned about the salvation of the cosmos as an integral enterprise than about the salvation of individuals considered separately. In Teilhard's eschatology, moreover, the Kingdom will be a transformation of our present world, not the substitution of a new world. It will not come by an arbitrary intervention of God but by the consummation of a universe already prepared for it. The actualization of the potentialities of creation is a necessary condition for the final advent of the Kingdom, even though the eschaton is a gift from God and not simply the world's own achievement. Man and nature collaborate with God in bringing the cosmos to completion:

> We continue from force of habit to think of the Parousia, whereby the Kingdom of God is to be consummated on Earth, as an event of a purely catastrophic nature—that is to say, liable to come about at any moment in history, irrespective of any definite state of Mankind. But why should we not assume, in accordance with the latest scientific view of Mankind in a state of anthropogenesis, that the parousiac

---

[76] See Teilhard de Chardin, *Hymn of the Universe*; *The Divine Milieu*, 102ff.; *The Phenomenon of Man*, 297.

370   Teilhard's Process Metaphysics (1969)

spark can, of physical and organic necessity, only be kindled between Heaven and a Mankind which has biologically reached a certain critical evolutionary point of collective maturity?[77]

Whitehead agrees that there will be a long future which will involve quite new types of orders. To this novel future both man and God will contribute. "Man's true destiny as cocreator in the universe is his dignity and his grandeur." For Whitehead also, God is primarily fulfiller of the world and only derivatively its judge. But Whitehead differs greatly from Teilhard in expecting no integrated cosmic convergence and no final consummation of history. He departs from classical Christianity in his assumption that time is infinite. Moreover, he disavows any detailed fixed divine plan. God has an unchanging general purpose, the maximum actualization of value and harmony; but he does not determine the world's free activity, and much that happens is contrary to his will. Within an over-all teleology, God envisages a plurality of goals which he continually revises in the light of the world's response to his initiative. Whitehead speculates that there may be various "cosmic epochs," some having types of orders unlike those with which we are familiar.[78] His vision of God does not guarantee any final victory of good in the world. But it does assure us that God is concerned for the world, that the future is not the product of human effort alone, and that God will not be finally defeated. Moreover, it does provide the confidence that whatever is of value will be preserved everlastingly in the divine memory. The only permanence lies in the world's contribution to God's consequent nature—which treasures without loss all that has been achieved, even while it remains open to further enrichment.[79]

In summary, Teilhard's process metaphysics, though not systematically developed, shows striking similarities with Whitehead's, especially in his views of temporality, interdependence, continuity, and the "within." There are close parallels in their presentations of continuing creation, interaction between God and the world, and the idea that the world's maturation is a condition for the fulfilment of God's purposes.

However, Whitehead's ontology is fundamentally pluralistic, whereas Teilhard has stronger monistic tendencies which are particularly evident in

---

[77] Teilhard, *The Future of Man*, 267; cf. 22; *The Divine Milieu*, 133–38; "Comment je vois," etc.

[78] Cf. Whitehead, *Process and Reality*, 139, 148, 171, 442; *Modes of Thought*, 78, 212. See also the last paragraph of *Religion in the Making*.

[79] Cf. Cobb, *A Christian Natural Theology*, 218–23.

his deterministic statements and in his expectation of cosmic convergence. Teilhard's beliefs in a beginning and end to history are closer to traditional representations of creation and eschatology, and his qualification of divine omnipotence is less extreme than Whitehead's. On some issues, however, Teilhard's monistic leanings seem to take him further from the biblical tradition—in his treatment of freedom, evil, and sin, for example, or in his apparent exaggeration of the unity and continuity of the world, or in his terminology concerning "the whole" and "the All," which often sound pantheistic despite his intentions. I hope to explore in another paper Teilhard's process theology in which is reflected the influence of his process metaphysics on his interpretation of such biblical themes as the integral nature of man, the significance of secular life, the unity of creation and redemption, and above all the idea of "the cosmic Christ."

Bibliography

Adams, Robert. "Idealism Vindicated." In *Persons: Human and Divine*, edited by Peter van Inwagen and Dean Zimmerman. Oxford: Oxford University Press, 2007.

Anderson, Bernhard W. *Creation versus Chaos*. New York: Association Press, 1967.

———. *From Creation to New Creation: Old Testament Perspectives*. Minneapolis: Fortress Press, 1994.

"Anthropology: Experts Meet but Ape-Man Link Is Still Lost." *Newsweek*, March 27, 1937, 30–31.

Arias, Alfonso Martinez. "Cells, Not DNA, Are the Master Architects of Life." *Noema*, May 30, 2023.

Artson, Bradley Shavit. *God of Becoming and Relationship: The Dynamic Nature of Process Theology*. Woodstock, VT: Jewish Lights, 2016.

Bailey, Lee Worth. *The Enchantments of Technology*. Urbana: University of Illinois Press, 2010.

Barbour, George B. *In the Field with Teilhard de Chardin*. New York: Herder & Herder, 1965.

Barbour, Ian. "Five Ways of Reading Teilhard." *Soundings* 51, no. 2 (1968): 115–45.

———. "The Significance of Teilhard." In *Changing Man: The Threat and the Promise*, edited by Kyle Haselden and Philip Hefner, 130–41. Garden City, NY: Doubleday, 1968.

———. "Teilhard's Process Metaphysics." *The Journal of Religion* 49, no. 2 (1969): 136–59.

———. "Teilhard's Process Metaphysics." In *Process Theology: Basic Writings*, edited by Ewert Cousins, 232–50. New York: Newman Press, 1971.

Barfield, Owen. *Saving the Appearances: A Study in Idolatry*. Middletown, CT: Wesleyan University Press, 1988.

Barrett, Nathaniel F. *Enjoyment as Enriched Experience: A Theory of Affect and Its Relation to Consciousness*. Cham, Switzerland: Palgrave, 2023.

374   *Bibliography*

Barthélemy-Maudale, Madeleine. *Bergson et Teilhard de Chardin*. Paris: Éditions du Seuil, 1963.

Baudry, Gérard-Henry. *Dictionnaire des Correspondants de Teilhard de Chardin*. Lille: Chez l'Auteur, 1974.

Bergson, Henri. *The Two Sources of Morality and Religion*. Translated by R. Ashley Audra and Cloudesley Brereton, with the assistance of W. Horsfall Carter. Garden City, NY: Doubleday Anchor Books, 1954 [1932].

Berry, Thomas. *The Dream of the Earth*. San Francisco: Sierra Club, 1998.

———. "Teilhard in the Ecological Age." In *Teilhard in the 21st Century: The Emerging Spirit of Earth*, edited by Arthur Fabel and Donald St. John, 57–73. Maryknoll, NY: Orbis Books, 2003.

Bertka, Contance M., ed. *Exploring the Origin, Extent, and Future of Life: Philosophical, Ethical, and Theological Perspectives*. Cambridge: Cambridge University Press, 2009.

Bjornerud, Marcia. *Timefulness: How Thinking Like a Geologist Can Help Save the World*. Princeton, NJ: Princeton University Press, 2018.

Bogaard, Paul, and Jason Bell, eds. *The Harvard Lectures of Alfred North Whitehead, 1924–1925: Philosophical Presuppositions of Science*. Edinburgh: Edinburgh University Press, 2017.

Bohm, David, and B. J. Hiley. *The Undivided Universe: An Ontological Interpretation of Quantum Mechanics*. London: Routledge, 1993.

Borowski, Susan. "Quantum Mechanics and the Consciousness Connection." *AAAS* (July 16, 2012).

Boudignon, Patrice. *Pierre Teilhard de Chardin: Sa Vie, son oeuvre, sa réflexion*. Paris: Éditions du Cerf, 2008.

Bracken, Joseph A., ed. *Christianity and Process Thought: Spirituality for a Changing World*. New Brunswick: Templeton Press, 2006.

———. *Creativity as Link between East and West*. Eugene, OR: Wipf & Stock, 2006.

———. *World without End: Christian Eschatology from a Process Perspective*. Grand Rapids, MI: Eerdmans, 2005.

Brion, Marcel. "Rencontre avec le Père Teilhard de Chardin. Entretien avec Marcel Brion," *Les Nouvelles Littéraires* (Paris), January 11, 1951. *See the translation by Donald Wayne Viney in the Appendix in the current volume.*

Bronstein, Noa. "Jeff Bezos' Cowboy Hat Photo Links Him to a Lineage of Images Depicting a Desire to Colonize and Claim." *Toronto Star*, special issue, February 21, 2020.

Brummer, Vincent. *The Model of Love: A Study in Philosophical Theology.* Cambridge: Cambridge University Press, 1993.

Brüntrup, Godehard. "Is Psycho-physical Emergentism Committed to Dualism? The Causal Efficacy of Emergent Mental Properties." *Erkenntnis* 48, nos. 2/3 (1998): 133–51.

———. "Zur Kritik des Funktionalismus." In *Ist der Geist berechenbar? Philosophische Reflexionen,* edited by Wolfgang Köhler and Hans-Dieter Mutschler (Hrsg.). Darmstadt: Wissenschaftliche Buchgesellschaft, 2003.

Byrne, Patrick H. "The Integral Visions of Teilhard and Lonergan: Science, the Universe, Humanity, and God." In *From Teilhard to Omega: Co-Creating an Unfinished Universe,* edited by Ilia Delio, 83–110. Maryknoll, NY: Orbis Books, 2014.

Caputo, John D. *What to Believe? Twelve Brief Lessons in Radical Theology.* New York: Columbia University Press, 2023.

Chalmers, David. *The Conscious Mind: In Search of a Fundamental Theory.* Oxford: Oxford University Press, 1996.

———. "Consciousness and Its Place in Nature." In *Philosophy of Mind: Classical and Contemporary Readings,* edited by David Chalmers, 247–72. New York: Oxford University Press, 2002.

Chapman, G. Clarke. "Jung and Christology." *Journal of Psychology and Theology* 25, no. 4 (December 1, 1997): 414–26.

Chester, Michael A. *Divine Pathos and Human Beings: The Theology of Abraham Joshua Heschel.* Elstree: Vallentine Mitchel, 2005.

Childs, Brevard S. *Biblical Theology of the Old and New Testaments: Theological Reflection on the Christian Bible.* Minneapolis: Fortress Press, 1993.

Chorost, Michael. "Where Thomas Nagel Went Wrong." *Chronicle of Higher Education,* May 13, 2013.

Christian, William. *An Interpretation of Whitehead's Metaphysics.* New Haven, CT: Yale University Press, 1959.

Cirkovic, Milan M. *The Great Silence: Science and Philosophy of Fermi's Paradox.* Oxford: Oxford University Press, 2018.

Clarke, David S. *Panpsychism: Past and Recent Selected Readings.* Albany: State University of New York Press, 2004.

Clayton, Philip. *Mind and Emergence: From Quantum to Consciousness.* Oxford: Oxford University Press, 2006.

Cobb, John B., Jr. *Is It Too Late? A Theology of Ecology.* Faith and Life Series. Beverly Hills, CA: Bruce, 1972. 50th anniversary edition published by Fortress Press in 2021.

376 Bibliography

———. *Christ in a Pluralistic Age*. Philadelphia: Westminster Press, 1975.

———. *Becoming a Thinking Christian: If We Want Church Renewal, We Will Have to Renew Thinking in the Church*. Nashville, TN: Abingdon Press, 1993.

———. "Teilhard and Whitehead." *Process Studies* 35, no. 1 (2006): 5–11.

———. "Teilhard and Whitehead." *Process in Praxis* (September 1, 2021).

Cobb, John B., Jr., and David Ray Griffin. *Process Theology: An Introductory Exposition*. Louisville, KY: Westminster John Knox Press, 1976.

Connes, Pierre, and James Lequeux. *History of the Plurality of Worlds: The Myths of Extraterrestrials through the Ages*. Cham, Switzerland: Springer, 2020.

Consolmagno, Guy, and Paul Mueller. *Would You Baptize an Extraterrestrial?: . . . and Other Questions from the Astronomers' In-box at the Vatican Observatory*. New York: Image, 2018.

Cooper, John. *Panentheism: The Other God of the Philosophers*. Grand Rapids, MI: Baker Academic, 2013.

Cooper, Keith. "8 Ways the James Webb Space Telescope Is Already Revolutionizing Astronomy." Space.com (2022).

Cousins, Ewert. "Teilhard and the Theology of the Spirit." *CrossCurrents* 19 (1969): 159–77.

Cowell, Sion. *The Teilhard Lexicon*. Brighton, UK: Sussex Academic Press, 2001.

Crespy, Georges. "The Problem of Evil in Teilhard's Thought." In *Process Theology: Basic Writings*, edited by Ewert Cousins, 283–98. New York: Newman Press, 1971.

Crowe, Michael J. *The Extraterrestrial Life Debate, 1750–1900: The Idea of a Plurality of Worlds from Kant to Lowell*. Mineola, NY: Dover Publications, 1999.

———. *The Extraterrestrial Debate: Antiquity to 1915*. Notre Dame, IN: University of Notre Dame Press, 2008.

Cuénot, Claude. *Pierre Teilhard de Chardin: Les Grandes Étapes de son Évolution*. Paris: Libraire Plon, 1958. Translated into English by Vincent Colimore as *Teilhard de Chardin: A Biographical Study*, edited by René Hague. Baltimore: Helicon Press, 1965.

D'Ouince, René. *Un Prophète en Procès: Teilhard de Chardin dans l'Église de son Temps*. Paris: Aubier-Montaigne, 1970.

Davis, Andrew M. *Mind, Value, and Cosmos: On the Relational Nature of Ultimacy*. Lanham, MD: Lexington, 2020.

————. *Metaphysics of Exo-Life: Toward a Constructive Whiteheadian Cosmotheology*. Grasmere, ID: SacraSage, 2023.

————. *From Force to Persuasion: Process-Relational Perspectives on Power and the God of Love*. Eugene, OR: Cascade, 2024.

Davis, Andrew M., and Roland Faber, eds. *Astrophilosophy, Exotheology, and Cosmic Religion: Extraterrestrial Life in a Process Universe*. Lanham, MD: Lexington, 2024.

Davison, Andrew. *Astrobiology and Christian Doctrine: Exploring the Implications of Life in the Universe*. Cambridge: Cambridge University Press, 2023.

Delio, Ilia. *Making All Things New*. Maryknoll, NY: Orbis Books, 2015.

————. "Trinitizing the Universe: Theogenesis and the Dynamism of Love." *Open Theology* 4 (2018): 158–69.

————. "Teilhard de Chardin and World Religions." *Journal of Ecumenical Studies* 54, no. 3 (Summer 2019): 306–27.

————. *The Not-Yet God: Carl Jung, Teilhard de Chardin, and the Relational Whole*. Maryknoll, NY: Orbis Books, 2023.

————, ed. *From Teilhard to Omega: Co-Creating an Unfinished Universe*. Maryknoll, NY: Orbis Books, 2014.

Dennett, Daniel C. *Consciousness Explained*. New York: Little Brown, 1991.

————. *Darwin's Dangerous Idea*. New York: Simon and Schuster, 1995.

Dennett, Daniel C., and Owen Flanagan. *The Problem of the Soul: Two Visions of Mind and How to Reconcile Them*. New York: Basic Books, 2002.

DeRose, Jason. "Religious 'Nones' Are Now the Largest Single Group in the US." *NPR*, January 24, 2024.

Desjardins, Joseph R. *Environmental Ethics: An Introduction to Environmental Philosophy*. Boston: Wadsworth Cengage Learning, 2006.

Dick, Steven J. *Plurality of Worlds: The Extraterrestrial Life Debate from Democritus to Kant*. Cambridge: Cambridge University Press, 1982.

————. *Life on Other Worlds: The 20th-Century Extraterrestrial Life Debate*. Cambridge: Cambridge University Press, 1998.

————. *Astrobiology, Discovery, and Societal Impact*. Cambridge: Cambridge University Press, 2020.

Disney, M. J. "Modern Cosmology: Science or Folktale?" *American Scientist* 95, no. 6 (2007).

Dobzhansky, Theodosius. "Teilhard de Chardin and the Orientation of Evolution." In *Process Theology: Basic Writings*, edited by Ewert Cousins, 229–48. New York: Newman Press, 1971.

378   Bibliography

Dombrowski, Daniel. *Analytic Theism, Hartshorne, and the Concept of God.* Albany: State University of New York Press, 1996.

———. *Kazantzakis and God.* Albany: State University of New York Press, 1997.

———. *Divine Beauty: The Aesthetics of Charles Hartshorne.* Nashville, TN: Vanderbilt University Press, 2004.

———. *A Platonic Philosophy of Religion: A Process Perspective.* Albany: State University of New York Press, 2005.

———. *Rethinking the Ontological Argument: A Neoclassical Theistic Response.* Cambridge: Cambridge University Press, 2006.

———. "Religion, Solitariness, and the Bloodlands." *American Journal of Theology and Philosophy* 36 (2015): 226–39.

———. *A History of the Concept of God: A Process Approach.* Albany: State University of New York Press, 2016.

———. *Whitehead's Religious Thought: From Mechanism to Organism, from Force to Persuasion.* Albany: State University of New York Press, 2017.

———. *Process Philosophy and Political Liberalism: Rawls, Whitehead, Hartshorne.* Edinburgh: Edinburgh University Press, 2019.

———. *Process Mysticism.* Albany: State University of New York Press, 2023.

Donceel, Joseph. "Teilhard de Chardin and the Body-Soul Relation." *Thought* 40, no. 3 (1965): 371–89.

Dourley, John P. *The Psyche As Sacrament: A Comparative Study of C. G. Jung and Paul Tillich.* Toronto: Inner City Books, 1981.

Dussel, Enrique. *Beyond Philosophy: Ethics, History, Marxism, and Liberation Theology.* Oxford: Rowan and Littlefield Publishers, 2003.

Eddington, Arthur. *Space, Time, and Gravitation.* Cambridge: Cambridge University Press, 1920.

Edinger, Edward F. *Ego and Archetype: Individuation and the Religious Function of the Psyche.* Boston: Shambhala, 1992.

Einstein, Albert. "Letter of 1950." *New York Times,* March 22, 1972.

Eloe, Laura. "Teilhard's Mathematical Analogies and the Tradition of the Church." *Teilhard Studies* 87 (Fall 2023): 1–23.

Enxing, Julia, and Klaus Müller, eds. *Perfect Changes: Die Religionsphilosophie Charles Hartshornes.* Regensburg: Verlag Friedrich Pustet, 2012.

Faber, Roland. "De-ontologizing God: Levinas, Deleuze, and Whitehead." In *Process and Difference: Between Cosmological and Poststructuralist Postmodernisms,* edited by Catherine Keller and Anne Daniell, 209–34. Albany: State University of New York Press, 2002.

Faricy, Robert L. "Teilhard de Chardin on Creation and the Christian Life." *Theology Today* 24, no. 3 (January 1967): 505–20.

Farrow, Douglas. "The Problem with Teilhard." *Nova et Vetera* [English edition] 16, no. 2 (2018): 377–85.

Ferré, Frederick. *Being and Value: Toward a Constructive Postmodern Metaphysics*. Albany: State University of New York Press, 1996.

———. *Knowing and Value: Toward a Constructive Postmodern Epistemology*. Albany: State University of New York Press, 1998.

———. *Living and Value: Toward a Constructive Postmodern Ethics*. Albany: State University of New York Press, 2001.

Ford, Lewis S. "The Power of God and the Christ." In *Religious Experience and Process Theology*, edited by Bernard Cargas and Harry J. Lee, 79–92. New York: Paulist Press, 1976.

———. *The Lure of God: A Biblical Background for Process Theism*. Philadelphia: Fortress Press, 1978.

———. "Theological Reflections on Extraterrestrial Life." In Davis, *Metaphysics of Exo-Life*, 153–78. Grasmere, ID: Sacrasage Press, 2023.

Forgan, Duncan H. *Solving Fermi's Paradox*. Cambridge: Cambridge University Press, 2019.

Foucault, Michel. *Discipline and Punish: The Birth of the Prison*. Translated by Alan Sheridan. New York: Vintage Books, 1979.

Francis, Pope. *Laudato Si': On Care for Our Common Home*. Maryknoll, NY: Orbis Books, 2016.

Fretheim, Terence. *The Suffering of God: An Old Testament Perspective*. Philadelphia: Fortress Press, 1984.

———. *God and World in the Old Testament: A Relational Theology of Creation*. Nashville, TN: Abingdon Press, 2005.

———. *God So Enters into Relationships That . . . A Biblical View*. Minneapolis: Fortress Press, 2020.

Frye, Northrop. *The Great Code: The Bible and Literature*. New York: HarperOne, 1982.

Gilkey, Langdon. *Maker of Heaven and Earth*. Garden City, NY: Doubleday & Co., 1959.

Gilson, Etienne. *Les Tribulations de Sophie*. Paris: J. Vrin, 1967.

———. *From Aristotle to Darwin and Back Again: A Journey in Final Causality, Species, and Evolution*. Translated by John Lyon. Notre Dame, IN: University of Notre Dame Press, 1984.

Goethe, Johann Wolfgang von. *Scientific Studies*. Edited and translated by Douglas Miller. New York: Suhrkamp, 1988.

380 Bibliography

Goff, Philip. *Consciousness and Fundamental Reality*. New York: Oxford University Press, 2017.

Gottlieb, A. E. "Nuclear Weapons in Outer Space." *Canadian Yearbook of International Law*, III (1965).

Gould, Stephen Jay. *Hen's Teeth and Horse's Toes: Further Reflections in Natural History*. New York: W. W. Norton & Company, 1983.

Gregersen, Niels Henrik. "Three Varieties of Panentheism. In *In Whom We Live and Move and Have Our Being: Panentheistic Reflections on God's Presence in a Scientific World*, edited by Philip Clayton and Arthur Peacocke. Cambridge: Eerdmans, 2004.

Griffin, David Ray. *Unsnarling the World-Knot: Consciousness, Freedom, and the Mind-Body Problem*. Berkeley: University of California Press, 1998.

——. *Religion and Scientific Naturalism: Overcoming the Conflicts*. Albany: State University of New York Press, 2000.

——. *Reenchantment without Supernaturalism: A Process Philosophy of Religion*. Ithaca, NY: Cornell University Press, 2001.

——. *Panentheism and Scientific Naturalism: Rethinking Evil, Morality, Religious Experience, Religious Pluralism, and the Academic Study of Religion*. Claremont: Process Century Press, 2014.

Grim, John, and Mary Evelyn Tucker. *Ecology and Religion*. Illustrated edition. Washington, DC: Island Press, 2014.

Grumett, David, and Paul Bentley. "Teilhard de Chardin, Original Sin, and the Six Propositions." *Zygon* 53, no. 2 (June 2018): 303–30.

Hacking, Ian. "Nineteenth Century Cracks in the Concept of Determinism." *Journal of the History of Ideas* 44, no. 3 (July-September 1983): 455–75.

Haight, Roger, SJ, Alfred Pach III, and Amanda Avila Kaminski, eds. *Spirituality of Creation, Evolution, and Work: Catherine Keller and Pierre Teilhard de Chardin*. New York: Fordham University Press, 2023.

Handley, George E. *New World Poetics: Nature and the Atlantic Imagination of Whitman, Neruda, and Walcott*. Athens: The University of Georgia Press, 2007.

Haqq-Misra, Jacob, and Seth D. Baum. "The Sustainability Solution to the Fermi Paradox." *American Indian Culture and Research Journal* 62 (2009): 47–51.

Hartshorne, Charles. "Ethics and the New Theology." *International Journal of Ethics* 45, no. 1 (1934): 90–101.

———. *The Philosophy and Psychology of Sensation*. Chicago: University of Chicago Press, 1934.

———. *Beyond Humanism: Essays in the Philosophy of Nature*. Chicago: Willett, Clark and Company, 1937.

———. *The Divine Relativity: A Social Conception of God*. New Haven, CT: Yale University Press, 1948.

———. *The Logic of Perfection: And Other Essays in Neoclassical Metaphysics*. LaSalle, IL: Open Court, 1962.

———. *Anselm's Discovery: A Re-examination of the Ontological Proof for God's Existence*. LaSalle, IL: Open Court, 1965.

———. *A Natural Theology for Our Time*. LaSalle, IL: Open Court, 1967.

———. *Creative Synthesis and Philosophic Method*. LaSalle, IL: Open Court, 1970.

———. *Born to Sing: An Interpretation and World Survey of Bird Song*. Bloomington: Indiana University Press, 1973.

———. "Whitehead's Revolutionary Concept of Prehension." *International Philosophical Quarterly* 19, no. 3 (September 1979): 253–63.

———. *Omnipotence and Other Theological Mistakes*. Albany: State University of New York Press, 1984.

———. *Creativity in American Philosophy*. Albany: State University of New York Press, 1984.

———. *Wisdom as Moderation: A Philosophy of the Middle Way*. Albany: State University of New York Press, 1987.

———. "Tolerance Test." Letter to the editor of the *Austin-American Statesman*, June 18, 1990.

———. *Creative Experiencing: A Philosophy of Freedom*, edited by Donald Wayne Viney and Jincheol O. Albany: State University of New York Press, 2011.

Hartshorne, Charles, and William L. Reese. *Philosophers Speak of God*. Chicago: University of Chicago Press, 1953.

Haugeland, John. "Pattern and Being." In *Dennett and His Critics*, edited by Bo Dahlbom. Oxford: Oxford University Press, 1993.

Haught, John F. "Theology after Contact: Religion and Extraterrestrial Intelligent Life." Annals of the New York Academy of Sciences, 950 (2001): 296–308.

———. "What's Going On in the Universe? Teilhard de Chardin and Alfred North Whitehead." *Process Studies* 35, no. 1 (2006): 43–67.

———. *The New Cosmic Story: Inside Our Awakening Universe*. New Haven, CT: Yale University Press, 2017.

Bibliography

———. *The Cosmic Vision of Teilhard de Chardin*. Maryknoll, NY: Orbis Books, 2021.

Henning, Brian. *Value, Beauty, and Nature: The Philosophy of Organism and the Metaphysical Foundations of Environmental Ethics*. Albany: State University of New York Press, 2023.

Heschel, Abraham Joshua. *Man Is Not Alone: A Philosophy of Religion*. New York: Farrar, Straus, and Giroux, 1976.

———. *The Prophets*. New York: Harper & Row, 1982.

Hesketh, Ian. "What Big History Misses." *Aeon Magazine*, December 16, 2021.

Higgins-Freese, Joanna, and Jeff Tomhave. "Race, Sacrifice, and Native Lands." In *This Sacred Earth: Religion, Culture, and Environment*, 2nd edition, edited by Roger S. Gottlieb, 716–20. New York: Routledge, 2004).

Highwater, Jamake. *The Primal Mind*. New York: Harper & Row, 1944.

Hopkins, Jasper. *Nicholas of Cusa on God as Not-Other: A Translation and an Appraisal of* De Li Non Aliud. Minneapolis: University of Minnesota Press, 1979.

———. *Nicholas of Cusa on Learned Ignorance: A Translation and an Appraisal of De Docta Ignorantia*. Minneapolis: The Arthur J. Banning Press, 1981.

Hughes, Donald J. *American Indian Ecology*. El Paso: Texas Western Press, 1987.

Huxley, Julian. "Introduction." In Pierre Teilhard de Chardin, *The Phenomenon of Man*, 11–28. London: Harper & Row, 1959.

Iqbal, Muhammad. *The Reconstruction of Religious Thought in Islam*. Stanford, CA: Stanford University Press, 2012.

James, William. *A Pluralistic Universe*. New York: Longmans, Green, and Co., 1909.

———. *The Principles of Psychology*, Volume I. New York: Dover, 1950.

Janzen, J. Gerald. "Metaphor and Reality in Hosea 11." *Semeia* 24 (1982): 1–26.

Jeans, James. *The Mysterious Universe*. New York: Macmillan, 1931.

Johnson, A. H. "Whitehead as Teacher and Philosopher." *Philosophy and Phenomenological Research* 29, no. 3 (March 1969): 351–76.

Johnson, Doug. "Decolonizing the Search for Extraterrestrial Life." *Undark* (April 4, 2022).

Jonas, Hans. *The Phenomenon of Life*. New York: Harper & Row, 1966.

Jung, C. G. *Aion: Researches into the Phenomenology of the Self.* Volume 9, Part 2. *The Collected Works of C. G. Jung.* Bollingen Series. New York: Pantheon Books, 1959.

———. *Memories, Dreams, Reflections.* Translated by Clara Winston and Richard Winston. New York: Pantheon Books, 1963.

———. *Psychology and Religion: West and East.* Translated by R. F. C. Hull. Corrected. Volume 11. *The Collected Works of C. G. Jung.* Bollingen Series. New York: Pantheon Books, 1963.

Jungel, Eberhard. *God as the Mystery of the World.* Translated by Darrell L. Guder. Grand Rapids, MI: Eerdmans, 1983.

Kafatos, Menas, and Robert Nadeau. *The Conscious Universe: Parts and Wholes in Physical Reality.* New York: Springer, 1990.

Kant, Immanuel. *Metaphysicae cum geometria iunctae usus in philosophia naturali, cuius specimen I. continet monadologiam physicam.* Academy edition, 1756.

———. *Critique of Pure Reason.* Translated by Norman Kemp Smith. New York: St. Martin's Press, 1965.

———. *Universal Natural History and Theory of Heaven.* Arlington, VA: Richer Resources Publications, 2008.

Kaufman, Gordon D. "Confucian and Christian Conceptions of Creativity: A Christian View of Creativity: Creativity as God." *Dao* 6 (2007): 105–13.

Keller, Catherine. *Apocalypse Now and Then: A Feminist Guide to the End of the World.* Boston: Beacon Press, 1996.

———. *Facing Apocalypse: Climate, Democracy, and Other Last Chances.* Maryknoll, NY: Orbis Books, 2021.

Kelly, Paul. "Did Whitehead Influence Teilhard?" *Process Studies* 11, no. 2 (1981): 106–7.

Kelsey, Morton T. *Encounter with God: A Theology of Christian Experience.* New York: Paulist Press, 1988.

Kenny, W. Henry. *A Path through Teilhard's Phenomenon.* Dayton, OH: Pflaum Press, 1970.

King, Thomas. *Teilhard's Mysticism of Knowing.* Fayetteville, NC: Seabury Press, 1981.

———. "Teilhard and the Environment." In *Teilhard de Chardin on People and Planet,* edited by Celia Deane-Drummond, 179–89. New York: Routledge, 2006.

King, Ursula. *Towards a New Mysticism: Teilhard de Chardin and Eastern Religions.* New York: Collins, 1980.

384 Bibliography

———. *Teilhard's Mysticism of Knowing*. New York: Seabury, 1981.

———. *The Spirit of One Earth: Reflections on Teilhard de Chardin and Global Spirituality*. St. Paul: Paragon House, 1998.

———. "Theories of Love: Sorokin, Teilhard and Tillich." *Zygon* 39, no. 1 (March 2004): 77–102.

———. *Teilhard de Chardin and Eastern Religions: Spirituality and Mysticism in an Evolutionary World*. Mahwah, NJ: Paulist Press, 2011.

———. "A Vision Transformed: Teilhard de Chardin's Evolutionary Awakening at Hastings." *The Heythrop Journal* 54 (2013): 590–605.

———. *Christ in All Things: Evolving Spirituality with Pierre Teilhard de Chardin*. Maryknoll, NY: Orbis Books, 2016.

———. "Teilhard de Chardin's Vision of Science, Religion, and Planetary Humanity: A Challenge to the Contemporary World." *Journal for the Study of Religion* 31, no. 1 (2018): 135–58.

Kingsley, Charles. *The Water-Babies*. Stamford: Longmeadow, 1994 [1863].

Kirsch, Adam. *The Revolt against Humanity: Imagining a Future without Us*. Columbia Global Reports 2023.

Kling, Sheri D. *A Process Spirituality: Christian and Transreligious Resources for Transformation*. Lanham, MD: Lexington Books, 2020.

Kosman, Aryeh. *The Activity of Being: An Essay on Aristotle's Ontology*. Cambridge: Harvard University Press, 2013.

Kugel, James L. *The God of Old: Inside the Lost World of the Bible*. New York: The Free Press, 2003.

Kuntz, Paul G. "Can Whitehead Be Made a Christian Philosopher?" *Process Studies* 12, no. 4 (Winter, 1982): 232–42.

Lakoff, George, and Mark Johnson. *Metaphors We Live By*. Chicago: The University of Chicago Press, 1980.

Lamarck, J. B. *Zoological Philosophy*. Translated by Hugh Elliot. New York: Bill Huth Publishing, 2006.

Laszlo, Ervin. "The Spirit of Einstein and Teilhard in 21st Century Science: The Emergence of Transdisciplinary Unified Theory." *Revista Portuguesa de Filosophia* 61 (2005): 129–36.

Leclerc, Ivor. *Whitehead's Metaphysics*. New York: Macmillan Co., 1958.

Lee, Bernard. *The Becoming of the Church: A Process Theology of the Structures of Christian Experience*. Mahwah, NJ: Paulist Press, 1974.

Lee, Keekok. *The Natural and the Artefactual: The Implications of Deep Science and Deep Technology for Environmental Philosophy*. Lanham, MD: Lexington Books, 1999.

Leibniz, Gottfried Wilhelm. *Die philosophischen Schriften von Gottfried Wilhelm Leibniz*, hg. von Carl Immanuel Gerhardt, 7 Bde., Berlin 1875–1890. Hildesheim: Olms, 1978.

Leroy, Pierre. *Lettres Familières de Pierre Teilhard de Chardin Mon Ami Les Dernières Années 1948–1955*. Vendôme: Le Centurion, 1976.

———. *Letters from My Friend Teilhard de Chardin*. Translated by Mary Lukas. New York: Paulist Press, 1980.

Levenson, Jon D. *Love of God: Divine Gift, Human Gratitude, and Mutual Faithfulness in Judaism*. Princeton, NJ: Princeton University Press, 2016.

Levin, Michael. "The Computational Boundary of a 'Self': Developmental Bioelectricity Drives Multicellularity and Scale-Free Cognition." *Frontiers in Psychology* 10 (2019). doi: 10.3389/fpsyg.2019.02688.

———. "Darwin's Agential Materials: Evolutionary Implications of Multiscale Competency in Developmental Biology." *Cellular and Molecular Life Sciences* 80, no. 6 (2023). doi: 10.1007/s00018-023-04790-z.

Levine, Michael. *Pantheism*. New York: Routledge, 1994.

Linafelt, Tod, and Timothy K. Beal, eds. *God Is the Fray: A Tribute to Walter Brueggemann*. Minneapolis: Fortress Press, 1998.

Lindbergh, Charles. *The Spirit of St. Louis*. New York: Scribner's and Sons, 1953.

Locke, John. *Second Treatise of Civil Government*.

Lockwood, Michael. *Mind, Brain, and the Quantum: The Compound 'I.'* Oxford: Balckwell, 1989.

Loomer, Bernard. "Two Conceptions of Power." *Criterion* 15, no. 1 (Winter 1976): 7–29.

Love, Alan C., and William C. Wimsatt. "Explaining Cultural Evolution." In *Beyond the Meme: Development and Structure in Cultural Evolution*. Minneapolis: University of Minnesota Press, 2019.

Lowe, Victor. "A.N.W.: A Biographical Perspective." *Process Studies* 12, no. 3 (1982): 137–47.

———. *Alfred North Whitehead: The Man and His Work. Volume I: 1861–1910*. Baltimore: The Johns Hopkins University Press, 1985.

———. *Alfred North Whitehead: The Man and His Work. Volume II: 1910–1947*. Edited by J. B. Schneewind. Baltimore: The Johns Hopkins University Press, 1990.

Lubac, Henri de. *The Religion of Teilhard de Chardin*. New York: Desclee, 1967.

386   Bibliography

———. "The Cosmic Christ." In *Process Theology: Basic Writings*, edited by Ewert Cousins, 257–67. New York: Newman Press, 1971.

Lubarsky, Sandra B., and David Ray Griffin, eds. *Jewish Theology and Process Thought*. Albany: State University of New York Press, 1996.

Ludlow, Peter, Yujin Nagasawa, and Daniel Stoljar. *There's Something about Mary: Essays on Phenomenal Consciousness and Frank Jackson's Knowledge Argument*. Boston: MIT Press, 2004.

Lupisella, Mark. *Cosmological Theories of Value: Science, Philosophy, and Meaning in Cosmic Evolution*. Cham, Switzerland: Springer, 2020.

Lyons, J. A. *The Cosmic Christ in Origen and Teilhard de Chardin: A Comparative Study*. Oxford: Oxford University Press, 1982.

Macauley, David. "Be-wildering Order: On Finding a Home for Domestication and the Domesticated Other." In *The Ecological Community: Environmental Challenges for Philosophy, Politics, and Morality*, edited by Roger S. Gottlieb, 104–37. New York: Routledge, 1997.

Mach, Ernst. *Die Analyse der Empfindungen und das Verhältnis des Physischen zum Psychischen*. Darmstadt: Wissenschaftliche Buchgesellschaft, 1991.

Malone-France, Derek. "Hell Is Other Planets: Extraterrestrial Life in the Western Theological Imagination." In *Social and Conceptual Issues in Astrobiology*, edited by Kelly C. Smith and Carlos Mariscal, 21–53. Oxford University Press, 2020.

Mann, Adam. "The James Webb Space Telescope Prompts a Rethink of How Galaxies Form." *PNAS* 120, no. 32 (2023)..

Mathews, Freya. *For the Love of Matter: A Contemporary Panpsychism*. Albany: State University of New York Press, 2001.

Mathews, Washington. "Navajo Legends." *American Folklore Society Memoirs* 5 (1879): 273–75.

McDaniel, Jay. "Process Thought and the Epic of Evolution Tradition." *Process Studies* 35, no. 1 (2006): 68–94.

McGinn, Bernard, ed. *Apocalyptic Spirituality: Treatises and Letters of Lactantius, Adso of Montier-En-Der, Joachim of Fiore, the Spiritual Franciscans, Savonarola*. Preface by Marjorie Reeves. New York: Paulist Press, 1979.

———. *The Complete Mystical Works of Meister Eckhart*. New York: Crossroad, 2007.

McIntosh, Steve. *Developmental Politics: How America Can Grow into a Better Version of Itself.* St. Paul: Paragon House, 2020.

Menacherry, Cheriyan. *Christ: The Mystery in History: A Critical Study on the Christology of Raymond Panikkar*. Frankfurt am Main: Peter Lang, 1996.

Mendonca, Valerian. "Panentheistic Interconnectedness: On the Revival of Metaphysics in A. N. Whitehead and P. Teilhard de Chardin." PhD dissertation. Katholieke Universiteit Leuven, 2019.

Mesle, C. Robert. *Process-Relational Philosophy: An Introduction to Alfred North Whitehead*. West Conshohocken: Templeton Press, 2008.

Mignolo, Walter D. *Local Histories Global Designs: Coloniality, Subaltern Knowledges, and Border Thinking*. Princeton, NJ: Princeton University Press, 2000.

———. *The Darker Side of Western Modernity: Global Futures, Decolonial Options*. Durham, NC: Duke University Press, 2011.

Miller, Clyde Lee. "God as *li Non-Aliud*: Nicholas of Cusa's Unique Designation for God." *Journal of Medieval Religious Cultures* 41 (2015): 24–40.

Miller, Sean. *Strung Together: The Cultural Currency of String Theory as a Scientific Imaginary*. Ann Arbor: University of Michigan Press, 2013.

Mitchell, Edgar. *The Way of the Explorer*. New York: Putnam's, 1996.

A Monk of the West. *Christianity and the Doctrine of Non-Dualism*. Hillsdale, NY: Sophia Perennis, 2004.

Mooney, Christopher. *Teilhard and the Mystery of Christ*. New York: Harper & Row, 1966.

———. "Teilhard de Chardin and Christian Spirituality." In *Process Theology: Basic Writings*, edited by Ewert Cousins, 299–320. New York: Newman Press, 1971.

Moran, Neuhof, Michael Levin, and Oded Rechavi. "Vertically- and Horizontally-Transmitted Memories—The Fading Boundaries between Regeneration and Inheritance in Planaria." *Biology Open* 5, no. 9 (2016): 1177–88.

Nagel, Thomas. *Mortal Questions*. London: Cambridge University Press, 1979/2006.

———. *Mind and Cosmos: Why the Materialist Neo-Darwinian Conception of Nature Is Almost Certainly False*. New York: Oxford University Press, 2012.

Nicholas of Cusa. *The Vision of God*. New York: Frederick Ungar, 1978.

North, Robert. "Teilhard and the Problem of Creation." *Theological Studies* 24 (1963): 577–601.

———. *Teilhard and the Creation of the Soul.* Milwaukee: Bruce Publishing Co., 1967.

Nussbaum, Charles. "Logic and the Metaphysics of Hegel and Whitehead." *Process Studies* 15, no. 1 (Spring 1986): 32–52.

O'Connor, Flannery. *The Habit of Being: Letters of Flannery O'Connor.* Edited by Sally Fitzgerald. New York: Farrar, Straus and Giroux, 1979.

O'Meara, Thomas F. *Vast Universe: Extraterrestrials and Christian Revelation.* Collegeville, MN: Liturgical Press, 2012.

O'Neil, Gerard. *The High Frontier: Human Colonies in Space.* New York: Morrow, 1977.

Oden, Thomas C. *The Living God.* San Francisco: Harper & Row, 1987.

Ortega, Mariana. *In-Between: Latina Feminist Phenomenology, Multiplicity, and the Self.* Albany: State University of New York Press, 2016.

Overbye, Dennis. "Who Will Have the Last Word on the Universe?" *New York Times,* May 2, 2023.

Overman, Richard. *Evolution and the Christian Doctrine of Creation.* Philadelphia: Westminster Press, 1967.

Paas, Stefan. *Creation and Judgement: Creation Texts in Some Eighth Century Prophets.* Leiden: Brill Academic Publishing, 2003.

Panikkar, Raimon. *Christophany: The Fullness of Man.* Maryknoll, NY: Orbis Books, 2004.

Passmore, John Arthur. *The Perfectability of Man.* Reprinted Edition. London: Duckworth, 1972.

Pearce, Jonathan M. S., and Aaron Adair. *Aliens and Religion: Where Two Worlds Collide: Assessing the Impact of Discovering Extraterrestrial Life on Religion and Theology.* Onus Books, 2023.

Petek, Joseph. *Unearthing the Unknown Whitehead.* Lanham, MD: Lexington Books, 2022.

Peters, Ted. *Cosmos as Creation: Theology and Science in Consonance.* Nashville, TN: Abingdon, 1989.

———. *Astrotheology: Science and Theology Meet Extraterrestrial Life.* Eugene, OR: Cascade, 2018.

Pinker, Steven. *The Blank Slate: The Modern Denial of Human Nature.* New York: Penguin Books, 2002.

Pinnock, Clark, et al. *The Openness of God: A Biblical Challenge to the Traditional Understanding of God.* Downers Grove, IL: InterVarsity Press, 1994.

Pittenger, W. Norman. *The Lure of Divine Love: Human Experience and Christian Faith in a Process Perspective.* New York: Pilgrim Press, 1979.

Playford, Richard, Stephen Bullivant, and Janet Siefert. *God and Astrobiology*. Cambridge Elements. Cambridge: Cambridge University Press, 2024.

Price, Lucien. *Dialogues of Alfred North Whitehead, as recorded by Lucien Price*. Boston: Little, Brown and Company, 1954.

"Priest Won't Agree Ape Man's Forebear: Monsignor Takes Issue with Jesuit Scholar's Opinion." *The Toronto Daily Star*, March 22, 1937.

Pryor, Adam. *Living with Tiny Aliens: The Image of God for the Anthropocene*. New York: Fordham University Press, 2020.

Rahner, Karl. "Marxist Utopia and the Christian Future of Man." In *Theological Investigations*, vol. 6, translated by Karl and Boniface Kruger. Baltimore: Helicon, 1969, 59–68.

———. *Foundations of Christian Faith*. New York: Crossroad, 1987.

Rasmussen, Larry. "Drilling in the Cathedral." *Dialog: A Journal of Theology* 42, no. 3 (August 2003): 202–25.

"Remarks by President Trump in State of the Union Address," February 4, 2020.

Renan, Ernest. *Averroès et L'Averroïsme: Essai Historique*. Third edition, revised and updated. Paris: Michel Lévy Frères Libraires Éditeurs, 1866.

Richardson, David. "Philosophies of Hartshorne and Chardin: Two Sides of the Same Coin?" *Southern Journal of Philosophy* 2 (1964): 107–15.

Robertson, Robin. *Jungian Archetypes: Jung, Gödel, and the History of Archetypes*. Revised edition. New York: iUniverse, 2009.

Rosenberg, Gregg. *A Place for Consciousness: Probing the Deep Structure of the Natural World*. Oxford: Oxford University Press, 2004.

Rubenstein, Mary Jane. *Pantheologies: Gods, Worlds, Monsters*. New York: Columbia University Press, 2018.

Russell, Bertrand. "Mind and Matter" (1950).

———. *Portraits from Memory and Other Essays*. London: George Allen & Unwin LTD, 1956.

———. *The Analysis of Matter*. London: Routledge, 1992.

Schlumpt, Heidi. "Time to Rehabilitate Teilhard de Chardin?" *National Catholic Reporter*, January 27, 2018.

Schmitz-Moormann, Nicole and Karl. *Pierre Teilhard de Chardin L'Oeuvres scientifique*, ten volumes. Olten und Freiburg im Breisgau: Walter-Verlag, 1971.

Schrödinger, Erwin. *What Is Life?* Translated by Verena Schrödinger. Reprint edition. Cambridge: Cambridge University Press, 2012.

Bibliography

Schwartz, James, SJ, and Tony Milligan. *The Ethics of Space Exploration.* Cham, Switzerland: Springer, 2016.

Searle, John R. *Mind: A Brief Introduction.* Oxford: Oxford University Press, 2004.

Segall, Matthew David. *Physics of World-Soul: Alfred North Whitehead's Adventure in Cosmology.* Grasmere, ID: SacraSage Press, 2021.

———. "Are There Alternatives to the Big Bang?" *Footnotes2Plato* (2022).

Sellars, Wilfried. "Some Reflections on Language Games." In *Science, Perception, and Reality.* New York: Humanities Press, 1963.

Shuch, H. Paul, ed. *Searching for Extraterrestrial Intelligence: SETI Past, Present and Future.* Chichester: Springer/Praxis, 2011.

Sia, Santiago, ed. *Charles Hartshorne's Concept of God: Philosophical and Theological Responses.* Dordrecht: Kluwer Academic Publishers, 1990.

Simpson, George Gaylord. *Scientific American* 202, no. 4 (April 1960): 204.

Singer, June K. *Boundaries of the Soul: The Practice of Jung's Psychology.* Revised edition. New York: Anchor Books, 1994.

Skrbina, David. *Mind That Abides: Panpsychism in the New Millennium.* Amsterdam: John Benjamins, 2009.

———. *Panpsychism in the West.* London: MIT Press, 2005.

Slattery, John. "Pierre Teilhard de Chardin's Legacy of Eugenics and Racism Can't Be Ignored." *Religion Dispatches*, May 21, 2018.

Smith, Kelly C., and Carlos Mariscal. *Social and Conceptual Issues in Astrobiology.* Oxford: Oxford University Press, 2020.

Smith, Wolfgang. *Theistic Evolution: The Teilhardian Heresy.* Brooklyn, NY: Angelico Press, 2012.

Smulders, Piet. *The Design of Teilhard de Chardin.* Westminster: Newman Press, 1967.

SpaceRef Editor. "Comments on Senate Floor Regarding Space by Sen. Bob Smith." *SpaceRef*, November 20, 2002.

Spitzer, Toba. *God Is Here: Reimaging the Divine.* New York: St. Martin's Essentials, 2022.

Sprigge, Timothy. *A Vindication of Absolute Idealism.* London: Routledge, 1983.

Stebbing, L. Susan. "Review of Alfred North Whitehead, *Process and Reality.*" *Mind* 39 (1930): 466–75.

Steiner, Rudolf. *Nature's Open Secret: Introduction to Goethe's Scientific Writings.* Great Barrington, MA: Anthroposophic Press, 2000.

———. *The Philosophy of Freedom.* East Sussex, UK: Steiner Press, 2011.

Stern, Chaim, ed. *Gates of Prayer: The New Union Prayerbook*. New York: Central Conference of American Rabbis, 1975.

Stoljar, Daniel. "Two Conceptions of the Physical." In *Philosophical and Phenomenological Research* 62, no. 2 (2001): 253–81.

———. *Ignorance and Imagination: The Epistemic Origin of the Problem of Consciousness*. Oxford: Oxford University Press, 2006.

Strawson, Galen. *Consciousness and Its Place in Nature: Does Physicalism Entail Panpsychism?* Exeter: Imprint Academic, 2006.

———. "Consciousness Isn't a Mystery. It's Matter." *New York Times*, May 16, 2016.

Stutter, Paul M. "As Creation Stories Go, the Big Bang Is a Good One." *Nautilus* (2022).

Swimme, Brian. "What Will You Do to Help Preserve the Possibilities?: Our Sacred Earth Is Dying." *The Ecozoic Reader* 3, no. 4 (2003).

Swimme, Brian Thomas, and Mary Evelyn Tucker. *Journey of the Universe*. Reprint edition. New Haven, CT: Yale University Press, 2014.

Tarnas, Richard. *The Passion of the Western Mind*. New York: Ballentine Books, 1991.

Teilhard de Chardin, Pierre. "Cosmic Life." *The Library of Consciousness* (1916).

———. "The Position of Man in Nature and the Significance of Human Socialization." *The Library of Consciousness* (1947).

———. *Le Phénomène humain*. Paris: Éditions du Seuil, 1955.

———. *La Vision du Passé*. Paris: Éditions du Seuil, 1957.

———. *The Phenomenon of Man*. Translated by Bernard Wall. New York: Harper & Row, 1959.

———. *The Divine Milieu*. Translated by Bernard Wall. New York: Harper & Row, 1960.

———. *Hymn of the Universe*. Translated by Simon Bartholomew. New York: Harper & Row, 1961.

———. *Letters from a Traveler*. New York: Harper & Row, 1962.

———. *The Future of Man*. Translated by Norman Denny. New York: Harper & Row, 1964.

———. *The Appearance of Man*. Translated by J. M. Cohen. New York: Harper & Row, 1965.

———. *Écrits du temps de la guerre* (1916–1919). Paris: Éditions Bernard Grasset, 1965.

———. *The Vision of the Past*. Translated by J. M. Cohen. New York: Harper & Row, 1966.

———. *Man's Place in Nature.* Translated by René Hague. New York: Harper & Row, 1966.

———. *Man's Place in Nature.* Translated by Noel Lindsay. New York: HarperCollins, 1966.

———. *Writings in the Time of War.* Translated by René Hague. New York: Harper & Row, 1968.

———. *Science and Christ.* Translated by René Hague. New York: Harper & Row, 1968.

———. *Human Energy.* Translated by J. M. Cohen. New York: Harcourt, Brace, Jovanovich, 1969.

———. *Letters to Léontine Zanta.* Translated by Bernard Wall. New York: Harper & Row, 1969.

———. *How I Believe.* Translated by René Hague. New York: Harper & Row, 1969.

———. *Activation of Energy.* Translated by René Hague. New York: Harcourt, Brace, Jovanovich, 1971.

———. *Christianity and Evolution.* Translated by René Hague. New York: Harcourt, Brace, Jovanovich, 1971.

———. *Let Me Explain.* New York: Harper & Row, 1972.

———. *Les Directions de L'Avenir.* Paris: Éditions du Seuil, 1973.

———. *Lettres Intimes de Teilhard de Chardin à Auguste Valensin, Bruno de Solages, Henri du Lubac, André Ravier: 1919–1955.* Introduction and notes by Henri de Lubac. Paris: Aubier Montaigne, 1974.

———. "My Universe." In *Process Theology: Basic Writings,* edited by Ewert Cousins, 249–43. New York: Newman Press, 1974.

———. *Toward the Future.* Translated by René Hague. London: Collins, 1975.

———. *Oeuvres de Teilhard de Chardin.* Thirteen volumes. Paris: Éditions du Seuil, 1955–76.

———. *The Heart of Matter.* Translated by René Hague. New York: Harcourt, Brace, Jovanovich, 1978.

———. *The Human Phenomenon.* Translated by Sarah Appleton-Weber. Brighton: Sussex Academic Press, 1999.

———. *Lettres à Édouard Le Roy (1921–1946): Maturation d'une pensée.* Éditions Facultés Jesuites de Paris, 2008.

———. *Le Rayonnement d'une Amitié, Correspondance avec la Famille Bégouën (1922–1955).* Bruxelles: Lessius, 2011.

Teilhard de Chardin, Pierre, and Lucille Swan. *The Letters of Teilhard de Chardin and Lucille Swan.* Edited by Thomas M. King, SJ, and

Mary Wood Gilbert. Scranton, PA: University of Scranton Press, 2001.

Teilhard de Chardin, Pierre, and Ursula King. *Pierre Teilhard de Chardin: Writings*. Modern Spiritual Masters Series. Maryknoll, NY: Orbis Books, 1999.

Thigpen, Paul. *Extraterrestrial Intelligence and the Catholic Faith: Are We Alone in the Universe with God and the Angels?* Gastonia: Tan Books, 2022.

Thomas Aquinas. *On the Truth of the Catholic Faith, Summa Contra Gentiles, Book Two: Creation*. Translated by James F. Anderson. Garden City, NY: Hanover House, 1956.

———. *Summa Theologiae*. Blackfriars edition. New York: McGraw Hill, 1972.

———. *The Power of God*. Translated by Richard J. Regan. Oxford: Oxford University Press, 2012.

Todd, Patrick. *The Open Future: Why Future Contingents Are All False*. New York: Oxford University Press, 2021.

Tracy, David. "Analogy, Metaphor, and God-Language: Charles Hartshorne." *Modern Schoolman* 62 (1985): 249–64.

Tresmontant, Claude. *Pierre Teilhard de Chardin: His Thought*. Baltimore: Helicon Press, 1959.

Tucker, Mary Evelyn, and John H. Berthrong, eds. *Confucianism and Ecology: The Interrelation of Heaven, Earth, and Humans*. Religions of the World and Ecology. Cambridge. Distributed by Harvard University Press for the Harvard University Center for the Study of World Religions, 1998.

Tucker, Mary Evelyn, John Grim, and Andrew Angyal. *Thomas Berry: A Biography*. Illustrated edition. New York: Columbia University Press, 2019.

Turner, Ben. "James Webb Telescope Spots Thousands of Milky Way Look-alikes That 'Shouldn't Exist' Swarming across the Early Universe." *LiveScience* (2023).

UN General Assembly, Resolution 1348 (XIII), December 13, 1958.

Unger, Peter. *All the Power in the World*. Oxford: Oxford University Press, 2006.

Vainio, Olli-Pekka Vainio. *Cosmology in Theological Perspective: Understanding Our Place in the Universe*. Grand Rapids, MI: Baker Academic, 2018.

Vanderwerth, W. C., ed. *Indian Oratory: Famous Speeches by Noted Indian Chieftains*. Norman: University of Oklahoma Press, 1971.

Bibliography

Viney, Donald Wayne. "Teilhard de Chardin and Process Philosophy Redux." *Process Studies* 35, no. 1 (Spring-Summer 2006): 12–42.

———. "Teilhard: Le Philosophe malgré l'Église." In *Rediscovering Teilhard's Fire*, edited by Kathleen Duffy, SSJ, 69–88. Philadelphia: Saint Joseph's University Press, 2010.

———. "Teilhard, Medawar, and the New Atheism." In *From Teilhard to Omega: Co-Creating an Unfinished Universe*, edited by Ilia Delio, 127–48. Maryknoll, NY: Orbis Books, 2014.

———. "Evolution's God: Teilhard de Chardin and the Varieties of Process Theology." *Teilhard Studies* 82 (Spring 2021): 1–22.

———. "Something Unheard Of: The Unparalleled Legacy of Jules Lequyer." *Process Studies* 51, no. 2 (Fall-Winter 2022): 143–68.

———, trans. "Meeting with Father Teilhard de Chardin." [Translation of a 1951 interview of Teilhard.] See Marcel Brion above and Appendix in current volume.

Viney, Donald Wayne, and George W. Shields. *The Mind of Charles Hartshorne: A Critical Examination*. Anoka, MN: Process Century Press, 2020.

Vlasic, Ivan. "The Relevance of International Law to Emerging Trends in the Law of Outer Space." In *The Future of the International Legal Order*, volume 2: *Wealth and Resources*, edited by Richard A. Falk and Cyril E. Black, 265–328. Princeton, NJ: Princeton University Press, 1970.

Wallace, Alfred Russel. *The World of Life: A Manifestation of Creative Power, Directive Mind and Ultimate Purpose*. London: Chapman and Hall, 1914.

Walsh, John Evangelist. *The Science Fraud of the Century and Its Solution: Unraveling Piltdown*. New York: Random House, 1996.

Weinandy, T. G. *Does God Change? The Word's Becoming in the Incarnation*. Still River, MA: St. Bede Publications, 1985.

Weintraub, David A. *Religions and Extraterrestrial Life: How Will We Deal with It?* Cham, Switzerland: Springer, 2014.

Whitehead, Alfred North. *The Concept of Nature*. Cambridge: Cambridge University Press, 1920.

———. *Science and the Modern World*. New York: Macmillan, 1925.

———. *Religion in the Making*. New York: Macmillan, 1926.

———. *Process and Reality*. New York: Macmillan, 1929.

———. *Adventures of Ideas*. New York: Macmillan, 1933.

———. *Modes of Thought*. New York: Macmillan, 1938.

———. *Essays in Science and Philosophy*. New York: Philosophical Library, 1948.

———. *The Function of Reason*. Boston: Beacon Press, 1958 [1929].

———. *Science and Philosophy*. Paterson: Littlefield, Adams & Co., 1964.

———. *Modes of Thought*. New York: The Free Press, 1968.

———. *Process and Reality: An Essay in Cosmology*. Corrected edition. Edited by David Ray Griffin and Donald Sherburne. New York: The Free Press, 1978 [1929].

———. *Religion in the Making*. Introduction by Judith A. Jones. Glossary by Randall E. Auxier. New York: Fordham University Press, 1996 [1927].

———. "Religious Psychology of the Western Peoples." March 30, 1939. ADDO20 Whitehead Research Library (2019).

———. "First Lecture." ADD018 Whitehead Research Library (1924).

Whitla, William. "Sin and Redemption in Whitehead and Teilhard de Chardin." *Anglican Theological Review* 47 (1965): 81–95.

Whitt, Laurie Anne, et al. "Indigenous Perspectives." In *A Companion to Environmental Philosophy*, edited by Dale Jamieson, 3–20. Malden: Blackwell Publishing, 2001.

Wieman, Henry Nelson. "A Philosophy of Religion: Review of *Process and Reality* by Alfred North Whitehead." *The Journal of Religion* 10, no. 1 (January 1930): 137–39.

Wieman, Henry Nelson, and Bernard Eugene Meland. *American Philosophies of Religion*. New York: Harper & Brothers, 1936.

Wildiers, N. M. "Cosmology and Christology." In *Process Theology: Basic Writings*, edited by Ewert Cousins, 269–82. New York: Newman Press, 1971.

Wilkinson, David. *Science, Religion, and the Search for Extraterrestrial Intelligence*. Oxford: Oxford University Press, 2013.

Williams, Rowan. *Christ the Heart of Creation*. London: Bloomsbury Continuum, 2018.

Wilson, David Sloan. "Reintroducing Pierre Teilhard de Chardin to Modern Evolutionary Science." *Brain, Religion and Behavior* 13, no. 4 (2021): 443–57.

Woods, Mark. "Wilderness." In *A Companion to Environmental Philosophy*, edited by Dale Jamieson, 349–61. Malden: Blackwell Publishing, 2001.

———. *Rethinking Wilderness*. Peterborough, Ontario, Canada: Broadview Press, 2017.

Wright, Jerry R. "Dreams and the Archetypal Christ." Presentation. Natural Spirituality Regional Gathering, Toccoa, Georgia. February 12, 2011.

Zimmerli, Walther. *The Old Testament and the World*. Translated by John J. Scullion. London: SPCK, 1976.

Zwart, Hub. *Continental Philosophy of Technoscience*. Cham, Switzerland: Springer, 2021.

Contributors

John Becker, PhD, is a lecturer of religious studies at California State University, Long Beach. In 2017, he received the International Process Network's Young Scholar Award. He is a member of the Society for Buddhist-Christian Studies and a research fellow for The Institute for Postmodern Development of China, USA. His research interests include process thought, comparative theology (Buddhism-Christianity), religions and ecology, and religious pluralism. He is co-editor of *Process Thought and Roman Catholicism*.

Godehard Brüntrup, SJ, PhD, is a German professor of philosophy and member of the Jesuit Order. He studied philosophy in Munich and later earned his PhD on mental causation in Berlin in 1993. He also holds a degree in Catholic theology. He currently teaches metaphysics and philosophy of mind at the Munich School of Philosophy and St. Louis University. He is one of the architects of the revival of panpsychism in analytic philosophy, for which he began arguing in his introduction to the mind-body problem in Germany in 1993. This book had a significant impact on German theology where younger scholars began to explore the connections between theology, panpsychism, and panentheism. He is co-editor of *Panentheism and Panpsychism: Philosophy of Religion Meets Philosophy of Mind* (2020).

Andrew M. Davis, PhD, is an American process philosopher, theologian, and scholar of the cosmos. He is program director for the Center for Process Studies, where he researches, writes, and organizes conferences on various aspects of process-relational thought. An advocate of metaphysics and meaning in a hospitable universe, he approaches philosophy as the endeavor to systematically think through what reality must be like because we are a part of it. He is an author, editor, and co-editor of several books, including *Mind, Value, and Cosmos: On the Relational Nature of Ultimacy*, which was nominated for the International Society of Science and Religion's

398 Contributors

2022 Book Prize; and most recently, *Metaphysics of Exo-Life: Toward a Constructive Whiteheadian Cosmotheology.* Follow and subscribe to his work at andrewmdavis.info.

Ilia Delio, PhD, is a Franciscan Sister of Washington, DC, and an American theologian specializing in the area of science and religion, with interests in evolution, physics, and neuroscience, and the import of these for theology. She currently holds the Josephine C. Connelly Endowed Chair in Theology at Villanova University. She is the author of twenty books, including *The Unbearable Wholeness of Being: God, Evolution, and the Power of Love*, which received the 2014 Silver Nautilus Book Award and a third-place Catholic Press Association Award for Faith and Science, and more recently, *The Not-Yet God: Carl Jung, Teilhard de Chardin, and the Relational Whole.* She holds two honorary doctorates, one from St. Francis University in 2015, and one from Sacred Heart University in 2020. She founded the Center for Christogenesis in 2016 to advance the evolutionary vision of Teilhard de Chardin.

Daniel A. Dombrowski, PhD, is professor of philosophy at Seattle University. Among his twenty-two books are *Rethinking the Ontological Argument: A Neoclassical Theistic Perspective*; *Contemporary Athletics and Ancient Greek Ideals*; *Process Philosophy and Political Liberalism: Rawls, Whitehead, Hartshorne*; and most recently, *Process Mysticism.* He is editor of the journal *Process Studies* and is past-president of the Metaphysical Society of America.

Kathleen Duffy, PhD, is professor emerita of physics, director of the Institute for Religion and Science at Chestnut Hill College, president of the American Teilhard Association, associate editor of Teilhard Studies, and serves on the board of Cosmos and Creation. She is the recipient of the Doctor of Humane Letters, Honoris Causa from Iona College, New Rochelle, New York, October 18, 2009; was inducted into the Hall of Fame for Catholic Witness, St. Hubert High School in 2005; and received the John Templeton Foundation Quality and Excellence in Teaching Award in 1998. She has published award-winning books, including *Teilhard's Mysticism: Seeing the Inner Face of Evolution* and *Teilhard's Struggle: Embracing the Work of Evolution.*

Paolo Gamberini, PhD, was born in Ravenna, Italy, in 1960 and entered the Jesuit Order in 1983. He earned his master of arts in philosophy at the Sacred Heart University in Milan. He studied theology in Germany

(Frankfurt and Tübingen), where he received his doctorate at the Jesuit School of Philosophy and Theology in Frankfurt. He has been working since 1985 in the Ecumenical movement especially with Anglicans and Lutherans, and has taught at various universities abroad and in the United States. From August 2015 to June 2018, he was associate professor at the University of San Francisco. He is the author of nearly a hundred articles and essays, and a few books, dealing with systematic theology, Christology, the doctrine of the Trinity, ecumenical theology, and spirituality. He has recently published a book titled *Deus 2.0. Rethinking the Christian Faith from the Post-Theistic Perspective.*

John F. Haught, PhD, is an American theologian. He is a Distinguished Research Professor at Georgetown University. He specializes in Roman Catholic systematic theology, with a particular interest in issues pertaining to physical cosmology, evolutionary biology, geology, and Christianity. He has authored numerous books and articles, including *The New Cosmic Story: Inside Our Awakening Universe*; *The Cosmic Vision of Teilhard de Chardin*; and *God after Einstein: What's Really Going On in the Universe?*

Catherine Keller, PhD, is George T. Cobb Professor of Constructive Theology in the Graduate Division of Religion, Drew University. She works amid the tangles of ecosocial, pluralist, feminist philosophy of religion and theology—and always as a process thinker. Among her many books are *Face of the Deep*; *On the Mystery*; *Cloud of the Impossible*; and *Political Theology of the Earth*. She has co-edited several volumes of the Drew Transdisciplinary Theological Colloquium, most recently *Political Theology on Edge: Ruptures of Justice and Belief in the Anthropocene*. Her latest monograph is *Facing Apocalypse: Climate, Democracy and Other Last Chances*.

Sheri D. Kling, PhD, is an author, speaker, singer, and spiritual mentor who draws from wisdom and mystical traditions, relational worldviews, depth psychology, and the intersection of spirituality and science to help people find meaning, belonging, and transformation. She regularly delivers dynamic "Music & Message" presentations to groups and offers courses, concerts, and spiritual retreats. Dr. Kling is director of Process & Faith and the John Cobb Legacy Fund and a faculty member of the Haden Institute. She sees her mission as midwifing wholeness in individuals, organizations, communities, and culture. She is the author *A Process Spirituality: Christian and Transreligious Resources for Transformation.*

400   *Contributors*

Steve McIntosh, JD, is an integral philosopher who has been greatly inspired by both Whitehead and Teilhard. He is author of the books *Developmental Politics, The Presence of the Infinite, Evolution's Purpose,* and *Integral Consciousness*. He is also coauthor of *Conscious Leadership*, with John Mackey and Carter Phipps. McIntosh is president of the Institute for Cultural Evolution think-tank, which is advancing a developmental approach to politics. His work has appeared in *USA Today, Real Clear Politics, The Daily Beast, The Hill, Areo Magazine,* and *The Developmentalist*. He has been interviewed on NPR, the Glenn Show, Rebel Wisdom, Oxford Review, and many other podcasts. His author website (stevemcintosh.com) includes extensive excerpts and videos on each of his books.

Robert Nicastro, is a PhD candidate in the Theology and Religious Studies program at Villanova University. He earned a bachelor of arts in philosophy from Gannon University in Erie, Pennsylvania, and a Master of Arts in Theology from Saint Mary's Seminary and University in Baltimore, Maryland. His research focuses on the interrelationship of cosmology, theology, and philosophy, and the implications of a coherent metaphysical worldview for addressing issues of social and enhancement technologies.

Elaine Padilla, PhD, is associate professor of philosophy and religion, Latinx/ Latin American Studies at the University of La Verne. Padilla constructively interweaves current philosophical discourse with Christianity, Latin American and Latino/a religious thought, mysticism, ecology, gender, and race. She is the author of *Divine Enjoyment: A Theology of Passion and Exuberance*, and co-editor of a three-volume project with Peter C. Phan: *Contemporary Issues of Migration and Theology; Theology of Migration in the Abrahamic Religions;* and *Christianities in Migration: The Global Perspective*. She has also published numerous articles and chapters, and is currently drafting a manuscript provisionally titled *The Darkness of Being*, in which she explores views on the soul and interiority with implications for race and gender.

Matthew David Segall, PhD, is associate professor in the Philosophy, Cosmology, and Consciousness program at California Institute of Integral Studies in San Francisco, California. He is the author of *Physics of the World-Soul: Whitehead's Adventure in Cosmology* and *Crossing the Threshold: Etheric Imagination in the Post-Kantian Process Philosophy of Schelling and Whitehead*. He is a multidisciplinary researcher focusing on applications of process philosophy across the natural and social sciences. He blogs regularly at footnotes2plato.com.

Donald Wayne Viney, PhD, earned degrees in philosophy from Colorado State University (BA, 1977) and the University of Oklahoma (MA, 1979; PhD, 1982). He is the first three-time recipient of the title of University Professor at Pittsburg State University (Kansas), having taught philosophy and religion at PSU from 1984 until 2022 before becoming professor emeritus. Professor Viney publishes mostly in the areas of the history of philosophy and the philosophy of religion with special interest in the works of Charles Hartshorne, Jules Lequyer, and Pierre Teilhard de Chardin. He sits on the editorial boards of *Process Studies*, *The American Journal of Theology and Philosophy*, and *The Midwest Quarterly*. In his spare time Viney performs and composes music.

Index

Aboux, Marie-Louise, 331
Abraham, 33, 313
absence-of-analysis argument, 74, 76
Adam, 10, 367
adventure, 34, 185
  of Christopher Columbus, 189
  novelty as an element of, 109–10
  right action as included in, 43
  unity of adventure, 190, 201
  the universe as an adventure, 310–11
  upward adventure, 197, 202
  as the urge of the universe, 179
  vividness, as inspiring, 199
  Whitehead's spirit of adventure, 3
  wild element in, 200
Analysis of Matter (Russell), 84
Anderson, Johan Gunnar, 343
Andrews, Roy Chapman, 344
angelism, 38
An hour with (periodical series), 338
Anselm, Saint, 53–54
Anthropocene, 28, 116
anthropocentrism, 137, 146–51, 292, 293, 294, 296
anthropocosmism, 137, 146–51, 165
anthropogenesis, 129, 369
anthropomorphism, 32, 73, 146, 150
anticipation, 310, 312–13, 314, 351
Appleton-Weber, Sarah, 212–13, 215
arcology (architectural ecology), 298
Aristotelian thought, 61, 145, 180, 362
Aristotle, 29, 93, 127, 167, 168
Arnold, Matthew, 308
Artson, Bradley Shavit, 255, 256, 260
astrotheology, 135–36. 176
Augustine of Hippo, Saint, 19, 29, 116, 361
axial religions, 239, 271

Bailey, Lee Worth, 188, 196, 198, 207–8
Baldwin effect, 55
baptism, 38
Barbour, Ian, 55–57, 174
Barfield, Owen, 130
Barrett, Nathaniel, 161
Bégouën, Max, 333, 336, 337
Bégouën, Simone, 6, 333
Berdyaev, Nicholas, 50
Bergson, Henri, 41, 86
  Creative Evolution, 9, 107
  on original unity and multiplicity, 359
  philosophical originality of, 116–17
  on stability as constituted by
    momentary actual occasions, 58
  Teilhard and Whitehead as inspired
    by, 3, 11, 37, 84, 107, 348
Berkeley, George, 62
Bernard of Clairvaux, Saint, 94, 96
Berry, Thomas, 47, 116, 300
Bezos, Jeff, 190
bifurcation of nature, 15, 57, 61, 63
Big History, 267, 280–81, 282
Billy, André, 335
biosphere, 24, 25, 193, 267, 274, 280
Bjornerud, Marcia, 25
Black, Davidson, 343
Boehme, Jacob, 231, 364
Bohm, David, 73, 217, 253
Boule, Marcellin, 18, 337, 342, 343
Boussac, Jean, 343
Breuil, Henri, 6
Brion, Marcel, *330*, 331–32, 336, 338, 339–44
Brummer, Vincent, 255
Bruno, Giordano, 114, 141
Burtt, E. A., 15
Byrne, Patrick, 220

404   Index

Cambridge Conversazione Society, 34
Carnap, Rudolf, 62
Catherine of Genoa, Saint, 101
cellular automata, 74–76
centration principle, 57, 82
   Christ as dynamic centration, 42
   convergence and, 235, 350
   in evolution, 219, 234
   Omega as a principle of, 219, 221
   as personalized, 39, 40
   Teilhard, emphasis on, 41, 56
Chalmers, David, 69–71, 76, 81
Chapman, G. Clarke, 109, 110
Chief Seattle, 206
chilarity, 125
Christian, David, 281
Christic, 325, 326
   Christic emergence, 318, 321–23, 327
   Christic sense of Teilhard, 321, 323,
      324, 327
   in *Creative Evolution,* 107
   third Christic nature, 236–37
Christification, 106, 107, 109, 110, 369
Christ in a Pluralistic Age (Cobb), 49, 291,
   293, 298
Christocentrism, 293, 299
Christogenesis, 293, 297
   anthropogenesis, as the end of, 129
   Center for Christogenesis, 35
   cosmogenesis as, 236
   Omega point of Christogenesis, 275,
      294, 323
Christology, 95, 115
   cosmic Christology, 56, 297
   evolution and, 114, 116
   of John Cobb, 293, 298
   secularization, problem of, 131
circular independence, 77
classical theism, 51, 53
   argument from design, 56
   creation ex nihilo as a central notion, 17
   creative transformation, missing in, 52
   on God as the fullness of existence, 58
   God's love in, 59, 60
   Greek philosophy and biblical
      imagery, reconciling, 245, 254
   monopolarity in, 39–40, 48, 102
   omnipotent God, belief in, 45, 46, 106
   supernaturality in, 42–43, 44, 53
   Teilhard and, 41–48

two extremes, viewing God from,
   253–54
Unmoved Mover of, 60, 92
climate change, 292–93, 299, 309
Cline, Michael, 7
Cobb, John B., Jr., 299, 361
   Christ, linking to the initial aim, 107
   on Christ as creative transformation,
      109
   Christ in a Pluralistic Age, 49, 291,
      293, 298
   as a process thinker, 50, 137
Columbus, Christopher, 189, 203
complexification, 157, 232
   continued development of, 241, 320
   cosmic urge toward, 125
   cosmogenesis and, 321
   in evolution, 154
   in movement from pre-life to life, 153
   something new as introduced
      through, 267
   as a Teilhardian term, 46, 218
   Whitehead on the trajectory toward,
      24
complexity-consciousness, 235, 345
   Christ as the Prime Mover of, 324
   evolution and, 222, 225
   monism and, 230–31
   Teilhard's law of complexity-
      consciousness, 13, 218
   universe as moving in the direction of,
      320–21
Comte de Buffon, Georges-Louis
   Leclerc, 126
concrescence, 157, 161
   completed concrescence, 21, 30
   as contrasted intensities, 273
   as a creative process, 16–17
   as discrete events in an interconnected
      series, 349–50, 354
   metaphysical unity of, 177–78
   physical and mental as united in, 156
   prehension of divine concrescence, 32
   process thought, concrescence in, 46
   the within as resonating with, 295
The Conscious Universe (Kafatos/Nadeau),
   217
consequent nature of God, 167, 297
   as everlasting, 365
   open-ended quality of, 33

Index   405

in panentheistic model, 99–100
primordial nature and, 40, 92, 173–74, 296, 299
   Whitehead as describing, 20–21, 30–31, 97, 132
   the world, contributing to, 174, 364, 370
Copernicus, Nicolaus, and Copernican thought, 61, 139, 140–41
cosmic convergence, 318, 319–21, 323, 327, 370
cosmic epochs, 28–29, 129, 174, 370
cosmic holism, 212–16
cosmic nature, 237, 324, 327
cosmic trinitarianism, 109
cosmocentric ethics, 86, 166
cosmogenesis, 120, 238
   as Christogenesis, 236, 325
   cosmos, replacing idea of, 13
   geocentric cosmos giving way to, 141, 145
   God at the center of, 96, 229
   law of complexity-consciousness in, 320–21
   noogenesis, as leading into, 321
   Omega, as consummated in, 332
   ontogenesis, presupposing, 154, 158
   as an unfolding process, 138, 168, 286
cosmological de-centering, 139–40, 143, 146, 150
cosmological solipsism, 143, 165, 169
cosmotheandrism, 230, 235, 237, 240
cosmotheology, 135, 176
counter-agency, 24, 123
Cowell, Sion, 46
Cox, David, 108
creatio ex nihilo, 11, 17, 22, 99–100, 169, 257, 360–61
creationism, 7, 126
Creative Evolution (Bergson), 9, 107
Creative Synthesis and Philosophic Method (Hartshorne), 37
creative transformation, 114, 298
   classical theism, as missing from, 52
   concrescence as related to, 16
   divine Seed as fueling, 101
   future fulfillment, for the sake of, 250
   in metaphysics of union, 11
   presence of Christ in, 109

in process thought, 49–50
   as a transreligious phenomenon, 110
creative union, 324, 360
   amortization of Christ in, 325–26
   God of, 256–60
   law of creative union, 235, 320
   metaphysics of, 11, 246
Crespy, Georges, 45
Darwin, Charles, 116, 123, 125–28, 141, 225, 253, 341
d'Aubarède, Gabriel, 338
Davis, Andrew M., 297
Dawson, Charles, 337, 341
death of thought, 305–9, 312, 313, 314
De consideratione libri quinque (Bernard of Clairvaux), 94
deep time, 26, 28, 119
Deism, 22–23
Delio, Ilia, 258, 268, 269, 275, 297, 302, 303
Dennett, Daniel, 124
Descartes, René, 62, 119
   Cartesian bifurcation, 57, 61, 67
   Cartesian ego and the wild other, 180
   cogito, ergo sum axiom, 182, 187
   concept of matter, critique of, 78–81
   dualism of, 14, 57, 64–65, 198, 354
   modern science and, 22, 179
   theory of evolution, prefiguring, 125
   turning point, representing, 181–82
Descent of Man (Darwin), 125
Desjardins, Joseph R., 184–85
determinism, 23, 313
   chaoticism as a logical contrary to, 59
   dialectical development and, 286
   freedom as linked with, 350, 355–58
   Omega, Teilhardian determinism in, 299, 301
   scientific materialism and, 240
Developmental Politics (McIntosh), 282
dialectical development, 285–86, 289
Dialogues Concerning Natural Religion (Hume), 22
differentiating union, 4, 221
   multiplicity not lost in, 90
   as organic union of the world, 301–2
   pantheism and, 172–73, 231, 233–34
   personalized evolution, as undergirding, 232–33

406 Index

true union as differentiating, 27, 31, 223, 235, 258, 345
Whiteheadian contrast and, 294
dipolarity, 48, 52
dipolarity of God, 33, 88, 102, 103, 171, 173
divine dipolarity, 132, 167
physical and mental poles of, 58, 156, 173
in process theism, 40, 99
divine entanglement, 97, 230, 232, 233, 236–38, 252, 277
divine eros, 208, 259
divine imperiality, 253–56
divine love, 54, 167
biblical portrait of, 39, 252, 253, 256, 260–62
Christ as entangled in, 236
in classical theism, 254
co-creation as part of, 251–53, 255, 257, 259
in exotheologies of Whitehead and Teilhard, 175
God as the energy of, 230, 233
memories as a permanent part of, 258
as relational, 12, 249, 250, 256, 259, 260
theology of divine love, 245
universe as grounded in, 237
divine lure, 4, 132, 203, 259, 293, 299
divine nature, 12, 30, 48, 133, 171–72
divine omnipotence, 45–46, 59, 140, 169, 355, 358, 361, 371
divine omnipresence, 51
divine omniscience, 46, 52
divine omni-sufficiency, 48, 169
divine transformation, 109
Dobzhansky, Theodosius, 52
Donceel, Joseph, 38
d'Ouince, René, 8, 331, 334
Dourley, John P., 104
"Dover Beach" (poem), 308
Duffy, Kathleen, 34
Dussel, Enrique, 182–83
dynamis, God as, 93
Earhart, Amelia, 190
ecotheology, 293, 299–300
Eddington, Arthur, 78, 83, 84
Edinger, Edward, 103
Einstein, Albert, 14–15, 116, 214, 216, 253, 310, 311, 313

emergence, 14, 233
Christic emergence, 318, 321–23, 327
evolutionary emergence, 151, 224, 236, 280–81
of human consciousness, 43, 75, 222–24, 226
of modernity, 61, 283–84
in the noosphere, 267, 283, 284, 287
panpsychist position on, 65, 72, 74
of progressive postmodernity, 284–85
sequential emergence, 282–83
strong *vs.* weak emergence, 66–69
energeia (activity), 93
enkrateia, practice of, 191
Enxing, Julia, 33
Eoanthropus (Piltdown Man), 336–37, 341–42
epistemic asymmetry, 64
Eros of the Universe, 190, 200, 202
Esse, metaphysics of, 167, 168
eugenics, 122, 132, 240
evil, 46, 54
in the evolutionary process, 45, 165, 167, 169, 365, 366
as growing alongside the good, 301
in Hellenistic thought, 361
the problem of evil, 12, 365–68
sin and evil, 367, 371
strength against strength, as the violence of, 194–95, 201
Whitehead on, 132, 170, 181, 361, 367
evolution, 278, 312
absolute values, as oriented toward, 161–62
beauty, as aiming for, 128–29
biological evolution, 139, 225, 281, 282, 342
of convergence, 218–19
cosmic evolution, 110, 139, 150, 151, 161, 163, 165, 167, 224, 226
cosmogenesis, evolutionary novelty in, 145
cultural evolution, 225, 279, 281, 282, 283, 285, 286, 288, 289
directed evolution, 211–12, 220, 223, 225, 226, 240
evolutionary cosmology, 113, 137–38, 151–54

evolutionary emergence, 151, 224, 236, 280–81

evolutive Christ, 42, 123, 236, 297, 302, 317–18, 322, 323, 324–26, 335

evolutive God, 38, 40, 87, 90, 91, 116, 133, 171

evolutive universe, 12, 45, 63, 87, 169

geocentrism collapse, evolutionist point of view following, 141

human consciousness as part of, 76, 155–56, 224, 320–21

love as core in, 50, 235, 257

mechanistic and mindless, as more than, 4, 124

morality, evolution of, 162–65

natural selection and, 24, 123, 127–28, 211, 220

neo-Christianity as coming to terms with, 41

of nonhumans, 294

noosphere evolution, 239, 267, 279, 281, 282, 283, 285, 287–89, 368

as Omega, 87–88, 106, 172, 219–21, 237–40, 243, 269, 295, 321, 325

pantheism and the God of evolution, 229–34

patience of the slow evolutionary process, 170

as personalized, 231, 232–33, 235–36, 240

radial energy as spiritualizing the evolutionary process, 268

religion as an aspect of, 238–40, 266–67, 327

as scientifically explicable, 361

Teilhard as an evolutionary scientist, 35, 55, 214, 319

theory of evolution, 116, 125–26, 253, 319, 327

three stages of evolution, 222–23

transformism, evolution as, 9, 126

exotheology, 135–38, 144, 145, 175

extension, modes of, 62, 79–81, 155, 156, 349

the extranatural, 42–43

extraterrestrial ethic, 166. *See also* outer space

Fermi Paradox, 159

Fermi solution, 207

Ferré, Frederick, 166

Ford, Lewis, 106, 109–10, 136, 145, 153, 159, 261–62

formal causality, 96

Foucault, Michel, 194

Francis, Pope, 314

Francis of Assisi, 56, 191

Fretheim, Terence, 247, 248, 250, 251–52, 256

the future, 193, 310

the convergent future, 27, 356, 368

directions of the future, 4, 22–33

ecotheology and the mattering future, 299–300

evolutive understanding of, 96, 161, 222, 240–41, 243

final thought in, 305–306

hope in the future, 49, 262, 273, 292, 314

humanity's pivotal role in, 251, 275

Omega in the future, 106, 172, 174, 219–20, 292, 364

open future, 13, 23, 27

radial energy and lure of the future, 122

religion of the future, 266–67, 268–70, 271, 272–74, 276–78, 326–27

Teilhard as confident towards, 5, 59, 114, 291

as unknown to God, 52, 251, 253, 364

Whitehead on, 28, 59, 201, 274, 292, 361, 364, 370

the world, future of, 26–27, 129, 222, 239, 242, 261, 368–71

Galileo, 61, 140–41, 270

geocentrism, 140, 141, 166

geosphere, 267, 274

Gilson, Etienne, 127

Goethe, Johann Wolfgang von, 121

Gould, Stephen Jay, 336

grace, 296, 298

the Great Fact, 283

Great Presence, 50

Griffin, David Ray, 50, 106, 107, 109, 137, 164, 288

Handley, George, 209

Harari, Yuval, 281

Hartshorne, Charles, 17, 32

Creative Synthesis and Philosophic Method, 37

408 Index

on distinction in the divine existence-
  actuality, 48
on emergent dualism, 14
finite minds, on the eternal existence
  of, 157
God, on the abstract essence of, 40
on God as a surpasser, 33
Jesuit motto, affinity with Teilhard
  over, 59–60
nature, on directionality in, 56
neoclassical theism of, 39, 51
*Omnipotence and Other Theological
  Mistakes*, 45–46
panpsychism, attributing to, 38
a priori rationality, emphasizing,
  53–54
as a process thinker, 41, 44, 47, 49, 52,
  55, 57–58
"Whitehead's Revolutionary Concept
  of Prehension," 16
on the withinness of other creatures, 13
Haught, John F., 35, 43, 47, 137, 159,
  171, 300
Hegel, G. W. F., 131, 231, 253, 286, 288,
  364
Henning, Brian, 166
Heschel, Abraham, 249, 254
Hesketh, Ian, 281
Heylighen, Francis, 211, 225
Higgins-Freese, Jonna, 192
Highwater, Jamake, 181, 184, 192, 205
Hinduism, 277, 332, 346
hope, 49, 242
  anticipation as putting on the virtue
    of hope, 313, 314
  Christian hope, 277, 327
  collective hope for the future, 292
  contrasting patterns of hope, 273–76
  optimism, replacing with hope, 299
  Teilhard, bringing a message of, 303,
    308, 339, 368
Hopkins, Gerard Manley, 56
Hughes, J. Donald, 207
Humani Generis encyclical, 10
Hume, David, 22, 80, 117, 119
Huxley, Julian, 155, 224
hylomorphism, 38, 40, 44, 49, 57
hyperphysics, 115, 230, 233
ideal ends, 190, 197, 199, 201, 203, 206
implosion, 40–41

Inge, Dean, 232
initial aim, 21, 103, 106, 132, 173, 295,
  296, 298, 299
integral philosophy, 282–83, 289
intelligent design, 116
interdependence of energy, 295
interiority, 24, 40–41, 42, 47, 84, 117,
  156, 218, 249, 352
intrinsic properties, 71, 76, 78, 80
Irenaeus of Lyons, 361
James, William, 28, 76, 129
James Webb Space Telescope, 135, 146,
  176, 324
Jeans, James, 217
Jesus Christ, 104, 191
  body of Christ, 110, 364
  Christ-Omega, 97, 107, 236, 323,
    324–26
  Cosmic Christ, 19, 38, 42, 53, 91, 233,
    322, 369, 371
  as creative transformation, 109
  divine love, Christ as entangled in,
    236
  in evolution, 42, 123, 236, 297, 302,
    317–18, 322, 323, 324–26, 335
  faith in Christ, 238, 299
  God's aim as fulfilled in the life of
    Jesus, 106
  on heaven as within us, 140–41
  Jung on the archetypal Christ, 108–9
  as Logos, 42, 106, 107, 110, 298
  the natural world as Christ incarnate,
    130
  as risen, 357
  Sacred Heart of Jesus, 318, 321–22
  second coming of Christ, 42
  Teilhard, mystical encounter with, 114
  third nature of Christ, 236–37
  Transcendent Christ, 327
  union in Christ, 321, 369
Joachim of Flora, 109
Johnson, A. H., 32
Johnson, Mark, 246–47
Jonas, Hans, 307
Jung, Carl, 103–4, 105, 106, 107–9, 110
"Jung and Christology" (Chapman), 109
Jungel, Eberhard, 245
Kafatos, Menas, 217
Kant, Immanuel, 63, 80–81, 119, 126
Kazantzakis, Nikos, 38

Kelsey, Morton, 107
King, Thomas, 117, 229
King, Ursula, 107, 241
   on deep evolution in the mind of
      Teilhard, 25, 26
   dual belonging, on the need for, 277
   harmonized complexity, on Teilhard
      advocating for, 268
   hope for the future, on Teilhard
      promoting, 242
   love, on Teilhard critiquing traditional
      concept of, 257
   on the mysticism of Teilhard, 101–2
   self-evolution, on responsibility for,
      274–75
   on spirit and matter as one in
      Teilhard, 106
Kirsch, Adam, 309
Kripke, Saul, 70
Kugel, James, 247, 249
Kuntz, Paul, 19
Lacroix, Alfred, 343
Lakoff, George, 246–47
Lamarck, J. B., 126–28
Lamarckian theory, 55, 124
LaPlace, Pierre-Simon, 23
Las Casas, Bartolomé de, 180
Laudato Si' encyclical, 314
law of recurrence, 213, 235, 345
Lazlo, Ervin, 216
Ledóchowski, Wlodimir, 18–19
Lee, Bernard, 54–55, 103
Lee, Keekok, 193
Lefèvre, Fréderic, 338
Lefevre, Luc, 335
Le Figaro Littéraire (periodical), 335
Leibniz, Gottfried W., 62, 73, 78–79, 80,
   81, 84–85, 86
Le Roy, Édouard, 321
Leroy, Pierre, 3, 6, 25, 144, 331
Levin, Janna, 306
*L'Evolution Rédemptrice du P. Teilhard de
   Chardin* (Lefevre), 335
Licent, Emile, 343
Lightyear (film), 188
Lindbergh, Charles, 189, 197–98
Logical Structure of the World (Carnap), 62
Loomer, Bernard, 259
Lowe, Victor, 34, 161
Lubac, Henri de, 42, 360

Lyons, James, 237
Macauley, David, 190, 192, 194, 195–96
Mach, Ernst, 72
Machado-Ruiz, Antonio, 205
Mathews, Freya, 80
McCown, J. H., 34–35
McDaniel, Jay, 47
Medawar, Peter, 35
Meeting (periodical series), 338
Meeting with Father Teilhard de Chardin
   (interview), 330, 331–37, 338–46
Mesle, C. Robert, 260
metanoia as a turn in direction, 198–99,
   200
Metaphors We Live By (Lakoff/Johnson),
   246–47
metaphysical zombies, 70, 76
Metaphysics of Exo-Life (Davis), 297
Mignolo, Walter, 178, 180, 187, 195
Mind (journal), 35
the mindless universe, 306–8
Minkowski, Hermann, 62
miracles, 42–43, 44
modernity, 63, 182
   commerce in, 183, 204
   darker side of western modernity,
      178–79, 209
   emergence of, 61, 283–84
   imperial Other as a transcendental
      aspect of, 195
   modern civilized/colonial savage
      divide, 180
   postmodernism as moving beyond,
      285, 287
   religious traditions, engaging with,
      265–66
   Teilhard and Whitehead as culturally
      modernist, 289
   the watchman as a god of modernity,
      194
monadology, 79, 84–85
Monadology (Leibniz), 84
monism, 89, 230
   Christianity as monist, 231
   dual-aspect monism, 156–57, 171,
      217–19
   monistic physicalism, 64
   neutral monism, 72
   parts *vs.* total process in, 349
   relative monism, 92–96, 100

410   Index

Russellian monism, 69, 81
Teilhard, monistic tendencies of, 90,
    217–18, 350, 368, 370–71
monogenism, 10
monopolarity, 39, 48, 102, 103–4
Mooney, Christopher, 40, 364
Mortier, Jeanne, 6–7, 317, 331, 333, 335
multiverse, 314–15
mutual relatedness, 97, 99, 120, 197, 259
mysticism of identification *vs.* mysticism
    of union, 358
Nadeau, Robert, 217
Nagel, Thomas, 13, 74, 308–9
natural science, 61, 62, 115, 116, 119–20,
    151, 354
natural theology, 56, 347
Nature Alive concept, 295
Naturphilosophie (Schelling), 121
Newman, John Henry, Saint, 17, 34
Newsweek (periodical), 7
Newton, Isaac, 15, 23, 61, 62, 270
Newtonian worldview, 14, 15, 23, 61, 349
New York Times (periodical), 305–6, 311
Nicholas of Cusa, 93, 94–95, 96, 97, 98
nones (no religious affiliation), 265, 276
noogenesis, 158, 226, 236, 296, 321, 323
noosphere, 241, 297
    communion of saints, resembling,
        293
    cone shape, visualizing noosphere as,
        321, 322
    earth, noospheric layer of, 129
    emergence in, 267, 283, 284, 287
    energy generated in, 326
    extraterrestrial noospheres, 145,
        158–59, 241
    global unification in future of the
        noosphere, 368
    human consciousness, role in, 268,
        274, 275
    as inwardness and centeredness in
        nature, 43
    noosphere evolution, 239, 267, 279,
        281, 282, 283, 285, 287–89, 368
    Omega as linked with, 211, 296, 301
    Omega Point and, 225, 292, 296
    as a single, closed system, 273–74
    as the thinking envelope of the earth,
        25–26, 342
North, Robert, 360

not-yetness, 97, 274
    mind as open to the not-yet, 312–13
    of the multiverse, 314–15
    not-yet future, God knowing only as
        possibility, 170, 253
    See also the future
Nouvelles Littéraires (periodical), 331–32,
    335, 339
Oakley, K. P., 336
O'Connor, Flannery, 34–35
Omega, 114, 129
    Christ as Omega, 97, 107, 236, 323,
        324–26
    consequent nature and, 167, 299
    differentiating union in, 4, 27, 31, 90,
        221, 232–33
    as direction and destiny, 300
    divine energy of love as centrating
        presence of, 230
    as evolution, 87–88, 106, 172, 219–21,
        237–40, 243, 269, 295, 321, 325
    in the future, 106, 131, 172, 174,
        219–20, 292, 364
    God as Omega, 171, 172, 229, 240,
        258, 294
    noosphere and, 211, 296, 301
    Omega optimism, 292, 293, 294
    Omega principle, 212, 219–21
    as partially actual/partially
        transcendent, 33
    as a personalized principle, 232, 332
    Segall on Teilhard's affirmation of,
        122–23, 132
    sphere of the person in, 32
    totality of love, emerging from, 227
    unifying process in, 90
    as the whole of the whole, 219–21
Omega Point, 89, 335
    consequent nature, similarity to, 31
    as entangled and not yet fulfilled, 97
    eschatological optimism of, 292
    of evolution, 87–88, 106, 269, 321
    God, distinguishing from, 92
    inevitable reaching of, 42, 268, 275
    no dissolution in, 91
    noosphere, on the level of, 225
    open endedness of, 293, 302
    as recurring actualization, 276
*Omnipotence and Other Theological
    Mistakes* (Hartshorne), 45–46

O'Neil, Gerard, 188
ontogenesis, 125, 154, 158
ontological expansion, 178, 182
original sin, 18, 43, 114, 116, 144, 190, 212, 366–67
Origin of Species (Darwin), 125
Ortega, Mariana, 178
orthogenesis, 211
Our Knowledge of the External World (Russell), 62
outer space, 195, 204
    coloniality in outer space, 185–86, 205
    domestication of outer space, 190, 193, 196–97, 200
    exploitation of, 201
    as the last frontier, 187
    otherness, making room for, 208
    outer-space ethics, 193, 203
    outer-space technology, 179, 180, 189, 191, 202
    politics of outer space, 200, 202
    space cowboy trope, 188–89
    weaponization of, 207
Overbye, Dennis, 305–6, 307–9, 311, 312, 313
paleontology, 54, 119
    China, excavation work in, 5–6, 18, 114, 334, 339, 343
    Piltdown dig, 5, 336–37, 341–42
    Teilhard as a paleontologist, 7, 9, 38, 113, 319, 332, 338, 344
panentheism, 47, 296
    Jung on cooperation with the divine, 110
    pantheism, as a superior form on, 301
    relative monism, panentheistic model of, 99–100
    Teilhard as a panentheist, 46, 87, 173, 174, 294
    transcendence and immanence in, 89
panexperientialism, 48, 51, 74, 88, 155, 157, 160–61, 230
Panikkar, Raimon, 230
panpsychism, 51, 65
    Chalmers, argument for, 69, 71–72
    dual-aspect monism, comparing to, 217
    experiential pantheism as building on, 230
    finite minds, on the eternal existence of, 157

genetic argument for, 74–76
hylomorphism and, 38, 40
intrinsic natures argument, 77–78
Leibniz on living mirrors in, 78–79
misunderstanding of, 72–74
in modern times, 61, 63, 80
scholarly skepticism toward, 57
Teilhard as a panpsychist, 47–48, 65, 81–86, 155–56, 218
"Panpsychism" (Nagel), 74
pantheism, 91, 301
    God and creation as merged in, 95
    immanence as prominent in, 174
    reformatted Christianity and, 235
    Teilhard as a pantheist, 46–47, 229–34, 294, 358, 371
    two kinds of pantheism, 172–73
Pantocrator, God as, 45, 46
parousia, 42, 369–70
Passmore, John, 226
Pensée Catholique (periodical), 335
personalized holism, 211–12
Petavius, Dionysius, 270
philosophy of organism, 28, 206
    as an atomic theory of actuality, 152
    Goethean science, as resonant with, 121
    metaphysics of union and, 23
    novelty in complex unity, aiming for, 209
    outer-space experience in, 196–97, 199
    in *Process and Reality*, 15
    subject emerging from the world in, 119
physicalism, 62, 64, 65, 69, 70, 72, 75
Piltdown excavation, 5, 336–37, 341–42
Pithecanthropus of Java, 343
Pittenger, Norman, 110, 145
Piveteau, Jean, 7, 8
Planck, Max, 78, 216
Plato, 21, 29, 30, 44, 170
pleromization, 42, 48, 91, 235–36, 238
postmodernism, 284–85, 286–87, 287–89
predestination, 300, 358
prehension, 15, 17
    adventure and, 55, 190, 197, 201
    as experiential, 58, 161
    as feelings, 16, 30
    God and prehending, 32, 46, 365

412 *Index*

as microscopic and nonsensory, 47, 73
of the past, 29–30
in past events and future possibilities,
199
prehensive unification, 119–20
Prime Mover, 167, 168, 269, 324
primordial nature of God, 106, 132
divine dipolarity and, 167
as primordial and consequent, 40,
92, 96
as the realm of all possibilities, 20, 29
Whitehead on, 40, 92, 96–97, 173–74,
296, 364–65
Principia Mathematica (Whitehead/
Russell), 4
process metaphysics, 10, 153
Barbour on, 56–57, 231
freedom and determinism in, 355–58
science and religion as synthesized
in, 347
Viney on, 57–58
Whitehead and Teilhard, similarities
in concepts, 175, 370–71
Process Mysticism (Dombrowski), 102
process philosophy, 43, 178
cosmology and theology, mutual
relevance of, 136–37
spiritual teachings of evolution in, 280
Teilhard as a process thinker, 37–38,
43, 47–48, 49, 55, 56, 58, 137
Whitehead as a process thinker, 31,
49–50, 137
process theology, 21, 40
anthropocentric tendencies, not
yielding to, 296
body of God, revelations of, 302
divine aim operating in, 299
in eschatological and apocalyptic
frameworks, 301
exotheology and, 137, 145
the future, role in, 52, 103, 170
Hartshorne as a process theist, 54
miracles, not resorting to, 44–45
noosphere, contemplating, 297
pluralism as key to, 293
process metaphysics and, 58, 371
Teilhard as a process theist, 37, 38, 41,
46, 110
Whitehead and, 9, 21, 37, 49, 87, 113,
137, 145, 291, 347

Protestant ethic, 183, 204
Protestant theology, 140
purity, 43, 102, 209
Putnam, Hilary, 70
quantum mechanics, 76, 216
quantum physics, 23, 198–99, 230, 348
radial energy, 24, 26
in dual aspect monism, 156–57
in evolutionary theory, 268, 274, 295
inverse form of gravitation and,
123–24
law of entropy, violating, 351
tangential energy, distinguishing from,
86, 122, 268–69, 295
withinness of matter as a type of, 218
Rahner, Karl, 90, 93, 94–96
Rasmussen, Larry, 191
rational religion, 271–72
reductionism, 124, 219
the Reformation, 181
relational holism, 97, 229, 230
Religion of Tomorrow, 327
religiosity, 130, 265, 266, 267, 270–72,
276, 277
Renan, Ernest, 23
Rethinking Wilderness (Woods), 183
retrospective induction, 151
The Revolt Against Humanity (Kirsch),
309
Richardson, David, 47
Rightness, 162, 311–12, 314–15
Rosenberg, Gregg, 74
Rubenstein, Mary Jane, 231
Russell, Bertrand, 4, 5
on the intrinsic quality of the physical,
81, 216–17
on the mental experience of reality, 78
Our Knowledge of the External World,
62
panpsychism, as linked with, 69, 72,
84, 86
salvation, 56, 130, 369
sanctification, 56
Sartre, Jean-Paul, 8, 338
Schelling, F. W. J. von, 121, 231, 364
Scholasticism, 114, 145
on the actualization of potentiality, 355
Aristotelian racism, adopting, 180
early modern method in response to,
179

Esse metaphysics and, 167
primary and secondary causes in, 362
static universe of, 168, 349
Teilhard and, 10, 56, 57–59, 131
Schrödinger, Erwin, 216
scientific essentialism, 70
scientific materialism, 15, 121, 160, 219, 240, 266, 309
scientific status, questioning, 117
scientism, 205, 240
Second Vatican Council, 35, 277
secularization, 131
Segall, Matthew David, 259
sensus fidelium, 266
Sepúlveda, Juan Ginés, 180
SETI (Search for Extraterrestrial Intelligence), 159
Simpson, George, 116
Sinanthropus (Peking Man), 5, 343
Singer, June, 107–8
Smith, Bob, 189
Smith, Wolfgang, 115–16
Smith-Woodward, Arthur, 341
Solages, Bruno de, 11–12, 21, 144–45
Soleri, Paulo, 298–99, 300
Sophist (Plato), 21, 30
Space, Time, and Gravitation (Eddington), 83
Spinoza, Baruch, 73, 131
"The Spirit of Einstein and Teilhard in the 21st Century" (Lazlo), 216
Spirit of St. Louis (Lindbergh), 197
spiritual but not religious (SBNR), 265, 276, 277
Spitzer, Toba, 252, 262
Stebbing, L. Susan, 35
Steiner, Rudolf, 121
Strawson, Galen, 72, 217
suffering, 39, 40, 45, 109, 322, 327, 366–67
supervenience, 68–69
survival of the fittest, 123, 241
sustainability solution, 207
Swan, Lucille, 333
Swimme, Brian, 47
Tarnas, Richard, 286
Teilhard de Chardin, Pierre
Auvergne, early life in, 318, 339, 340, 342
Bergson, as inspired by, 116–17

bifurcation of nature, attempting to overcome, 57, 63
as censured, 18, 34–35, 113–14, 115, 334
clandestins, distribution of, 6, 8, 333–34, 335
classical theism and, 41–48
on continuing creation, 358–62, 370
on the Cosmic Christ, 38, 42, 53, 91, 322, 369, 371
cosmic holism of, 212–16
cosmic sense of, 118, 323, 324
cosmological consciousness of, 138, 141–46
on creative union, 11, 235, 256–57, 320, 324, 325–26, 360
creativity in evolutionary vision of, 91–92
on the death of cosmos and consciousness, 8, 306–7
on divine love, 246, 256–58, 261–62
on the divine milieu, 91, 227–28, 302
dual-aspect monism, affirming, 171, 217–19
eschatology of, 292, 300, 301, 350, 357, 369, 371
evil, on the problem of, 12, 365–68
as an evolutionary scientist, 35, 55, 214, 319
exile from France, 6, 18, 34, 317
faithful priesthood of, 5, 54
fire imagery, use of, 98–99, 102, 107, 227, 335
the future, as confident towards, 5, 59, 114, 291
geological work, linking with spirituality, 228, 319
on God and time, 362–65
in the Great War, 5, 10, 114
hope, bringing a message of, 212, 292, 303, 308, 339, 368
human distinction, describing, 224
integral philosophy building on the spirit of, 282, 289
as a Jesuit, 7, 18, 59–60, 113, 115, 306, 339
Marcel Brion, interview with, *330,* 331–37, 338–46
on the metaphysics of union, 11, 16, 23, 27, 131, 169, 230, 335, 360

millennialism, as accused of, 332, 345
the mind in ontology of, 155–60
monistic tendencies of, 90, 217–18, 350, 368, 370–71
as a mystic, 101–2, 121
on the nonliving, 152–53
on noogenesis, 158, 226, 236, 296, 321, 323
on the oneness of God, 98–99
optimism, offering, 292, 293, 294, 297, 299 303, 345, 368
as a paleontologist, 7, 9, 38, 113, 319, 332, 338, 344
panentheist view of God, 87, 89, 99
as a panpsychist, 47–48, 65, 79, 81–86, 155–56, 218
as a pantheist, 46–47, 229–34, 294, 358, 371
personalistic universe of, 234, 235, 237
as a process theist, 12, 37, 38, 41, 46, 110, 113
Sacred Heart, devotion to, 318, 321–22
as a scientist, 7, 8, 55, 117–18, 120, 130, 151, 211, 246, 256, 306–7, 308, 319, 337, 339, 344
Shiva, keen interest in, 277
Soleri as a disciple of, 298–99
on spirit and matter as intertwined, 105–6
on the stuff of things, 13, 228, 340
temporalistic outlook of, 347, 348–49, 358–59, 370
on the third nature of Christ, 236–37
on totalitarianism, 226–27
truth, on the essential criterion of, 132–33
on unclear narrative of the universe, 313–14
as an unsatisfied theist, 265, 266–70, 274, 276
value, as reawakening an ontology of, 160–62, 164–66
vision of God, 301–2
war essays, 10, 11, 101, 332, 333
on the within, 13–14, 17, 40, 118, 282, 293, 294–95, 370
See also complexity-consciousness; differentiating union; noosphere; Omega; process metaphysics; radial energy

Teilhard de Chardin, works of
"The Christic," 317–28
Divine Milieu, 56, 91, 302, 317, 334
"Evolution," 9
Future of Man, 225, 242, 291
"God of Evolution," 229
"Heart of Matter," 63, 81–82, 228, 318, 332
Human Phenomenon, 24, 36, 54, 55, 114, 115, 116, 118, 212–14, 221, 222, 226, 240, 321
Hymn of the Universe, 56
"Hymn to Matter," 227–28
"Mass on the World, 317
Phenomenon of Man, 35, 147, 154, 212, 265, 267, 301, 335
"Sketch of a Personalistic Universe," 234
Toward the Future, 269
Writings in Time of War, 101
"Zest for Living," 25
Teilhard de Chardin Album (ed. Mortier/ Aboux), 331
Teilhard-Chambon, Marguerite, 320, 333
theodicy, 45, 46
theogenesis, 48, 171–72, 229
theory of relativity, 62
Thomas Aquinas, Saint, 58, 116
on God's relation to the creature, 93–94
on God's relation to the world, 88, 167
substance and being as basic categories for, 56
Thomistic theology, 11–12, 44, 57, 168
thought outside of nature, 308–10, 311, 312
Tillich, Paul, 97, 104
Timaeus (Plato), 21
Tomhave, Jeff, 192
Toronto Daily star, 7
totalitarianism, 180, 193, 194, 226–27, 346, 368
Toy Story (film), 187–88
Tracy, David, 38
transcendentals, 311–12
Treatise of Human Nature (Hume), 80
Tresmontant, Claude, 363–64
tribal religion, 271, 272

Trump, Donald, 189
Tucker, Mary Evelyn, 300
ultra-hominization, 321
Unger, Peter, 79
Unire, metaphysics of, 168–69, 175
Valensin, Auguste, 18, 19, 36
Valladolid Debate, 180
Vatican II, 35, 277
via tertia, overcoming dualism via, 82
Viney, Donald Wayne, 55, 57–59
Vlasic, Ivan, 185–86, 191, 200
Wall, Bernard, 212
Wallace, Alfred Russel, 126
Way of the Explorer (Mitchell), 198
Wegner, Alfred, 25
Weismann, August, 124
Whitehead, Alfred North
  beauty, on the maximizing of, 310, 314
  Bergson, inspired by, 3, 116, 348
  bifurcation of nature, attempting to
    overcome, 15, 57, 61, 63
  causal efficacy and, 55, 119
  Christopher Columbus, in praise of,
    189, 203
  complex unity of, 120, 178, 199, 286
  contrast, on the concept of, 119–20,
    272, 294, 301
  convergence of thought with Teilhard,
    116–18, 131
  on cosmological decentering, 139–41,
    143, 146, 150
  creation out of nothing, rejecting,
    360–61
  creativity in vision of reality, 91, 92
  critique of modern science, 179–82
  on divine indestructibility, 307, 308
  on divine love, 246, 256, 258–59
    261–62
  on the divine lure, 53, 293, 299
  on empty entities, 79–80
  on Eros of the Universe, 190, 200, 202
  evil, God as exonerated from
    responsibility for, 366, 367
  evolutionary views, 14, 47, 279–81,
    288
  on the experiential process, 58, 234
  fellow sufferer, on God as, 89, 260
  future, view of, 278, 370
  on historical continuity of the past,
    351, 353

  immediacy, understanding of, 30, 55,
    124, 260, 354, 365
  on the initial aim, 21, 103, 106, 132,
    173, 295, 296, 298, 299
  integral philosophy as building on the
    spirit of, 282, 289
  on the many as increased by one, 31,
    223
  metaphysics, defining, 148–49
  the mind in ontology of, 155–60
  misplaced concreteness, on the fallacy
    of, 17, 43, 79, 119
  on modernity, 63, 81, 283
  ontology of, life and living in, 152–54
  panentheism and, 87, 99
  panexperientialism of, 88, 155,
    160–61
  philosophy of organism, 15–16, 28,
    119, 121, 152, 196–97, 266
  pluralism in the scheme of, 56, 349–50
  on the primordial nature of God, 40,
    92, 96–97, 173–74, 296, 364–65
  as a process theist, 9, 21, 37, 49, 87,
    113, 137, 145, 291, 347
  radically open universe, envisioning,
    292, 293
  on reciprocal interaction between
    God and the world, 362–63
  on religiosity, 270–72, 277
  on scientific materialism, 15, 121, 160,
    266, 309
  on the subjective pole, 57, 352
  Teilhard not sufficiently aware of, 3, 48
  temporalistic outlook, 348, 358–59
  on the universe as an ongoing process,
    88, 275
  as an unsatisfied theist, 266, 270–73,
    276
  value as reawakened in ontology of,
    160–66
  See also adventure; concrescence;
    consequent nature of God
Whitehead, Alfred North, works of
  Adventures of Ideas, 20–21, 104–5
  *Enquiry into the Principles of Natural
    Knowledge,* 5
  Function of Reason, 25
  Principia Mathematica, 4
  Process and Reality, 15, 20, 29–30,
    35–36, 86, 122, 274

416 Index

Religion in the Making, 3, 19–20, 21, 270–71, 288

Science in the Modern World, 3, 19, 20, 270

Whitehead, Eric, 4–5

Whitehead, Evelyn, 4, 17

Whitla, William, 46

Wieman, Henry Nelson, 30, 35–36

Wilber, Ken, 282

Wild, Roger, 331

Wildiers, N. M., 42, 131

Wilson, David Sloan, 211–12, 225

Wimsatt, William, 281

withinness, 13, 296

  in the elements of the world, 268

  evolution, contribution of the within to, 55

  of inert matter, 294–95

  matter, withinness and withoutness of, 218

  natural selection as lacking a within, 127

  spontaneity and freedom, as linked with, 14

  subjective pole, as resembling, 57

  as taking many forms, 17

  Teilhard on the within, 13–14, 17, 40, 118, 282, 293, 294–95, 370

  the "within," describing and defining, 351–55

Woods, Mark, 183

Wordsworth, William, 43, 160

World Soul, 44, 46, 57

World War I, 4–5, 10, 11, 101, 114, 320, 332–33

World War II, 6, 8, 114, 185, 189, 334

Wright, Wilbur and Orville, 189

Zimmerli, Walther, 252

Zoological Philosophy (Lamarck), 126